剑桥应用语言学年度评论 2002
Annual Review of Applied Linguistics

话语和对话
Discourse and Dialogue

主编 〔美〕Mary McGroarty

导读 王振华

2016年·北京

Originally published by Cambridge University Press in 2002. This reprint edition is published with the permission of the Syndicate of the Press of the University of Cambridge, Cambridge, England.

原书由英国剑桥大学出版社于 2002 年出版。

本版经英国剑桥大学出版社授权出版。

This edition is licensed for sale in the People's Republic of China only (excluding Hong Kong SAR, Macao SAR and Taiwan Province). No part of this publication may be reproduced or distributed by any means, or stored in a database or retrieval system, without the prior written permission of the publisher.

本版仅限在中华人民共和国境内（不包括香港特别行政区、澳门特别行政区及台湾）销售。未经出版者书面许可，不得以任何方式复制或发行本书的任何部分。

剑桥应用语言学年度评论
专家委员会

主　任　胡壮麟
副主任　田贵森　朱永生
委　员　曹　进　何　伟　靳　琰　赖良涛　李战子
　　　　　彭宣维　齐振海　孙迎晖　王振华　辛志英
　　　　　杨信彰　于　晖　张　辉　张　琳　张　薇
　　　　　郑　萱

CONTENTS

总序 ··· 胡壮麟 1
导读 ··· 王振华 11

EDITOR'S INTRODUCTION
··· Mary McGroarty i

APPROACHES TO DISCOURSE ANALYSIS

1. CONVERSATION ANALYSIS AND APPLIED LINGUISTICS
   ············ Emanuel A. Schegloff, Irene Koshik, Sally Jacoby, and David Olsher 3
2. QUANTITATIVE AND QUALITATIVE APPROACHES TO
   DISCOURSE ANALYSIS
   ··· Anne Lazaraton 36
3. MEANING BEYOND THE CLAUSE: SFL PERSPECTIVES
   ··· J. R. Martin 57
4. CORPUS LINGUISTIC APPROACHES FOR DISCOURSE ANALYSIS
   ··· Susan Conrad 82
5. BEYOND SCIENCE AND IDEOLOGY CRITIQUE:
   DEVELOPMENTS IN CRITICAL DISCOURSE ANALYSIS
   ··· Allan Luke 105

APPLICATIONS OF DISCOURSE ANALYSIS

6. GENRE: LANGUAGE, CONTEXT, AND LITERACY
   ··· Ken Hyland 125
7. DISCOURSE ANALYSIS AND STYLISTICS
   ··· Paul Simpson and Geoff Hall 151

8. DISCOURSE ISSUES IN CROSS-CULTURAL PRAGMATICS
.... Diana Boxer   168

DISCOURSE IN THE CLASSROOM

9. PEER-PEER DIALOGUE AS A MEANS OF SECOND LANGUAGE
   LEARNING
   .... Merrill Swain, Lindsay Brooks, and Agustina Tocalli-Beller   191
10. TEACHER-STUDENT INTERACTION AND
    LANGUAGE LEARNING
    .... Joan Kelly Hall and Meghan Walsh   208
11. TEACHERS' USES OF THE TARGET AND FIRST LANGUAGES IN
    SECOND AND FOREIGN LANGUAGE CLASSROOMS
    .... Miles Turnbull and Katy Arnett   229

DISCOURSE ANALYSIS AND ASSESSMENT

12. DISCOURSE AND ASSESSMENT
    .... Tim McNamara, Kathryn Hill, and Lynette May   247
13. DISCOURSE APPROACHES TO ORAL LANGUAGE ASSESSMENT
    .... Richard F. Young   271
14. DISCOURSE APPROACHES TO WRITING ASSESSMENT
    .... Ulla Connor and Aymérou Mbaye   293

BIOGRAPHICAL INFORMATION ON CONTRIBUTORS

总　　序

自 2013 年 8 月起，商务印书馆与剑桥大学出版社开始商洽在大陆出版《应用语言学年度评论》(*Annual Review of Applied Linguistics*)事宜，至 2014 年春末签约。此后，商务印书馆英语编辑室领导栾奇和马浩岚并责任编辑杨子辉博士先后来访，约我办三件事，一是代为组织国内学者为各卷写导读，二是承担导读的审稿任务，三是为商务版《应用语言学年度评论》写一个总序。作为对我的照顾，同意我邀请复旦大学朱永生教授[①]和北京师范大学田贵森教授[②]参加导读审定工作。就总序而言，多次思考之后，想谈以下四个方面。

一、刊物方针

《应用语言学年度评论》（以下简称《年度评论》）是美国应用语言

[①] 朱永生：复旦大学教授、博导，杭州师范大学钱塘学者，高校功能语言学研究会副会长，高校语篇分析研究会副会长，*Linguistics and Human Sciences* 编委及《中国外语》等杂志编委。曾任苏州大学外语系主任、复旦大学外文系主任和国际文化交流学院院长、国际系统功能语言学研究会执委、国务院学科评议组成员、全国高校外语教学指导委员会委员等职务。著有《系统功能语言学多维思考》《系统功能语言学再思考》《语境动态研究》《系统功能语言学概论》等。

[②] 田贵森：北京师范大学外文学院教授、博导，中国功能语言学学会常务理事、中国社会语言学学会理事。1976 年河北师范大学外语系毕业后留校任教，1987 年北京外国语大学硕士，1991 年纽约市立大学硕士，1997 年北京大学博士。曾任河北师大外国语学院院长，河北省高校外语教学研究会会长，中国教育学会外语教学专业委员会副理事长。著有《禁忌语的功能研究》《英语专业毕业论文写作教程》《新编英语词汇学教程》等。

学学会（American Association for Applied Linguistics，简称 AAAL）主办的一部书刊结合的出版物，自 1980 年起每年一卷，至 2014 年已出版 34 卷。该刊最初由 Newbury House 出版社出版，自第 5 卷起改为剑桥大学出版社出版，延续至今。美国南加州大学美国语言研究所主任 Robert B. Kaplan 教授筹划第 1 卷《年度评论》时，邀请犹他州布里格姆-扬大学日耳曼语系 Randall L. Jones 教授和华盛顿大学应用语言学中心主任 G. Richard Tucker 教授三人合作主编。在他们领导下的编委会对办刊宗旨确定这样一个基本认识：尽管 1941 年美国密执安大学率先成立了将语言学理论应用于语言教育的英语学院，1956 年英国爱丁堡大学成立了应用语言学系，1959 年美国华盛顿大学建立了应用语言学中心，1966 年 TESOL Quarterly 出版，1977 年美国应用语言学学会成立，《年度评论》编委会无意选定其中之一作为应用语言学界共同遵循的蓝图，而是决定走自己的路。在此基础上编委会确定的方针有如下特点：（1）《年度评论》不是杂志，因为它一年只出一本；它又被看作是一本杂志，因为它由出版社的杂志部负责编辑、发行事务。[①]（2）该出版物不对应用语言学做面面俱到的报道，而是对应用语言学学科的现状进行专题评论、综述和文献式的归纳。（3）应用语言学具有高度的跨学科性，因此该刊重点结合双语教育、语言教育学、心理语言学和社会语言学四个方面进行选题。考虑到这四个学科枝叶蔓生，年刊会对一个学科的某一领域做全面的综述和评论。（4）即使上述四个学科也不是应用语言学的唯一研究领域，因为该刊遵循美国应用语言学学会所倡导的功能导向，着眼于具体应用更甚于理论。（5）所有的文章由编委会组织某一领域的专家撰写，不转载已在其他刊物上发表的文章，也不采用在某个学术会议上已经宣读的论文，更不对某一部具体的学术著作进行评论。因此，《年度评论》的主要任务是收集和突出被学术界很少报道或研究的领域，不重复已有工作，更不企图贬低某一

---

① 《应用语言学年度评论》问世后，受到国际学术界的高度重视，被权威的《社会科学引文索引》（SSCI）、《艺术和人文科学引文索引》（AHCI）和《科学引文索引》（SCI）所收录。

个方面,或对本学科内某项研究的价值进行排队。这样,《年度评论》对二语习得和语言干扰等内容谈得不多,因为这方面的研究成果已经发表很多。反之,微语言学、符号语言学、计算机辅助教学等受到重视。(6)《年度评论》本身应当正确面对来自不同领域实践者的认同或挑战。[1][2] 鉴于上述情况,《年度评论》每卷都有一个主题,如"语言和语言教育政策"(卷2)、"书面话语"(卷3)、"读写教育"(卷4)等。这些选题均具有学术性、实用性、时代性和独特性。与此同时,该刊每隔四五年会有一卷就应用语言学的整体研究从不同方面进行总结式的调研和讨论,内容涉及语言学习和教学、话语分析、教学创新、二语习得、计算机辅助教学、职场语境下的语言用途、社会语言学、语言政策和语言评估(如卷1、5、10、15、19等)。每年向读者提供500多个新的文献,以帮助本学科教学科研人员能深入掌握情况,点面结合。《年度评论》原计划的第1卷在1980年出版,由于组稿和印刷的原因,实际上在1981年问世。这一脱节现象直到1994年第14卷才得到扭转,即每卷标明的年度与出版年度取得一致。[3]

二、主编更迭

三十多年来,《年度评论》的总主编大约十年更换一次。美国南加利福尼亚大学美国语言研究所主任 Robert B. Kaplan 教授从创刊起任总主编,连续十年。Kaplan 曾任美国应用语言学会会长、英语作为第二语言教

---

[1] Rota, A. (1982). ANNUAL REVIEW OF APPLIED LINGUISTICS (ARAL). Robert B. Kaplan (Gen. Ed.); Randall L. Jones and G. Richard Tucker (Co-Eds.). *TESOL Quarterly*, 16, 398–404.

[2] Kaplan, Robert B. (1980). Introduction. *Annual Review of Applied Linguistics*, 1, vii–xi.

[3] Kaplan, Robert B. and William Grabe. (2000). Applied Linguistics and the Annual Review of Applied Linguistics. in *Annual Review of Applied Linguistics*, 20, 3–17. Cambridge University Press.

学学会会长、《牛津应用语言学手册》总主编、《国际语言学百科全书》编委等。① 在 Kaplan 主编的《牛津应用语言学手册》中,他认为应用语言学家至少应该具备以下领域的一些知识:人类学、社会学、经济学、政治学、教育学、老年人学、历史学、国际关系、语言学习和教学、词典编纂学、政策研究、心理学和神经科学、公共管理、教师培训和文本生成等。此外,每一位应用语言学家都应精于计算机使用,能够对数据进行统计分析。②③

自第 11 卷起,William Grabe 任主编。Grabe 是美国北亚利桑那州大学负责科研的副校长,曾先后在该校英语系和应用语言学系任教。Grabe 认为应用语言学的核心是"试图解决人们在日常生活中遇到的与语言相关的问题",是一种"研究现实世界语言问题的、实践驱动的学科"。④ 鉴于这个原因,应用语言学必然是一个交叉学科,涉及许多其他领域。这可见之于他对每卷的选题,如"读写教育"(卷 12)、"二语教学"(卷 13)、"语言政策和规划"(卷 14)、"技术和语言"(卷 16)、"多语现象"(卷 17)、"二语教育基础"(卷 18)、"应用语言学的学科性"(卷 19,20)。Grabe 任总主编至 2000 年卸任。在他最后一次负责的第 20 卷,他和 Robert Kaplan 合写了一篇回顾应用语言学和《年度评论》发展历程的总结性文章。

自 2001 年起任总主编的是北亚利桑那大学英语系的 Mary McGroarty 教授。她主要研究双语现象、语言政策、语言教育和课堂研究、社会语言学、二语教学的文化影响等。由于第一次出任主编,McGroarty 邀请了美

---

① Bruthiaux, Paul, Dwight Atkinson, William G. Egginton, William Grabe, Viadehi Ramanathan. Eds. (2005). *Directions in Applied Linguistics in Honour of Robert B. Kaplan.* Clevedon: Multilingual Matters Ltd.
② Kaplan, Robert B. (1999). *The Oxford Handbook of Applied Linguistics.* Edinburgh: Edinburgh University Press.
③ 刘海涛. 从比较中看应用语言学. 北华大学学报(社会科学版),2007,8(2):4.
④ Grabe, William. (2000). Introduction. *Annual Review of Applied Linguistics*, 20, 1–2. Cambridge University Press.

国著名外语教学法专家 Wilga M. Rivers 为第 21 卷"语言和心理学"写序,题为"沿着记忆巷道的漫长旅程"。此后,McGroarty 在她任期内主编了"话语和对话"(卷22)、"语言接触和演变"(卷23)、"语言教育学的进展"(卷24)和"通用语语言"(卷26)。《年度评论》第27和28卷的主题分别为"语言与科技"和"神经语言学和认知语言处理",但未见到这两卷本应由总主编执笔的引言,在目录中也未出现,原因不详。作为总主编的 McGroarty 在第29卷"语言政策和语言评估"中再次出现,不过她邀请了著名学者 Bernard Spolsky 作为客座主编。Spolsky 教授长期在以色列的 Bar-Ilan 大学任教,曾任该校人文学院院长,并创建语言政策研究中心。在编辑业务方面,他曾任国际刊物 Language Policy(《语言政策》)的总主编,Asia TEFL(《亚洲英语作为外语教学》)杂志的出版部主任和总编辑。Spolsky 的专著都与语言政策和语言教育有关,如《教育语言学导论》(1978)、《二语学习的条件》(1991)、《社会语言学》(1998)、《以色列诸语言:政策、意识和实践》(1999)、《语言政策》(2004)、《语言管理》(2009)等。[①] 由此看来,Spolsky 无力全心投入《年度评论》的编辑工作,这次只是扮演一次客串角色而已。

自第30卷起,总主编一职由美国密执安州立大学的 Charlene Polio 教授担任。Polio 的主要研究领域为二语写作、二语习得、外语课堂话语、新技术和有经验教师之间的行为差异。她在编辑工作上有较多经验,除接受《年度评论》的总主编任务外,也是 Modern Language Journal(《现代语言杂志》)的编辑,此前曾为 Journal of Second Language Writing(《二语写作杂志》)和 TESOL Quarterly 杂志编委会委员。[②] Polio 为《年度评论》各卷确定的选题为"应用语言学专题"(卷30)、"第二语言教育研究"(卷31)、"公式化语言研究"(卷32)、"多语现象研究"(卷33)、"研究方法专题"(卷34)。这体现了她作为总主编延续了该刊创办时的主导思

---

① Spolsky, Bernard. Homepage. http://www.biu.ac.il/faculty/spolsky/. 2015. 1. 3.
② Polio, Charlene. http://www.wsu.edu/~oikui/. 2015. 1. 5.

想,即每卷的稿子都是就某一领域的特定问题而精选的。

为《年度评论》写稿的作者中不乏名人,如 Henry G. Widdowson、James R. Martin、Bernard Spolsky、Alan Davies 等都是国际著名语言学家。

三、国人参与

我国大陆、港台地区和国际华人圈对《应用语言学年度评论》很为重视。

台湾学者郑锦全(Chan-chuan Cheng)在第 7 卷上发表"语言和计算机"一文。郑当时任台湾师范大学华语文教学研究所讲座教授、台湾地区研究院语言所研究员和人文社会科学研究中心通信研究员(Cheng, 2014)。[①] 另一位是台湾清华大学培养的许静芬(Ching-fen Hsu)博士,现在台湾华梵大学人文学院师资培养研究中心工作,专攻威廉姆斯综合征(Williams Syndrome)发育障碍的语言习得研究,是第 28 卷"威廉姆斯综合征:基因型和认知表型描述"一文的第一作者。[②] 香港教育学院语言教学研究中心主任的李楚成(David C. S. Li)教授在第 26 卷上发表"作为大中华通用语的汉语"一文。[③] 在《年度评论》第 30 卷独立发表有关传承语学习的社会文化维度一文的何纬芸(Agnes Weiyun He)教授,早期毕业于北京外国语大学,现为 Stony Brook 大学应用语言学和亚洲研究专业的教授,筹建了该校多语和跨文化交际中心。何纬芸主要研究语言语境和语篇的结合,人们如何通过日常互动逐步构建和重构概念、社团和文化。近十年来,她专门研究不同时期和不同背景下汉语作为传承语的社会化。[④] 在《年度评论》第 27 卷与 John Flowerdew 联名发表"多语制和二语写作在电

[①] Cheng, Chan-chuan(郑锦全). http://doc88.com/P-795557797523.html. 2014.12.9.
[②] Hsu, Ching-fen(许静芬). http://www.docin.com/p-2898691.html & key. 2015.1.5.
[③] Li, David, C. S.(李楚成). http://dfl.shufe.edu.cn/structure/ xueshu-com-142410-1.htm. 2014.12.9.
[④] He, Agnes Weiyun(何纬芸). http://www.stonybrook.edu/commcms/asian/PROGRAMS.html. 2014.12.9.

子时代的关系"一文的李咏燕博士（Yongyan Li）任教于香港大学教育学院英语教育系，其研究范围包括专业写作、多语学者的研究和发表实践、言而有据的写作、科学文章的整篇抄袭现象、在职教育等。①令人瞩目的是，上述学者与大陆高校和研究单位保持良好的学术联系，如郑锦全教授曾担任四川大学文学与新闻学院兼职教授、厦门大学嘉庚学院中文系兼职教授、北京大学汉语语言学研究中心兼职研究员；李楚成教授曾在上海财经大学举行关于中国外语学习者和使用者常见错误的纠正讲座；何纬芸教授与上海交通大学苗瑞琴副教授合作编写了"继承语之习得及其社会化"一文。②

大陆学者对《年度评论》也做出了应有的反应和贡献。早在1981年《年度评论》第1卷问世后，我国学者左焕琪教授便在国内语言学权威刊物《当代语言学》上作了报道，既介绍了编者Kaplan的背景，也对该卷四个部分作了近似导读的介绍。作者当时就以敏锐的眼光指出这是"近年来美国应用语言学领域引人瞩目的新刊物"。③较近的可举2012年方秀才的"程式语面面观介绍"一文，对《年度评论》第32卷从认知视角、教学应用、社会学进展和未来展望四个部分深入介绍。作者特别注意到，为了从多种视角讨论程式语这一主题，总主编没有限定程式语的定义、内涵，也没有统一术语，让每篇文章的作者采用自己认同的术语和定义，④这表明《年度评论》并没有因为总主编的变动而放弃原有的风格。

行文至此，有必要提一下以Charlene Polio为首的新编委会所作的一个重大决定，那就是她代表编委会聘请了我国广东外语外贸大学王初明教授从第31卷起任《年度评论》顾问委员会的委员。这是对我国应用语言

---

① Li, Yongyan（李咏燕）. http://www_researchgate. net/profile/Yongyan_Li/publications. 2014. 12. 9.
② 何纬芸，苗瑞琴. 继承语之习得及其社会化. 载姬建国，蒋楠主编：应用语言学（西方人文社会科学前沿述评）. 北京：中国人民大学出版社，2007. 239–255.
③ 左焕琪. 应用语言学年度评述（1980）.《国外语言学》，1983，(3)：46–49.
④ 方秀才.《程式语面面观》介绍.《当代语言学》，2013，15（4）：492–495.

学研究发展和水平的肯定。我与王初明教授结识于1995年9月,当时我是香港中文大学的访问学者,他是英语系的博士生。我们经常一起讨论学术问题。长江后浪推前浪,2011年我从北京外国语大学中国外语教育研究中心学术委员会主任退下后,他接替了此职。王初明教授现在的学术兼职有国务院学位委员会外国语言文学学科评议组成员、中国高等教育学会外语教学研究分会副会长。他的主要研究方向为第二语言习得研究及其在外语教学中的应用,主要学术创见有外语写长法、语境补缺假说、外语语音学习假设、外语学习的学伴用随原则、读后续写的理论和应用价值。

四、"商务"特色

除保留剑桥版《应用语言学年度评论》的原有特色外,商务版《应用语言学年度评论》有它自己的特色。

商务版《年度评论》从第20卷开始,而不是从第1卷开始。我认为商务印书馆此举着眼于让读者以更多的精力把握应用语言学在新世纪的发展,急读者之所急。我们还应该看到,《年度评论》第20卷实际上起到承前启后的作用。在该卷中,为上世纪创刊时立下汗马功劳的Robert Kaplan、William Grabe和G. Richard Tucker分别对应用语言学和《年度评论》在二十年中的发展作了系统的总结,帮助读者对前二十年有个总体了解,又寄厚望于这门新学科在新世纪、新千年的发展,把握前进的方向。其次,商务版《年度评论》增加了满足中国读者需求的新内容,那就是每卷都有一篇1.5万字左右的中文导读。这便于帮助读者掌握每卷的基本内容和背景材料,特别是汉语界的教师、研究者和学生。

参与此任务的导读作者有国内外语界著名学者,也有新生代的中青年学者。这些专家学者对自己撰写的内容比较熟悉。作为此项目的组织者,我没有向他们摊派任务,而是让各位学者根据自己熟悉的领域自由选题。对各位作者的努力我在此谨表谢意。如前所述,导读初稿完成后均由上海复旦大学朱永生教授和北京师范大学田贵森教授分别先行审读。对两位教授退休后仍能不辞辛苦、鼎力相助的感激之情,难以言表。

由于《年度评论》涉及多个学科和领域,各卷原版的体例不全相同,而各位导读作者的学术生涯也不尽相同,我们对导读编写体例上只作大致要求,不强调绝对统一。总的印象是,每位导读作者对本卷各章内容都能做提纲挈领的介绍和解释,帮助读者理解和抓住要点,这是共同的优点。导读作者各自的特色则表现在:(1)能在正文之前对本卷的总主编、客座编辑做介绍,并对总主编的引言深入分析,起到画龙点睛的作用;(2)对本卷主题进行了解释;(3)对有关主题在20世纪的研究状况或《年度评论》已经发表过的专辑作必要回顾;(4)对每卷论文内容进行归纳,指出其特点;(5)坦率指出某卷内容的不足之处;(6)结合国内现状进行讨论,并进行反思;(7)在讨论中,引入当代先进理论;(8)向我国学界和领导部门提出今后有待深入展开研究的问题。

在结束本序之际,再次感谢各位导读作者,以及永生教授和贵森教授的共同努力,使本项艰巨任务得以顺利完成;祝贺商务版《应用语言学年度评论》正式出版;祝愿商务印书馆今后在应用语言学和理论语言学等领域为外语教育界和学术界做出更多更大贡献!

北京大学蓝旗营寓所

2015年元月

导　读

王振华[①]

一、引言

剑桥大学出版社 2002 年出版的《应用语言学年度评论》第 22 卷主题是"话语和对话"。在此以前，1982 年第 3 卷的主题为"书面话语"，表明了当时的学术界偏重于书面语而不是口语。尽管如此，这已经说明了时任总主编美国南加利福尼亚大学美国语言研究所主任 Robert B. Kaplan 教授对话语很为重视。8 年后，Kaplan 教授在作为总主编任期的最后一年，又与美国北亚利桑那州大学英语系和应用语言学系 William Grabe 教授合作主编了 1990 年第 11 卷，主题为"话语分析"，深入分析构建话语的众多元素。

如今呈现在我们眼前的第 22 卷，内容从话语延伸至对话，浓缩了从 80 年代开始的发展过程。本卷共收入论文 14 篇，既有理论综述性文章、也有理论应用性文章，如语篇分析在语言教学实践中的应用。第 1 篇文章讨论会话分析与应用语言学的关系，第 2-6 篇主要讨论语篇研究的方法或

[①] 王振华：上海交通大学教授、博导、英语系主任、马丁适用语言学研究中心执行主任；兼任中国功能语言学研究会副会长、中国英汉语篇研究会副会长、中国法律语言学研究会副会长、中国政法大学法律语言学研究中心研究员和副主任。*International Journal of Law, Language and Discourse* 和《当代外语研究》等多家国内外学术期刊编委。在 *Semiotica* 等国内外学术刊物上发表论文 65 篇，出版著作和教材 19 部。主持国家和省部级科研项目 3 项，教育部重大项目子项目 1 项，其他项目 16 项，参与项目 5 项。

视角，其中第 2 篇讨论语篇分析的定量和定性方法，第 3 篇讨论语篇研究的系统功能语言学方法，第 4 篇介绍语篇分析的语料库方法，第 5 篇介绍批评语篇分析的新发展，第 6 篇介绍语篇研究的语类视角。第 7 篇和第 8 篇文章分别讨论语篇分析与文体学和语用学之间的关系。第 9 篇到第 11 篇文章关注外语教学实践中的生生互动与外语学习，师生互动与二语学习，教师课堂教学使用一语和二语的问题。最后的第 12-14 篇的三篇文章关注的主要是语篇分析与教与学的评估问题，如运用语篇分析的研究成果评估口语能力和写作能力等。

本书中许多文章作者都是相关领域里的专家和领军人物，如承担开篇之作的 Emannel Schegloff 是美国洛杉矶加利福尼亚大学社会学教授，他、Harvey Sacks、Gail Jefferson 三人于二十世纪六七十年代开创了会话分析（conversation analysis）这个研究领域。另外，他对互动语言学的贡献也很显著。第 3 篇文章的作者 James Martin 是澳大利亚悉尼大学语言学教授，国际著名系统功能语言学家。他于 20 世纪 90 年代创立了评价理论（appraisal theory）。另外，他对语类理论和语篇语言学的贡献显著，代表作有 English Text: System and Structure(1982), Working with Discourse: Meaning Beyond the Clause(2003/2007), Genre Relations: Mapping Culture(2008)。第 4 篇作者 Susan Conrad 是美国俄勒冈州波特兰大学应用语言学教授，主要研究语篇文体、写作、教育语言学，并对基于语料库的语法研究有重大贡献，常与 Geoffrey Leech, Douglas Biber 等国际著名语言学家合作，代表作有 Register, Genre and Style(2009)。作为第 6 篇作者的 Ken Hyland 是香港大学应用语言学中心教授，研究领域有话语分析、语言教育、外语教育、写作、修辞学等。他的著作 Metadiscourse 是国内外语篇分析学者耳熟能详的学术名作。至于编写第 7 篇论文的 Paul Simpson 则是英国女王大学英语学院教授，主要研究批评语篇分析、语用学、社会学和文体学，代表作有 Language, Ideology, and Point of View(1993)。这些学者所提出的语篇分析理论，有的一问世就是经典，有的通过一段时间的应用也成为经典。

二、各篇内容[①]

1. 会话分析与应用语言学

本篇由 Emannel Schegloff、Irene Koshik、Sally Jacob 和 David Olsher 四位作者合作完成。文章首先综述会话分析(conversation analysis, CA)的研究成果,然后讨论 CA 与应用语言学 (applied linguistics, AL) 的交叉研究。作者认为,CA 研究的领域和 AL 关注的许多焦点相交叉,在 AL 的研究中运用 CA 的研究资源和工具,必然提升特定语言环境下对语言的理解,助推 AL 研究的发展,同时也可检验和深化 CA 的研究成果。本文全面系统地提出了 CA 理论对 AL 研究的意义,提供了二者结合的途径,明确了二者交叉研究应注意的问题。

本文的价值在于,通过 CA 理论解释和描述日常话语的结构,发掘人类语言交际中反复出现的交际行为模式,并通过研究言语交际的序列性和组织性等来解释人类社会交往的组织规律,为关注语言教学和语言习得的 AL 研究的诸多实践提供参考和指导。

2. 话语分析的定量和定性方法

第 2 篇文章由 Anne Lazaraton 完成。作者从 70 余本期刊中甄选 16 篇基于定性或定量的论文进行研究,通过对前人的研究成果在论文结构、数据收集分析、结果呈现、结论分析和科研价值等方面进行分析,发现语篇分析在学术界的定性研究缺少评估标准,并对存在的问题提出了可行的解决方案。本文对语篇分析定性和定量研究进行开创性总结,将各类分析模型和研究理念介绍例析,不但对"定性"与"定量"、"自上而下"与"自下而上"分析法、话语分析、民族志传播学进行了通俗、系统的解释,还对各类概念加以阐明和扼要区分,以支持文中的实例描述和观点论证。

---

① 第二部分谈到的作者和有关论文请参见各篇文章后的参考文献。

本文对方法论的反思具有前瞻性和指导意义。作者透过纷繁的研究，对宏观的方法论进行探讨，提出了定性研究的评价标准，是一种学术突破。

3. 跨越小句的意义：系统功能语言学视角

第3篇论文的作者为James R. Martin。本文综述了基于系统功能语言学（systemic-functional linguistics, SFL）的话语分析研究，诸如：与连贯有关的语法连贯、词汇连贯、连贯纽带，与语篇语义有关的协商、识别、连接、概念等系统网络，以及与社会语境有关的语类和语域理论。此外，作者详细阐述了SFL视角下语篇分析的新进展，如：DA研究开始向音系层和词汇语法层拓展；语篇人际意义的研究开始关注日常话语和机构话语的评价资源等。作者通过对已有研究进行梳理，指出了目前研究的不足，并对该领域未来的发展提出建议。作者认为，SFL框架对话语分析研究的适用性主要源于其对语类和功能语法的详尽描写，及其在多模态研究中的适应性。该领域未来应该关注基于语料库的语篇语义学和语域研究。这种综述方式对进行相关论述提供了很好的范式，对撰写学术论文和做研究有一定启示。

4. 话语分析的语料库语言学视角

文章作者Susan Conrad介绍了以语料库语言学为基础的语篇分析方法。文章首先概括了基于语料库的语言研究的总体特征：以语料库为基础；使用计算机辅助技术；强调语言使用模式的实证性分析；使用定量与定性分析相结合的技术。Conrad接着介绍了适用于语篇分析的四种主要方法：(1)研究某一语言特征的使用特点，如导致补语从句中that的省略与保留的因素；(2)研究某一语言功能的实现方式，如描述英语中表达立场的所有语法结构；(3)描述语言变体的特征，如对大学里不同场合所使用的语域之间的关系进行多维度分析；(4)研究整个文本中某一语言特征的出现情况，如作者是如何通过指称自己和读者来建构权威的。针对每种方法，作者简要回顾该领域已开展的相关研究，并围绕实例说明其分析步骤、过程、结果、意义及局限，旨在表明语料库语言学能从多方面帮助人们对语篇的理解。文章在结论部分简要介绍了语料库语言学中的其他焦点问题，并指出未来语料库语言学在语篇分析中面临的挑战。

本文的一大亮点在于介绍了以语料库和计算机技术为基础的多维度分析法。该方法旨在利用"因素分析法"对语域变异中语言特征的共现模式进行分析。作者通过实例证明，多维度分析法能够在不同的语言变体之间进行复杂的比较，比研究单独的语言特征更能全面地揭示语域的特征。同时，该方法有助于在不同的层次间进行语域之间的比较，语域之间定量的变异也可以在功能上得到解释。

本文还提出了其他一些焦点问题，如跨语言比较、平行语料库、语料库语言学在翻译及语言教学中的应用、机器翻译，以及词语重复序列的语料库研究，对今后的研究具有非常有益的指导和借鉴意义。值得注意的是，以语料库为基础的语篇研究未来也面临着一定的挑战，包括用于语篇层面语料库研究的计算机工具的利用率问题以及语料库的设计问题，值得语言研究者高度重视。

5. 超越科学和意识形态批判：批评话语分析的诸种发展

作者 Allan Luke 认为，在全球化背景下，新的跨国机构、社会构型、物质经济矛盾催生了公共话语、意识形态、身份认同等议题的多元化，对批评话语分析所涉及的语言理论和社会理论提出了新的要求。文章通过评述批评话语分析的本质和当前困境，指出了摆脱困境的突破口，勾勒了批评话语分析的发展图景，旨在为新时期中的批评话语分析重新定位。

Luke 指出，批评话语分析是一系列关乎政治立场和认识论的集合。就分析方法而言，批评话语分析履行着"往返转换"的职责，即通过语言学、符号学与文学的不同微观分析工具，对文本所建构的社会、制度和权力关系展开宏观评述。就政治内涵而言，批评话语分析是在不断变化的社会、经济、文化环境中,对语言、话语、文本和图像的潜在权势含义所作的批评解读(Luke,1997;van Dijk,1993)。更进一步讲,批评话语分析本身甚至也可以被看作话语,即一个由力量、权力与社会关系构成的场域。

  盛行的批评话语分析是一个意识形态批判的方案,"研究在社会政治语境下,语篇和谈话如何实施、再现和抵制社会权势滥用、统治和不平等"(van Dijk,2001)。然而,该方案可能使批评话语分析陷入新阿尔都塞主义范式(neo-Althussarian paradigm)的危险,即假定所有的媒体都是被霸权集中控制的质询,普通民众均是该霸权意识的受害者和攻击目标,进而限制了批评话语分析的视野。作者认为,困境的出路在于超越对意识形态批判的强烈专注,重新审视政治、经济、文化全球化形势下话语对权力的生产性使用。换言之,话语及其伴随的知识或权力构造既可以是积极的,也可以是消极的。因此,批判性话语分析有着捕捉、描述和批判更为广泛的话语规范性秩序的潜能,包括那些以生产性的、公正的、解放性的方式建构和转变知识与权力的话语关系。就此而言,新时期中的批评话语分析亟待新的研究对象、新的社会和文化理论概念的介入与融合。

  本文创新点主要有二。其一,作者拓展了话语对权力的生产性使用范畴,指出话语兼具积极性、消极性(McKenna,2006),因而新的时代需要比意识形态分析更为延展的、专注于各种新的文本构造,而不仅仅是统治阶级压迫下散居群体身份认同的研究议程。其二,作者勾勒了批评话语"积极性"的雏形,与积极话语分析(Martin,2004)的主张十分相近:批评话语分析对社会实践和事实的解析可采取更为积极的态度,从而加强人与人的相互理解,构建宽松和谐的社会。

  文章对批评话语分析在全球化背景下的发展具有重要理论价值和启示。它不但巩固并审视了新形势下批评话语分析的研究地位,促进了诸如互联网作为全球话语环境的研究(Koutsogiannis & Mitsikopoulou,2004)、亚裔移民者的国家身份认同感调查(Yamaguchi,2005)等研究发展,还特别连结了批评话语分析与新时期中教育研究的桥梁,包括教育政策

(Rizvi & Lingard，2013；Taylor，2007)、语言教学中的文化价值观(Liu，2005)、双语教室中的二语教学(Lam，2004)等。

6. 语类：语言、语境和读写能力

作者 Ken Hyland 在本文中综述了新修辞学派、悉尼学派和特殊用途英语等语类研究的三个流派及其特点，并在此基础上探讨了语类意识及其在外语教学中提高读写能力的作用，提出读写教学语类的意识理论框架。这一理论框架为提高读写教学质量、培养大学生在话语社团里开展研究、发表研究成果提供了借鉴，也为教学理念的转变、教学中的课堂任务设计和教材开发提供了指导。

本文由 7 节组成：(1)语类理论的背景知识，(2)语类整体性，(3)语类资源与功能变异，(4)语类变异与文化语境，(5)互为话语性、语类混淆以及语类集，(6)语类、读写能力与意识形态，(7)基于语类的教学法。本文介绍的主要是功能语言学的语类理论，该理论认为语类是分阶段有目的的社会过程。语类方法虽然有缺点，但它把语言、目的与语境连接在一起，有助于对话语、读写能力以及话语社团的理解。

文章认为，近20年来，应用语言学界对语类研究的关注日益增加，其中一点就是将语类理论应用于英语教学中的读写能力和语言特点研究。

文中谈到，语类存在于社会现实之中，同时又建构社会现实。在一个社团中，语类是社团社会活动的一种"样板"，社团成员通过按照它来发展相互间的关系，计划、调整和实施他们的交际行为。同时，语类也是一种选择，人们运用语类在约定俗成的交际活动中高效地"做事"，以期达到既定的交际目的。

文章指出，语类的模式不是僵化的、一成不变的。国际上不断变化的社会、政治和经济因素不断地对语类产生影响。基于语类理论的读写教学引导学习者提高对语类变化的敏感性：变化是常态，是一种意义表达的需要，所以在强调语类的规约性的同时，必须同时注意语类的适应性、协同性和多重性。

外语学习本质上是一个不断语境化的过程。基于语类理论的读写教学要求学习者不断地反思自己的语类实践；审视专业学科话语社团的文化和"做事"的规范，明确交际目的和读者对象。从提高学习者的语类意识入手，在读写教学过程中，学习者参与到这一不断语境化的互动过程之中。

7. 语篇分析与文体学

本文由 Paul Simpson 和 Geoff Hall 合写。文中涉及文学与非文学语篇的界定，以及当代语篇文体学研究方法及进展。文章以所选文学和非文学的重要专题研究、文章和书籍等为主线，考察综合应用多种理论和研究框架的文体学研究。文章指出，文学与非文学语篇的界定不是纯语言层面的，而是依赖于文本、读者、制度、社会文化语境的多元交叉，语篇文体学研究的跨学科性、研究方法的多样性。

文章认为，语篇分析既要研究文本也要把握社会语境，日常对话的语言分析对文学文本意义研究具有促进作用，文体学的研究方法和原则对于非文学语篇研究也具有重要意义。本文的主要观点有 5：(1) 诗学和语言学 (特别是新历史主义和语用学) 结合是语篇文体学研究的重要方法。莎士比亚戏剧中人物的话语交际应放在具体历史语境中研究。(2) 对话分析应用于文学语篇意义研究，对话是日常交际中的自我维护，话语修正可以揭示人物关系及性格化，话语交际也是建立某种权力关系的社会政治交际，同时说话者的社会地位比所说内容更能影响语篇意义和价值。(3) 读者对戏剧人物的理解是认知因素与文本因素交互作用的结果，读者在日常社交中形成的交际能力是理解小说对话的概念模型，对话结构对阅读过程具有引导作用。(4) 叙事学来源于日常对话，语用研究必不可少，自然叙事与文学作品叙事有共性与差异。当前英语小说叙事有"类似自传转向"的特点，即从第三人称标准英语转向第一人称英语方言，日常口语的语言特征使用增多。(5) 当前语篇文体学研究在研究焦点和范围上都跨越了文学和非文学的界限。语言行为理论、行为类型理论、对话分析、话语心理学和普遍语用学模型等理论框架可以应用于日常语言、法庭证词、公众媒体话语等非文学话语研究。

8. 跨文化语用学中的话语议题

作者 Diana Boxer 在本文中综述了跨文化语用学（Cross-cultural Pragmatics，简称 CCP）及其应用的最新研究成果。

CCP 认为来自不同社会或社区的个体根据各自的语用规则进行交流，往往会造成话语期盼的冲突，最终导致误解。这种误解具有典型的双向性，即群体之间相互误解。因此，不同的语言规则有可能使一个群体对另一个群体产生成见、偏见甚至歧视。绝大多数 CCP 研究都采用人种学研究方法或交际社会语言学的方法来收集和分析数据，即对已记录话语中的语言失误进行微观分析。

文章指出，与 CCP 研究最相关的三大领域为社会互动、教育和职场。

在社会互动领域，不同的世界观会导致群体之间的误解，因为世界观的不同可能会使人们对同一语境产生不同的理解。跨文化语用差异会使对话者无法达成一致理解，从而无法建立友谊，进而妨碍社会和谐。因此，跨文化语用研究要求双方跨越彼此文化的局限性、追求理解一致性。

在教育领域，CCP 涉及教育的各个层面，从早期幼儿教育到高等教育。作者列举了大量的前人研究成果来证明 CCP 在这一领域的重要性。例如，高校外籍教师和本土学生之间哪些语言和行为被认为是恰当的；是否有一些语言和行为在美式语境中被视为与性相关而在其他语境中却不是；国际助教（international teaching assistants，简称 ITA）与学生之间的语言交际研究等。

在工作场所，CCP 研究不仅处理不同社会之间也处理社会内部的文化或语言不一致问题。例如，Bilbow（1997）通过使用命令和建议探索了香港多文化工作环境中的跨文化交际。CCP 对职场的研究有助于消除成见或偏见，促进相互理解，还有助于纠正职场中的权力不公正现象，通过使双方意识到并理解各自的言语和行为规则、权力和统治问题等，实现双方平等。

作者指出，在不同的语言和文化环境中，跨文化交际能力尤为重要，对跨文化语用的忽视会导致偏见、成见甚至疏离。意识和理解不同语言和文化中的规则和差异性能够帮助人们相互协商、互相靠拢、消除隔阂、促进相互理解。

9. 同伴对话是二语学习的途径之一

本文由 Merrill Swain、Lindsay Brooks 和 Agustina Tocalli-Beller 三人合写而成。

文章从社会文化理论视角探讨同伴对话对二语学习产生的影响。作者首先阐述了社会文化理论的核心内容，即语言调节论、内化论和最近发展的理论；其次，分别阐述了写作、口语、听力以及阅读活动中同伴对话与二语学习之间的联系。文章认为，虽然相关研究没有证实同伴对话对二语学习产生显著影响，但告知二语学习者如何合作学习以及为何合作学习对促进同伴调节学习是非常重要的。

文章介绍了写作活动中同伴对话和同伴反馈对二语学习产生的影响。Swain and Lapkin (1998) 运用"微观起源"分析了两个 8 年级学生在法语沉浸课堂上共写一个故事的对话，结果表明同伴对话调节了二语的学习。Swain and Lapkin (2001) 考察了两个 7 年级学生在法语沉浸课堂上完成不同阶段写作任务的情况，结果显示同伴反馈有助于二语学习。Spielmam Davidson (2000) 研究了一个 8 年级的班级在法语课堂上共同学习条件句的形式和意义的情景，发现学生在有干预的写作学习活动中取得了明显进步。De Guerrero and Villamil (2000) 采用"微观起源"方法分析了 16 篇"读者"和"作者"的原始作文和修改后重写作文的片段，发现无论是作者还是读者和其同伴讨论并得到反馈后，二语知识都得到了强化和重组。其他学者的研究，如 Tang and Tithecott (1999)，Storch (1999，2000，2001a，2001b)，DiCamilla and Anton (1997)，Paulus (1999)，也证实了同伴对话和同伴反馈对语言的学习能产生一定的影响。Lynch and Maclean (2001)，Lynch (2001) 和 Ohta (2001) 的研究表明，口语活动中同伴对话能提升学习者的二语水平。Garcia and Asencion (2001)的调查结果表明,听力活动结束后同伴互动能帮助学习者提升听力理解能力。Klingner and Vaughn(2000)的研究表明,阅读过程中同伴对话能帮助学生运用理解策略和共构知识。

文章在"社会文化理论"框架内探讨"同伴合作对话"这种学习者个体间的互动学习形式是否有助于二语学习,为理解和研究二语学习提供了新的视角。"同伴合作对话"可以促进语言的内化过程,在此过程中突显了语言的交际观,即语言是交流的工具,也是认知的工具。同时,与同伴合作对话时,学习者个体的学习也是其知识建构的过程,学习者二语知识的发展是在与同伴的互动中实现的。

本文给我们的启示是,对教师来说,应更新语言观念,了解学生的知识发展水平,创设和组织有效的同伴对话活动,在学生个体间的互动中发挥好中介作用;对学习者来说,二语知识的发展产生于与同伴的互动中,因此,应积极参与和构建与同伴的互动。对研究人员来说,可以更全面地审视和研究第二语言学习的过程。

10. 师生互动与语言学习

本文由 Joan Kelly Hall 和 Meghan Walsh 两人合作写成。

文章立足于第一语言课堂、第二语言课堂以及外语课堂,围绕怎样的师生互动话语方式有利于语言学习这一问题,展开对三种语言课堂中老师与学生的面对面互动的研究,重点对比"教师引发-学生应答-教师评价"(IRE)和"教师引发-学生应答-教师后续话语"(IRF)三话步会话结构对学生语言学习的影响,然后从认识论角度对教师的会话结构选择进行解释并呈现实证研究。所归纳出的结论如下:(1)不同的三话步会话结构可造成不同的语言学习环境:IRE 会话结构的频繁使用会限制学生的课堂参与性;IRF 会话结构可以创造有效的语言学习环境,教学效果显著。(2)不同的课堂互动类型反映教师潜在的认识差异:采用 IRE 的老师将教学当成知识传播过程,采用 IRF 的老师则将教学当成师生共同参与的社会过程。(3)新近的研究已从实证角度定性、定量地证明了语言学习和课堂互动之间的关系。

论文的要点包括：语言学习与课堂互动的社会文化视角研究日益重要。IRE会话结构（Lemke，1990）作为三种课堂普遍存在的模式，在近来的研究（Cazden，1988；Barnes，1992；Gutierrez，1994；Nystrand，1997；Lin，2000）中被证明存在弊端：IRE会话结构的过度使用，不利于学生发展复杂的语言知识和技能，并且影响学生在社会文化层面上学习英语的兴趣。而三种语言课堂的实证研究（Wells，1993；Hall，1998；Nassji & Wells，2000；Rex & McEachen，1999；Sullivan，2000）表明IRF会话结构能促使学生思考，学生可陈述观点或讲述自身经历，促进师生互动。最后，作者以实证研究（Johnston，Woodside-Jiron & Day，2000）证明了课堂互动类型与教师观念之间的联系。

本文的亮点有：（1）将IRE和IRF三话步会话结构进行对比，充分论证了IRF会话结构的潜在价值和应用前景，改变人们对西方传统教育话语的认识。（2）全面展现了三种语言课堂的实证研究：第一语言课堂、第二语言课堂和外语课堂，所涉及的实证研究时间跨度较大（1988年-2000年），调查课堂范围广，成功对研究问题进行分析，使研究结论具有说服力。（3）不仅成功解析了不同语言课堂的会话结构研究中的社会文化因素，而且在此基础上对未来的研究进行了展望。

11. 二语或外语课堂中教师对目标语和母语的使用

Miles Turnbull和Katy Arnett两位作者从理论研究和实证研究两个方面做了文献综述，总结了近年来在二语或外语课堂中教师对目标语和母语使用的研究。论文分理论研究、实证研究、研究前景三个部分。

（1）理论研究。文章回顾了目标语输入、学习者动机、学习者认知水平、语码转换、使用母语的条件这五个方面。就目标语输入而言，二语或外语课堂中，应该只使用目标语，还是最大程度上使用目标语，或是优化目标语和母语之间的搭配？针对这些问题，作者（2001b）认为，适量使用母语可以使学习者更好地理解、吸收目标语。就学习者动机而言，大多数研究者认为二语或外语教学课堂上尽可能使用或者全部使用目标语,可以激发学习者的学习动机。关于学习者的认知水平,大部分研究者认为学习者的认知水平与教师在课堂上使用没有关系。关于语码转换的研究,学者认为,课堂上教师应该进行自然的语码转换。就什么情况下使用母语,文章主要回顾了 Cook(2001)和 Turnbull(2001b)两人的观点。

(2)实证研究。文章通过教师课堂话语,分析教师在二语或外语教学中使用目标语和母语的情况,作者从社会语言学语码转换的视角和功能教学法两个方面,回顾了三个实证研究。文章首先谈到教师对于使用目标语和母语的观点和态度,大部分教师认为在课堂上要以目标语为主,在一定情况下使用母语。文章还谈到学习者对这个问题的看法,主要介绍了两个调查,大部分学生认为教师在二语或外语教学中应该以目标语为主,辅以适量的母语。

(3)研究前景。作者认为未来的研究重点是在二语或外语教学中如何理解目标语和母语的使用数量和质量,如何使用学习者的母语才能使之更容易接受、学习更有成效。更重要的是,要进行过程-效果研究从而判断使用目标语和母语与学习者目标语水平和成绩的关系。

本文从理论研究成果和实证研究成果两个方面进行了综述,为二语或外语课堂中使用目标语和母语提供了更为全面的视角。就其理论价值而言,在综述前人研究的基础上,为二语或外语课堂优化使用目标语和母语提供了理论依据,同时,为未来的研究方向做了铺垫。就其应用价值而言,为二语或外语教学实践提供了更为可靠的方法依据,有助于教师们根据课堂教学内容的需求,适时地选择全部使用目标语,或者优化目标语和母语的使用比率,以更好地实现课堂教学效果。

12. 语篇与语言评估

本文由 Tim McNamara、Kathryn Hill 和 Lynette May 三人合作写成。

文章讨论的焦点是基于语篇研究的口语能力评估方法,探讨测试背景下的对话者、任务、表现、应试者和评估者。对话者角色对于口语测试的作用越来越引起大家的注意。考官与应试者之间的不同之处对测试的影响可以通过使用语篇分析方法来研究。Berry（1997）发现，个性因素（外向或内向）和性别影响着语篇。就任务而言，Komos(1999) 使用语篇分析来对比口语测试中访谈对话和角色扮演这两种形式，Riggenbach（1998）使用语篇分析来建议学习者在课堂外选择母语对话者，并记录下他们的对话。就任务和表现而言，Skehan(1998) 提出任务结构和在何种状况下被实行能够影响任务的难度；在非测试情境下的这项研究需要仔细分析不同任务类型下以及不同表现状况下生成的语篇。就应试者性格特征而言，测试更多的是一种交流，这意味着很难分开讨论应试者和测试者的性格特征给测试带来的效应。因此应该考虑到多种因素，比如双方参与者的性别，应试者和测试者的文化背景和语言背景。就评分标准而言，口语测试研究加深理解评分者的语言与行为对测试分数的影响，完善评分等级有利于分析应试者语篇。

文章还谈到社会语用能力，认为跨语言语用学研究主要是在语篇完成任务的帮助下完成的，语篇完成任务通常是以书面形式呈现出来的，在给定的社交情境下，应试者选择在这种情境下要说的话。文章指出，目前有关课堂测试情境下的语篇分析研究还不多。

文章还讨论了语篇分析与技术问题，如半直接语言测试、在线语用测试、语料库的使用等。

文章的创新之处在于，它进行了以语篇为基础的口语评估方法研究。这些研究起初侧重于传统的口语面谈，继而延伸到新的测试形式，包括两人交流和小组交流。语篇分析已经被证明有助于研究评分者的行为和完善评分等级。另一创新之处在于紧跟最新研究关注口语评估内的语用能力评估和技术应用，包括半直接和直接的评估方法以及电脑数据库的使用。

13. 口头语言评估的语篇分析方法

作者 Richard F. Young 通过对口语测试文本解读方法的批判性分析，结合学术界目前对口语测试的评判标准，提出语言形式、非语言交流、语言文本等对口语测试者的影响。

文章首先研究了一段样本对话，审视了学界不同的构建解读方法，如语言形式、非语言交流、语言学情景解读等，然后综述了可以测试的语言文本和不能测试的语言文本。作者强调了之前测试中没有关注到的因素——交流的语言形式和沟通背景以及参与者意图达到的结果与口语交流和参与者文化的密切关系，并强调了面对面交流的完整性对于语言传递的重要性。

语言能力测试一个重要的层面就是非语言因素的角色发挥和影响。如 Birdwhistell 关于母子对话的非语言情景解读，从单纯的语言文本分析到语言和非语言因素的分析迈出了一小步。

口语是一个复杂的现象，理解一个二语习得者在多大程度上可以灵活运用语言是语言测试中的一个难点。50 年来，录音机和再现技术已经使研究取得了进步。近年来，研究者开始运用文本分析来审视已有的测试方法，并且提出新的测试的方法。本文提出了二语习得者口语测试中尚未得到深度研究的问题：语言形式的分析和语言情景的分析以及文化因素的影响，这对研究语言口语测试的准确性和全面性有所启示。

14. 写作评估的语篇分析方法

Ulla Connor 和 Aymerou Mbaye 两位作者通过研究两次大型英语写作考试的评分过程，对比最新的文本分析研究成果，发现基于语篇结构分析的写作能力的评分标准和英语写作能力的实际评估有较大差异。

文章分析和归纳了教学和测试评估在 EFL、ESL 写作中的语篇分析方法。作者指出，尽管写作测试评估日益受到重视，但是，很多研究忽视了近期语篇分析研究的新成果。对于写作评估和评判标准而言，二者之间所存在的差距亟待语篇结构理论的介入。作者基于近期的语篇分析研究成果，对 EFL、ESL 写作测试实践中存在的写作评价——评判标准的差距进行了语篇特征分析，在综述原因的基础上，提出了一个同时满足语言学和语篇特征分析要求的写作评估模型。

两作者将修辞学和交际特征引入到写作评估之中,并指出,一般的测试研究倾向于对文本的语言学特征(语法、词汇和文本结构)进行分析,但是这样做忽略了对读者而言同样重要的写作效力问题,如策略性和社会语言学能力。因此,写作评价需要强调语篇、社会语言学和策略能力等诸多方面。

两作者高度总结并归纳了当时第二语言能力评价的最新研究以及文本分析的最新研究进展,并在此基础上提出文本分析需要在以下三个方面有所提高:(1)语篇能力:强调的能力应该高于语篇结构和段落的衔接与连贯;(2)社会语言学能力:强调的能力应该包括对正确写作问题以及语篇语气(语调)和语域的写作意识培养;(3)策略能力:读者和观众意识的培养。

最后,作者提出了写作能力模型的交际能力分析框架和评估标准。

三、评述

从本卷《年度评论》各篇文章可以看到,语篇分析的经典理论应用于语言教学实践已取得了卓越成效。不过语言教学是个常谈常新的话题,是个动态的实践活动,因此,新的问题随着教学实践的发展会不断涌现。同理,语篇的研究活动也一直在持续不断地进行。但本卷《年度评论》出版于 2002 年,所涉及的理论是距今十多年的理论和应用。另外,本卷《年度评论》涉及的理论以英美学派为主,很少涉及欧洲大陆学者和澳大利亚学者对语篇分析的研究成果。作为扩展阅读,这里介绍一下以 de Beaugrande 为代表的欧洲大陆学者的语篇语义研究和以 Martin 为代表的悉尼学派的语篇语义研究,以飨读者。

1. 欧洲大陆学派的语篇语义观

以 de Beaugrande 为代表的篇章语言学家们受 20 世纪 80 年代认知科学思潮的影响,强调语篇的交际过程,与忽视语境研究的传统语法学者们泾渭分明,形成独具一格的欧洲大陆学派。de Beaugrande(1980,

1981)提出语篇性的七大标准,即衔接、连贯、意向性、情境性、信息性、可接受性和互文性,是欧洲大陆学派语篇语义研究的基石。欧洲大陆学派语篇语义研究的代表作包括 de Beaugrande (1981) 撰写的《篇章语言学导论》和 van Dijk (1980) 的《宏观结构》等。

de Beaugrande 在语篇语义学的研究中提出了规程说,并在实践中综合了多学科的知识,特别是 Wood 在20世纪70年代提出的扩展网络技术 (Augmented Transition Network),旨在研究语篇的实际 (actual) 信息动态生成和处理过程,强调人类语言的实质是人类活动。传统语法旨在发现语法规则,规程说则致力于语篇动态生成的动机、策略、规律、优先选择和常规选择,研究语篇操作系统的构建、调节和运作,并提出语篇管制的三个原则:效益性 (efficiency)、效能性 (effectiveness) 和合适性 (appropriateness)(de Beaugrande,1980:21)。

van Dijk(1980) 从认知角度区别了自然语言中的宏观结构 (macro-structure) 和微观结构 (microstructure),整体结构 (global structure) 和局部结构 (local structure),使用认知模型解析宏观结构的产生、转换、知识储存等,以及其在人类互动交际中如何组织复杂的信息,并阐明其与人类认知之间的关系。van Dijk 提出超结构 (superstructure) 的概念,认为它与宏观结构是内容与形式的关系。van Dijk 还关注语篇的语境模式,解析语境如何影响篇章话语的产生、结构、理解等,研究话语、语言使用者和语境三者之间的关系(陈春燕,2010)。

整体而言,欧洲大陆学派的语篇语义学不仅研究语篇的表层形式,而且在宏观意义上强调语篇互动性的交际语境。欧洲大陆学派指出语篇的实质是人类活动,并将其视为一种与语境相关联的操作过程,在语言使用者的交际事件 (communicative occurrence) 中不断地维持其元稳定 (meta-stability)。

2. 悉尼学派的语篇语义观

悉尼学派的理论基础是以 Halliday 为代表的系统功能语言学。Halliday 主要研究英语小句的语法,认为一个小句中同时具有谋篇、概念和人际等三种元功能。对应小句的三种元功能得出小句的三种意义：谋篇意义、概念意义及人际意义（王振华，2009）。Martin 继承了 Halliday 的三大元功能思想，认为超越小句的大语篇同样具有这三大元功能生成的意义。他以系统思想和功能思想为核心，开拓了语篇语义学的新视野，是悉尼学派的代表人物（王振华，2012）。

悉尼学派的语篇语义研究代表作有：1992 年 Martin 的《英语语篇：系统和结构》和 2003 年（2007 年再版）Martin & Rose 合著的《语篇研究——跨越小句的意义》，以及 2005 年 Martin 和 White 合著的《评价性语言：英语中的评价系统》。Martin 认为他的语篇语义系统"研究的是语义与语法自然联系的语篇"（Martin，1992：1）。他提出与三大元功能相联系的语篇语义资源体系，认为分析语篇语义有六种维度，即协商系统（negotiation）、评价系统（appraisal）、概念系统（ideation）、联结系统（conjunction）、识别系统（identification）和语篇格律系统（periodicity）（Martin & Rose，2003，2007）。他关注语篇中与语境相关联的词汇语法资源，试图解释语言使用者如何在语篇层面建构意义，拓展了语言的语篇语义层。

Martin 引领悉尼学派将 Halliday 的横组合、纵聚合的概念应用到语篇层面，扩展了 Halliday 的语境观和 Halliday & Hasan 的衔接理论，并解析了语域、语类和意识形态的关系，为自然语篇提供了系统的、操作性强的分析工具。

3. 欧洲大陆学派和悉尼学派的语篇语义研究对比

语篇本身是一个系统，语篇语义学研究的内容就是该系统中的生产者、文本/话语及语篇的消费者这三个要件以及三者之间的关系（王振华，2008）。语篇语义的研究路径多种多样，而一个范式、两个脉络、三种功能、四种语义、五个视角的研究路径基于系统科学和系统功能语言学（王振华，2009），能够较全面、系统地阐释语篇语义的研究范式、研究目标和研究内容。我们试图从这三个角度对悉尼学派和欧洲大陆学派的异同进行对比分析。鉴于学派内部观点的多样性,本文重点对比 Martin 和 de Beaugrande 这两个代表人物的语篇语义观。

(1)研究范式对比

从研究范式上看,悉尼学派和欧洲大陆学派都可以看作是在系统科学的范式下展开的,对理论的应用都比较广泛。系统科学"把研究重心放在探究各个系统的本质规律上(http://zh.wikipedia.org/wiki/系统科学)。"悉尼学派的语篇语义研究侧重在社学科学领域,继承了系统功能语言学中系统这个核心概念:"系统功能语言学研究的是系统,即不同语言单位之间的关系"(Martin, 1992:4)。他们在对语篇意义研究的过程中,建构了各级各类的系统网络,将使用中的语言和语言的使用者纳入不同的系统中进行研究。欧洲大陆学派在系统科学的范式下,结合自然科学的研究成果,以语篇生产者及消费者的心理操作为中心,解释文本/话语的生成和理解。

两个学派的不同点是:悉尼学派从社会学、符号学及语言学的理论出发,将语言和语境有机地结合起来研究意义,用同切圆系统地将语境和语言分层(stratum),语境分语类和语域,语言分语篇语义、词汇语法和音系字系。在此基础上,研究各个层次之间的附生关系,认为语类附生于语域之上,语类是各种语域意义模式的模式;语篇语义附生于词汇语法之上,词汇语法附生于音系字系之上,语篇语义由词汇语法实现,词汇语法由音系字系实现。悉尼学派既研究使用中的语言,也研究语言的使用者,既研究语境系统,也研究语言系统,既研究系统之间的实现关系,也研究系统的实例化和个体化关系(马丁、王振华,2008)。因此,悉尼学派通过系统网络对精密阶进行描写,语言及语言使用者的意义潜势,为语篇语义研究提供了极具实用性的分析工具,是语篇语义学从宏观到微观研究的典范。欧洲大陆学派受认知科学、心理学及语言学等影响,强调语篇语义的宏观研究,他们综合认知科学等多学科知识,重点利用流行的扩展网络技术表征语篇操作,并从宏观层面研究语篇生成及接收的程序过程。欧洲大陆学派认为语言系统是虚拟(virtual)的,从语言到语篇有赖于现实化

（actualization）的操作进程，需从语言系统中进行选择组合，最终形成语篇的功能单位。其思想带有明显的人工智能学科特征。

（2）研究目标对比

从研究目标上看，悉尼学派和欧洲大陆学派都研究超越句子的大语篇，不仅重视语篇的表层形式，而且强调语篇的深层意义。两个学派都承认语篇是语言生产者和消费者选择/激活的结果，有盖然性，理论都比较成熟。欧洲大陆学派指出语言是具造义潜势的虚拟系统，语篇是语言选择后以特定结构展现的现实系统。这与悉尼学派认为语言是意义潜势的观点有共通之处。

两大学派亦有不同。悉尼学派研究语篇功能的实现，属于功能主义。悉尼学派发展了系统功能语言学，在三个元功能的基础上，提出语篇有协商系统、联结系统、格律系统、识别系统、概念系统、评价系统等。该学派重视语篇在人际交往中的功能：评价系统与协商系统、参与系统（involvement）（Martin & White, 2005）属于人际意义范畴下语篇语义的三个次系统。概念系统是指语言使用者把对现实的理解以语篇的形式体现，意义的体现具有序列性；联结系统主要从联结词语角度体现语篇内部的逻辑关系；识别系统从入篇资源（introducing resources）和追踪资源（tracking resources）入手识别文本中具体的或抽象的参与者，入篇资源、追踪资源的实现手段分别是呈现性指称（presenting reference）和认定性指称（presuming reference）；语篇格律研究语篇节奏和信息流，小波浪、大波浪和浪潮是分析大语篇的有效手段，语篇格律探索信息流规律，研究信息峰相连的规律模型，并预测波的层级（王振华，2009）。理论中各系统的关联性较强，突出系统性。

欧洲大陆学派研究语篇的动态生成。该学派利用认知科学和认知语言学的已有成果，强调语言使用者的交际过程，提出语篇性七大标准，但受宏观研究影响，各个标准的研究较为独立，关联性不强，缺乏系统性。de Beaugrande 把语篇生成看作可调节的自动操作系统，认为语篇操作模式的决定性因素是操作性（operationality）和人类的主观认可性（human plausibility)(de Beaugrande,1981:33)。语篇生成阶段包括生成计划（planning），概念形成（ideation），概念拓展（development），概念表达（expression），语法化解析（parsing）(de Beaugrande,1981:42)。理解的过程与生成的过程则基本相反。

（3）研究内容对比

从研究内容上看，悉尼学派和欧洲大陆学派都从文本/话语及语言使用者（生产者和消费者）角度进行研究，讨论文本/话语的语篇衔接、连贯、知识建构和会话研究，关注语言使用者生成语篇的语境，但亦有异同。

a）关于文本/话语的研究。

在文本/话语的衔接上，悉尼学派和欧洲大陆学派很大程度上都受到Halliday & Hasan（1976）衔接理论的影响，但由于研究范式的不同，对衔接的研究角度有一定的区别。

Martin将重点放在联结词语上，并用来洞悉语篇中事件之间的逻辑关系。他提出了四种逻辑关系：加和关系、比较关系、时序关系以及解释小句间的因果、目的或条件等关系。他从横组合、纵聚合的角度研究语篇的衔接，形成联接系统网络，研究大语篇的表层衔接和深层连贯。此外，Martin的联结系统还涉及格律方面的衔接，同时还提出了逻辑隐喻的概念（王振华，2007）。

De Beaugrande探讨了短程语段衔接（short-term stretches）和长程语段衔接（long-term stretches）的方式和作用。短程语段衔接主要靠语法的依赖关系（grammatical dependencies）。长程语段衔接有利于组织表层语篇（surface text），节省语篇笔墨，与效益性（efficiency）这一语篇管制原则相联系（de Beaugrande,1981:54）。衔接的方式包括词组、小句和句子的语法化，涵盖了重现（recurrence）、冠词（articles）、共指（co-reference）、省略（ellipsis）及连接（junction）(de Beaugrande,1980:19)。de Beaugrande从认识科学角度讨论连贯，把连贯看作知识激活的操作过程，语篇世界是由概念的相互关系构建的网络系统。连贯手段包括：第一，因果关系和类属关系；第二，事件、动作、物品及情景是如何组织的；第三，连贯的实现需要借助互文性的连续互动得以实现（de Beaugrande, 1980：19）。

关于文本/话语的知识构建，Martin 在系统功能语言学的框架下，认为知识通过概念意义体现，并结合从 Bernstein & Muller 的社会学研究，从社会符号学角度解读语域作为语境变量与知识结构的关系，研究不同语类、不同学科的知识编码，阐明术语形成、术语关联性及术语间因果关系阐释的内部机制，强调语法隐喻构建垂直话语的重要性（杨信彰，2012）。与 Martin 对知识的社会符号学研究不同，de Beaugrande 从心理学及人工智能角度强调交际过程中的知识激活，指出知识不论是在储存或使用过程中，都可被看成是框架（frame）或图式（schema），强调知识的排列性质和实现性操作进程。他认为知识与语言使用者实现交际目的的计划紧密相关，是参与者在交流中实现自我角色的脚本（script）指南。框架和图式更倾向于知识的内部排列，而计划和脚本体现日常互动的交际目的（de Beaugrande, 1980：163-164）。他也探讨人们的知识体系对于语篇生成和理解所起的作用（de Beaugrande, 1980：259），并指出，句子依赖语法知识，而语篇更注重经验知识（de Beaugrande, 1980：14）。

关于文本/话语的会话研究，Martin 侧重从元功能出发，析出言语功能的语义层次（semantic stratum）。从结构类型角度探讨日常会话中的交换结构，分析与三大元功能对应的结构类型：粒子结构、韵律结构和格律结构，并研究话步、话轮转换的结构类型，强调会话的人际功能（王振华、张大群、张先刚，2010）。de Beaugrande 对会话进行宏观分析，认为语篇是人类社会实践。语言生产者有目的地通过语篇将信息传递给语言消费者，以建立各种关系。对话行为可以认为是人们运用有目的地监听和操纵交际情景，并进行协商的结果。会话交流情景的即时性很大程度上取决于互文性，会话中的衔接、连贯和可接受性不同于其他语类的语篇性标准（de Beaugrande, 1980：242）。de Beaugrande（2004）还重点从重音（stress）、音高（pitch）、音量（volume）和语速（pace）四个方面对会话片段进行格律研究。这一点 Martin 很少论及。

b)关于语言的生产者、消费者及相关语境的研究。

悉尼学派和欧洲大陆学派的语篇语义研究都关注了语言的生产者和消费者。从语言使用者的角度出发,悉尼学派提出了语篇语义的评价系统,强调赋值语义(evaluation of semantics),从社会学视野将文本中评价性词汇纳入研究范围,在语篇层面上进一步拓展了人际元功能的研究。他提出的协商系统也关注语言使用者在会话语篇中的互动作用。de Beaugrande 提出的意图性、可接受性,关注语言生产者、消费者在语篇生成时的心理机制。意图性关注语言的生产者是否有意地致力于语篇的衔接和连贯。在语篇操作模式中,语篇被当成将语言生产者的心理安排(plan)转换成传信目的(goal)的通道(de Beaugrande, 1980: 164)。他认为,一个语篇的可接受性往往取决于对话双方是否愿意成功交际的态度,即谈话人是否主观认可语篇的连贯性(de Beaugrande, 1980: 20)。

关于语篇生成的语境研究,悉尼学派借鉴了叶尔姆斯列夫的符号学理论,强调语境对语篇语义研究的重要作用,认为语境有三个层面:语类、语域及意识形态(Martin, 1992)。Martin 的语境模型是这三个层面的"外延式符号"和其自身的"内包式符号"层层叠加起来的,其语境理论的着眼点是语篇的图式结构(胡壮麟、朱永生、张德禄、李战子,2008:426—427)。de Beaugrande 同样强调语境的作用,他提出的语篇标准的情景性及互文性关注语篇生成的语境。情景性使语篇联系当时或可追溯的情景因素,而互文性指的是一个指定文本和其他先前相关文本的关系。语言使用者的意图影响互文性的运用。互文性是形成语篇类型的主要因素(de Beaugrande, 1980:20)。可见悉尼学派从语篇功能实现出发研究互文性,而欧洲大陆学派是从语篇动态交际程序出发研究互文性。

欧洲大陆学派的语篇语义研究具有很强的跨学科性,将人工智能和心理学领域的研究成果运用于语篇研究,动态地表征语篇的生成和理解机制,是从认知角度研究语篇语义的有效尝试,对语篇语义形式化的研究具有参考价值。由于这种宏观研究的复杂性,欧洲大陆学派缺乏对语篇语义成分关系的基础研究,以至成为制约其形式化发展的障碍。悉尼学派则从社会学、符号学角度,阐明了语篇语义的六个系统,为语篇语义分析提供了可操作的社会科学工具。从一定意义上讲,这两大学派的语篇语义研究具有一定的互补性。

参考文献

de Beaugrande, R.(1980). *Text, Discourse and Process: Toward a Multidisciplinary Science of Texts*. Group Norwood: Ablex.

de Beaugrande, R.(2004). *A New Introduction to The Study of Text and Discourse*. http://www.beaugrande.com/new_intro_to_study.htm.

de Beaugrande, R. & W. Dressler.(1981). *Introduction to Text Linguistics*. London: Longman Publishing Group.

Halliday, M. A. K.(1978/2001). *Language as Social Semiotic:The Social Interpretation of Language and Meaning*. London: Edward Arnold/Beijing:Foreign Language Teaching and Research Press.

Halliday, M. A. K.(1994). *An Introduction to Functional Grammar*. London: Arnold.

Halliday, M. A. K. & R. Hasan.(1976). *Cohesion in English*. London: Longman.

Halliday, M. A. K. & C. Matthiessen.(2004/2008). *An Introduction to Functional Grammar*. London:Arnold.

Koutsogiannis, D., & Mitsikopoulou, B.(2004). The Internet as a global discourse environment. *Language Learning & Technology*, 8(3), 83–89.

Lam, W. S. E. Second language socialization in a bilingual chat room: Global and local considerations. *Language Learning & Technology*, 8(3), 44–65.

Liu, Y.(2005). The construction of cultural values and beliefs in Chinese language textbooks: A critical discourse analysis. *Discourse: Studies in the Cultural Politics of Education*, 26(1), 15–30.

Luke, A.(1997). The material effects of the word: Apologies, 'stolen children' and public discourse. *Discourse: Studies in the Cultural Politics of Education*, 18(3), 343–368.

Luke, A.(2002). Beyond science and ideology critique: Developments in Critical Discourse Analysis. *Annual Review of Applied Linguistics*, 22, 96–110.

Martin, J.(1992). *English Text: System and Structure*. Amsterdam: Benjamins.

Martin, J.(2007). Construing Knowledge: a Functional Linguistic Perspective. In Frances Christie and J. R. Martin(eds.)*Language, Knowledge and Pedagogy: Functional Linguistic and Sociological Perspectives*[C]. London: Continuum. 34–64.

Martin, J. R.(2004). Positive discourse analysis: Solidarity and change. *Revista Canaria de Estudios Ingleses*, 49, 179–200.

Martin, J. & D. Rose.（2003/2007）. *Working with Discourse:Meaning Beyond the Clause*. London: Continuum.

Martin, J. & P. White.（2005）. *The Language of Evaluation: Appraisal in English*. London: Palgrave.

McKenna, B.（2004）. Critical discourse studies: Where to from here? *Critical Discourse Studies*, *1*（1）, 9–39.

Rizvi, F. , & Lingard, B.（2013）. *Globalizing Education Policy*. Routledge.

Taylor, S.（2004）. Researching educational policy and change in 'new times': Using critical discourse analysis. *Journal of Education Policy*, *19*（4）, 433–451.

van Dijk, T. A. *Text and Context.*（1977）. London and New York: Longman.

van Dijk, T. A.（1980）. *Macrostructures: An Interdisciplinary Study of Global Structures in Discourse, Interaction, and Cognition.* New Jersey: Laurence Erlbaum Associates.

van Dijk, T. A.（1993）. Principles of critical discourse analysis. *Discourse & Society*, *4*（2）, 249–283.

van Dijk, T. A.（2001）. Critical discourse analysis. *The Handbook of Discourse Analysis*, 352–371.

van Dijk, T. A.（2008）. *Discourse and Context: A Sociocognitive Approach.* Cambridge: Cambridge University Press.

Woods, W.（1970）. Transition Network Grammars for Natural Language Analysis. *Communications of the ACM*, *13*: 591–606.

Yamaguchi, M.（2005）. Discursive representation and enactment of national identities: The case of generation 1. 5 Japanese. *Discourse & Society*, *16*（2）, 69–299.

陈春燕, van Dijk. 新著话语与语境介绍.《外语教学与研究》, 2010,（1）:75–77.

范文澜.《文心雕龙注》. 北京：人民文学出版社, 1962.

胡壮麟, 朱永生, 张德禄, 李战子.《系统功能语言学概论》, 北京：北京大学出版社, 2008.

姜望琪.《语篇语言学研究》. 北京：北京大学出版社, 2011.

刘辰诞, 赵秀凤.《什么是篇章语言学》. 上海：上海外语教育出版社, 2011.

刘熙载.《艺概》. 上海：上海古籍出版社, 1978.

马丁, 王振华. 实现化、实例化和个性化——系统功能语言学的三种层次关系.《上海交通大学学报》, 2008,（5）：73–81.

王振华. 评价系统及其运作——系统功能语言学的新发展.《外国语》, 2001,（6）：13–20.

王振华. 语篇研究新视野——《语篇研究——跨越小句的意义》述介.《外语教学与研究》, 2007,（5）：415–418.

王振华. 作为系统的语篇,《外语学刊》, 2008,（3）：50–57.

王振华. 语篇语义的研究路径——一个范式、两个脉络、三种功能、四种语义、五个视角.《中国外语》,2009,(6):26–38.
王振华.编者的话.载王振华(编)《马丁文集》.上海:上海交通大学出版社,i–iv. 2012.
王振华,张大群,张先刚.马丁对语篇语义的研究,《当代外语研究》,(10):43–49. 2010.
杨信彰.导读[A].载王振华(编)《马丁文集(4)——语域研究》.上海:上海交通大学出版社,i–ix. 2012.

EDITOR'S INTRODUCTION

Mary McGroarty

Overview of Volume 22

As a phenomenon, discourse does not belong only to applied linguistics, although applied linguistics figures among the disciplines in which discourse is a central focus. For approximately the last three decades, applied linguists and scholars in allied disciplines have developed more detailed theoretical foundations, more sophisticated research techniques, and a wider range of applications for discourse analysis. Heterogeneity of theoretical perspectives, of contexts of application, and of research methods has been a hallmark of contemporary discourse research, as many of the volumes in the influential series *Advances in Discourse Processes* attest (see, for example, Tannen, 1988). Papers in the 1990 volume of the *Annual Review of Applied Linguistics* (Grabe, 1990) similarly testify to the already well-established variety of discourse analytic approaches and applications. The classroom has never been the only setting with which discourse analysts and applied linguists have concerned themselves, although educational applications of discourse analytic techniques have been common in North American scholarship ever since *The Language of the Classroom* (Bellack, Kliebard, Hyman, & Smith, 1966), *Functions of Language in the Classroom* (Cazden, John, & Hymes, 1972), and *Towards an Analysis of Discourse* (Sinclair & Coulthard, 1975). It remains a context of major consequence for many applied linguists because of their connection to the world of teaching practice and assessment. The theme of this year's volume, *Discourse and Dialogue*, revisits some of the topics discussed in these earlier volumes, adds some new areas of consideration, and captures some of the richness of recent discourse-related work.

The chapters in the first section, Approaches to Discourse Analysis, situate the study of discourse in several of the disciplines for which it offers a principal mode of investigation. Different disciplines employ different rationales and approaches to discourse analysis, and the reviews in this first section illustrate the epistemological and methodological diversity driving different approaches. Differences arise because of the comparative prominence of discourse data as contrasted with social theory. Some epistemologies attempt to accord equal prominence to both, some privilege a particular perspective on social theory, and some are avowedly agnostic with respect to theory and proceed on a largely inductive basis such that patterns in (typically, large) samples of linguistic data constitute principal findings. The chapters in this first section illustrate the entire range of approaches. Schegloff, Koshik, Jacoby, and Olsher outline the areas in which Conversation Analysis, rooted in sociology, has special relevance to applied linguistic concerns. Lazaraton's review of empirical work in discourse analysis raises important issues of research design and analytic choices as revealed in a set of recent empirical articles. Martin sets out the conceptual foundations of Systemic Functional Linguistics and shows how it has recently been employed across several areas of investigation, including social semiotics as well as applied linguistics. Conrad explains the types of research questions particularly suitable for investigation using corpus linguistic techniques and notes that increasingly powerful computing tools as well as the availability of several large corpora will enable wider impact for corpus-based research. Luke's discussion of developments in critical discourse analysis takes on the issue of the link between social theory and linguistic analyses.

The second section illustrates some typical applications of discourse analysis. Hyland shows how current discourse analytic work based on the Systemic Functional approach has helped to refine definitions of genre and consequently affected approaches to applied linguistic research and language instruction. Simpson and Hall demonstrate that recent work in literary stylistics reflects several approaches to discourse analysis, many of them employed to challenge prior reliance on exclusively formalist interpretations. In her review of pragmatic issues in cross-cultural communication, Boxer provides several examples of insights drawn from research using discourse analytic techniques, techniques that have helped to identify some of the areas in which parties to an interaction can experience difficulties despite the outward appearance of 'speaking the same language.'

The third section features research that employs discourse analysis in classrooms, mainly language classrooms, as a means to better understand the interactional processes that constitute teaching and learning. Much of the work discussed in this section illustrates growing awareness of the potential of sociocultural theory to reveal new insights about language learning (Lantolf, 2000). Swain, Brooks, and Tocalli-Beller show that students can support each other's learning through their interactions with each other; thus peer-peer dialogue serves as both medium and evidence of language learning. In their presentation of teacher-student interaction, Hall and Walsh demonstrate that teachers and students apparently exert reciprocal influences on each other during the course of exchange such that, even while engaged in similar tasks, students in a classroom may experience different interactional environments. Turnbull and Arnett review recent work on teachers' classroom language use in order to revisit the perennially important question about proportion of native and second language use during instruction. They note that identification of the proportion of native versus target language used does not in itself inspire much insight unless it is coupled with more precise accounts of learning tasks and outcomes in different contexts.

The papers on assessment in the fourth section testify to increasing sophistication about the nature of discourse as an interactionally determined phenomenon. McNamara, Hill, and May present a variety of approaches to oral language assessment and emphasize that individual, occupational, and situational factors can impinge on oral language assessments in ways that make them atypical of interactions not conducted for purposes of evaluation. Through dissecting a conversation between a mother and son, Young shows the many layers of meaning conveyed and interpretations derived from the different lenses of various discourse analytic approaches; this chapter makes the important point that most research on oral assessment to date has privileged the verbal at the expense of the nonverbal channel and contends that new technologies expand the possibilities for recording and analysis of nonlinguistic aspects of interaction. In their consideration of writing assessment, Connor and Mbaye note that sentence-level criteria have for too long dominated the evaluation of second language writing and propose new criteria that include discourse competence for use in writing assessment as well as instruction.

Taken as a whole, the papers in this volume offer some selective updates to many of the topics addressed in *ARAL 11* (Grabe, 1990) and extend into new directions as well. Some of these chapters illustrate the influence of constructivist epistemologies and more nuanced understandings of instructional environments, two areas crucial for advances in applied linguistic scholarship (McGroarty, 1998). They further exemplify awareness of the connections between research questions amenable to discourse analytic approaches and technological developments, notably computer-based technologies, to facilitate data collection and analysis. But technological developments alone cannot address many of the crucial pedagogical questions related to interactional processes that promote learning, both the learning of languages and other kinds of learning. To render a more complete picture, concomitant research on the various social networks that surround and support uses of new technologies is required (Brown & Duguid, 2000). With respect to instructional and assessment applications, as with other arenas of applied linguistics, technological improvements that enable the collection of more, better quality, and more precisely cataloged units of data must be linked to questions of theoretical and pedagogical import. Thus the tensions between data- and theory-driven discourse research exemplified by the chapters in the first section here continue and suggest several promising avenues for future investigations.

Procedural Notes

Because one of the goals of *ARAL* has been to serve as a reference tool, this volume carries the usual three indexes—an *Author* index for authors cited in the past five volumes, a *Subject* index for subjects discussed in the past ten volumes, and a *Contributor* index of contributors to the past ten volumes, along with their topics—that enable readers to trace the influence of particular scholars and the trearment of particular topics over time. The *ARAL* indexes thus reflect the continuity and shifts in the field of applied linguistics. Because applied linguistics is an international field, contributors are invited from all geographic areas and asked to provide original articles on their topics in English. While English is an international language, spelling of a few items varies by country and region. For the sake of uniformity in presentation, all spelling in the text follows North American conventions, but titles (and, if used, direct quotations) retain the spellings used in the original publications.

The content of each chapter is the sole responsibility of the author or authors, as are all judgments conveyed therein; neither the editor nor the editorial directors intervene in content choices made, beyond extending the initial invitation to write about a certain topic. In keeping with the goal of providing a useful reference tool, all reasonable efforts have been made to ensure the accuracy of references, and the editor apologizes in advance if any inaccuracies in referencing have inadvertently been allowed to persist in the final version of each chapter. (This has proven a special challenge in the case of citations for internet resources, a protean realm where the number of sources and conventions for referring to them are constantly evolving.)

This volume marks the first time that *ARAL* carries the designation 'an official journal of the American Association for Applied Linguistics,' an arrangement proposed over a year ago and approved by a majority vote of the AAAL membership in the summer of 2001. I look at this relationship as an opportunity to bring *ARAL* to a wider audience, including the students pursuing advanced degrees who typically constitute between a quarter and a third of the Association's membership. In giving AAAL members access to a wide range of solid and current scholarship, *ARAL* should help AAAL's members "promote principled approaches to language-related concerns," a central goal of the organization, as well as fulfill its traditional role of bringing sound, original overviews of recent research to the international scholarly community. Even though applied linguistics remains "a relatively ill-defined and interdisciplinary domain" (Grabe, 2000, p. vii), *ARAL* reflects the major emphases of the field and directs academic attention to new developments that warrant consideration. Like my editorial predecessors, I expect that *ARAL* will "continue to chart the field, to contribute to its development, and to serve as an important resource both to practitioners and to future applied linguists" (Kaplan & Grabe, 2000, p. 16). It is my hope that the relationship between AAAL and *ARAL* will contribute to the vibrancy of both.

Acknowledgments

Many different individuals and organizations provide the support necessary to sustain the series and produce each volume. The Editorial Directors of the series have offered substantial and continued support and helped to identify many of the contributors to this volume, as have members of the Editorial Advisory Board. I am particularly indebted to all contributors for their willingness to share their perspectives on discourse analysis and thus make this volume of *ARAL* a reality. Many of them are senior scholars; all are active researchers and teachers who had to deal with competing obligations while preparing their chapters. I am additionally grateful to the staff of the Cambridge University Press Journals Division: manager Ed Barnas, editorial assistant Julie Lee, and production manager Ed Carey, whose timely and professional work serve both the journal and the discipline well.

The persons more closely involved in the editorial process have again proven their poise and professionalism, and I am fortunate to benefit from their skills. Beth Yule, the *ARAL* Editorial Assistant, has once again managed to take manuscripts submitted in a variety of formats and render them coherent and consistent, sometimes through several iterations. Moreover, her meticulous attention to maintenance and revision of the indexes makes them valuable resources. Julie McCormick's expertise in publication design and page layout has once more shaped the final version of *ARAL 22* and made it attractive and clear despite occasional initial glitches in draft versions of the texts, tables, or diagrams for the various chapters. At all stages of manuscript preparation, our work has been facilitated by the efforts of Marc Lord, who established a server through which we can share work quickly in electronic format. Careful proofreading assistance was provided by Camilla Vásquez and Heidi Vellenga; each of them has helped to ensure a higher level of accuracy in this volume. All facets of the work needed to produce *ARAL* benefit from the in-kind support of the English Department and the College of Arts and Sciences at Northern Arizona University. Each of these entities has absorbed some of the incidental costs associated with the planning, preparation, and production of the series. In this connection, I am most grateful to William Grabe, English Department Chair, and David Best, Dean of Arts and Sciences, for their commitment to scholarship in applied linguistics as embodied in *ARAL*. My thanks to all concerned.

Mary McGroarty
Flagstaff, Arizona
January 2002

APPROACHES TO DISCOURSE ANALYSIS

1. CONVERSATION ANALYSIS AND APPLIED LINGUISTICS[1]

Emanuel A. Schegloff, Irene Koshik, Sally Jacoby, and David Olsher

Conversation Analysis (CA) as a mode of inquiry is addressed to all forms of talk and other conduct in interaction, and, accordingly, touches on the concerns of applied linguists at many points. This review sketches and offers bibliographical guidance on several of the major relevant areas of conversation-analytic work—turn-taking, repair, and word selection—and indicates past or potential points of contact with applied linguistics. After covering these areas, we include a brief discussion of some key themes in CA's treatment of talk in institutional contexts. Finally, we discuss several established areas of applied linguistic work in which conversation analytic work is being explored—native, nonnative, and multilingual talk; talk in educational institutions; grammar and interaction; intercultural communication and comparative CA; and implications for designing language teaching tasks, materials, and assessment tasks. We end with some cautions on applying CA findings to other applied linguistic research contexts.

Its name to the contrary notwithstanding, "conversation analysis" (CA) is not concerned with conversation alone. The term "conversation analysis" as used here refers specifically to what some have referred to as "ethnomethodological conversation analysis," a line of work whose earliest contributions are often identified with authors such as Sacks, Schegloff, Jefferson, Pomerantz, and others, and not to the literatures also sometimes referred to by that name (or by the term "conversational analysis") associated with such authors as Grice, Gumperz, Hatch, Tannen, and others—some in the applied linguistics community—whose declared intent is to describe conversational uses of language. CA's broader provenance extends to the study of talk and other forms of conduct (including the disposition of the body in gesture, posture, facial expression, and ongoing activities in the setting) in all forms of talk in interaction. To be sure, work so far has suggested that talk in ordinary conversation is the locus of the basic or default practices of talk in interaction, and that talk in specific institutional or functionally specified contexts is often characterized by describable modifications of those organizations of practice. But wherever humans engage in talk in interaction, or in interaction in which talk can spontaneously "break out," there will be an orientation by the participants to the practices of talking in interaction. Understanding interaction in such settings can be enhanced by the findings of conversation analysis, and by the research practices underlying those findings. This is to say that "CA" refers to not only a corpus of findings and accounts of talk-in-interaction, but also—perhaps preeminently—to a method of inquiry, one addressed to distinctive data and embodying a distinctive research stance.

 A substantial proportion of the research and professional preoccupations of applied linguists and of applied linguistics falls into the domain for which CA resources are well-suited. Whether the area is the properties of native and nonnative language use in a variety of settings and contexts, the organization of discourse and interaction in the classroom and in other pedagogic settings in which teaching and learning are meant to occur, the assessment of such learning, or the like, much of what makes up the substance of these professional and research domains is found in the real world in situations of talk in interaction. Applied linguists can therefore potentially benefit from bringing the resources and tools of conversation analysis to bear on those domains which engage their interest and professional concerns—whether in conversation or in institutionally specific talk. This chapter offers analytical and bibliographical guidance on a few main areas of CA work, and examines their past and potential future intersection with phenomena, problems, and settings of distinctive interest to an applied linguistic constituency. The sections that follow next begin by sketching areas of conversation analytic work and some of their prime bibliographical resources and then suggest areas of potential intersection with applied linguistics. Then we take up some long-standing areas of interest in applied linguistics and suggest some ways in which conversation analytic resources might prove fruitful for them, along with some exemplars of work where this promise may already be bearing fruit.

Some Fundamental Aspects of the Organization of Conversation

Whether speaking their native language or another, whether fluently or not, whether to another or others doing the same or not, whether in ordinary conversation or in a classroom or in the work place or in some other institutionally or functionally specialized situation, there are certain issues all participants in talk-in-interaction will find themselves dealing with. They will, for example, need some way of organizing the order of their participation—usually one person speaking at a time (turn-taking). They will fashion their contributions to be recognizable as some unit of participation—some "turn-constructional unit" (turn organization). They will have practices for forming their talk so as to accomplish one or more recognizable actions (action formation). They will deploy resources for making the succession of contributions cohere somehow, either topically or by contributing to the realization of a trajectory of action or interaction (sequence organization). They will avail themselves of practices for dealing with problems in speaking, hearing and/or understanding the talk (the organization of repair). They will select and deploy and understand the words used to compose the talk, and will do that in a timely fashion (word/usage selection). They will do all of this with an eye to their co-participants (recipient design) and to the occasion and context, its normative parameters or boundaries of duration, appropriate activities and their order, etc., (overall structural organization of the occasion of interaction). All of the preceding, and others, compose the preoccupations and major topical areas of Conversation Analysis. It is the premise of this chapter that many of the topics and concerns which preoccupy applied linguists intersect these aspects of the organization of interaction and are shaped by them. The remainder of this section will sketch several of these areas with bibliographical citations, and suggest their potential bearing on applied linguistic interests. Ensuing sections start from the applied linguistic end and touch on work which has drawn on conversation analytic resources.

To begin with, however, it will be worthwhile to underscore a single underlying premise of this work which should be relevant to applied linguists as well. People use language and concomitant forms of conduct to do things, not only to transmit information; their talk and other conduct *does* things, and is taken as doing things—things such as requesting, offering, complaining, inviting, asking, telling, correcting, and the myriad other actions which talk in interaction can accomplish. By "actions" here we are not referring to physical actions but to ones accomplished through the talk; and we are referring not only to actions with familiar vernacular names like those just mentioned, but recognizable and describable actions without such names (such as "confirming allusions," cf. Schegloff, 1996c). Understanding analytically what action is (or actions are) being done by some unit of talk is not accessible to casual inspection and labeling; it requires examination of actual specimens of naturally occurring talk in interaction and analysis of what they are designed to accomplish by their speakers and understood to have accomplished by their recipients, and what practices implement that design. (This stance toward action is, accordingly, quite distinct from that of speech act theory; cf. Schegloff, 1988a, 1992a, 1992b).

The practices of talking in interaction are grounded jointly in dealing with the contingencies of managing to sustain talking together as an orderly arena of action, on the one hand, and, on the other hand, the contingencies of producing and recognizing determinate actions, combinations of actions and sequences of actions. For those trying to understand a bit of talk, the key question about any of its aspects is—why that now (Schegloff & Sacks, 1973)? What is getting done by virtue of that bit of conduct, done that way, in just that place? This is, in the first instance, the central issue for the parties to the talk—both for its construction and for its understanding. And for that reason, it is the central issue for academic/professional students of the talk. If we are to understand language in its contexts of deployment, we need in the first instance to understand how and for what it is deployed by its participants, and how its deployments are understood by them and reflected in their own responsive conduct. The CA literature to which we refer the reader should be appreciated and assessed by reference to this criterion. The examination of empirical materials of interest to applied linguists should be guided by this question: what interactional project, what action that composes it, does some bit of talk embody and exemplify? All the organizations of practice discussed below are meant to provide resources for dealing with this question.

Turn-Taking

The practices of turn-taking organize distribution of opportunities to talk among parties to interaction and constrain the size of turns, by making the possible completion of a turn "transition-relevant." This interactive dimension—in which possible completion can (but need not always) occasion or trigger the start of a next turn by another—has consequences for speakers' construction of turns, and thereby for the form which turns (and the: ir building blocks, "turn-constructional units") take. The main bibliographical resources in this area are Sacks, Schegloff, and Jefferson (1974) on turn-taking and Schegloff (1982, 1996a) on turn organization, but see also Sacks, 1992, Jefferson (1973, 1984), Lerner (1991, 1996, in press) and Schegloff (1999a, 2000a, 2001a).

Of the many ways turn-taking and turn organization should matter to applied linguists, we mention only one here. The unmarked value of the transition space is one beat of silence; that is, after possible completion of a turn, a next speaker ordinarily allows one beat of silence to pass before starting a next turn (Jefferson, 1984); departures from that value (shorter or longer) are potentially marked and import-laden. One place where trouble can become apparent—for example, trouble in understanding—is in longer silences at the transition space. Furthermore, depending on the character of the turn which the silence follows, silence can be taken as incipient rejection of, or disalignment from, what preceded it (Pomerantz, 1984; Sacks, 1987; Schegloff, 1988b, 1995). This can be problematic for those with delayed understanding or impaired capacity to start a next turn "on time," and this is one place where orientation to nonnativeness can be invoked, for example, to discount the rejection-implication of delayed next turn start (e. g., Carroll, 2000).

Repair

The practices of repair constitute the major (though not the sole) resource for parties to talk-in-interaction for displaying that they are dealing with trouble or problems in speaking, hearing, or understanding the talk. The main bibliographical resources are Schegloff, Jefferson and Sacks (1977); Schegloff (1979, 1987, 1992c, 1997a, 1997b, 2000b); and Jefferson (1974, 1987).

Three points are worth special emphasis in explicating CA's treatment of this area, so apparently relevant to diverse applied linguistic interests:

1. The practices of repair at issue for CA are discursive and interactional, not cognitive. Initiating repair is an action or a move in interaction, one

which claims a problem; that is so whatever may cognitively be the case. Displaying a delay before a next word is a move in interaction, quite distinct from some delay in the "speech planning process."

2. The courses of conduct treated as "repair" in CA involve the parties stopping the course of action otherwise in progress—whether turn or sequence or activity—to address a trouble/problem of speaking, hearing or understanding the talk, and resuming that course of action upon completion of the repair segment (either with success in dealing with the trouble or with failure). Undertakings to deal with trouble en passant, without stopping the ongoing activity to do so, are empirically different in various respects (cf. Jefferson, 1987), and are distinct from repair organization.

3. Note in particular the phrase "understanding the *talk*" which appears recurrently in accounts of repair. This is meant to discriminate dealing with problems of understanding the talk (ordinarily the just-preceding talk) from other problems of understanding (e. g., understanding the events, conduct, etc., being described, as compared to understanding the talk describing them).

The importance of points (2) and (3) comes to a focus in one area which is very likely of special interest to applied linguists, and that is talk in pedagogical contexts—whether in formal classrooms or otherwise organized. In such settings, explaining and understanding are very likely to constitute the main line of activity occupying the talk, and problems of understanding and dealing with such problems are endogenous to the core activities of the setting. In language teaching classrooms, trouble in speaking and correcting that trouble may similarly constitute the main line of activity, and not a departure from it. Discriminating the main trajectory of the interaction from temporary suspension of it for repair can be far less clear than in other, nonpedagogical settings. Yet this is crucial for the application of this domain of CA's resources to be warranted. Not every correction is repair; not every problem in understanding implicates the operations of *repair* for its solution (cf. Koshik, 2001a). Classroom and other overtly pedagogical settings are not necessarily the most inviting settings, or the most relevant ones, for the application of conversation-analytic work on repair. What settings might appeal more?

Among several prima facie candidates we may mention here only a few. What is treated in applied linguistics (as elsewhere) as "fluency/disfluency" refers in substantial measure to a speaker's same-turn self-repair initiation and other problems of progressivity—that is, the practice of "progressing" or advancing the utterance being produced (Schegloff, 1979). What disrupts "fluency" are cut-offs (or self-interruptions), sound stretches, delay markers (such as "uh") and pauses, repeats of earlier said items, and the like. Many of these figure in CA treatments of "same-turn repair," which is not to say that they should all be treated as repair initiators, but does suggest the possibility of useful interchange. Applied linguists often have to deal with trouble in understanding a speaker's talk—the sources of that trouble, ways of displaying that there is trouble, ways of displaying what the trouble is, and ways of undertaking to resolve it. Here CA work on other-initiated repair can be a resource (cf. Schegloff, 2000b; Wong, 2000a), as can work on repair in which already displayed problematic understandings are addressed (cf. Schegloff, 1992c).

Word Selection

The final area of CA work which can be taken up here is that of word selection by speakers in the course of talk in interaction. There are two main lines of inquiry in this area. One examines the deployment of words or multiword usages by reference to other words or usages in the immediate environments of the talk—for example, for its "punning" relationship to that talk (Sacks, 1973) or its sound relationship to the surrounding talk, which can, it appears, even induce misspeakings (Jefferson, 1996). The other line of work examines the practices for referring within semantic domains, such as person reference, place reference (Schegloff, 1972), measurement formulations (Sacks, 1989), etc. The discussion below is focused on reference to persons; the main bibliographic resources are Sacks (1972a, 1972b, 1992 passim); Schegloff (1991, 1996b, 1997c, 1999b, 1999c, 2001a); and Sacks and Schegloff (1979).

Two aspects of the work in CA on word selection, and person reference in particular, may be of special interest and relevance to applied linguists. First, work on person reference has brought to explicit notice various practices that inform fluent, idiomatic, "competent" language use, but which have no established place in linguistic or pragmatic description, and therefore may easily escape pedagogical attention. For example, there is a preference for "recognitional" reference if possible; that is, if a recipient is figured by a speaker to know the person to be referred to, the speaker should do the reference in a fashion that invites and enables such recognition (i. e., by personal name or other recognitional descriptor fitted to the terms of the recipient's recognition of the referent, e. g., "the person sitting next to you;" cf. Sacks & Schegloff, 1979; Schegloff, 1996b). Failure to do so when the recipient was known to be acquainted with the referent can be understood as "withholding." Such practices of talk-in-interaction might well be a proper part of the teaching of a language.

The second point bears on the very conduct of applied linguistic research and discourse itself. As early as the mid-1960s Sacks pointed out that referring to persons by category terms—male/female, child/adult, American/Canadian/ Egyptian/Italian/ Kenyan/ Korean/Russian..., native/nonnative speaker—can be profoundly equivocal (Sacks, 1972a, 1972b, 1992; Schegloff, 1991). Since every person who is a member of some category in one of these sets is also a member of a category in each of the other sets, referring to someone as "a woman" is not warranted simply by being, in fact, a woman; that "someone" is also an adult, a native speaker, and the like. The issue is not only factuality; it is relevance. (In fact, factuality turns out not always to be required.) When a speaker in conversation refers to someone by a category term, we can then cogently ask—we need to ask— what made that category a relevant one for the speaker to use in that context? What was being done thereby? The fact that the referent is actually a member of that category is not sufficient; people are actually members of many categories.

And the same issue arises for academic or professional researchers; referring to people being studied by category terms cannot be sufficiently warranted by their actually being members of those categories; the relevance of the categories being used has to be warranted. And for many purposes, the pertinent relevance is not relevance to the investigator, but relevance to the persons being categorized while engaged in the activities being studied. The emergent issue for applied linguists, then, is: when is it warranted to characterize the persons being discussed as "native" or "nonnative" speakers of the language? When do they—the objects of inquiry—orient to these category memberships? How should that bear on and constrain the usage by the applied linguistic researcher (cf. Hosoda, 2001)?

We have omitted from this part of the chapter some of the most central areas of conversation-analytic inquiry—in particular, sequence organization (Schegloff, 1990, 1995) and the analysis of the formation or construction of actions organized into the sequences which are described in sequence organization (on action formation, cf. inter alia, Drew, 1984; Heritage, 1998; Jefferson, 1993; Pomerantz, 1980; Sacks, 1992; Schegloff, 1988c: 118–31, 1996c, 1997b). These are no less important to the chapter than the topics which we have addressed, only less tractable to compressed treatment. Their importance extends the point just made in the preceding paragraph. What figures most centrally for the persons whose language use we study and hope to contribute to is what they get done by talking, and what they understand about what their interlocutors are getting done. Those actions, organized into interactionally co-produced trajectories of action, are what talk-in-interaction is all about. Language control is relevant to the achievement of actions and the understanding of the actions of others—what are they doing by saying what they're saying and saying it in that way? How can I do what I want to do? Applied linguists might wish to consider focusing on these themes to get to the heart of talking in interaction, just as they should consider the importance of getting at which categories of participation are relevant to the parties who are participating, not to those who are studying the participation. These are issues of disciplined inquiry in the human or social sciences more generally, not limited to applied linguistics. But they apply to applied linguistics as well.

Talk in Institutional Contexts

From the beginning, CA has included in its research data material from so-called institutional settings, such as a suicide prevention hotline (Sacks, 1972a, 1992), group therapy sessions with adolescents (Sacks, 1992), or calls to the police (Schegloff, 1967, 1968), though the practices analyzed were, for the most part, not distinctively institutional ones. Subsequent work has examined talk in a variety of institutional or functionally specialized settings, such as legal settings (e. g., Atkinson & Drew, 1979; Drew, 1992; Manzo, 1993; Maynard, 1984), broadcast media (e. g., Clayman, 1992; Clayman & Heritage, in press; Greatbatch, 1988, 1992; Heritage, 1985; Heritage & Greatbatch, 1991), business organizations (e. g., Atkinson, Cuff, & Lee, 1978; Boden, 1994), pedagogical settings (e. g., Koshik, in press a, b; Lerner, 1995; Mori, 2002; Olsher, 2001), research work groups (e.

g., Jacoby, 1998c, Jacoby & Gonzales, 1991, in press), medical settings (e. g., Heritage & Maynard, in press; Heritage & Stivers, 1999; Lutfey & Maynard, 1998; Robinson, 1998), emergency dispatch centers (e. g., Whalen & Zimmerman, 1987; Whalen, Zimmerman & Whalen, 1988; Zimmerman, 1984, 1992), airport operations rooms (e. g., Goodwin, 1996; Goodwin & Goodwin, 1996), and counseling sessions (e. g., Peräkylä, 1993, 1995; He, 1995, 1998b), among others.

The key point about talk in such "special" contexts is that one cannot properly understand how the parties come to talk as they do and to understand one another as they do without making reference to special features to which they are oriented—whether legal constraints as, for example, in the case of broadcast news interviews (cf. Heritage, 1985; or Clayman, 1988, 1992, on "neutralism"), or organizational and functional ones, as, for example, in some classroom settings, etc. Institutional talk has often been of special interest to applied linguists because of the bearing of such special contextual features on the special populations with which applied linguists are concerned—as, for example, with second language learners targeted at a special purpose usage, a special purpose which can impinge and have a bearing on how talk in such settings is organized.

We limit ourselves here to only a few points about CA's treatment of such specialized environments of talk-in-interaction. (Among the main bibliographic sources here are Drew and Heritage, 1992b, and Heritage and Greatbatch, 1991.)

First, conversation-analytically speaking, the sheer fact that the physical environment or social occasion in which talk is conducted can be characterized as a courtroom, a hospital, or a TV studio does not render that talk "institutional." As with the earlier mentioned categorization of individuals, it is the relevance and procedural consequentiality (Schegloff, 1991) of that character (qua courtroom, hospital, etc.) to the participants, manifested in the talk, which underlies its potential bearing on their production and understanding of the talk; if they are not oriented to it, it cannot be shown to be implicated in their construction of the interactional activity. For example, in a famous broadcast interview in the late 1980s, an interviewer's interaction with a presidential candidate turned into a verbal confrontation mid-course, though the physical setting and public identities remained constant. But as their practices of talking changed, they progressively showed that they were no longer treating that physical and social context as procedurally consequential for their conduct of the talk (Clayman & Whalen, 1988/89; Schegloff,

1988/89). Treating episodes of talk in interaction as "institutional" involves showing how that institutional character is embodied—is "done"—in the details of the talk and other conduct. As Heritage and Greatbatch (1991) suggest, where a distinctive turn-taking organization (or other such omnipresent organization) is involved, the sheer turn-by-turn development of the talk displays the parties' orientation to the institutional character of the interaction, as in news interviews or courtrooms; in its absence, discrete practices of talking need to be elucidated to warrant the characterization of the interaction as relevantly institutional.

Second, there is no sharp segregation between the practices of ordinary talk and interaction and the practices of talk in institutional settings. People engage in ordinary conversation in institutional settings, e. g., when coworkers chat around the water cooler or intersperse bits of ordinary conversation in the course of task-related institutional interaction, talk which commonly has a bearing on the setting's "business," but which is organized by the practices of ordinary conversation. Institutional activities which have distinctive "speech exchange systems" (Sacks et al., 1974) can also transform themselves into everyday activities, as in the case of the news interview just described or when classroom group work or a business meeting or group therapy session goes off task and turns into small talk. Likewise, specific conversational practices, such as the sequential organization of searching for a word (Goodwin & Goodwin, 1986), can emerge in the course of a spate of institutional talk, such as a teacher's grammar explanation during an ESL writing conference (Koshik, in press a). General conversational practices can also be deployed to serve institutionally specific purposes, e. g., when teachers use repair initiation as a pedagogical prompt to get students to self-correct their own language errors, even when the teachers experienced no problem in hearing or understanding the student's talk (Koshik, in press a). And specialized institutional practices of talk (what Levinson, 1979, terms "activity types") can also be deployed (and can be topicalized as such) in everyday settings in order to accomplish specialized tasks. For example, parents can "interrogate" their teenager when she asks for an increase in allowance or comes home after curfew, or can make use of "display question" sequences in the course of reading a storybook to a toddler. Of relevance to applied linguists is the implication that communicative competence includes knowing, to various degrees, when, how, with whom, and when not to use both conversational and institutional practices of talk and interaction in both institutional and noninstitutional settings, and understanding what is being done by users of these various practices in both kinds of settings.

As noted, there do appear to be distinctive practices for various aspects of talk in institutional contexts, which generally involve a reduction and specialization of practices, fitted to the character and focal activities of the institutional setting (Drew & Heritage, 1992a). But much of the talk in institutional settings is the product of the practices of talk in ordinary contexts; resolving overlapping talk, the practices of repair, word selection by reference to recipient design, the practices of turn and sequence construction, and many other practices figure in institutional settings in much the same way as they do in everyday conversation. So the default analytic orientation needs to be to address "institutional" data in much the same way as one addresses talk in unspecialized contexts, while being alert to modifications best understood by reference to participants' orientation to the particular circumstances and constraints of the occasion, whether institutional or functional in character. Limiting one's interest and analytic tool kit only to institutional talk, to a particular domain of institutional talk, or only to practices of everyday conversation can result in missing the complexity of all kinds of talk and interaction and in restricting particular findings to one domain or the other.

CA Research in Areas of Interest to Applied Linguists

This section will focus on specific areas of intersection between applied linguistics and recent CA and CA-informed research. One type of intersection concerns CA and CA-informed research on talk-in-interaction in various contexts, including nonnative talk and talk in educational contexts, which are of special interest to applied linguists. The second intersection concerns ways in which CA research on talk-in-interaction has the potential to inform various domains of interest to applied linguists, such as grammar, intercultural communication, and language pedagogy.

Native, Nonnative, and Multilingual Talk

From the seminal work of Dell Hymes (1972) onward, there has been an ongoing interest among applied linguists in communicative competence as a conceptual frame for the range of skills and knowledges involved in understanding and participating in the use of language to accomplish social actions (e. g., Bachman, 1990; Canale, 1983; Canale and Swain. 1980; and Celce-Murcia, Dörnyei, & Thurrell, 1995). As a field of sociology, CA has been concerned with describing the interactional practices that are competences of ordinary conversation (Heritage, 1984b). From an applied linguistic perspective, Markee (2000) argues for the importance of interactional competence as a collaborative, socially constituted domain of communicative competence that includes practices such as turn-taking and repair. Since CA research is theoretically and methodologically grounded as a study of publicly observable phenomena, the view of competence it supports is one of situated practices rather than psycholinguistic models of learning processes and knowledge structures (Jacoby & McNamara, 1999). CA and CA-informed studies which investigate the conversational competence of second language speakers can help us to understand how the categories of native (NS) and nonnative (NNS) speaker are understood by participants and what practices are specific to this talk as it occurs in natural, as opposed to experimental, settings (Wagner, 1996).

Conversation analytic studies have the potential to bring some clarity to the problematic categories of "native" and "nonnative" speaker. Researchers from a number of different perspectives have either questioned the native-nonnative speaker distinction or challenged the ways in which these categories have been interpreted (e. g., Firth & Wagner, 1997; Kachru & Nelson, 1996; Kasper, 1997). Firth and Wagner's (1997) critique of second language acquisition methodology sparked a fruitful scholarly debate in the *Modern Language Journal* (1997, 1998), centered in part around how these categories are interpreted. Even if it were possible to objectively define these categories, from a conversation analytic perspective the relevance of one's nonnative speaker status may at times be demonstrably oriented to by the use of special practices of talk on the part of the "native" or the "nonnative" speakers, and at other times language expertise and nativeness may be virtually irrelevant (cf. Hosoda, 2001; Jacoby & Gonzales, in press; Jacoby & McNamara, 1999).

At least to some extent, conversation analytic studies of talk involving "nonnative speakers" can reveal that identities related to nativeness and nonnativeness, such as expert and novice language speakers, are locally constituted within the ongoing communication. In studying this talk, we can come to understand how participants themselves understand and express native/nonnative identities, and what special practices of talk may be involved. Hosoda (2001), for example, describes various practices of repair (as well as their nondeployment) that display participants' orientation at that moment to the relevance of relative competence in the language, and thereby provide a data-internal warrant for the use of terms such as "native/nonnative speaker" as relevant characterizations of the parties. Such a demonstration of the possibility of empirically warranting such characterizations presents an invitation and challenge to others to address the same or similar issues.

Since the early work by Jordan and Fuller (1975), Gaskill (1980) and Schwartz (1980), CA and CA-informed studies of naturally-occurring nonnative talk have more recently begun to expand in focus and number, including an edited volume of such studies currently in preparation (Gardner & Wagner, 2001). Researchers have looked at NNS-NNS, or *lingua franca*, talk (e. g, Carroll, 2000; Firth, 1996; Wagner, 1996) and NS-NNS talk (e. g. Hosoda, 2000; Wong, 2000 a, b) involving both 'native' and 'nonnative' speakers. Two studies which, together, compared interactional phenomena in 'native' and 'nonnative' discourse are Wong's (2000a) study of delayed next turn repair-initiations found in the nonnative English talk of Mandarin speakers, and Schegloff's (2000b) companion article which investigated occurrences of the practice in ordinary, "native" English talk.

Talk in Educational Institutions

A small but increasing amount of CA and CA-informed research on talk in educational institutions directly addresses issues of interest to applied linguists. Markee (2000) explains how this research "can help refine insights into how the structure of conversation can be used by learners as a means of getting comprehended input and producing comprehended output" (p. 44). Markee's (1994, 1995) and Ohta's (2001) work, informed by both CA and discourse analysis and, in Ohta's case, set within a sociocognitive framework, point to possible new avenues of exploration for SLA research. Willey (2001) adds to our understanding of communication strategies by analyzing what researchers have called "appeals for assistance" as used in naturally-occurring classroom talk. He shows how "appeals" that occur during word searches embedded within a student's turn at talk differ from those used to initiate a new sequence.

Even though CA methodology may be appropriate to answer some existing applied linguistic questions, most CA research, including some research on talk in educational institutions, is not built to answer theoretically motivated research questions of the type that applied linguists often ask. However, applied linguists may also usefully be informed by this research, as it addresses issues of how talk in educational contexts is organized, how particular goal-oriented actions are accomplished through this talk, and ways that this talk differs from ordinary conversation and from talk in other educational contexts. Recent CA research on L2 pedagogy has explored a variety of practices. Lerner (1995) focuses on the use of incomplete turn-constructional units to structure participation by students in a bilingual elementary school classroom. Koshik (in press a, b) analyzes the functions of particular teacher question types in ESL writing conferences. Mori (2002) studies how instructional design affects ways in which students' talk develops in a Japanese language classroom. Olsher (2001) describes the uses language learners make of special practices for combining talk and gesture in order to facilitate small-group interaction in an EFL class. CA work on other school contexts encountered by language learners includes physics research team interactions (Jacoby & Gonzales, in press), language institute front-desk encounters (Kidwell, 2000), and academic counseling sessions (Guthrie, 1997; He, 1994, 1995, 1998b).

CA research can also illuminate what is going on in particular interactional L2 assessment encounters, not only so as to monitor interrater reliability and potential contamination of oral proficiency scores by interaction with the examiner, but also to discover routine and unique communication practices through which participants co-construct the assessment format itself as well as the actions these practices accomplish (Egbert, 1998; He, 1998a; Marlaire & Maynard, 1990; Lazaraton, 1991, 1997; McNamara, Hill, & May, this volume; Riggenbach, 1998; Young, this volume).

Grammar and Interaction

Despite its origins in sociology, CA research has always had a keen interest in the lexical and grammatical details of everyday and institutional talk. From the syntactic typology of turn-constructional units (Sacks, Schegloff, & Jefferson, 1974), through discussions of reference terms for persons (Sacks & Schegloff, 1979; Schegloff, 1996b), lexical phenomena such as "and" -prefacing (Heritage &

Sorjonen, 1994), "okay" (Beach, 1993, 1995), "uh-huh" (Schegloff, 1982), "yeah" and "mm hm" (Jefferson, 1984), "oh" (Heritage, 1984a), and "actually" (Clift, 1999, 2001), reported speech (Golato, 2000, in press, a, b; Holt, 1996), and the collaborative construction of one turn unit by more than one participant (Lerner, 1991, 1996), CA treats grammar and lexical choices as sets of resources which participants deploy, monitor, interpret, and manipulate as they design turns, sort out turn-taking, co-construct utterances and sequences, manage intersubjectivity and (dis) agreement, accomplish actions, and negotiate interpersonal trajectories as real-time talk and interaction unfold (e. g., Ford, 1993; Ford, Fox, & Thompson, in press, Ford & Wagner, 1996; Fox, 1987; Goodwin, 1979, 1986; Hayashi, 1999, in press; He & Tsoneva, 1998; Heritage & Roth, 1995; Ochs, Schegloff, & Thompson, 1996; Schegloff, 1972, 1979, 1990; Selting & Couper-Kuhlen, in press). Recently, the number of studies has begun to expand and benefit not only from the insights of scholars rooted in CA studies of language use, but also from scholars rooted in linguistic traditions of analysis who have embraced a CA perspective, in some instances under the rubric "interactional linguistics." These scholars discuss not only ways in which 'grammar organizes social interaction, ' but also ways in which 'social interaction organizes grammar' and how grammar, itself, can be seen as a mode of social interaction (Schegloff, Ochs, & Thompson, 1996).

Intercultural Communication and Comparative CA

Another area of research where conversation analysis offers the potential for a useful contribution is the study of intercultural communication and interlanguage pragmatics. While much research on interlanguage pragmatics (e. g., Kasper & Blum-Kulka, 1993) has been based on data collected with written "discourse completion" surveys, there has been a call for increased attention to the sequential organization (Kasper & Dahl, 1991) of practices with which participants carry out social action through talk. CA studies of speaking practices across languages and cultures can provide a basis for comparison of L2, or language learner, speaking practices with native speaker norms in both Ll and L2. There is an expanding body of research using conversation analysis to study talk-in-interaction in a variety of languages, including German (Egbert, 1996, 1997a, b; Golato, 2000, in press a, b, c), Finnish (Sorjonen, 1996, 2001, in press a, b); Swedish (Lindström, 1994,

1997, 1999); Japanese (Hayashi, 1999, in press; Hayashi, Mori, & Takagi, in press; Tanaka, 1999), Mandarin (Wu, 1997, 2000); Korean (Kim, 1999a, 1999b, 200la, 200lb; Park, 1998a, 1998b, 1998c, 1999, in press; Suh & Kim, 2001); findings from such studies may inform our understanding of the mother-tongue practices of learners of English from various linguistic backgrounds. Golato (in press c), for example, noted similarities and differences in responses to compliments in English and German, and there is a substantial literature on commonalities and differences between societies in the ways in which conversational openings on the telephone are organized (Godard, 1977; Hopper, 1992; Hopper & Koleilat-Doany, 1989; Hopper & Chen, 1996; Houtkoop-Steenstra, 1991; Lindström, 1994; Park, in press; Schegloff, 1968, 1979, 1986, 1993, 2002a, b, c, in press).

However, a caution remains in considering ways that conversation analysis might contribute to interlanguage pragmatics research. While CA studies sequences of actions carried out through naturally-occurring talk based on instances found in the data, interlanguage pragmatics begins with a linguistic pragmatic inventory of speech acts, defined according to speakers' intent, and then looks for the instances of these categories. A strict application of CA to interlanguage pragmatic research may not be wholly appropriate. On the other hand, CA work on familiar social actions such as invitations (Davidson, 1984; Drew, 1984), complaints (Schegloff, 1988a), disputes (Goodwin & Goodwin, 1990), and assessments (Pomerantz, 1984), or unfamiliar actions such as "confirming allusions" (Schegloff, 1996c), as well as work on other aspects of social action and sequential organization of talk-in-interaction such as conversational openings and closings (Schegloff & Sacks, 1973), story tellings and participation of recipients (Goodwin, 1984; Jefferson, 1978; Sacks, 1974; Schegloff, 1997d), may offer a broader construal of interlanguage pragmatics as a basis for future research in this field.

Implications of CA Research for Design of Language Teaching Tasks, Materials, and Assessment

CA research has obvious implications for the design of tasks and materials based on "authentic" talk from ordinary conversation and from a wide range of real-life institutional settings in which L2 learners are likely to be involved, both as professionals and as clients. Textbooks using invented dialogue based on intuitions of how certain language functions are accomplished do not always offer students accurate knowledge of language use. Wong's (1984, 2002) research on phone conversations in ESL textbooks exemplifies this discrepancy between textbook language and naturally-occurring talk. She found that most of the ESL text phone conversations which she studied were inaccurate and misleading, both in terms of their organization and the preferences which are displayed in the talk. Wong's research also suggests a fruitful direction for further applied linguistic research. Especially where learners' languages differ, e. g., not all languages share the American English preference for recognition over identification in phone conversations (see citations in the preceding section), it is especially important that textbooks accurately convey how these practices are done in the L2.

CA research on institutional talk also has implications for the design of syllabi, tasks, and materials for learning Language for Specific Purposes (Jacoby, 1998a, 1998b, 2001; Koshik, 2000). Competent and successful special purpose communication is a challenge for anyone, NS or NNS, professional expert or novice, lay person or client. Since most CA research on institutional discourse is not explicitly concerned with NNSs or with externally evaluating and isolating instructable aspects of professional communication, applied linguists and LSP practitioners may need to create their own thoughtful and specific bridges between the findings of CA research and the content of particular LSP courses and materials.

CA research can also inform the design of L2 assessment tasks (e. g., role-plays) as well as clarify the pluses and minuses of particular testing formats (e. g., role-play, group discussion, face-to-face interview, or candidate talking to tape-recorded prompts). CA research also raises fundamental issues regarding the positing of appropriate assessment criteria and the interactional processes through which assessment criteria are applied and negotiated not only by insider members in their own indigenous formal and informal assessment activities but also by outsider language testing experts when actually engaged in the categorizing, judging, and rating of particular communication performances in formal assessment settings (Jacoby, 2001; Jacoby & McNamara, 1999).

Cautions in Applying CA Findings

We end this section with a caution about applying findings extracted from conversation analysis literature to other research contexts. CA analyses are grounded on recurrent patterns of talk studied with detailed attention to the specific sequential contexts in which these practices are found. Specific findings should not be used to categorize talk in other settings without investigating whether similar practices are used to accomplish similar actions in the new setting. This is especially relevant for those investigating institutional contexts such as classrooms. As we have seen, CA research on institutional talk, including pedagogical talk, has shown that, although conversational practices of talk are used in institutional settings, both for conversational and institutional purposes, many of the practices of talk in institutional settings have been developed to meet institution-specific goals and are specific to the settings in which they are used. Even small variations in the way a particular turn is designed can reflect the actions these turns are being used to accomplish (Koshik, in press a). Conversely, similarly-formed turns can accomplish different actions in different contexts and even in different sequential contexts within one setting (Koshik, 2001b). These actions can only be discovered by a close, turn-by-turn sequential analysis of the talk. It is therefore especially important that researchers of talk investigate individual practices for what they are being used to accomplish in a particular sequence and setting, rather than relying on categories imported from other, even similar, settings.

Conclusion

Although the areas of intersection between applied linguistics and CA touched on in this review have of necessity been limited, there are indications that the relationship between the two fields is growing. The topics touched on in the present chapter range from the more theoretical and analytical stance which examines the nature of language use and of its acquisition to the more practical one concerned with actual pedagogy, assessment, and the like. One might even venture the suggestion that exposure to conversation-analytic accounts of conversational episodes can itself be a powerful resource in advancing the learning of a language by those with moderate to advanced proficiency in it. This possibility has just begun to be explored (Barraja-Rohan & Pritchard, 1997). There is open terrain for inquiry in this whole area for those who will undertake to bring together the necessary training in CA with engagement with the issues which applied linguistics brings to the fore.

Notes

1. We would like to thank Marianne Celce-Murcia, Fred Davidson, Makoto Hayashi, Numa Markee, and Jane Zuengler for their valuable comments on earlier drafts of this paper.

REFERENCES

Atkinson, J. M., & Drew, P. (1979). *Order in court: The organisation of verbal interaction injudicial settings*. London: Macmillan.

Atkinson, J. M., Cuff, M., & Lee, J. (1978). The recommencement of a meeting as a member's accomplishment. In J. Schenkein (Ed.), *Studies in the organization of conversational interaction* (pp. 133–153). New York: Academic Press.

Bachman, L. F. (1990). *Fundamental considerations in language testing*. Oxford: Oxford University Press.

Barraja-Rohan, A., & Pritchard, C. R. (1997). *Beyond talk: A course in communication and conversation for intermediate adult learners of English*. Melbourne: Western Melbourne Institute of TAFE Publishing Service.

Beach, W. A. (1993). Transitional regularities for 'casual' "Okay" usages. *Journal of Pragmatics, 19*. 325–352.

Beach, W. A. (1995). Preserving and constraining options: "Okays" and 'official' priorities in medical interviews. In G. H. Morris & R. J. Chenail (Eds.), *The talk of the clinic: Explorations in the analysis of medical and therapeutic discourse* (pp. 259–289). Hillsdale, NJ: Lawrence Erlbaum.

Boden, D. (1994). *The business of talk: Organizations in action*. Cambridge: Polity Press.

Canale, M. (1983). From communicative competence to communicative language pedagogy. In J. C. Richards & R. W. Schmidt (Eds.), *Language and Communication* (pp. 2–27). New York: Longman.

Canale, M., &Swain, M. (1980). Theoretical bases of communicative approaches to second language teaching and testing. *Applied Linguistics, 1*, 1–47.

Carroll, D. (2000). Precision timing in novice-to-novice L2 conversations. *Issues in Applied Linguistics, 11*(1), 67–110.

Celce-Murcia, M., Dörnyei, Z., & Thurrell, S. (1995). Communicative competence: A pedagogically motivated model with content specifications. *Issues in Applied Linguistics, 6*(2), 5–35.

Clayman, S. E. (1988). Displaying neutrality in television news interviews. *Social Problems, 35*(4), 474–492.

Clayman, S. E. (1992). Footing in the achievement of neutrality: The case of news-interview discourse. In P. Drew & J. Heritage (Eds.), *Talk at work: Interaction in institutional settings* (pp. 163–198). Cambridge: Cambridge University Press.

Clayman, S., & Heritage, J. (in press). *The news interview: Journalists and public figures on the air.* Cambridge: Cambridge University Press.

Clayman, S. E., & Whalen, J. (1988/1989). When the medium becomes the message: The case of the Rather-Bush encounter. *Research on Language and Social Interaction, 22,* 241–272.

Clift, R. (1999). *Grammar in interaction: The case of 'actually'* (Essex Research Reports in Linguistics No. 26). University of Essex.

Clift, R. (2001). Meaning in interaction: The case of 'actually.' *Language, 77,* 245–291.

Davidson, J. (1984). Subsequent versions of invitations, offers, requests, and proposals dealing with potential or actual rejection. In J. M. Atkinson & J, Heritage (Eds.), *Structures of social action* (pp. 102–128). Cambridge: Cambridge University Press.

Drew, P. (1984). Speakers' reportings in invitation sequences. In J. M. Atkinson & J. Heritage (Eds.), *Structures of social action* (pp. 152–164). Cambridge: Cambridge University Press.

Drew, P. (1992). Contested evidence in courtroom cross-examination: The case of a trial for rape. In P. Drew & J. Heritage (Eds.), *Talk at work: Interaction in institutional settings* (pp. 470–520). Cambridge: Cambridge University Press.

Drew, P., & Heritage, J. (1992a). Analyzing talk at work: An introduction. In P. Drew & J. Heritage (Eds.), *Talk at work: Interaction in institutional settings* (pp. 3–65). Cambridge: Cambridge University Press.

Drew, P., & Heritage, J. (Eds). (1992b). *Talk at work: Interaction in institutional settings.* Cambridge: Cambridge University Press.

Egbert, M. (1996). Context-sensitivity in conversation analysis: Eye gaze and the German repair initiator 'Bitte.' *Language in Society, 25,* 587–612.

Egbert, M. (1997a). Schisming: The collaborative transformation from a single conversation to multiple conversations. *Research on Language and Social Interaction, 30*(1), 1–51.

Egbert, M. (1997b). Some interactional achievements of other-initiated repair in multiperson conversation. *Journal of Pragmatics, 27,* (61), 1–34.

Egbert, M. (1998). Miscommunication in language proficiency interviews of first-year German students: A comparison with natural conversation. In R. Young & A. He (Eds.), *Talking and testing: Discourse approaches to the assessment of oral proficiency* (pp. 147–169). Amsterdam: Benjamins.

Firth, A. (1996). The discursive accomplishment of normality: On 'Lingua franca' English and conversation analysis. *Journal of Pragmatics, 26,* 237–260.

Firth, A., & Wagner, J. (1997). On discourse, communication, and (some) fundamental concepts in SLA research. *Modern Language Journal, 81* , 285–300.

Ford, C. E. (1993). *Grammar and interaction: Adverbial clauses in American English conversations*. Cambridge, UK: Cambridge University Press.

Ford, C. E., Fox, B. A., & Thompson, S. A. (Eds.) (in press). *The language of turn and sequence*. Oxford, UK: Oxford University Press.

Ford, C. E., & Wagner, J. (Eds.) (1996). Interaction-based studies of language. [Special issue of *Pragmatics, 6* (3)].

Fox, B. (1987). *Discourse structure and anaphora*. Cambridge: Cambridge University Press.

Gardner, R., & Wagner, J. (Eds.) (2001). *Second language talk: Studies of native and nonnative interaction*. Manuscript submitted for publication.

Gaskill, W. (1980). Correction in NS-NNS conversation. In D. Larsen-Freeman (Ed.), *Discourse analysis in second language acquisition research* (pp. 125–137). Rowley, MA: Newbury House.

Godard, D. (1977). Same setting, different norms: Phone call beginnings in France and the United States. *Language in Society, 6*, 209–219.

Golato, A. (2000). Und ich so / und er so [and I'm like / and he's like]: An innovative German quotative for reporting on embodied actions. *Journal of Pragmatics, 32*(1), 29–54.

Golato, A. (in press a). Grammar and interaction: reported discourse and subjunctive in German. *Zeitschrift für Sprachwissenschaft*.

Golato, A. (in press b). Self-quotation in German: Reporting on past decisions. In T. Güldemann, & M. v. Roncador (Eds.), *Reported discourse: A meeting ground for different linguistic domains*. Amsterdam: John Benjamins.

Golato, A. (in press c). German compliment responses. *Journal of Pragmatics*.

Goodwin, C. (1979). The interactive construction of a sentence in natural conversation. In G. Psathas (Ed.), *Everyday language: Studies in ethnomethodology* (pp. 97–112). New York: Irvington.

Goodwin, C. (1984). Notes on story structure and the organization of participation. In M. Atkinson & J. Heritage (Eds.), *Structures of social action* (pp. 225–246). Cambridge: Cambridge University Press.

Goodwin, C. (1986). Between and within: Alternative treatments of continuers and assessments. *Human Studies, 9*, 205–217.

Goodwin, C. (1996). Transparent vision. In E. Ochs, E. A. Schegloff, & S. A. Thompson (Eds.), *Interaction and grammar* (pp. 370–404). Cambridge: Cambridge University Press.

Goodwin, C., & Goodwin, M. H. (1990). Interstitial argument. In A. Grimshaw (Ed.), *Conflict talk* (pp. 85–117). Cambridge: Cambridge University Press.

Goodwin, C., & Goodwin, M. H. (1996). Formulating planes: Seeing as a situated activity. In Y. Engstrom & D. Middleton (Eds.), *Cognition and communication at work* (pp. 61–95). Cambridge: Cambridge University Press.

Goodwin, M. H., & Goodwin, C. (1986). Gesture and co-participation in the activity of searching for a word. *Semiotica, 62* (1/2), 51–75.

Greatbatch, D. (1988). A turn-taking system for British news interviews. *Language in Society, 17*, 401–430.

Greatbatch, D. (1992). On the management of disagreement between news interviewees. In P. Drew & J. Heritage (Eds.), *Talk at work: Interaction in institutional settings* (pp. 268–301). Cambridge: Cambridge University Press.

Guthrie, A. (1997). The systematic deployment of "okay" and "mmhmm" in academic advising sessions. *Pragmatics, 7* (3), 397–415.

Hayashi, M. (1999). Where grammar and interaction meet: A study of co-participant completion in Japanese conversation. *Human Studies, 22*, 475– 499.

Hayashi, M. (in press). Postposition-initiated utterances in Japanese conversation: An interactional account of a grammatical practice. In M. Selting & E. Couper-Kuhlen (Eds.), *Studies in interactional linguistics*. Amsterdam: John Benjamins.

Hayashi, M., Mori, J., & Takagi, T. (in press). Contingent achievement of co-tellership in a Japanese conversation: An analysis of talk, gaze, and gesture. In C. Ford, B. Fox, & S. A. Thompson (Eds.), *The language of turn and sequence*. Oxford: Oxford University Press.

He, A. W. (1994). Withholding academic advice: Institutional context and discourse practice. *Discourse Processes, 18* (3), 297–316.

He, A. W. (1995). Co-constructing institutional identities: The case of student counselees. *Research on Language and Social Interaction, 28* (3), 213–231.

He, A. W. (1998a). Answering questions in LPIs: A case study. In R. Young & A. He (Eds.), *Talking and testing: Discourse approaches to the assessment of oral proficiency* (pp. 101–117). Amsterdam: Benjamins.

He, A. W. (1998b). *Reconstructing institutions: Language use in academic counseling encounters*. Stamford, CT: Ablex Publishing.

He, A. W., & Tsoneva, S. (1998). The symbiosis of choices and control: Toward a discourse-based account of CAN. *Journal of Pragmatics, 29*, 615–637.

Heritage, J. (1984a). A change-of-state token and aspects of its sequential placement. In J. M. Atkinson & J. Heritage (Eds.), *Structures of social action: Studies in conversation analysis* (pp. 299–345). Cambridge, UK: Cambridge University Press.

Heritage, J. (1984b). *Garfinkel and Ethnomethodology*. Cambridge: Polity Press.

Heritage, J. (1985). Analyzing news interviews: Aspects of the production of talk for an overhearing audience. In T. A. van Dijk (Ed.), *Handbook of discourse analysis, Vol. 3*, (pp. 95–119). New York: Academic Press.

Heritage, J. (1998). *Oh*-prefaced responses to inquiry. *Language in Society, 27*, 291–334.

Heritage, J., & Greatbatch, D. (1991). On the institutional character of institutional talk: The case of news interviews. In D. Boden & D. H. Zimmerman (Eds.), *Talk and social structure* (pp. 93–137). Cambridge: Polity Press.

Heritage, J. C., & Maynard, D. W. (in press). *Practicing medicine: Talk and action in primary care encounters.* Cambridge: Cambridge University Press.

Heritage, J., & Roth, A. 1. (1995). Grammar and institution: Questions and questioning in the broadcast news interview. *Research on Language and Social Interaction, 28* (1), 1–60.

Heritage, J., & Sorjonen, M. 1. (1994). Constituting and maintaining activities across sequences: *And*-prefacing as a feature of question design. *Language in Society, 23,* 1–29.

Heritage, J., & Stivers, T. (1999). Online commentary in acute medical visits: A method of shaping patient expectations. *Social Science and Medicine, 49,* 1501–1517.

Holt, E. (1996). Reporting on talk: The use of direct reported speech in conversation. *Research on Language and Social Interaction, 29,* 219–245.

Hopper, R. (1992). *Telephone conversation.* Bloomington: Indiana University Press.

Hopper, R., & Koleilat-Doany, N. (1989). Telephone openings and conversational universals: A study in three languages. In S. Ting-Toomey & F. Kevizing (Eds.), *Language, Communication and Culture* (pp. 157–179). Newbury Park: Sage.

Hopper, R., & Chen, C. (1996). Languages, cultures, relationships: Telephone openings in Taiwan. *Research on Language and Social Interaction, 29,* 291–313.

Hosoda, Y. (2000). Other-repair in Japanese conversations between nonnative and native speakers. *Issues in Applied Linguistics, 11* (1), 39–63.

Hosoda, Y. (2001). Conditions for other-repair in NS/NNS conversation. *The Language Teacher, 25* (11), 29–31.

Houtkoop-Steenstra, H. (1991). Opening sequences in Dutch telephone conversations. In D. Boden & D. H. Zimmerman (Eds.), *Talk and social structure: Studies in Ethnomethodology and conversation analysis* (pp. 232–250). Cambridge: Polity Press.

Hymes, D. (1972). On communicative competence. In J. B. Pride & J. Holmes (Eds.), *Sociolinguistics* (pp. 269–285). Harmondsworth: Penguin.

Jacoby, S. (1998a). How can ESP practitioners tap into situated discourse research—And why should we? (Part l). *English for Specific Purposes News, 7* (1), 1, 4, 9–10.

Jacoby, S. (1998b). How can ESP practitioners tap into situated discourse research—And why should we? (Part 2). *English for Specific Purposes News, 7* (2), 4–5, 10.

Jacoby, S. (1998c). *Science as performance: Socializing scientific discourse through the conference talk rehearsal.* Unpublished Ph. D. dissertation. University of Califomia, Los Angeles.

Jacoby, S. (2001). Rethinking English for Science and Technology (EST): What can "indigenous assessment" tell us about the communication culture of science? Manuscript submitted for publication.

Jacoby, S., & Gonzales, P. (1991). The constitution of expert-novice in scientific discourse. *Issues in Applied Linguistics, 2*, 149–181

Jacoby, S., & Gonzales, P. (in press). Saying what wasn't said: Negative observation as a linguistic resource for the interactional construction of performance feedback. In C. Ford, B. Fox, & S. A. Thompson (Eds.), *The language of turn and sequence*. Oxford: Oxford University Press.

Jacoby, S., & McNamara, T. (1999). Locating competence. *English for Specific Purposes, 18* (3), 213–241.

Jefferson, G. (1973). A case of precision timing in ordinary conversation: Overlapped tag-positioned address terms in closing sequences. *Semiotica, 9*, 47–96.

Jefferson, G. (1974). Error correction as an interactional resource. *Language in Society, 2*, 181–199.

Jefferson, G. (1978). Sequential aspects of story-telling in conversation. In J. Schenkein (Ed.), *Studies in the organization of conversational interaction* (pp. 219–248). NY: Academic Press.

Jefferson, G. (1984). Notes on some orderlinesses of overlap onset. In V. D'Urso & P. Leonardi (Eds.), *Discourse analysis and natural rhetorics* (pp. 11–38). Padova: CLEUP Editore.

Jefferson, G. (1987). Exposed and embedded corrections. In G. Button & J. R. E. Lee (Eds.), *Talk and social organisation* (pp. 86–100). Clevedon, England: Multilingual Matters Ltd.

Jefferson, G. (1993). Caveat speaker: Preliminary notes on recipient topic-shift implicature. *Research on Language and Social Interaction, 26*(1), 1–30.

Jefferson, G. (1996). On the poetics of ordinary conversation. *Text and Performance Quarterly, 16* (1), 1–61

Jordan, B., & Fuller, N. (1975). On the non-fatal nature of trouble: Sense-making and trouble-managing in lingua franca talk. *Semiotica, 13*, 11–32.

Kachru, B. B., & Nelson, C. 1. (1996). World Englishes. In S. L. McKay & N. H. Hornberger (Eds.), *Sociolinguistics and language teaching* (pp. 71–102). Cambridge: Cambridge University Press.

Kasper, G. (1997). Beyond reference. In G. Kasper & E. Kellerman (Eds.), *Communication strategies: Psycholinguistic and sociolinguistic perspectives* (pp. 345–359). London: Longman.

Kasper, G., & Blum-Kulka, S. (Eds.) (1993). *Interlanguage pragmatics*. New York: Oxford University Press.

Kasper, G., & Dahl, M. (1991). Research methods in interlanguage pragmatics. *Studies in Second Language Acquisition, 13*, 215–247.

Kidwell, M. (2000). Common ground in cross-cultural communication: Sequential and institutional contexts in front desk service encounters. *Issues in Applied Linguistics, 11* (1),

17–37.

Kim, K. H. (1999a). Phrasal unit boundaries and organization of turns and sequences in Korean conversation. *Human Studies*, 22, 425–446.

Kim, K. H. (1999b). Other-initiated repair sequences in Korean conversation: Types and functions. *Discourse and Cognition*, 6 (2), 141–168.

Kim, K. H. (2001a). The Korean topic marker *nun* as tying device: Grounding referents and actions. *Discourse and Cognition*, 7 (1), 155–184.

Kim, K. H. (2001b). Confirming intersubjectivity through retroactive elaboration: Organization of phrasal units in other-initiated repair sequences in Korean conversation. In M. Selting & E. Couper-Kuhlen (Eds.), *Studies in interactional linguistics* (pp. 345–372). Amsterdam: John Benjamins.

Koshik, I. (2000). Conversation analytic research on institutional talk: Implications for TESOL teachers and researchers. *TESOL Research Interest Section Newsletter*, 7 (2), pp. 3, 8–11.

Koshik, I. (in press a). Designedly incomplete utterances: A pedagogical practice for eliciting knowledge displays in error correction sequences. *Research on Language and Social Interaction*.

Koshik, I. (in press b). A conversation analytic study of yes/no questions which convey reversed polarity assertions. *Journal of Pragmatics*.

Koshik, I. (2001a). Teacher practices for oral treatment of student errors in second language writing. Manuscript submitted for publication.

Koshik, I. (2001b). Reinvestigating the category of display questions in ESL pedagogical discourse. Manuscript submitted for publication.

Lazaraton, A. (1991). *A conversation analysis of structure and interaction in the language interview*. Unpublished Ph. D. dissertation, University of California, Los Angeles.

Lazaraton, A. (1997). Preference organization in oral proficiency interviews: The case of language ability assessments. *Research on Language and Social Interaction*, 30 (1), 53–72.

Lerner, G. H. (1991). On the syntax of sentences-in-progress. *Language in Society*, 20, 441–458.

Lerner, G. H. (1995). Turn design and the organization of participation in instructional activities. *Discourse Processes*, 19, 111–131.

Lerner, G. H. (1996). On the 'semi-permeable' character of grammatical units in conversation: Conditional entry into the turn space of another speaker. In E. Ochs, E. A. Schegloff & S. A. Thompson (Eds.), *Interaction and grammar* (pp. 238–276). Cambridge: Cambridge University Press.

Lerner, G. H. (in press). Turn-sharing: the choral co-production of talk in interaction. In C. E. Ford, B. A. Fox & S. A. Thompson (Eds.), *The language of turn and sequence*. Oxford: Oxford University Press.

Levinson, S. (1979). Activity types and language. *Linguistics, 17*, 365–399. Reprinted in P. Drew & J. Heritage (Eds.), *Talk at work: Interaction in institutional settings* (pp. 66–100). Cambridge: Cambridge University Press.

Lindström, A. B. (1994). Identification and recognition in Swedish telephone conversation openings. *Language in Society, 23*(2), 231–252.

Lindström, A. B. (1997). Designing social actions: Grammar, prosody, and interaction in Swedish conversation. PhD dissertation, Department of Sociology, University of California. Los Angeles.

Lindström, A. B. (1999). Directives and the negotiation of work tasks in the Swedish home help service. In P. Linell, L. Ahrenberg & L. Jönsson (Eds.) *Samtal och Språkänvandning i Professionerna [Conversation and language use in the professions]* (pp. 157–168). Uppsala, Sweden: Association Suedoise de Linguistique Appliquée.

Lutfey, K., & Maynard, D. (1998). Bad news in oncology: How the physician and patient talk about death and dying without using those words. *Social Psychology Quarterly, 61*, 321–341.

Manzo. J. F. (1993). Jurors'narratives of personal experience in deliberation talk. *Text, 13* (2), 267–290.

Markee, N. (1994). Toward an ethnomethodological respecification of second-language acquisition studies. In E. E. Tarone, S. M. Gass, & A. D. Cohen (Eds.), *Research Methodology in second language acquisition* (pp. 89–116). Mahwah, NJ: Lawrence Erlbaum Associates.

Markee, N. (1995). Teachers' answers to students' questions: Problematizing the issue of making meaning. *Issues in Applied Linguistics, 6*, 63–92.

Markee, N. (2000). *Conversation analysis.* Mahwah, NJ: Lawrence Erlbaum.

Marlaire, C., & Maynard, D. (1990). Standardized testing as an interactional phenomenon. *Sociology of Education, 63*, 83–101.

Maynard, D. (1984). *Inside plea bargaining: The language of negotiation.* New York: Plenum.

McNamara, T., Hill, K., & May, L. (this volume). Discourse and assessment.

Mori, J. (2002). Task design, plan, and development of talk-in-interaction: An analysis of a small group activity in a Japanese language classroom. *Applied Linguistics, 23* (3).

Ochs, E., Schegloff, E. A., & Thompson, S. A. (Eds.). (1996). *Interaction and grammar.* Cambridge, UK: Cambridge University Press.

Ohta, A. S. (2001). *Second language acquisition processes in the classroom.* Mahwah, NJ: Lawrence Erlbaum.

Olsher, D. (2001). Embodied completion of sequential action in ESL small group work. In R. Gardner & J. Wagner (Eds.), *Second language talk: Studies of native and nonnative interaction.* Manuscript submitted for publication.

Park, Y. Y. (1998a). A discourse analysis of contrastive connectives in English, Korean, and Japanese conversation: With special reference to the context of dispreferred responses. In A. Jucker & Y. Ziv (Eds.), *Discourse markers* (pp. 277–300). Amsterdam: John Benjamins.

Park, Y. Y. (1998b). Interactive grammar: The turn-final use of *nuntey* in Korean and *kedo* in Japanese. In D. Silva (Ed.), *Japanese/Korean Linguistics, Vol.* 8 (pp. 45–59). Stanford, CA: Center for the Study of Language and Information.

Park, Y. Y. (1998c). A discourse analysis of the Korean connective *ketun* in conversation. *Crossroads of Language, Interaction, and Culture, 1*, 71–79.

Park, Y. Y. (1999). The Korean connective *nuntey* in conversational discourse. *Journal of Pragmatics, 31*, 191–218.

Park, Y. Y. (in press). Recognition and identification in Japanese and Korean telephone conversation openings. In K. K. Luke & T. S. Pavlidou (Eds.), *Telephone calls: Unity and diversity in conversational structure across languages and cultures*. Amsterdam: John Benjamins.

Peräkylä, A. (1993). Invoking a hostile world: Discussing the patient's future in AIDS counseling. *Text, 13* (2), 291–316.

Peräkylä, A. (1995). *AIDS counselling: Institutional interaction and clinical practice*. Cambridge: Cambridge University Press.

Pomerantz, A. M. (1980). Telling my side: 'Limited access' as a 'fishing' device. *Sociological Inquiry, 50*, 186–198.

Pomerantz, A. (1984). Agreeing and disagreeing with assessments: Some features of preferred/ dispreferred turn shapes. In J. M. Atkinson & J. Heritage (Eds.), *Structures of social action: Studies in conversation analysis* (pp. 57–101). Cambridge: Cambridge University Press.

Riggenbach, H. (1998). Evaluating learner interactional skills: Conversation at the micro level. In R. Young & A. He (Eds.), *Talking and testing: Discourse approaches to the assessment of oral proficiency* (pp. 53–68). Amsterdam: John Benjamins.

Robinson, J. D. (1998). Getting down to business: Talk, gaze, and body orientation during openings of doctor-patient consultations. *Human Communication Research, 25* (1), 97–123.

Sacks, H. (1972a). An initial investigation of the usability of conversational materials for doing sociology. In D. N. Sudnow (Ed.), *Studies in social interaction* (pp. 31–74). New York: Free Press.

Sacks, H. (1972b). On the analyzability of stories by children. In J. J. Gumperz & D. Hymes (Eds.), *Directions in sociolinguistics: The ethnography of communication* (pp. 325–345). New York: Holt, Rinehart and Winston.

Sacks, H. (1973). On some puns with some intimations. In R. W. Shuy (Ed.), *Report of the Twenty-Third Annual Georgetown Round Table Meeting on Linguistics and Language Studies* (pp. 135–144). Washington, DC: Georgetown University Press.

Sacks, H. (1974). An analysis of the course of a joke's telling in conversation. In R. Bauman & J. Sherzer (Eds.), *Explorations in the ethnography of speaking* (pp. 337–353). Cambridge: Cambridge University Press.

Sacks, H. (1987 [1973]). On the preferences for agreement and contiguity in sequences in conversation. In G. Button & J. R. E. Lee (Eds.), *Talk and social organisation* (pp. 54–69). Clevedon, England: Multilingual Matters.

Sacks, H. (1989). On members' measurement systems. *Research on Language and Social Interaction, 22*, 45–60.

Sacks, H. (1992). *Lectures on conversation*, (2 vols). (Ed. G. Jefferson, with Introductions by E. A. Schegloff.) Oxford: Blackwell.

Sacks, H., & Schegloff, E. A. (1979). Two preferences in the organization of reference to persons in conversations and their interaction. In G. Psathas (Ed.), *Everyday language: Studies in ethnomethodology* (pp. 15–21). New York: Irvington.

Sacks, H., Schegloff, E. A., & Jefferson, G. (1974). A simplest systematics for the organization of turn-taking for conversation. *Language, 50*, 696–735.

Schegloff, E. A. (1967). *The first five seconds: The order of conversational openings.* Unpublished Ph. D. dissertation, University of California, Berkeley.

Schegloff, E. A. (1968). Sequencing in conversational openings. *American Anthropologist, 70*, 1075–1095.

Schegloff, E. A. (1972). Notes on a conversational practice: Formulating place. In D. Sudnow (Ed.), *Studies in social interaction* (pp. 75–119). New York: Free Press.

Schegloff, E. A. (1979). The relevance of repair to a syntax-for-conversation. In T. Givon (Ed.), *Syntax and semantics* [vol. 12]: *Discourse and syntax* (pp 261–286). New York: Academic Press.

Schegloff, E. A. (1982). Discourse as an interactional achievement: Some uses of "uh huh" and other things that come between sentences. In D. Tannen (Ed.), *Georgetown University Roundtable on Languages and Linguistics.* (pp. 71–93). Washington, DC: Georgetown University Press.

Schegloff, E. A. (1986). The routine as achievement. *Human Studies, 9*, 111–151.

Schegloff, E. A. (1987). Some sources of misunderstanding in talk-in-interaction. *Linguistics, 25*, 201–218.

Schegloff, E. A. (1988a). Presequences and indirection: Applying speech act theory to ordinary conversation. *Journal of Pragmatics, 12*, 55–62.

Schegloff, E. A. (1988b). On an actual virtual servo-mechanism for guessing bad news: A single case conjecture. *Social Problems, 35* (4), 442–457.

Schegloff, E. A. (1988c). Goffman and the analysis of conversation. In P. Drew & A. Wootton (Eds.), *Erving Goffman: Exploring the interaction order* (pp. 89–135). Cambridge: Polity

Press.

Schegloff, E. A. (1988/1989). From interview to confrontation: Observations on the Bush/Rather encounter. *Research on Language and Social Interaction, 22*, 215–240.

Schegloff, E. A. (1990). On the organization of sequences as a source of 'coherence' in talk-in-interaction. In B. Dorval (Ed.), *Conversational organization and its development* (pp. 51–77). Norwood, NJ: Ablex.

Schegloff, E. A. (1991). Reflections on talk and social structure. In D. Boden & D. H. Zimmerman (Eds.), *Talk and social structure* (pp. 44–70). Cambridge: Polity Press.

Schegloff, E. A. (1992a). To Searle on conversation: A note in return. In J. R. Searle et al. (Eds.), *(On) Searle on conversation* (pp. 113–128). Amsterdam: John Benjamins.

Schegloff, E. A. (1992b). Introduction, Volume 1. In G. Jefferson (Ed.), *Harvey Sacks: Lectures on Conversation* (pp. ix–lxii). Oxford: Blackwell.

Schegloff, E. A. (1992c). Repair after next turn: The last structurally provided place for the defence of intersubjectivity in conversation. *American Journal of Sociology, 95*(5), 1295–1345.

Schegloff, E. A. (1993). Telephone conversation. In R. E. Asher (Ed.), *Encyclopedia of Language and Linguistics* (pp. 4547–4549). Oxford, England: Pergamon Press.

Schegloff, E. A. (1995). Sequence organization. Unpublished manuscript.

Schegloff, E. A. (1996a). Turn organization: One intersection of grammar and interaction. In E. Ochs, E. A. Schegloff, & S. A. Thompson (Eds.), *Interaction and grammar* (pp. 52–133). Cambridge: Cambridge University Press.

Schegloff, E. A. (1996b). Some practices for referring to persons in talk-in-interaction: A partial sketch of a systematics. In B. A. Fox (Ed.), *Studies in anaphora* (pp. 437–485). Amsterdam: John Benjamins.

Schegloff, E. A. (1996c). Confirming allusions: Toward an empirical account of action. *American Journal of Sociology, 102*, 161–216.

Schegloff, E. A. (1997a). Third turn repair. In G. R. Guy, C. Feagin, D. Schiffrin, & J. Baugh (Eds.), *Towards a social science of language: Papers in honor of William Labov. Volume 2: Social interaction and discourse structures* (pp. 31–40). Amsterdam: John Benjamins.

Schegloff, E. A. (1997b). Practices and actions: Boundary cases of other-initiated repair. *Discourse Processes, 23*, 499–545.

Schegloff, E. A. (1997c). Whose text? Whose context? *Discourse and Society, 8*(2), 165–87.

Schegloff, E. A. (1997d). 'Narrative analysis' thirty years later. *Journal of Narrative and Life History, 7* (1–4), 97–106.

Schegloff, E. A. (1999a). Discourse, pragmatics, conversation, analysis. *Discourse Studies. 1* (4), 405–435.

Schegloff, E. A. (1999b). '*Schegloff*'s texts' as '*Billig*' s data:' A critical reply to Billig.

Discourse and Society, 10, 558–571.

Schegloff, E. A. (1999c). Naivete vs. sophistication or discipline vs. self-indulgence: A rejoinder to Billig. *Discourse and Society, 10,* 577–582.

Schegloff, E. A. (2000a). Overlapping talk and the organization of turn-taking for conversation. *Language in Society, 29*(1), 1–63.

Schegloff, E. A. (2000b). When 'others' initiate repair. *Applied Linguistics, 21,* 205–243.

Schegloff, E. A. (2001). Accounts of conduct in interaction: Interruption, overlap and turn-taking. In J. H. Turner (Ed.), *Handbook of sociological theory* (pp. 287–321). New York: Plenum.

Schegloff, E. A. (2002a). Beginning in the telephone. In J. E. Katz & M. Aakhus (Eds.), *Perpetual contact: Mobile communication, private talk, public performance* (pp. 284–299). Cambridge: Cambridge University Press.

Schegloff, E. A. (2002b). On 'opening sequencing' : An introductory note. In J. E. Katz & M. Aakhus (Eds.), *Perpetual contact: Mobile communication, private talk, public performance* (pp. 319–324). Cambridge: Cambridge University Press.

Schegloff, E. A. (2002c). Opening sequencing. In J. E. Katz & M. Aakhus (Eds.), *Perpetual contact: Mobile communication, private talk, public performance* (pp. 326–385). Cambridge: Cambridge University Press.

Schegloff, E. A. (in press). Reflections on research on telephone conversation openings: Issues of cross-cultural scope and scholarly exchange, interactional import and consequences. In K. K. Luke & T. S. Pavlidou (Eds.), *Telephone calls: Unity and diversity in conversational structure across languages and cultures.* Amsterdam: John Benjamins.

Schegloff, E. A. . Jefferson, G., & Sacks, H. (1977). The preference for self-correction in the organization of repair in conversation. *Language, 53,* 361–382.

Schegloff, E. A., Ochs, E., & Thompson, S. A. (1996). Introduction. In E. Ochs, E. A. Schegloff, & S. A. Thompson (Eds.), *Interaction and grammar* (pp. 1–51). Cambridge: Cambridge University Press.

Schegloff, E. A., & Sacks, H. (1973). Opening up closings. *Semiotica, 8,* 289–327.

Selting, M., & Couper-Kuhlen, E. (Eds.). (in press). *Studies in interactional linguistics.* Amsterdam: John Benjamins.

Schwartz, J. (1980). The negotiation for meaning: Repair in conversations between second language learners of English. In D. Larsen-Freeman (Ed.), *Discourse analysis in second language acquisition research* (pp. 138–153). Rowley, MA: Newbury House.

Sorjonen, M. (1996). On repeats and responses in Finnish conversations. In E. Ochs, E. A. Schegloff, & S. A. Thompson (Eds.), *Interaction and grammar* (pp. 277–327). Cambridge: Cambridge University Press.

Sorjonen, M. (2001). *Responding in conversation: A study of response particles in Finnish.*

Amsterdam: John Benjamins.

Sorjonen, M. (in press a). Recipient activities: The particle "no" as a go-ahead response in Finnish conversations. In C. E. Ford, B. A. Fox, & S. A. Thompson (Eds.), *The language of turn and sequence*. Oxford: Oxford University Press.

Sorjonen, M. (in press b). Simple answers to yes-no questions: The case of Finnish. In E. Couper-Kuhlen & M. Selting (Eds.), *Interactional linguistics*. Amsterdam: John Benjamins.

Suh, K. H., & Kim, K. H. (2001). The Korean modal marker *keyss* revisited: A marker of achieved state of intersubjectivity. *Berkeley Linguistic Society, 26*, 271–282.

Tanaka, H. (1999). *Turn-taking in Japanese conversation: A study in grammar and interaction*. Amsterdam: John Benjamins.

Wagner, J. (1996). Foreign language acquisition through interaction—a critical review of research on conversational adjustments. *Journal of Pragmatics, 26*, 215–235.

Whalen, M. R., & Zimmerman, D. H. (1987). Sequential and institutional contexts in calls for help. *Social Psychological Quarterly, 50* (2), 172–185.

Whalen, J., Zimmerman, D. H., & Whalen, M. R. (1988). When words fail: A single case analysis. *Social Problems, 35* (4), 335–362.

Willey, B. (2001). Examining a "communication strategy" from a conversation analytic perspective: Eliciting help from native speakers inside and outside word search sequences. Unpublished M. A. Thesis, University of Illinois at Urbana-Champaign.

Wong, J. (1984). Using conversational analysis to evaluate telephone conversation in English as a second language textbooks. Unpublished master's thesis, University of California, Los Angeles.

Wong, J. (2000a). Delayed next turn repair initiation in native/nonnative speaker English conversation. *Applied Linguistics, 21* , 274–297.

Wong, J. (2000b). The token 'yeah' in nonnative speaker English conversation. *Research on Language and Social Interaction, 33*, 39–67.

Wong, J. (2002). "Applying" conversation analysis in applied linguistics: Evaluating English as a second language textbook dialogue. *International Review of Applied Linguistics in Language Teaching, 40* (2), 37–60.

Wu, R. J. R. (1997). Transforming participation frameworks in multi-party Mandarin conversation: The use of discourse particles and body behavior. *Issues in Applied Linguistics, 8* (2), 97–118.

Wu, R. J. R. (2000). Final particles in Mandarin Chinese: A conversation analysis of *A* and *OU*. Unpublished Ph. D. dissertation, Department of Applied Linguistics, University of California, Los Angeles.

Young, R. F. (this volume). Discourse approaches to oral language assessment.

Zimmerman, D. H. (1984). Talk and its occasion: The case of calling the police. In D.

Schiffrin (Ed.), *Meaning, form, and use in context: Linguistic applications* (pp. 210–228). Washington, DC: Georgetown University Press.

Zimmerman, D. H. (1992). The interactional organization of calls for emergency service. In P. Drew & J. Heritage (Eds.), *Talk at work: Interaction in institutional settings* (pp. 418–469). Cambridge: Cambridge University Press.

2. QUANTITATIVE AND QUALITATIVE APPROACHES TO DISCOURSE ANALYSIS

Anne Lazaraton

This chapter summarizes 16 empirical studies that employ quantitative and/or qualitative discourse analytic techniques published in applied linguistics journals over the last five years. These studies tend to analyze spoken discourse in formal contexts, produced by both adults and children who are native and nonnative speakers of English. Unfortunately, all studies focus only on English discourse, which suggests that analyses of discourse in other languages are clearly needed; moreover, it was extremely difficult to find published discourse analytic studies which employ only quantitative research methods. Although each of these discourse analytic studies presents segments of transcribed discourse, researchers collect data of the type and in the amount prescribed by the analytical tradition employed—those working within the conversation analytic tradition collect, transcribe, analyze, and present only recorded social interaction, while researchers who situate themselves in the ethnography of communication framework collect and present various forms of "triangulated" data to support their conclusions. The chapter concludes by mentioning the problem of evaluative criteria for qualitative research, and by suggesting that applied linguists need to address this issue and articulate some reasonable solutions, so that all published research is, in fact, quality research.

The applied linguist who is interested in learning about (or brushing up on) the many facets of discourse analysis has a number of sources from which to choose. For example, Cook (1989) covers a number of theories of discourse (discourse as structure, as dialogue, and as knowledge), as do Brown and Yule (1983), although they take a more linguistic perspective on issues such as context, information structure, reference, and coherence. Hatch (1992) illustrates a number of approaches to discourse analysis that she judges are important tools for the language teacher (e. g., system and ritual constraints, speech act and speech events, cohesion and coherence). McCarthy (1991) examines various models of discourse analysis and how they relate to the teaching of grammar, vocabulary, and phonology, as well as features of spoken and written language. Celce-Murcia and Olshtain (2000) discuss various fields of study that employ discourse analysis (cohesion and coherence analysis, information structure analysis, conversation analysis and critical discourse analysis). Finally, Schiffrin (1994) provides a very comprehensive overview of six approaches to discourse (speech acts, Gricean pragmatics, ethnography of communication, variation analysis, conversation analysis, and interactional sociolinguistics) with data illustrating how each approach works. It is also worth mentioning that discourse analysis is seen as an increasingly important tool for language teaching (e. g., Riggenbach, 1999), for second language acquisition research (e. g., Markee, 2000), and for language test development and validation (e. g., Lazaraton, in press).

What is unfortunate, though, when considering this set of resources, is that none deals with the broader methodological issues in quantitative and qualitative discourse analysis, as it is practiced by applied linguists, in any detail. From a larger disciplinary perspective, dichotomies like those shown in Figure 1 are often used to distinguish qualitative and quantitative research:

Qualitative Research	Quantitative Research
naturalistic	controlled
observational	experimental
subjective	objective
descriptive	inferential
process-oriented	outcome-oriented
valid	reliable
holistic	particularistic
'real', 'rich', 'deep' data	hard, replicable data
ungeneralizable single case analysis	generalizable aggregate analysis

Figure 1 : Characteristics of qualitative and quantitative research (from Larsen-Freeman & Long 1991, p. 12. Used by permission of Sage Publications).

From this vantage point, very few empirical studies using discourse analysis seem to be aligned with the characteristics of quantitative research that Larsen-Freeman and Long mention. Perhaps the most basic consideration in distinguishing the two for the present purpose is whether the data are analyzed in numerical or nonnumerical form. Johnstone (2000) puts it this way: Are the research questions answered in mechanical ways (for example, counting instances, computing means, calculating statistics) or nonmechancial (asking about, watching, or listening to phenomena of interest)? In other words, quantitative discourse analysts seek to determine how often something happens, while why and how things happen are the focus of qualitative discourse analyses.

Nunan (1992), the only applied linguistics research methods text to discuss discourse analysis as a research tool, contends that the relevant question to ask in distinguishing qualitative from quantitative research is, "To what extent should I attempt to (a) prespecify (b) isolate and control the phenomena under investigation?" (p. 8). With respect to discourse analysis specifically, Nunan proposes four criteria that one may use for distinguishing among the various discourse analytic approaches:

- the method of generating data: Are the data invented, elicited, or naturalistic?
- the mode of communication: Are the data in the form of speech or writing?
- the units of analysis: Are the units analyzed linguistic or nonlinguistic?
- the type of analysis: Is the analysis primarily categorical or interpretive?

While gleaning answers to the first two questions is relatively straightforward for most empirical studies using discourse analysis, the line between categorical and interpretive data analysis is fuzzier, and research may strive to do both, as an analysis of published discourse analytic research over the last five years reveals. In perusing over seventy issues of *Applied Linguistics, Language Learning, Studies in Second Language Acquisition,* and *TESOL Quarterly,* it became clear that (1) discourse analytic studies are not prevalent, and (2) quantitative discourse analytic studies are rare. In this chapter, I describe 16 empirical research studies in applied linguistics that are representative of recent discourse analytic work; from this review, I hope that we can infer the current methodological preoccupations in this work. I begin by looking at two studies which employ a quantitative approach to understanding spoken language common in many SLA studies, then review a study which uses VARBRUL, a multivariate statistical procedure, as well as qualitative discourse to understand first and second language use in an immersion classroom. Then studies carried out using more qualitative approaches, including conversation analysis, ethnography of communication, and genre analysis are summarized. The chapter concludes with an appendix that summarizes the relevant methodological and analytic features of the research mentioned here, so that the interested reader can locate studies that meet certain criteria, and with a brief discussion of some persistent, unresolved methodological issues in carrying out discourse analysis.

Quantitative Approaches

Remarkably, it was impossible to locate a published applied linguistics study which claims to be both discourse analytic and quantitative in nature. While many published SLA studies analyze spoken language, this language is almost always elicited by some research task, rather than produced naturalistically. The audiotapes are generally transcribed using conventional spelling, with the resulting transcriptions coded for features of interest, which are then counted and analyzed using statistical procedures such as ANOVA. Transcripts, or data excerpts, if given at all, are usually presented in the articles' Method section as an example of a coding category, or in an appendix. That is, the data are not analyzed in their original, or more accurately, transcribed form, which is the case in every qualitative study summarized here. It is important to note that researchers who work in this way do not claim that their studies are discourse analytic, nor am I doing so. Still, two examples will suffice to show the methodological decisions made concerning the analysis of produced discourse in this sort of SLA research. On the more "interpretive" end (and I use this term loosely), Williams (1999) looked at 8 adult ESL learners representing four levels of proficiency in order to determine "attention to form" (how, when, what kinds). Sixty hours of IEP listening-speaking classes were audiorecorded while the learners were engaged in many different activities. Williams isolated cases of learner-learner interaction and then located "language-related episodes" (LREs), "discourse in which the learners talk or ask about language, or question, implicitly or explicitly, their own language use or that of others" (p. 595). She coded all 255 LREs in her data for numerous features, including requests to teacher or another learners, learner-learner negotiation, metatalk, and other correction. Descriptive statistics and bar charts are used to show the frequency of LREs by level, per session, and per 1000 words. Her results, which indicated that attention to form is influenced by proficiency level and activity type and is more often of a lexical rather than a syntactic nature, are several steps removed from the naturalistic classroom language data that were collected. Data fragments are presented as examples of different types of attention to form in the Methods section, but not as "results."

An example of more categorically-oriented SLA research can be found in Shehadeh's (1999) study of the "modified comprehensible output" of second language learners. Here, 16 dyads (8 NS-NNS, 8 NNS-NNS) engaged in two experimental elicitation tasks—a picture dictation and an opinion exchange, both of which were audiotaped. The researcher then selected 5-minute samples from the audiotapes to transcribe "in detail," and presented a few segments as examples of the many coding categories used (e. g., self-vs. other-initiation of clarification requests; responses to these; c-units). Frequencies, percentages, and results from ANOVA procedures are reported to support the conclusion that self-initiations are more frequent, and that the picture dictation task produced more modifications. Again, the discourse data themselves are not presented as results of the study.

However, the most interesting quantitative discourse analytic study from a methodological point of view is Broner's (2000) dissertation (see also Broner 2001), a noteworthy example of a primarily quantitative investigation integrating data and insights from qualitative discourse analysis. Broner's study is rooted in variation analysis, a sociolinguistic approach to the analysis of language that views discourse as a reflection of one's speech community and looks to social and linguistic factors to understand patterns of language variation and change. She used a case study approach to look at first and second language use of three English-speaking fifth graders who attended a Spanish full immersion program. These three children were audiorecorded for 13 hours over a period of five months in order to get a detailed and measurable description of their language use in classroom interactions with their teacher and peers as well as in academic task work. As with the ethnographic studies mentioned later in this chapter, Broner also collected data in the form of observations, notebooks, interviews with children and their teachers, and a schoolwide survey. The verbal interactions were analyzed qualitatively, using a general discourse analytic technique based on transcribed data fragments, as well as descriptively with percentages and statistically with chi-square tests. The numerical analyses of the data allowed Broner to determine that "second language use is *not* independent of the variables of interlocutor, activity, content, and on/off task" (p. 206). These results are of limited use, though, in that no more than two factors could be examined at any one time, so there is no way "to account for the multiple and cross-cutting and intersecting factors that influence learner speech" (Young & Bayley, 1996, pp. 303–304).

In fact, Broner's study went much further, in that a third "layer" of analysis was used to construct a language use model for the three children using Variable Rule Analysis, or VARBRUL, so that she could "go beyond reporting data based on unsystematic observations of very few instances of language use and analysis of percentages" (p. 3). Specifically, VARBRUL was used to pinpoint the conditions (specifically, task and interlocutor, the two independent variables in the study) under which the three children used Spanish or English (the dependent variable). Broner maintains that VARBRUL is uniquely suited to this task, because the alternative, Analysis of Variance (ANOVA), perhaps the most widely used multivariate statistical procedure in published applied linguistics research (Lazaraton, 2000), requires a fairly even distribution of observations across represented (rather than empty) cells. An in-depth explanation of the details of VARBRUL (or Goldvarb for Macintosh) is beyond the scope of this chapter (though Young & Bayley, 1996, give an extremely detailed introduction to this statistical procedure); nevertheless, some general methodological points can be made:

1. It is based on the principles of quantitative modeling and multiple causes.
2. It tests multiple hypotheses that are motivated by a particular linguistic, social, and/or psychological theory.
3. It is based on the analysis of a large number of tokens of the variable form (500–3000 tokens are mentioned by Young and Bailey, 1996).
4. What counts as a token and what doesn't is a theory-based decision with analytical consequences, and accurate coding of hypothesized independent variables for each is crucial.
5. VARBRUL performs a regression analysis of the data to generate a statistical model of factor weights and probabilities, including the smallest

list of contextual factors that significantly contribute to variation. It also approximates the overall probability that the rule being investigated will apply (input probability) and the weight of each factor group. VARBRUL usually requires several "runs" to achieve the best fitting model for the tested hypotheses.
6. There are conventional procedures for interpreting VARBRUL results and for determining whether the results confirm or disconfirm stated hypotheses.

In order to perform her analysis, Broner coded 4843 utterances from the children's classroom language use for both interlocutor (e. g., student, teacher, self, overhearers) and for task features (e. g., goal, content, on vs. off task). She also coded a number of linguistic contexts (e. g., clause type, style). Many interesting results emerged from this study, such as the finding that L1 (English) vs L2 (Spanish) use was significantly affected when the teacher was the interlocutor (Spanish use was more likely). Spanish was also more likely to be used when the goal of the task required focusing on the L2.

Perhaps the real value of the study, however, is shows what is possible using this technique of "top-down" data analysis, one based primarily on theory, rather than data. As Young and Yandell (1999) observe, "the tools [VARBRUL] help us to answer questions that a theory has helped us to ask. Bottom-up analyses of interlanguage, no matter how sophisticated the tools of analysis, produce facts without a context in which those facts can be interpreted" (p. 485). Or, as Preston notes, "many a good study seems foolishly criticized by the post-hoc recriminations the investigators have directed towards their own work when they note that other variables may have confounded the one they set out to study. Of course they have! Why not deal realistically with this inevitable variety, while focusing on how the factor one delights most in does (or does not) influence the data" (1996, p. 31).

Qualitative Approaches

The majority of discourse analytic studies in our field are apt to employ one of two qualitative research methodologies: conversation analysis or ethnography of communication. *Conversation analysis* (or CA), which views discourse as a local construction of social order, is a sociological approach that attempts to uncover the systematic properties of the sequential organization of talk and the social practices displayed by and embodied in talk-in-interaction. CA employs inductive methods to search for recurring patterns across many cases without appeal to intuitive judgments of what speakers "think" or "mean." The analyst attempts to model the procedures and expectations employed by the participants by proceeding as the talk does: on a turn-by-turn basis. Briefly (see Schegloff, Koshik, Jacoby, and Olsher's chapter in this volume, and Pomerantz and Fehr, 1997, for an explication of some analytic "tools" for doing CA), the conversation analyst generally subscribes to the following methodological tenets:

1. using authentic, recorded data which are carefully transcribed;
2. using "unmotivated looking" rather than pre-stated research questions;
3. employing the "turn" as the unit of analysis;
4. analyzing single cases, deviant cases, and collections thereof;
5. disregarding ethnographic and demographic particulars of the context and participants;
6. eschewing the coding and quantification of data.

Conversation analytic studies have only recently begun to appear in applied linguistics journals, a fact which is somewhat remarkable given that conversation analysis has been going strong for nearly forty years now. In reading such studies, one is struck by the similarities in how the researchers describe their databases, transcribe their data into turns at talk using conventional notation (as in Atkinson & Heritage, 1984), analyze exemplar cases which are neither tallied nor coded, and suggest ways in which the interactional practices displayed are implicative of certain identities. For example, Wong (2000a), working within the CA framework, begins with the assumption that initiations of repair on some problem in hearing or understanding are overwhelmingly initiated in the next turn following the trouble source (as in Schegloff, Jefferson, & Sacks, 1977). She then analyzes some potentially contrary data taken from a database of 12 transcribed native speaker-nonnative speaker (Mandarin L1) telephone conversations. Wong shows that the NNSs do not always initiate and do repair "as early as possible," in fact, other-initiation of repair is often delayed within the next turn of these speakers. These delayed other-initiations "aim at averting, avoiding, or correcting miscommunication and misunderstanding in the talk" (p. 244.) Using the same database, Wong (2000b) also examined the use of "yeah" in the speech of these same learners. Although this token appears in the same-turn repair environment, it functions as means by which a speaker can present him or herself as "competently managing throughout disfluency and repair" (p. 39). Wong proposes that interactional practices such as these are ways in which the learners can construct and display an identity of 'nonnative speaker.'

Seedhouse (1997) also used conversation analysis to make sense of how repair is accomplished in numerous published and unpublished extracts taken from many second language classrooms. This work is consistent with recent CA studies on "institutional talk" (e. g., Drew & Heritage, 1992), where the analyst tries to understand how everyday conversational practices are employed, or modified to achieve certain institutional goals. In this article, Seedhouse uses many data fragments to show how the pedagogical goals of the second language classroom (i. e., promoting second language acquisition) may, in fact, be at odds with the interactional practices of repair (i. e., hearers rarely correct speakers overtly) in this particular context. His findings document that repair done by the teachers he studied was accomplished without direct, negative evaluation using "no" for language related problems, although procedural issues in classroom management were repaired directly.

The potential for miscommunication in cross-cultural encounters is one that second language educators and researchers are quite aware of (see Boxer, this volume). What is unique about Cameron and Williams's (1997) study of the interactions among a NNS student nurse from Thailand, her supervisor, and two patients at a U. S. psychiatric hospital is how, despite the "daunting odds" against successful communication when medicine, culture, and language interact, the tasks at hand are competently co-achieved by the participants. The nurse in question not only used non-targetlike pronunciation (shown in the data fragments through using phonetic transcription); she rarely marked verbs for past tense. Yet, Cameron and Williams demonstrate how participants in the interactions are able to use inferences and communication strategies to ensure that interpretations they make are relevant ones. The authors also argue that the displayed professional knowledge of the nurse was a crucial element in the successful interactions that occurred.

A final representative conversation analysis study is Boyle's (2000) examination of implicit compliments in a third institutional context, that of broadcast radio interviews. Boyle's study was motivated by what he sees as the limitations of our current understanding of explicit compliments (i. e., Manes & Wolfson, 1981). He explicates how interactants employ various interpretive procedures to understand both the constitution and the effect of these implicit compliments. Drawing on a database of transcribed radio programs in the United Kingdom, Boyle demonstrates in the data extracts how the person being complimented (and the hearing audience) can infer that when an assessment of an achievement is noted or a comparison to someone notable is made, these are, in fact, implicit compliments, to which recipients respond appropriately. Unlike much of the existing research on explicit compliments, which seeks to count and classify this speech act, Boyle, in the CA tradition, shows "the skillful ways in which individuals constitute them" (p. 43).

The second major qualitative approach to discourse analysis in applied linguistics research can be found in the *ethnography of communication*, an anthropological approach to language and culture which views discourse as a reflection of cultural and social reality and seeks to find holistic explanations for cultural conceptions and constructions of meaning and behavior. Ethnographers generally subscribe to the following methodological tenets (Davis & Henze, 1998, p. 401):

1. understanding that realities are multiple, constructed, and holistic;
2. overtly recognizing the researcher's own positionality;
3. documenting variation and cultural change across a community;
4. ensuring prolonged engagement and persistent observation;
5. triangulating data sources;
6. generating working hypotheses;
7. giving a thick description of participants and context;
8. applying research findings to social issues.

Obviously, there is both overlap and some clear differences between ethnography and conversation analysis; space limitations preclude a discussion of this topic here (but see, for example, Moerman, 1988). The most salient difference that emerges from reviewing the following studies, though, is that transcribed interactional data are just one (and not necessarily the most important) source of information that should be considered in documenting cultural practices.

One fruitful strand of ethnographic discourse analysis in applied linguistics is an examination of the language socialization of second language speakers, especially children. For example, Toohey's (2001) study followed six nonnative speaker elementary school children in the second grade to understand the nature of "disputes" in this context. Her triangulated data, consisting of observations, field notes, and audiotaped and videotaped interactions among the children, yielded evidence of three kinds of disputes: material disputes about places or resources in the classroom; opinion disputes about the worth of produced work; and disputes about the nature of play. Each of these is illustrated with a transcribed data fragment of actual talk. One of the children she followed seemed to be frequently marginalized in this educational setting, suggesting that the findings are relative to issues of language use and power, and racism, and further suggest that "recognizing the expertise of children might assist them in speaking from powerful and desirable positions with other children" (p. 275).

Another educational ethnographic study of elementary classroom language use can be found in Klingner and Vaughn (2000), who were interested in both how and how often the children they followed (nearly all L1 speakers of Spanish) helped each other in group work on "collaborative strategic reading" in a fifth grade English language classroom. Again, their triangulated data come from multiple sources: audiorecordings of group discourse, a pretest/posttest vocabulary measure, and a researcher log. Unlike the other studies summarized so far, these researchers actually counted the number of utterances of various types (e. g., reading aloud, using reading strategies). Both discourse samples and frequency counts are presented to illustrate the types and frequencies of helping behaviors (such as comprehension checks or feedback) in which the students engaged, as well as how students responded to unknown vocabulary. Students made significant gains on the vocabulary measure, as indicated by t-test results. They concluded that peer assistance in learning groups can be successful if students are given specific instruction in how and when to help classmates.

Morita's (2000) ethnographic study of the language socialization of adults is also notable for its focus on oral practices and academic discourse socialization.

She analyzed the academic culture of two TESL courses at a Canadian university taught by two instructors and attended by 21 graduate students, 15 native speakers of English and 6 nonnative speakers. Her triangulated data consisted of classroom observations, class session videotapes and transcriptions, interviews with participants, questionnaires, and relevant documents, which led her to choose the Oral Academic Presentation (OAP) as her unit of analysis. Morita found that oral presenters learned how to (a) indicate an "epistemic stance," either as relative experts or relative novices, towards the material in question, and (b) engage the audience by showing a personal connection to the material. The NNS participants reported various unique difficulties with the task at hand, for example, an unfamiliarity with the form of classroom interaction in the Canadian university, a (perceived) lack of ability in critical thinking, and a (perceived) lack of confidence Perhaps the most interesting empirical finding, clearly evident from the data transcripts she presents, is that Oral Academic Presentation performance is "socially and collaboratively constructed by the presenter, audience, backup, and instructor" (Morita, 2000, p. 292).

Parks and Maguire (1999) analyzed a very specific form of written language from a constructivist-discourse perspective, namely, the ways in which francophone nurses learned to write nursing notes in English. Their triangulated data consisted of on-site observations (which were recorded and transcribed) of clinical educators and the 11 nurses who took part in the study; drafts of written notes and medical charts; and oral interviews with each nurse. The results are reported in the form of copies of notes and transcribed interactions; their analysis of both the micro-and macro-levels of text production and the overt and covert processes of collaboration in producing the notes are used to support their conclusions about how L2 writers succeed or fail at becoming members of communities of practice, and how workplace practices and institutional culture affect this process.

One recent study of identity construction is reported by Nelson (1999), who examined how sexual identity is discussed in university ESL classes. She observed two such classes, collected classwork, conducted interviews, and recorded class discussions. The focus of her analysis is a 3-minute transcript from one grammar class lesson for which she provides retrospective commentary. The lesson, which was based on a modals practice worksheet containing the prompt "Those two women are walking arm in arm," began with a grammar discussion, but then moved on to the word "lesbian" after one student speculated "they could be lesbians." Nelson then documents how the task itself, which was based on speculation, encouraged the discussion, and how the discussion revealed the participants' own positioning with respect to sexual identity.

Lin (1999) reports on a critical ethnographic study of four Hong Kong middle school classrooms representing a range of socioeconomic levels using data collected from surveys, interviews with students, and an audiorecording of a reading lesson in order to understand the students' use of and views about English. Lin claims that, for example, the use of the L1 or the L2 in the classroom matters less than "how a teacher uses either language to connect with students and help them transform their attitudes, disposition, skills, and self-image—their habitus or social world" (p. 410). Lin maintains that an understanding of existing classroom practices provided by ethnographic studies such as this provide is a vital first step in this transformative process.

Using a narrative inquiry approach to analyze 16 full-length language learning memoirs and 7 additional essays, Pavlenko (2001) believes that viewing such memoirs as a genre, rather than just a source of ethnographic data with a certain informational value, allows us to understand the larger "social and rhetorical forces that shape them" (p. 218). Pavlenko was particularly interested in the cultural construction of gender in the 23 written texts published between 1975 and 2000. Her analysis identified references to gender relations and gendered subjects; she also counted the references which contained links between gender and language learning for both male and female narrators. The numerous extracts from the texts demonstrate how the writers construct gendered voices in their stories.

To conclude this section on qualitative approaches to discourse analysis, one final study that merits attention is the genre analysis of the social services oral intake interview reported by Tarone and Kuehn (2000), where genre is defined as a "class of oral communicative events that share a set of communicative purposes, which in turn determine the structure of the genre" (p. 101). Their goal was to determine the structure of this form of institutional talk, which they accomplished by collecting four sorts of data: an intuitive representation of the interview format; three actual audiotaped social services interviews which were later transcribed; the written application form used in the interview; and follow-up interviews with the two financial workers themselves. They established that the written application form structures, but is not identical to, the actual interview. Furthermore, the one NNS applicant responded differently than the two NS applicants did, which Tarone and Kuehn view as potentially problematic if misunderstandings result in, for example, welfare fraud. They conclude by noting that their study "demonstrates the usefulness of genre analysis as a tool for describing important speech events in the social life of nonnative-English-speaking immigrants and refugees in U. S. society" (p. 124).

Conclusion

A summary of these studies (see Appendix) indicates that recent published discourse analytic research (1) focuses more on formal contexts, such as classrooms or medical settings, than on informal conversation; (2) with few exceptions, uses spoken, rather than written discourse for data; and (3) considers such data produced by both adults and children who are both native speakers and learners of English. All of the qualitative studies present segments from the transcribed discourse as results, although the two SLA studies reviewed do not. Both the amounts and types of data collected and presented reflect the epistemological commitments of the particular research tradition in which the analyst works.

Other methodological decisions in discourse analysis are still debated, including the need (and the justification) for quantification and coding discourse data (cf. Schegloff, 1993, who presents a cogent argument against quantification of conversational data); the most appropriate way(s) to transcribe discourse data and present them as results (see Edwards & Lambert, 1993, on this issue; Green, Franquiz, & Dixon, 1997, and Roberts, 1997, discuss some philosophical and ideological issues in transcription), the appropriate unit of analysis for discourse research–the turn, the utterance, or another unit altogether (e. g., Crookes, 1990; Foster, Tonkyn, & Wigglesworth, 2000); and perhaps most fundamentally, the nature of context in discourse (e. g, Fitch, 1998). Also, all of the research cited in this chapter is based on analysis of English discourse; studies of the discourse of other languages are clearly lacking (although Young & He, 1998, contains several studies of discourse in other languages).

A final pressing problem for those engaged in qualitative research is determining a standard, or standards, that should be used in evaluating this research (Lazaraton, 2001). While quantitative research has a number of conventional numerical criteria for evaluating the "soundness" of a study (via probability levels, interrater reliability estimates, and the like), qualitative research has no such neat and tidy correlates. It is imperative for those of us working within "interpretive" research traditions to address these issues and to explicate some reasonable solutions, so that we can ensure that all published research, both qualitative and quantitative, is truly quality research.

ANNOTATED BIBLIOGRAPHY

Broner, M. (2001). *Impact of interlocutor and task on first and second language use in a Spanish immersion program*. CARLA Working Paper #18. Center for Advanced Research on Language Acquisition, University of Minnesota, Minneapolis, MN.

This shorter version of Broner's dissertation is available through CARLA at the University of Minnesota (http: //carla. acad. umn. edu; 8/15/01).

Young, R., & Bayley, R. (1996). VARBRUL analysis for second language acquisition research. In R. Bayley & D. R. Preston (Eds.), *Second language acquisition and variation* (pp. 253–306). Amsterdam: John Benjamins.

This lengthy, clearly written appendix to Bayley and Preston's edited collection explains the steps in using VARBRUL in its DOS and Macintosh platforms by using data from their own research and other variation studies of Ll and L2 interlanguage.

Young, R., &He, A. W. (Eds.). (1998). *Talking and testing: Discourse approaches to the assessment of oral proficiency*. Philadelphia: John Benjamins.

Although this edited collection deals with talk in only one setting—the oral proficiency interview—the studies included represent a wide range of analytic approaches (conversation analysis, ethnography of communication, interactional sociolinguistics, knowledge structure analysis, topical structure analysis) and analyze data in languages other than English, including Spanish, German, and Korean.

OTHER REFERENCES

Atkinson, J. M., & Heritage, J. (Eds.). (1984). *Structures of social action: Studies in conversation analysis.* Cambridge: Cambridge University Press.

Boxer, D. (this volume). *Discourse issues in cross-cultural pragmatics.*

Boyle, R. (2000). 'You' ve worked with Elizabeth Taylor!' : Phatic functions and implicit compliments. *Applied Linguistics, 21* , 26–46.

Broner, M. (2000). *Impact of interlocutor and task on first and second language use in a Spanish immersion program.* Unpublished Ph. D. dissertation, University of Minnesota, Minneapolis, MN.

Brown, G., & Yule, G. (1983). *Discourse analysis.* Cambridge: Cambridge University Press.

Cameron, R., & Williams, J. (1997). Senténce to ten cents: A case study of relevance and communicative success in nonnative-native speaker interactions in a medical setting. *Applied Linguistics, 18,* 415–445.

Celce-Murcia, M., & Olshtain, E. (2000). *Discourse and context in language Teaching.* Cambridge: Cambridge University Press.

Cook, G. (1989). *Discourse.* Oxford: Oxford University Press.

Crookes, G. (1990). The utterance, and other basic units for second language discourse analysis. *Applied Linguistics, 11,* 183–199.

Davis, K. A., & Henze, R. C. (1998). Applying ethnographic perspectives to issues in cross-cultural pragmatics. *Journal of Pragmatics, 30,* 399–419.

Drew, P., & Heritage, J. (Eds.). (1992). *Talk at work: Interaction in institutional settings.* Cambridge: Cambridge University Press.

Edwards, J. A., & Lambert, M. D. (Eds.). (1993). *Talking data: Transcription and coding in discourse research.* Hillsdale, NJ: Lawrence Erlbaum.

Fitch, K. 1. (1998). Text and context: A problematic distinction for ethnography. *Research on Language and Social Interaction, 31,* 91–107.

Foster, P., Tonkyn, A., & Wigglesworth, G. (2000). Measuring spoken language: A unit for all reasons. *Applied Linguistics, 21,* 354–375.

Green, J., Franquiz, M., & Dixon, C. (1997). The myth of the objective transcript: Transcribing as a situated act. *TESOL Quarterly, 31,* 172–176.

Hatch, E. (1992). *Discourse and language education.* New York: Cambridge University Press.

Johnstone, B. (2000). *Qualitative methods in sociolinguistics.* New York: Oxford University Press.

Klingner, J. K., & Vaughn, S. (2000). The helping behaviors of fifth graders while using collaborative strategic reading during ESL content classes. *TESOL Quarterly, 34,* 69–98.

Larsen-Freeman, D., & Long, M. H. (1991). *An introduction to second language acquisition research.* London: Longman.

Lazaraton, A. (2000). Current trends in research methodology and statistics in applied linguistics. *TESOL Quarterly*, 34, 175–181.

Lazaraton, A. (2001). *Evaluative criteria for qualitative research: Whose standards? And whose research?* Manuscript submitted for publication.

Lazaraton, A. (in press). *A qualitative approach to the validation of oral language tests.* Cambridge: Cambridge University Press.

Lin, A. M. Y. (1999). Doing-English-lessons in the reproduction or transformation of social worlds? *TESOL Quarterly*, 33, 393–412.

Manes, J., & Wolfson, N. (1981). The compliment formula. In F. Coulmas (Ed.), *Conversational routine: Explorations in standardized situations and prepatterned speech* (pp. 115–132). The Hague: Mouton.

Markee, N. (2000). *Conversation analysis.* Mahwah, NJ: Lawrence Erlbaum.

McCarthy, M. (1991). *Discourse analysis for language teachers.* Cambridge: Cambridge University Press.

Moerman, M. (1988). *Talking culture: Ethnography and conversation analysis.* Philadelphia, PA: University of Pennsylvania Press.

Morita, N. (2000). Discourse socialization through oral classroom activities in a TESL graduate program. *TESOL Quarterly*, 34, 279–310.

Nelson, C. (1999). Sexual identities in ESL: Queer theory and classroom inquiry. *TESOL Quarterly*, 33, 371–391.

Nunan, D. (1992). *Research methods in language learning.* Cambridge: Cambridge University Press.

Parks, S., & Maguire, M. H. (1999). Coping with on-the-job writing in ESL: A constructivist-semiotic perspective. *Language Learning*, 49, 143–175.

Pavlenko, A. (2001). Language learning memoirs as a gendered genre. *Applied Linguistics*, 22, 213–240.

Pomerantz, A., & Fehr, B. J. (1997). Conversation analysis: An approach to the study of social action as sense making practices. In T. A. van Dijk (Ed.), *Discourse as social action, discourse studies: A multidisciplinary introduction, Volume 2* (pp. 64–91). London: Sage Publications.

Preston, D. (1996). Variationist perspectives on second language acquisition. In R. Bayley and D. R. Preston (Eds.), *Second language acquisition and linguistic variation* (pp. 1–45). Amsterdam: John Benjamins.

Riggenbach, H. (1999). *Discourse analysis in the language classroom. Volume 1: The spoken language.* Ann Arbor, MI: University of Michigan Press.

Roberts, C. (1997). Transcribing talk: Issues of representation. *TESOL Quarterly*, 31, 167–172.

Schegloff, E. A. (1993). Reflections on quantification in the study of conversation. *Research on*

Language and Social Interaction, 26, 99–128.

Schegloff, E. A., Jefferson, G., & Sacks, H. (1977). The preference for self-correction in the organization of repair in conversation. *Language, 53*, 361–382.

Schegloff, E. A., Koshik, I., Jacoby, S., & Olsher, D. (this volume). Conversation analysis and applied linguistics.

Schiffrin, D. (1994). *Approaches to discourse.* Oxford: Basil Blackwell.

Seedhouse, P. (1997). The case of the missing "no" : The relationship between pedagogy and interaction. *Language Learning, 47*, 547–583.

Shehadeh, A. (1999). Non-native speakers' production of modified comprehensible output and second language learning. *Language Learning, 49*, 627–675.

Tarone, E., & Kuehn, K. (2000). Negotiating the social services oral intake interview: Communicative needs of nonnative speakers of English. *TESOL Quarterly, 34*, 99–126.

Toohey, K. (2001). Disputes in child L2 learning. *TESOL Quarterly, 35*, 257–278.

Williams, J. (1999). Learner-generated attention to form. *Language Learning, 49*, 583–625.

Wong, J. (2000a). Delayed next turn repair initiation in native/non-nonnative speaker English conversation. *Applied Linguistics, 21*, 244–267.

Wong, J. (2000b). The token "yeah" in nonnative speaker English conversation. *Research on Language and Social Interaction, 33*, 39–67.

Young, R., & Yandell, B. (1999). Top-down versus bottom-up analysis of interlanguage data: A reply to Saito. *Studies in Second Language Acquisition, 21*, 477–488.

APPENDIX

Methodological/Analytic Features of 16 Summarized Studies

Author (date)	Context	Participants	Data	Transcription System	Analytic Method	Code/Counts Provided	Data given in results section
Boyle(2000)	UK radio programs	NS British English	audiotapes	CA system	CA of implicit compliments	No	4 fragments
Broner(2000)	Spanish immersion classes in US	3 5th graders	audiotapes, observations, notebook, interviews, survey	CA system	Discourse analysis	No	30 fragments of talk
							4 interview fragments
							percentages X^2 statistics
					VARBRUL model to predict L1/L2 use	Yes	VARBRUL statistics
Cameron & Williams (1997)	U.S. psychiatric hospital	1 NNS nurse (Thai L1) 2 NS patients 1 NS supervisor	audiotapes	rough (some phonetic)	CA of participants' understanding despite nurse's NNS speech	No	12 fragments
Klingner & Vaughn (2000)	5th grade reading class in US	37 Ss; all but 2 NSs of Spanish	audiotapes, vocabulary test, research log	rough	ethnography of helping behaviors	Yes	8 fragments
					t-test of vocabulary gains	Yes	t-test results

2. QUANTITATIVE AND QUALITATIVE APPROACHES TO DISCOURSE ANALYSIS

Author (date)	Context	Participants	Data	Transcription System	Analytic Method	Code/Counts Provided	Data given in results section
Lin (1999)	Hong Kong middle school classrooms	4 classes, different socioeconomic backgrounds	audiotapes, survey, interviews	detailed	critical ethnography of English use and students' perception of value	No	3 class fragments 1 interview fragment
Morita (2000)	TESL courses in Canada	2 instructors, 21 graduate students (5 NNSs)	observations, CA-like audiotapes, videotapes, interviews, questionnaire, course documents		ethnography of oral academic presentations	No	fragments of 6 presentations; responses from 5 questionnaires
Nelson (1999)	ESL grammar class in US	26 Ss, 1 instructor	observations, worksheets, interviews	rough (some symbols given)	queer-informed inquiry of sexual identity discussion	No	3-minute transcript with retrospective commentary
Parks & Maguire (1999)	English hospital in Quebec	11 nurses, all French L1	audiotapes, videotapes, nursing notes and charts, interviews	rough	constructivist-semiotic analysis of nursing notes	No	fragments of nursing notes, researcher notes, interviews
Pavlenko (2001)	published language learning memoirs	15 female, 7 male writers	written texts	N/A	narrative inquiry of gendered voice	No/Yes	22 text excerpts
Seedhouse (1997)	multiple SL classrooms	NS teachers, L2 learners	audiotapes, videtapes	rough	CA of teachers' repair initiations	No	30+ fragments

Author (date)	Context	Participants	Data	Transcription System	Analytic Method	Code/Counts Provided	Data given in results section
Shehadeh (1999)	experiment	16 dyads: 8 NS-NNS, 8 NNS-NNS	audiotapes of picture dictation and opinion tasks	'detailed'	ANOVA of repair initiations by task and partner	Yes	percentages ANOVA results
Tarone & Kuehn (2000)	social services intake interview in US	2 NS workers; 2 NS, 1 NNS applicants	audiotapes written application form intuitions about interview structure interviews	rough	genre analysis of interview	No No	43 fragments outline of interview structure
Toohey (2001)	2nd grade class in Canada	2 female NNSs and NS peers	audiotapes, videotapes	rough	ethnography of disputes	Yes	6 fragments
Williams (1999)	IEP oral skills class	8 adult NNS students	audiotapes of classroom language use	rough	numerical analysis of language-related episodes (LREs)	Yes	means, standard deviations of LREs bar charts
Wong (2000a)	telephone conversations	12 NS-NNS dyads; all NNSs had Mandarin L1	audiotapes	CA	CA of delayed other initiations	No	7 fragments
Wong (2000b)	telephone conversations	12 NS-NNS dyads; all NNSs had Mandarin L1	audiotapes	CA	Use of "yeah" by NNSs	No	17 fragments

3. MEANING BEYOND THE CLAUSE: SFL PERSPECTIVES

J. R. Martin

This chapter takes note of the longstanding orientation Systemic Functional Linguistics (SFL) to discourse studies before moving to a more detailed and selective presentation of current developments in SFL with respect to discourse models, developing research methodologies, and applications to different domains. The reinterpretation of cohesion as discourse semantics (identification, negotiation, conjunction, and ideation) is reviewed with respect to metafunctions (textual, interpersonal, and ideational). This work on texture is then related to social context through the register variables tenor, field and mode alongside genre. The chapter then reviews recent SFL-inspired research that applies these models to analysis of discourse across languages, modalities of communication, and domains. Work done on school and workplace discourse has raised new questions about appropriate units of discourse structure and their relationship to register analysis. It is predicted that some of these questions may be answered by the development of improved software for discourse analyses affording greater specificity in mapping the relationships among genres.

Systemic Functional Linguistics (hereafter SFL) has a longstanding interest in discourse analysis, deriving historically from Firth's (1957) concern with meaning as function in context and Mitchell's canonical (1957) study of service encounters in the Moroccan marketplace. Halliday (1967) built a focus on discourse function into his grammar through his work on Theme/Rheme and (Given)/New structure; and his perspective on textual meaning beyond the clause (i. e., cohesion) is outlined in Halliday and Hasan (1976). In addition his model of social context (e. g., Halliday, 1978 on field, tenor, and mode) stimulated SFL register studies around the world and led to the development of genre analysis, particularly in Australia (e. g., Hasan, 1977; Martin, 1985). There are many SFL publications featuring discourse analysis, including Benson, Cummings, and Greaves, 1988; Benson and Greaves, 1985; Davies and Ravelli, 1992; Fries and Gregory, 1995; Ghadessy, 1993, 1995, 1999; Gregory and Carroll, 1978; Hasan and Fries, 1995; Sánchez-Macarro and Carter, 1998; Stainton and Devilliers, 2001; Steiner and Veltman, 1988; Ventola, 1991, 2000; special issues of *Word* (*40*, 1-2, 1989), *Language Sciences* (*14*, 4, 1992) and *Cultural Dynamics*, (*6*, 1, 1993) and many issues of *Functions of Language*.

In the next section, one reading of the theory informing this work will be outlined, based on Martin (1992) and Martin and Rose, in press. Following this, some recent developments and current trends in SFL discourse analysis will be reviewed.

Modeling Discourse

Early work on cohesion was designed to move beyond the structural resources of grammar and consider discourse relations which transcend grammatical structure. Halliday (1973) treated cohesion as involving non-structural relations beyond the sentence, within what he refers to as the textual metafunction (as opposed to ideational and interpersonal meaning). In Halliday and Hasan (1976) the inventory of cohesive resources was organized as

- reference
- ellipsis
- substitution
- conjunction
- lexical cohesion

Gutwinski (1976) develops a closely related framework, including these resources (and in addition grammatical parallelism). Reference refers to resources for identifying a participant or circumstantial element whose identity is recoverable. In English the relevant resources include demonstratives, the definite article, pronouns, comparatives, and the phoric adverbs here, there, now, and then. Ellipsis refers to resources for omitting a clause, or some part of a clause or group, in contexts where it can be assumed. In English conversation, rejoinders are often made dependent through omissions of this kind: 'Did they win?' 'Yes, they did.' Some languages, including English, have in addition a set of place holders which can be used to signal the omission—e. g., so and not for clauses, do for verbal groups and one for nominal groups. This resource of place holders is referred to as substitution. Ellipsis and substitution are sometimes treated as a single resource (e. g., Halliday, 1994). From the perspective of English, ellipsis is substitution by zero; more generally, looking across languages, it might be better to think of substitution as ellipsis (signaled) by something. Reference, ellipsis, and substitution involve small closed classes of items or gaps, and have together been referred to as grammatical cohesion (Gutwinski, 1976; Hasan, 1968).

Also included as grammatical cohesion is the typically much larger inventory of connectors which link clauses in discourse, referred to as conjunction For Halliday and Hasan (1976), this resource comprises linkers which connect sentences to each other, but excludes paratactic and hypotactic (coordinating and subordinating) linkers within sentences, which are considered structural by Halliday. Gutwinski, however, includes all connectors, whether or not they link clauses within or between sentences.

The complement of grammatical cohesion involves open system items, and so is referred to as lexical cohesion. Here the repetition of lexical items, synonymy or near synonymy (including hyponymy), and collocation are included. Collocation was Firth's term for expectancy relations between lexical items (e. g., the mutual predictability of strong and tea, but not powerful and tea).

The relationship between a cohesive item and the item it presupposed in a text is referred to as a cohesive tie. Gutwinski (1976) contrasts the different kinds of cohesive ties that predominate in writing by Hemingway and James, with Hemingway depending more on lexical cohesion than does James. Halliday and Hasan (1976) provide a detailed coding scheme for analyzing cohesive ties, which takes into account the distance between a cohesive item and the item presupposed.

Later work concentrated on the semantics of these cohesive resources and their relation to discourse structure. Martin (1992) worked on reformulating the notion of cohesive ties as discourse semantic structure, inspired by the text-oriented conception of semantics of the Hartford stratificationalists (Gleason, 1968; Gutwinski, 1976) with whom he studied in Toronto. In his stratified account, cohesion was reformulated as a set of discourse semantic systems at a more abstract level than lexicogrammar, with their own metafunctional organization. Halliday's nonstructural textual resources were thus reworked as semantic systems concerned with discourse structure, comprising

- identification
- negotiation
- conjunction
- ideation

Identification is concerned with resources for tracking participants in discourse. This system subsumes earlier work on referential cohesion in a framework which considers both the ways in which participants are introduced into a text and kept track of once introduced. In addition, the ways in which phoric items depend on preceding or succeeding co-text, on assumed understandings, or on other relevant phenomena (images, activity, sound etc.) are considered. For definitions of 'phora' terms (e. g., *anaphora, cataphora, endophora, exophora, homophora*), see Martin (1992).

Negotiation is concerned with resources for exchanging information and goods and services in dialogue. This system subsumes some of the earlier work on ellipsis and substitution in a framework which considers the ways in which interlocutors initiate and respond in adjacency pairs. Drawing on earlier work at Birmingham (Sinclair & Coulthard, 1975) and Nottingham (Berry, 1981), a framework for exchanges consisting of up to five moves was developed, alongside provision for additional tracking and challenging side-sequences (Ventola, 1987). This work is closely related to studies in conversation analysis (CA) but with a stronger grammatical orientation (such as that canvassed in Ochs, Schegloff, & Thompson, 1996). Eggins and Slade (1997) introduce ongoing SFL research in this area in relation to wider questions of discourse structure and social context; Coulthard (1992) updates the Birmingham-based work.

Conjunction is concerned with resources for connecting messages, via addition, comparison, temporality, and causality. This system subsumes earlier work on linking between clauses in a framework which considers, in addition, the ways in which connections can be realized inside a clause through verbs, prepositions, and nouns (e. g., result in, because of, reason). Drawing on Gleason (1968), a framework for analyzing internal[1] (pragmatic/rhetorical) and external (semantic/propositional) conjunctive relations was proposed, including the possibility of connections realized simply by the contiguity of messages (i. e., links unmarked by an explicit connector).

Ideation is concerned with the semantics of lexical relations deployed to construe institutional activity. I use 'construe' to emphasize the role texts play in making meaning—that is, knowledge—and thus constructing social context—that is, reality; cf. Halliday and Matthiesen, 1999. This system subsumes earlier work on lexical cohesion in a framework which considers how activity sequences and taxonomic relations (of classification and composition) organize the field of discourse (Benson & Greaves, 1992). Drawing on Hasan (1985), a model for a more detailed account of lexical relations including repetition, synonymy, hyponymy, and meronymy was proposed; in addition, collocation was factored out into various kinds of 'nuclear' relations. involving elaboration, extension, and enhancement (as developed by Halliday, 1994. for the clause complex).

The result of these reformulations is a semantic stratum of text-oriented resources dedicated to the analysis of cohesive relations as discourse structure. Once stratified with respect to lexicogrammar, these resources can be aligned with metafunctions in the following proportions:

- identification   textual meaning
- negotiation   interpersonal meaning
- conjunction   logical[2] meaning
- ideation   experiential meaning

This brings us the question of modeling social context in a functional theory which looks at what cohesion is realizing alongside the ways in which it is realized. In SFL, social context is modeled through register and genre theory. Following Halliday (1978) a natural relation is posited between the organization of language and the organization of social context, built up around the notion of kinds of meaning (Mattheissen, 1993). Interpersonal meaning is related to the enactment of social relations (social reality), or tenor; ideational meaning is related to the construction of institutional activity('naturalized reality'), or field; and textual meaning is related to information flow across media (semiotic reality), or mode. A summary of these relationships between types of meaning and register variables is outlined in Table 1.

Table 1: Types of meaning in relation to social context

	'Reality construal'	Contextual variable
Interpersonal	social reality	tenor
Ideation	(logical, experiential)	'natural' reality field
Textual	semiotic reality	mode

Following Martin (1992), field is concerned with systems of activity, including descriptions of the participants, process and circumstances these activities involve. For illustrative work, see Halliday and Martin (1993) and Martin and Veel (1998). Tenor is concerned with social relations as these are enacted through the dimensions of power and solidarity. For foundational work on tenor see Poynton (1985). Mode is concerned with semiotic distance, as this is affected by the various channels of communication through which we undertake activity (field) and simultaneously enact social relations (tenor). For exemplary work on differences between speech and writing, see Halliday (1985).

In Martin (1992), an additional level of context, above and beyond tenor, field, and mode, referred to as genre, has been deployed. This level is concerned with systems of social processes, where the principles for relating social processes to each other have to do with texture, that is, the ways in which field, mode and tenor variables are phased together in a text. In Australian educational linguistics, genres have been defined as staged, goal-oriented social processes (Martin, 1999), a definition which flags the way in which most genres take more than a single phase to unfold, the sense of frustration or incompletion that is felt when phases don't unfold as expected or planned, and the fact that genres are addressed (i. e. formulated with readers and listeners in mind), whether or not the intended audience is immediately present to respond. In these terms, as a level of context, genre represents the system of staged goal-oriented social processes through which social subjects in a given culture live their lives. An overview of this stratified model of context is presented in Figure 1; this image includes Lemke's (1995) notion of metaredundancy, whereby more abstract levels are interpreted as patterns of less abstract ones. Thus register is a pattern of linguistic choices, and genre a pattern of register choices (i. e., a pattern of a pattern of texture). For further discussion, see Christie and Martin (1997), Eggins (1994), Eggins and Martin (1997), Martin (1992, 2001a), and Ventola (1987).

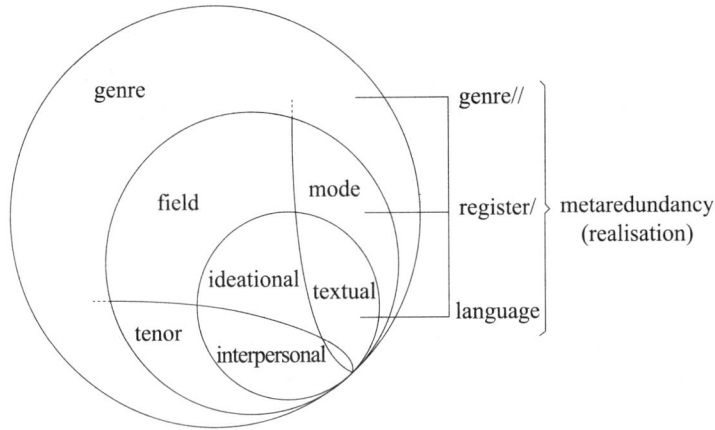

Figure 1: Metafunctions in relation to register and genre.

Recent Developments

Throughout the 1990s, SFL discourse analysis developed along several parameters, including relevant aspects of phonology and grammar. Higher levels of phonological analysis, pushing well beyond the tone group as far as rhythm is concerned, are pursued in van Leeuwen (1991), Martinec (2000a), and Watt (2001). In grammar, research expanded across languages and language families, including relevant work on textual meaning. Caffarel, Martin, and Matthiessen (in press) includes chapters on French, German, Telegu, Chinese, Japanese, Vietnamese, Tagalog, and Pitjantjatjara, each with an emphasis on showing how the various grammars operate in discourse. The papers in Steiner and Yallop (2000) explore the implications of functional descriptions of this kind for translation and multilingual text production.

For English, one significant trend has been the development of computer assisted analysis programs which facilitate the coding of large quantities of text for SFL grammar and discourse features. These programs include O'Halloran and

Judd (2001); Matthiessen and Wu's SysAm (http: //minerva. ling. mq. edu. au/ Resources/AnalysisTools/Tools. htm); O'Donnell's Systemic Coder (O'Donnell, 1995; http: //www. wagsoft. com/Coder/index. html); and Webster's Functional Grammar Processor (e. g. Webster, 1995; Webster & Kit, 1995). These tools are making it possible to undertake large scale semantic analyses with a view to quantitative interpretation and have given new impetus to longstanding SFL interests in corpus based research (Halliday, 1991, 1992, 1993; Halliday & James, 1993; Matthiessen, 1999, in press; Nesbitt & Plum, 1988; Plum & Cowling, 1987). This work on automated discourse analysis is complemented by work on synthesis, in, for example, the text generation research introduced in Bateman (2001), Bateman, Matthiessen, and Licheng (1999), Bateman and Rondhuis (1997), Matthiessen and Bateman (1991), and Teich (1999).

At the level of discourse semantics, some of the most important developments have to do with interpersonal meaning. Eggins and Slade (1997) present a rich model of speech function, especially designed for analyzing initiating moves and responses in casual conversation. Recently this has been insightfully applied to human/bonobo interaction (Benson, Fries, Gredves, Iwamoto, Savage-Rumbaugh, & Taglialatela, in press). Hasan and her colleagues (Hasan, 1996) have developed a finely tuned set of semantic networks designed for the study of adult-child interaction in home and school. These have been instrumental in exploring Bernstein's theories of language and socialization (Bernstein, 1996), especially in relation to gender and social class, and represent the most important linguistically informed body of research into semantic styles and their implications for education (see especially Cloran, 1989, 1999a, b; Hasan, 1990, 1991, 1992, 2001; Hasan & Cloran, 1990; Williams, 1995, 1996, 1999, 2001). Hasan (1995a) and Halliday (1995) insightfully review the implications of close textual analysis for Bernstein's work, and deal incisively with populist misunderstandings; Cloran (2000) provides an accessible introduction to semantic networks and their deployment in the study of sociosemantic variation.

Another major development in interpersonal discourse semantics has been the emergence of appraisal theory (see Martin, 2000a, and the website designed by Peter White at http: //www. grammatics. com/appraisal/index. html). Appraisal complements negotiation from the perspective of resources for evaluation, including systems of attitude, engagement, and graduation. Attitude focuses on resources for construing affect, judgment, and appreciation (roughly the lexically realized realms of emotion, ethics, and aesthetics); engagement is concerned with the sourcing of attitude and acknowledgment of alternative voices (heteroglossia); and graduation covers force (intensification of inherently gradable meanings) and focus('fuzzification' of inherently nongradable categories). Work on this dimension of intersubjective meaning has refocused attention on prosodic realization (across ideational boundaries) in various registers, such as history (Coffin, 1997); narrative and literary criticism (Rothery & Stenglin, 1997, 2000); news stories (White, 1997); casual conversation, including humor and gossip and their implications for generation, ethnicity, and gender (Eggins & Slade, 1997); and popular science (Fuller, 1998).

Ideational semantics is elaborated in Halliday and Matthiessen (1999), who are particularly concerned with establishing a semiotic perspective on what is generally viewed as cognition. Their project includes work on what they call sequences which is relevant to conjunction. Van Leeuwen (1996) develops a complementary perspective on agency which has been influential in critical discourse analysis. Matthiessen (in press) explores Rhetorical Structure Theory (RST) from the perspective of this research, continuing a dialogue between SFL conjunction analysis and RST (Mann, Matthiesen, & Thompson, 1992), which began in the 1980s (Martin, 1992). For relevant work on causation in Dutch, see Degand (2001). From the perspective of discourse analysis, what has been slow to emerge is an understanding of different kinds of expectancy relations linking clauses across registers. Temporal sequencing and causal reasoning tend to be foregrounded over tropes of other kinds, such as description, classification, composition, comparison, critique, review, stirring, coaxing, serving, and so on; research is urgently required in these areas.

As far as participant identification is concerned, the main developments have come from language typology through consideration of the ways in which nominal group resources interact with Theme, and in some languages with conjunction (the so-called subject-switching systems found in Papua and Australia). These issues are explored in Caffarel et al. (in press) in relation to Martin (1983). Textual meaning has also been investigated in relation to information flow in general across languages (Downing & Lavid, 1998; Hasan & Fries, 1995; Lavid, 1997) and in relation to layers of Theme and New in English discourse (Ghadessy,

1995; Halliday & Martin, 1993). Martin (1992, 1993, 1995a) explores the ways in which texts use higher level Themes to predict information flow and higher level News to retrospectively distill the point of preceding discourse, thus following up suggestions by Pike and Halliday about 'hierarchy of periodicity' as a form of textual organization (Fries, 1981). Halliday's work on grammatical metaphor as a resource for packaging meaning has been instrumental in this area of inquiry (Halliday, 1998; Halliday & Matthiessen, 1999; Simon-Vandenbergen, Taverniers, & Ravelli, in press).

This raises the question of higher-level units in discourse, which has been explored in various ways. One useful tool has been Hasan's cohesive harmony (Cloran, 1999b; Hasan 1984, 1985; Parsons, 1991). In cohesive harmony analysis, we are asking how ideation and identification interact as far as experiential grammar is concerned, based on the degree to which cohesively related items enter into the same kind of experiential relationship with other cohesively related items. Breaks in the pattern of interaction are associated with discourse boundaries of one kind or another and so relevant to the recognition of higher-level units. This style of analysis is not unrelated to the work of Gregory and his colleagues on phasal analysis (Gregory, 1995, 2001; Stainton & Devilliers, 2001), which, however, takes into account a full metafunctional spectrum of meaning (ideational, interpersonal, and textual) in order to determine phases and transitions in discourse.

Cloran's work on rhetorical units (RU), on the other hand, is more selective in its parameters, having been designed to focus on the register variable mode (Cloran, 1994, 1995, 1999a, b, 2000). She looks in particular at the context dependency of the participant functioning as subject in a clause and at the tense of that clause's verb (the 'deixis' of the clause, in other words) and on this basis sets up classes of RU ranging from those positioning language as ancillary to the task at hand to those in which language constitutes the social activity. The inter-dependencies among RUs are explored through her concept of embedding, and used to investigate parent-child interaction in the home as part of Hasan's language and socialization project outlined above.

The relation of all three of these perspectives on units of discourse to work on genre structure is an important issue which has not been resolved. Certainly the conversational data that Gregory and his colleagues and Cloran are investigating is not the kind that has generally attracted genre analysts (see, however, Eggins &

Slade, 1997), presumably because of the difficulty in recognizing clear stages of the kind found in the analysis of narrative, exposition, service encounters, appointment making, or classroom discourse. As a result, the issue of generalizing discourse units across registers remains a pressing one in SFL-informed discourse analysis (cf. Taboada, 2000, in press).

As far as register analysis is concerned, there has been significant work in tenor, mode, and field. The main tenor initiative draws on appraisal analysis to explore solidarity, as exemplified in Eggins and Slade (1997) and White (2000) who analyze the face work done through casual conversations involving family members, friends, and coworkers. The outstanding mode initiative is multi-modal discourse analysis, inspired by the work of O'Toole (1994) and Kress and van Leeuwen (1996) on images (see also van Leeuwen & Jewitt, 2001). Martinec (1998, 2000b, c, 2001) extends this work to the modality of action, and van Leewuen (1999) to the modality of music and sound. These tools have encouraged SFL discourse analysts to consider the ways in which language negotiates meaning in cooperation with other semiotic systems (Baldry, 1999; Eggins & Iedema, 1997; Iedema, 2001; Kress & van Leeuwen, 2001; O'Halloran, 1999a) and to focus on some of the new kinds of discourse evolving in the print and electronic media (Lemke, 1998; Veel, 1998).

Research into field has explored several kinds of school and workplace discourse. Work on institutionalized learning includes mathematics (O'Halloran, 1999a, b, 2000; Veel, 1999), science (Halliday & Martin, 1993; Kress, Jewitt, Ogborn, & Tsatsarelis, 2001; Martin & Veel, 1998; Unsworth, 1998), geography (Martin, 2001b; van Leeuwen & Humphrey, 1996; Wignell, Martin, & Eggins, 1990), history (Coffin, 1997; Martin, 200lc; Martin & Wodak, in press; Veel & Coffin, 1996) English (Martin, 1996a; Rothery & Stenglin, 1997, 2000), and English for academic purposes (Lewin, Fine, & Young, 2001; Ravelli & Ellis, in press; Ventola, 1998; 1999, Ventola & Mauranen, 1995). Work on workplace communication includes administration (Iedema, 1997a, 1998, 2000; Iedema & Degeling, 2001; Iedema & Scheeres, in press), science and technology (Rose, 1997, 1998; White, 1998), speech disorders (Armstrong, 1987, 1992; Fine, 1994, 1995; Fine, Bartolucci, & Szatmari, 1989; Oram, Fine, Okamoto, & Tannock, 1999; Ovadia & Fine, 1995), medicine (Jordens, Little, Paul, & Sayers, 2001), law (Gibbons, in press; Iedema, 1993, 1995), and museums and galleries (Ferguson,

MacLulich, & Ravelli, 1995; Ravelli, 1996, 1998).

The range of this research has had a number of implications for genre analysis, including analysis of generic structures and intertextual relations with one another. Work on administrative directives (Iedema, 1997a; Martin, 1998) and print media news stories (Iedema, 1997b; White, 1997), for example, revealed genres that are best characterized as having a nucleus/satellite structure (as opposed to a more traditional part/whole beginning, middle, and end organization), a kind of orbital structure with an obligatory core stage and optional elaborating stages that are not strictly sequenced. Martin (1995b, 1996b) follows up the implications of this for experiential structures in general, analogizing from genre structure back to grammar. Across fields, the problem of longer texts arose and attempts were made to model these as series of smaller genres drawing on Halliday's 1994 categories of expansion (elaboration, extension, and enhancement). This serial perspective on macro-genres as genre complexes is introduced in Martin 2001b (see also Iedema, 2000; Jordens et al., 2001) and further developed in Christie (1999, in press) for classroom discourse.

Another important dimension of genre analysis across fields has to do with mapping relationships among genres from both typological and topological perspectives. Using paradigms and system networks to model valeur, narrative and factual genres are explored typologically in Martin (2001a) and Martin and Plum (1997); this kind of analysis depends on categorical distinctions. The notion of genres as more gradient semantic regions is explored topologically in Martin (2001b, c), Rose (1997, 1998), and Veel (1997) for a range of factual genres from science, geography, and history. The relation of work on macro-genres and genre topology to the question of 'genre mixing' is discussed in Martin (2001b). For SFL work on genre in relation to other approaches, see Hyon (1996) and Hyland (this volume).

Connections

Obviously in a survey of this kind I have had to be selective. One of the most obvious extensions would be to the work of present and past staff and students at the University of Birmingham. Fortunately, this work is ably surveyed in Coulthard (1992, 1994) and Caldas-Coulthard and Coulthard (1996). Of these colleagues, special mention should be made of Michael Hoey, who has developed the Hatfield Polytechnic strain of discourse analysis inspired by Eugene Winter (Hoey 1991, 2001; Scott & Thompson, 2000). In America, the clearest links are with west coast functionalism, especially Fox (1987), because she brings several discourse semantic regions (CA, RST, and participant identification) to bear on the 'grammar' of text development. Some further connections are explored in Martin and Rose (in press).

The strength of SFL work on discourse probably lies in its relatively well developed descriptions of genre and functional grammar, and the adaptability of SFL modeling across modalities (to image, music, and action, for example). This grounds research firmly in the materiality of both global and local perspectives on meaning. The challenge for future work lies in filling in the middle ground between text and clause through intensive corpus-based work on discourse semantics and register. The success of this enterprise depends on the development of relevant software to both enhance and supplant manual analysis. I expect this technology to affect our conception of language and attendant semiotic systems as radically as the invention of writing and the tape recorder have shaped our discipline in the past, since for the first time we'll be able to manage large-scale sociosemantic analyses of data.

Notes

1. The terms *internal* and *external* are from Halliday and Hasan (1976); van Dijk (1977) opposes pragmatic to semantic relations. The contrast is between *He came, because I just saw him* (internal = 'why I'm saying he came') and *He came because I saw him and told him to* (external = 'why he came').

2. In SFL the ideational metafunction includes two subcomponents, the experiential and the logical; experiential meaning is associated with orbital structure (mononuclear), and logical meaning with serial structure (multinuclear; Martin 1996b).

ANNOTATED BIBLIOGRAPHY

Martin (1992) outlines the reading of SFL discourse analysis assumed here. Martin and Rose (in press) provide an accessible introduction to this work, focussing on writing and incorporating recent developments; Eggins and Slade

(1997) complement this with a focus on spoken discourse. Halliday and Martin (1993), Christie and Martin (1997), and Martin and Veel (1998) illustrate this kind of analysis across a range of fields. Unsworth (2000) is designed for prospective researchers who want to take up these tools. Hasan (1996) surveys her pioneering work on cohesion, genre, semantic networks, and the relation of language to social context.

OTHER REFERENCES

Armstrong, E. (1987). Cohesive harmony in aphasic discourse and its significance in listener perception of coherence. In R. H. Brookshire (Ed.), *Clinical aphasiology: Conference proceedings*, Vol. 17 (pp. 210–215). Minneapolis, MN: BRK Publishers.

Armstrong, E. (1992). Clause complex relations in aphasic discourse: A longitudinal study. *Journal of Neurolinguistics, 7*(4), 261–275.

Baldry, A. (Ed.) (1999). *Multimodality and multimediality in the distance learning age.* Campo Basso: Lampo.

Bateman, J. A. (2001). Between the leaves of rhetorical structure: Static and dynamic aspects of discourse organization. *Verbatum. 23*(1), 31–58.

Bateman, J. A., Matthiessen, C. M., & Licheng, Z. (1999). Multilingual language generation for multilingual software: A functional linguistic approach. *Applied Artificial Intelligence, 13*(6), 607–639.

Bateman, J. A., & Rondhuis, K. (1997). Coherence relations: Towards general specification. *Discourse Processes, 24*, 3–49.

Benson, J. D., Fries, P. Greaves, W. S. Iwamoto, K., Savage–Rumbaugh, S., & Taglialatela, J. (in press). Confrontation and support in bonobo-human discourse. *Functions of Language, 9*, 2.

Benson, J. D., & Greaves, W. S. (Eds.). (1985). *Systemic perspectives on discourse: Selected theoretical papers from the 9th International Systemic Workshop.* Norwood, NJ: Ablex.

Benson, J. D., & Greaves, W. S. (1992). Collocation and field of discourse. In W. A. Mann & S. A. Thompson (Eds.), Discourse description: *Diverse analyses of a fund raising text* (pp. 397–409). Amsterdam: John Benjamins.

Benson, J. D., Cummings, M. J., & Greaves, W. S. (Eds.). (1988). *Linguistics in a systemic perspective.* Amsterdam: John Benjamins.

Bernstein, B. (1996). *Pedagogy, symbolic control and identity: Theory, research, critique.* London: Taylor & Francis.

Berry, M. (1981). Systemic linguistics and discourse analysis: A multi-layered approach to exchange structure. In M. Coulthard & M. Montgomery (Eds.), *Studies in discourse analysis* (pp. 120–145). London: Routledge & Kegan Paul.

Caffarel, A., Martin, J. R., & Matthiessen, C. M. (Eds.). (in press). *Language typology: A functional perspective*. Amsterdam: John Benjamins.

Caldas-Coulthard, C., & Coulthard, M. (Eds.). (1996). *Text and practices: Readings in critical discourse analysis*. London: Routledge.

Christie, F. (Ed.). (1999). *Pedagogy and the shaping of consciousness: Linguistic and social processes*. London: Cassell.

Christie, F. (in press). *Classroom discourse analysis*. London: Continuum.

Christie, F., & Martin, J. R. (Eds.) (1997). *Genre and institutions: Social processes in the workplace and school*. London: Pinter.

Cloran, C. (1989). Learning through language: The social construction of gender. In R. Hasan & J. R. Martin (Eds.). *Language development: Learning language, learning culture* (pp. 361–403). Norwood, NJ: Ablex.

Cloran, C. (1994). Rhetorical units and decontextualisation: An enquiry into some relations of context, meaning and grammar. *Monographs in Systemic Linguistics, 6*. Nottingham: School of English Studies, Nottingham University.

Cloran, C. (1995). Defining and relating text segments: Subject and theme in discourse. In R. Hasan & P. Fries (Eds.), *On subject and theme: A discourse functional perspective* (pp. 361–403). Amsterdam: Benjamins.

Cloran, C. (1999a). Contexts for learning. In F. Christie (Ed.), *Pedagogy and the shaping of consciousness* (pp. 31–65). London: Cassell.

Cloran, C. (1999b). Context, material situation and text. In M. Ghadessy (Ed.), *Text and context in functional linguistics* (pp. 177–217). Amsterdam: Benjamins.

Cloran, C. (2000). Socio-semantic variation: Different wordings. different meanings. In L. Unsworth (Ed.), *Researching language in schools and communities* (pp. 152–183). London: Cassell.

Coffin, C. (1997) Constructing and giving value to the past: An investigation into secondary school history. In F. Christie & J. R. Martin (Eds.), *Genre and institutions: Social processes in the workplace and school* (pp. 196–230). London: Pinter.

Coulthard, M. (Ed.). (1992). *Advances in spoken discourse analysis*. London: Routledge.

Coulthard, M. (Ed.). (1994). *Advances in written text analysis*. London: Routledge.

Davies, M., & Ravelli, L. J. (Eds.). (1992). *Advances in systemic linguistics: Recent theory and practice*. London: Pinter.

Degand, L. (2001). Form and function of causation: A theoretical and empirical investigation of causal constructions in Dutch. [*Studies op het gebied van de Nederlandse taalkunde, 5.*] Peeters: Leuven.

Downing, A., & Lavid, J. (1998). Information progression strategies in administrative forms: A cross-linguistic study. In A. Sánchez-Macarro & R. Carter (Eds.), *Linguistic choice across genres* (pp. 99–115). Amsterdam: John Benjamins.

Eggins, S. (1994). *An introduction to systemic functional linguistics*. London: Pinter.

Eggins, S., & Iedema, R. (1997). "Difference" without diversity: The semantics of women's magazines. In R. Wodak (Ed.), *Gender and discourse* (pp. 165–196). Thousand Oaks, CA: Sage.

Eggins, S., & Martin, J. R. (1997). Genres and registers of discourse. In T. A. van Dijk (Ed.), *Discourse as structure and process*, Vol. 1 (pp. 230–256). London: Sage.

Eggins, S., & Slade, D. (1997). *Analysing casual conversation*. London: Cassell.

Ferguson, L., MacLulich, C., & Ravelli, L. J. (1995). *Meanings and messages: Language guidelines for museum exhibitions*. Sydney: Australian Museum.

Fine, J. (1994). *How language works: Cohesion in normal and nonstandard communication*. Norwood, NJ: Ablex.

Fine, J. (1995). Towards understanding and studying cohesion in schizophrenic speech. *Applied Psycholinguistics, 16*, 25–41.

Fine, J., Bartolucci, G., & Szatmari, P. (1989). Textual systems: Their use in creation and miscalculation of social reality. *Word, 40* (1–2), 65–80.

Firth, J. R. (1957). A synopsis of linguistic theory, 1930–1955. *Studies in Linguistic Analysis* [Special volume of the Philological Society] (pp. 1–31). London: Blackwell.

Fox, B. A. (1987). *Discourse structure and anaphora: Written and conversational English*. Cambridge: Cambridge University Press.

Fries, P. H. (1981). On the status of theme in English: Arguments from discourse. *Forum Linguisticum, 6*(1), 1–38.

Fries, P., & Gregory, M. (Eds.). (1995). *Discourse in society: Systemic functional perspectives*. Norwood, NJ: Ablex.

Fuller, G. (1998). Cultivating science: Negotiating discourse in the popular texts of Stephen Jay Gould. In J. R. Martin & R. Veel (Eds.), *Reading science* (pp. 35–62). London: Routledge.

Ghadessy, M. (Ed.). (1993). *Register analysis: Theory and practice*. London: Pinter.

Ghadessy, M. (Ed.). (1995). *Thematic development in English texts*. London: Pinter.

Ghadessy, M. (Ed.). (1999). *Text and context in functional linguistics*. Amsterdam: John Benjamins.

Gibbons, J. P. (in press). Forensic linguistics. Oxford: Blackwell.

Gleason, H. A., Jr. (1968). *Contrastive analysis in discourse structure. Monograph Series on Languages and Linguistics, 21*. Washington, DC: Georgetown University (Georgetown University Institute of Languages and Linguistics).

Gregory, M. (1995). *Before and towards communication linguistics: Essays by Michael Gregory and Associates*. (Jin Soon Cha, Ed.). Seoul: Sookmyng Women's University.

Gregory, M. (2001). Phasal analysis within communication linguistics: Two contrastive discourses. In P. Fries, M. Cummings, D. Lockwood, & W. Sprueill (Eds.), *Relations and functions within and around language* (pp. 316–345). London: Continuum.

Gregory, M., & Carroll, S. (1978). *Language and situation: Language varieties and their social contexts*. London: Routledge & Kegan Paul.

Gutwinski, W. (1 976). *Cohesion in literary texts: A study of some grammatical and lexical features of English discourse*. The Hague: Mouton.

Halliday, M. A. K. (1967). Notes in transitivity and theme in English: Part 1. *Journal of Linguistics, 3*(1), 37–81.

Halliday, M. A. K. (1973). *Explorations in the functions of language*. London: Edward Arnold.

Halliday, M. A. K. (1978). *Language as a social semiotic: The social interpretation of language and meaning*. London: Edward Arnold.

Halliday, M. A. K. (1985). *Spoken and written language*. Geelong, Victoria: Deakin University Press.

Halliday, M. A. K. (1991). Towards probabilistic interpretations. In E. Ventola (Ed.), *Functional and systemic linguistics* (pp. 39–61). Berlin: Mouton deGruyter.

Halliday, M. A. K. (1992). Language as system and language as instance: The corpus as a theoretical construct. In J. Svartvik (Ed.), *Directions in corpus linguistics: Proceedings of Nobel Symposium 82*, Stockholm, 4–8 August, 1991, (pp. 61–77). Berlin: De Gruyter.

Halliday, M. A. K. (1993). Quantitative studies and probabilities in grammar. In M. Hoey (Ed.), *Data, description, discourse: Papers on English language in honour of John McH. Sinclair* [on his sixtieth birthday] (pp. 1–25). London: Harper Collins.

Halliday, M. A. K. (1994). An introduction to functional grammar. London: Edward Arnold.

Halliday, M. A. K. (1995). Language and the theory of codes. In A. Sadovnik (Ed.), *Knowledge and pedagogy: The sociology of Basil Bernstein* (pp. 127–144). Norwood, NJ: Ablex.

Halliday, M. A. K. (1998). Things and relations: Regrammaticising experience as technical knowledge. In J. R. Martin & R. Veel (Eds.), *Reading science* (pp. 185–235). London: Routledge.

Halliday M. A. K., & Hasan, R. (1976) *Cohesion in English*. London: Longman.

Halliday, M. A. K., & Hasan, R. (1985) *Language, context, and text: Aspects of language in a social-semiotic perspective*. Geelong, Victoria: Deakin University Press.

Halliday, M. A. K., & James, Z. (1993). A quantitative study of polarity and primary tense in the English finite clause. In J. M. Sinclair, M. Hoey, & G. Fox (Eds.). *Techniques of description: Spoken and written discourse* (pp. 32–66). London: Routledge.

Halliday, M. A. K., & Martin, J. R. (1993). *Writing science: Literacy and discursive power*. London: Falmer.

Halliday, M. A. K., & Matthiessen, C. M. (1999). *Construing experience through language: A language-based approach to cognition*. London: Cassell.

Hasan, R. (1968). Grammatical cohesion in spoken and written English, Part I. Papers of the Programme in Linguistics and English Teaching, Series I, No. 7. London: Department of General Linguistics, University College.

Hasan, R. (1977). Text in the systemic-functional model. In W. Dressler (Ed.), *Current trends in textlinguistics* (pp. 228–246). Berlin: Walter de Gruyter.

Hasan, R. (1984). Coherence and cohesive harmony. In J. Flood (Ed.), *Understanding reading comprehension: Cognition, language and the structure of prose* (pp. 181–219). Newark, DE: International Reading Association.

Hasan, R. (1985). The texture of a text. In M. A. K. Halliday & R. Hasan (Eds.), *Language, context and text* (pp. 70–96). Geelong, Victoria: Deakin University Press.

Hasan, R. (1990). Semantic variation and sociolinguistics. *Australian Journal of Linguistics* 9(2), 221–276.

Hasan, R. (1991). Questions as a mode of learning in everyday talk. In M. McCausland (Ed.), *Language education: Interaction and development* (pp. 70–119). Launceston: University of Tasmania.

Hasan, R. (1992). Meaning in sociolinguistic theory. In K. Bolton & H. Kwok (Eds.), *Sociolinguistics today: International perspectives* (pp. 80–119). London: Routledge.

Hasan, R. (1995a). On social conditions for semiotic mediation: The genesis of mind in society. In A. Sadovnik (Ed.), *Knowledge and pedagogy* (pp. 171–196). Norwood, NJ: Ablex.

Hasan, R. (1995b). The conception of context in text. In P. Fries & M. Gregory (Eds.), *Discourse in society* (pp. 183–283). Norwood, NJ: Ablex.

Hasan, R. (1996). *Ways of saying, ways of meaning: Selected papers of Ruqaiya Hasan* (Edited by C. Cloran, D. Butt, & G. Williams). London: Cassell.

Hasan, R. (1999). Speaking with reference to context. In M. Ghadessy (Ed.), *Text and context in functional linguistics* (pp. 219–328). Amsterdam: John Benjamins.

Hasan, R. (2001). The ontogenesis of decontextualised language: Some achievements of classification and framing. In A. Morais, I. Neves, B. Davies, & H. Daniels (Eds.), *Towards a sociology of pedagogy: The contribution of Basil Bernstein to research* (pp. 47–79). New York: Peter Lang.

Hasan, R., & Cloran, C. (1990). A sociolinguistic interpretation of everyday talk between mothers and children. In M. A. K. Halliday, J. Gibbons, & H. Nicholas (Eds.), *Learning, keeping and using language*, Vol. 1 (pp. 67–99). Amsterdam: John Benjamins.

Hasan, R., & Fries, P. (Eds.). (1995). *On subject and theme: A discourse functional perspective*. Amsterdam: John Benjamins.

Hoey, M. J. (1991). Another perspective on coherence and cohesive harmony. In E. Ventola (Ed.), *Functional and systemic linguistics* (pp. 385–414). Berlin: Mouton de Gruyter.

Hoey, M. J. (2001). *Textual interaction: An introduction to written discourse analysis*. London:

Routledge.

Hyland, K. (this volume). Genre: Language, context, and literacy.

Hyon, S. (1996). Genre in three traditions: Implications for ESL. *TESOL Quarterly, 30*, 693–722.

Iedema, R. (1993). Legal English: Discipline specific literacy and genre theory. *Australian Review of Applied Linguistics, 16*(2), 86–122.

Iedema, R. (1995). Legal ideology: The role of language in common law appellate judgments. *The International Journal for the Semiotics of Law, 7*(22), 21–36.

Iedema, R. (1997a). The language of administration: Organizing human activity in formal institutions. In F. Christie & J. R. Martin (Eds.), *Genre and institutions* (pp. 73–100). London: Pinter.

Iedema, R. (1997b). The history of the accident news story. *Australian Review of Applied Linguistics, 20*(2), 95–119.

Iedema, R. (1998). Hidden meanings and institutional responsibility. *Discourse and society, 9*, 481–500.

Iedema, R. (2000). Bureaucratic planning and resemiotisation. In E. Ventola (Ed.), *Discourse and community* (pp. 47–70). Tubingen: Gunter Narr.

Iedema, R. (2001). Analysing film and television. In T. van Leeuwen & C. Jewitt (Eds.), *Handbook of visual analysis* (pp. 183–204). London: Sage.

Iedema, R., & Degeling, P. (2001). From difference to divergence: The logogenesis of interactive tension. *Functions of Language, 8*(1), 33–56.

Iedema, R., & Scheeres, H. (in press). From doing to talking work: Renegotiating knowing, doing and identity. In C. Candlin & S. Sarangi (Eds.), *Applied Linguistics* [special issue for 2002].

Jordens, C. F., Little, M., Paul, K., & Sayers, E. J. (2001). Life disruption and generic complexity: A social linguistic analysis of narratives of cancer illness. *Social Science and Medicine, 53*, 1227–1236.

Kress, G., & van Leeuwen, T. (1996). *Reading images: The grammar of visual design*. London: Routledge.

Kress, G., & van Leeuwen, T. (2001). *Multimodal discourse—The modes and media of contemporary communication*. London: Arnold.

Kress, G., Jewitt, C., Ogborn, J., & Tsatsarelis, C. (2001). *Multimodal teaching and learning: The rhetorics of the classroom*. London: Continuum.

Lavid, J. (1997). Specifying the discourse semantics of grammatical theme for multilingual text generation: Preliminary findings. *Revista de la Sociedad Espanola para el Procesamiento del Lenguaje Natural, 21* , 57–79.

Lemke, J. (1995). *Textual politics: Discourse and social dynamics*. London: Taylor & Francis.

Lemke, J. (1998). Multiplying meaning: Visual and verbal semiotics in scientific text. In J. R. Martin & R. Veel (Eds.), *Reading science* (pp. 87–113). London: Routledge.

Lewin, B., Fine, J., & Young, 1. (2001). *Expository discourse: A genre based approach to social science texts*. London: Continuum.

Mann, W. C., Matthiessen, C. M., & Thompson, S. A. (1992). Rhetorical structure theory and text analysis. In W. C. Mann & S. A. Thompson (Eds.), *Discourse description: Diverse linguistic analyses of a fund-raising text* (pp. 39–78). Amsterdam: Benjamins.

Mann, W. C., & Thompson, S. A. (Eds.). (1992). *Discourse description: Diverse linguistic analyses of a fund-raising text*. Amsterdam: Benjamins.

Martin, J. R. (1983). Participant identification in English, Tagalog and Kâte. *Australian Journal of Linguistics*, *3*(1), 45–74.

Martin, J. R. (1985). *Factual writing: Exploring and challenging social reality*. Geelong, Victoria: Deakin University Press.

Martin, J. R. (1992). *English text: System and structure*. Amsterdam: Benjamins.

Martin, J. R. (1993). *Life as a noun*. In M. A. K. Halliday & J. R. Martin (Eds.), *Writing science* (pp. 221–267). London: Falmer.

Martin, J. R. (1995a). More than what the message is about: English theme. In M, Ghadessy (Ed.), *Thematic development in English texts* (pp. 223–258). London: Pinter.

Martin, J. R. (1995b). Text and clause: Fractal resonance. *Text*, *15*(1), 5–42.

Martin, J. R. (1996a). Evaluating disruption: Symbolising theme in junior secondary narrative. In R. Hasan & G. Williams (Eds.), *Literacy in society* (pp. 124–171). London: Longman.

Martin, J. R. (1996b). Types of structure: Deconstructing notions of constituency in clause and text. In E. H. Hovy & D. R. Scott (Eds.), *Computationat and conversational discourse: Burning issues—an interdisciplinary account* (pp. 39–66). Heidelberg: Springer.

Martin, J. R. (1998). Practice into theory: Catalyzing change. In S. Hunston (Ed.), *Language at work* (pp. 151–167). Clevedon: Multilingual Matters.

Martin, J. R. (1999). Modelling context: A crooked path of progress in contextual linguistics (Sydney SFL). In M. Ghadessy (Ed.), *Text and context in functional linguistics* (pp. 25–61). Amsterdam: Benjamins.

Martin, J. R. (2000a). Beyond exchange: Appraisal systems in English. In S. Hunston & G. Thompson (Eds.), *Evaluation in text: Authorial stance and the construction of discourse* (pp. 142–175). Oxford: Oxford University Press.

Martin, J. R. (2000b). Close reading: Functional linguistics as a tool for critical analysis. In L. Unsworth (Ed.), *Researching language in schools and communities* (pp. 275–303). London: Longman.

Martin, J. R. (2000c). Design and practice: Enacting functional linguistics in Australia. *Annual Review of Applied Linguistics*, *20*, 116–126.

Martin, J. R. (2001a). A context for genre: modelling social processes in functional linguistics. In R. Stainton & J. Devilliers (Eds.), *Communication in linguistics* (pp. 1–41). Toronto: GREF (Collection Theoria).

Martin, J. R. (2001b). From little things big things grow: Ecogenesis in school geography. In R. Coe, L. Lingard, & T. Teslenko (Eds.), *The rhetoric and ideology of genre: Strategies for stability and change* (pp. 243–271). Cresskill, NJ: Hampton Press.

Martin, J. R. (2001c). Writing history: Construing time and value in discourses of the past. In C. Colombi & M. Schleppergrell (Eds.), *Developing advanced literacy in first and second languages* (pp. 87–118). Mahwah, NJ: Erlbaum.

Martin, J. R. (2001d). Giving the game away: Explicitness, diversity and genre-based literacy in Australia. In R. Wodak et al. (Eds.), *Functional Ill/literacy* (pp. 155–174). Vienna: Verlag der Osterreichischen Akadamie der Wissenschaften.

Martin, J. R., & Plum, G. (1997). Construing experience: Some story genres. *Journal of Narrative and Life History. 7*(1–4), 299–308.

Martin, J. R., & Rose, D. (in press). *Working with discourse: Meaning beyond the clause*. London: Continuum.

Martin, J. R., & Veel, R. (Eds.). (1998). *Reading science: Critical and functional perspectives on discourses of science*. London: Routledge.

Martin, J. R. & Wodak, R. (Eds.). (in press) *Re/reading the past: Critical and functional perspectives on discourses of history*. Amsterdam: John Benjamins.

Martinec, R. (1998). Cohesion in action. *Semiotica, 120*(1/2), 161–180.

Martinec, R. (2000a). Rhythm in multimodal texts. *Leonardo, 33*(4), 289–297.

Martinec, R. (2000b). Types of process in action. *Semiotica, 130*(3/4), 243–268.

Martinec, R. (2000c). Construction of identity in M. Jackson's 'Jam'. *Social Semiotics, 10*, 313–329.

Martinec, R. (2001). Interpersonal resources in action. *Semiotica, 135*(1/4), 117–145.

Matthiessen, C. M. I. M. (1993). Register in the round: Diversity in a unified theory of register analysis. M. Ghadessy (Ed.), *Register analysis: Theory and practice* (pp. 221–292). London: Pinter.

Matthiessen, C. M. I. M. (1999). The system of TRANSITIVITY: An exploratory study of text-based profiles. *Functions of Language, 6* (1), 1–51.

Matthiessen, C. M. I. M. (in press). Combining clauses into clause complexes: A multi–faceted view. In J. Bybee & M. Noonan (Eds.), *Complex sentences in grammar and discourse: Essays in honor of Sandra, A. Thompson* (pp. 237–322). Amsterdam: John Benjamins.

Matthiessen, C. M. I. M. & Bateman, J. (1991). *Text generation and systemic linguistics: Experiences from English and Japanese*. London: Pinter.

Matthiessen, C. M. I. M. & Wu, C. (2001). SysAm. [Programs for computational analysis].

Available at: http : //minerva. ling. mq. edu. au/Resources/AnalysisTools/Tools. htm.

Mitchell, T. F. (1957). The language of buying and selling in Cyrenaica: A situational statement. *Hesperis*, *26*, 31–71.

Nesbitt, C., & Plum, G. (1988). Probabilities in a systemic-functional grammar: The clause complex in English. In R. P. Fawcett & D. Young (Eds.), *New developments in systemic linguistics*, vol. 2: *Theory and application* (pp. 6–38). London: Pinter.

Ochs, E. Schegloff, E. A., & Thompson, S. A. (Eds.). (1996) *Interaction and grammar.* Cambridge: Cambridge University Press.

O'Donnell, M. (1995). From corpus to codings: Semiautomating the acquisition of linguistic features. In Proceedings of the AAAI Spring Symposium on Empirical Methods in Discourse Interpretation and Generation (pp. 120–123). Stanford, CA: Stanford University.

O'Halloran, K. L. (1999a). Interdependence, interaction and metaphor in multisemiotic texts. *Social Semiotics*, *9*, 317–354.

O'Halloran, K. L. (1999b). Towards a systemic functional analysis of multisemiotic mathematics texts. *Semiotica*, *124*(1/2), 1–29.

O'Halloran, K. L. (2000). Classroom discourse in mathematics: A multisemiotic analysis. *Linguistics and Education*, *10*, 359–388.

O'Halloran, K. L., & Judd, K. (2001). Systemics (CD ROM). Singapore: Singapore University Press.

Oram, J, Fine, J., Okamoto, C., & Tannock, R. (1999). Assessing the language of children with Attention Deficit Hyperactivity Disorder. *American Journal of Speech-Language Pathology*, *8*, 72–80.

O'Toole, M. (1994). *The language of displayed art.* London: Leicester University Press.

Ovadia, R., & Fine, J. (1995). A functional analysis of intonation in Asperger's Syndrome. In J. Siegfried (Ed.), *Therapeutic and everyday discourse as behavior change: towards a microanalysis in psychotherapy process research* (pp. 491–510). Norwood, NJ: Ablex.

Parsons, G. (1991). Cohesion and coherence: Scientific texts. In E. Ventola (Ed.), *Functional and systemic linguistics* (pp. 415–430). Berlin: Mouton de Gruyter.

Plum, G., & Cowling, A. (1987). Some constraints on grammatical variables: Tense choice in English. In R. Steele & T. Threadgold (Eds.), *Language Topics: Essays in honor of Michael Halliday*, Vol. II (pp. 281–305). Amsterdam: John Benjamins.

Poynton, C. (1985). *Language and gender: Making the difference.* Geelong, Victoria: Deakin University Press.

Ravelli, L. J. (1996). Making language accessible: Successful text writing for museum visitors. *Linguistics and Education*, *8*, 367–387.

Ravelli, L. J. (1998). The consequences of choice: Discursive positioning in an art institution. In A. Sánchez-Macarro & R. Carter (Eds.), *Linguistic choice across genres* (pp. 137–154).

Amsterdam: John Benjamins.

Ravelli, L. J. (2000). Beyond shopping: Constructing the Sydney Olympics in three-dimensional text. *Text, 20* (4), 1–27.

Ravelli, L. J., & Ellis, R. A. (Eds.). (in press). *Academic writing in context: Social-functional perspectives on theory and practice.* London: Continuum Press.

Rose, D. (1997). Science, technology and technical literacies. In F. Christie & J. R. Martin (Eds.), *Genre and institutions* (pp. 40–72). London: Pinter.

Rose, D. (1998). Science discourse and industrial hierarchy. In J. R. Martin & R. Veel (Eds.), *Reading science* (pp. 236–265). London: Routledge.

Rothery, J., & Stenglin, M. (1997). Entertaining and instructing: Exploring experience through story. In F. Christie & J. R. Martin (Eds.), *Genre and institutions* (pp. 231–263). London: Pinter.

Rothery, J., & Stenglin, M. (2000). Interpreting literature: The role of appraisal. In L. Unsworth (Ed.), *Researching language in schools and communities* (pp. 222–244). London: Cassell.

Sanchez-Macarro, A., & Carter, R. (Eds.) (1998). *Linguistic choice across genres: Variation in spoken and written English.* Amsterdam: John Benjamins.

Scott, M., & Thompson, G. (Eds.). (2000). *Patterns of text: In honour of Michael Hoey.* Amsterdam: John Benjamins.

Simon-Vandenbergen, A. M., Taverniers, M., & Ravelli, L. J. (Eds.). (in press). *Metaphor: Systemic and functional perspectives.* Amsterdam: John Benjamins.

Sinclair, J. M., & Coulthard, R. M. (1975). *Towards an analysis of discourse: The English used by teachers and pupils.* London: Oxford University Press.

Stainton, R., & Devilliers, J. (Eds.). (2001). *Communication in linguistics.* Toronto: Groupe de recherche en études francophones (GREF).

Steiner, E., & Veltman, R. (1988). *Pragmatics, discourse and text: Some systemically-inspired approaches.* London: Pinter.

Steiner, E., & Yallop, C. (Eds.). (2000). *Exploring translation and multilingual text production: Beyond content.* Berlin: Mouton de Gruyter.

Taboada, M. (2000). Cohesion as a measure in generic analysis. In A. Melby & A. Lommel (Eds.), *LACUS Forum XXVI* (pp. 35–49). Fullerton, CA: The Linguistic Association of Canada and the United States.

Taboada, M. (in press). Rhetorical relations in dialogue: A contrastive study. In C. L. Moder & A. Martinovic-Zic (Eds.), *Discourse across languages and cultures.* Amsterdam: John Benjamins.

Teich, E. (1999). *Systemic functional grammar in natural language generation: Linguistic description and computational representation.* London: Cassell.

Unsworth, L. (1998). "Sound" explanations in school science: A functional linguistics perspective on effective apprenticing texts. *Linguistics and Education, 9*(2), 199–226.

Unsworth, L. (Ed.). (2000). *Researching language in schools and communities: Functional linguistic perspectives*. London: Cassell.

van Dijk, T. A. (1977). *Text and context: Explorations in the semantics and pragmatics of discourse*. London: Longman.

van Leeuwen, T. (1991). Rhythm and social context. In P. Tench (Ed.), *Studies in systemic phonology* (pp. 231–262). London: Pinter.

van Leeuwen, T. (1996). The representation of social actors. In C. Caldas-Coulthard & M. Coulthard (Eds.), *Texts and practices: Readings in critical discourse analysis* (pp. 32–70). London: Routledge.

van Leeuwen, T. (1999). *Speech, music, sound*. London: Macmillan.

van Leeuwen, T., & Humphrey, S. (1996). On learning to look through a geographer's eyes. In R. Hasan & G. Williams (Eds.), *Literacy in society* (pp. 29–49).

van Leeuwen, T., & Jewitt, C. (2001). *Handbook of visual analysis*. London: Sage.

Veel, R. (1997). Learning how to mean—scientifically speaking: Apprenticeship into scientific discourse in the secondary school. In F. Christie & J. R. Manin (Eds.), *Genre and institutions* (pp. 161–195). London: Pinter.

Veel, R. (1998). The greening of school science: Ecogenesis in secondary classrooms. In J. R. Martin & R. Veel (Eds.), *Reading science* (pp. 114–151). London: Routledge.

Veel, R. (1999). Language, knowledge and authority in school mathematics. In F. Christie (Ed.), *Pedagogy and the shaping of consciousness* (pp. 185–216). London: Cassell.

Veel, R., & Coffin, C. (1996). Learning to think like an historian: the language of secondary school history. In R. Hasan & A. Williams (Eds.), *Literacy in society* (pp. 191–231). London: Longman.

Ventola, E. (1987). *The structure of social interaction: A systemic approach to the semiotics of service encounters*. London: Pinter.

Ventola, E. (Ed.). (1991). *Functional and systemic linguistics: Approaches and uses*. Berlin: Mouton de Gruyter.

Ventola, E. (1998). Interpersonal choices in academic work. In A. Sánchez-Macarro & R. Carter (Eds.), *Linguistic choices across genres* (pp. 117–136). Amsterdam: Benjamins.

Ventola, E. (1999). Semiotic spanning at conferences: Cohesion and coherence in and across conference papers and their discussions. In W. Bublitz, U. Lenk, & E. Ventola (Eds.), *Coherence in spoken and written discourse: How to create it and how to describe it* (pp. 101–125). Amsterdam: John Benjamins.

Ventola, E. (Ed.). (2000). *Discourse and community: Doing functional linguistics*. Tubingen: Gunter Narr.

Ventola, E., & Mauranen, A. (Eds.). (1995). *Academic writing: Intercultural and textual issues*.

Amsterdam: Benjamins.

Watt, D. L. E. (2001). Intonational cohesion and tone sequences in English. In Stainton, R., & Devilliers, J. (Eds.), *Communication in linguistics* (pp. 361–378). Toronto: Groupe de recherche en études francophones (GREF).

Webster, J. (1995). Studying thematic development in on-line help documentation using the functional semantic processor. In M. Ghadessy (Ed.), *Text and context in functional linguistics* (pp. 259–271). London: Pinter.

Webster, J., & Kit, C. (1995). Computational analysis of Chinese and English texts with the functional semantic processor and the C-LFG Parser. *Journal of Literary and Linguistiic Computing, 10*, 203–211.

White, P. (1997). Death, disruption and the moral order: The narrative impulse in mass 'hard news' reporting. In F. Christie & J. R. Martin (Eds.), *Genre and institutions* (pp. 101–133). London: Pinter.

White, P. (1998). Extended reality, proto-nouns and the vernacular: Distinguishing the technological from the scientific. J. R. Martin & R. Veel (Eds.), *Reading science* (pp. 266–296). London: Routledge.

White, P. (2000). Dialogue and inter-subjectivity: Reinterpreting the semantics of modality and hedging. In M. Coulthard, J. Cotterill, & F. Rock (Eds.), *Working with dialogue* (pp. 67–80). Tubingen: Neimeyer.

Wignell, P., Martin, J. R., & Eggins, S. (1990). The discourse of geography: Ordering and explaining the experiential world. *Linguistics and Education, 1*, 359–392.

Williams, G. (1995). Joint book-reading and literacy pedagogy: A socio-semantic examination. Volume 1. *Current Original Resources in Education (CORE), 19*(3). Fiche 2 B01-Fiche 6 B01.

Williams, G. (1996). Joint book-reading and literacy pedagogy: A socio-semantic examination. Volume 2. *Current Original Resources in Education (CORE), 20*(1). Fiche 3 B01-Fiche 8 E10.

Williams, G. (1999). The pedagogic device and the production of pedagogic discourse: A case example in early literacy education. In F. Christie (Ed.). *Pedagogy and the shaping of consciousness* (pp. 88–122). London: Cassell.

Williams, G. (2001). Literacy pedagogy prior to schooling: Relations between social positioning and semantic variation. In A. Morais, I. Neves, B. Davies, & H. Daniels (Eds.), *Towards a sociology of pedagogy: The contribution of Basil Bernstein to research* (pp. 17–45). New York: Peter Lang.

4. CORPUS LINGUISTIC APPROACHES FOR DISCOURSE ANALYSIS

Susan Conrad

This chapter provides an overview of approaches within corpus linguistics that address discourse-level phenomena. The shared characteristics of all corpus-based research are first reviewed. Then four major approaches are covered: (1) investigating characteristics associated with the use of a language feature, for example, analyzing the factors that affect the omission or retention of *that* in complement clauses; (2) examining the realizations of a particular function of language, such as describing all the constructions used in English to express stance; (3) characterizing a variety of language, for example, conducting a multi-dimensional analysis to investigate relationships among the registers used in different settings at universities; and (4) mapping the occurrences of a feature through entire texts, for example, tracing how writers refer to themselves and their audience as they construct authority in memos. For each approach, a variety of studies are reviewed to illustrate the diverse perspectives that corpus linguistics can bring to our understanding of discourse. The chapter concludes with a brief overview of some other foci in corpus linguistics and suggests that two areas require particular attention for the advancement of discourse-oriented corpus studies: the need for more computer tools and computer programmers for corpus linguistics, and the need for further studies about how best to represent language varieties in a corpus.

Corpus linguistics encompasses a great variety of approaches for studying language use. For many readers, concordance listings may be the most familiar form of corpus linguistics. These listings display all the occurrences of a word or structure in a database, with a small amount of context on each side. Overall, they appear quite divorced from a situation of use, and may therefore give the impression that corpus linguistics has little to offer discourse analysis. However, concordance listings represent only a small piece of the work that goes on in corpus linguistics. Full corpus-based studies provide complex information about social and textual factors that influence language choices, and therefore can contribute greatly to our understanding of discourse.

In this chapter, I provide an overview of approaches within corpus linguistics that are especially applicable to discourse analysis. I begin with an introduction to the features that characterize all corpus linguistic work, and then focus on four approaches:

- investigating the characteristics associated with the use of a language feature; for example, what factors are associated with a speaker's use of past perfect ("I'd done a lot") rather than past tense ("I did a lot")?
- examining the realizations of a particular function of language, for example, describing all the constructions in English that are used to express stance.
- characterizing a variety of language, such as describing the similarities and differences between casual conversations and academic writing.
- mapping the occurrence of language features through a text, for example, tracking the terms that writers use to refer to themselves and their audience.

Within each approach, I briefly review studies to illustrate the diverse research that has been conducted. I conclude by mentioning some additional foci in corpus linguistics, and briefly consider the future challenges for corpus linguistics in discourse analysis. Throughout, I emphasize work that has been conducted since the late 1990s; useful earlier work and bibliographies can be found in many sources including Biber, Conrad, and Reppen (1996); McEnery and Wilson (1996); Svartvik (1992); and Thomas and Short (1996). I also give most coverage to studies of English, since the majority of corpus work has been done with English; however, the approaches are equally applicable to other languages.

Characteristics of Research in Corpus Linguistics

Four features, described briefly below, characterize work within corpus linguistics (for more details, see introductory corpus linguistics books such as Biber,

Conrad and Reppen, 1998; Kennedy, 1998; and, on statistics in corpus linguistics, Oakes, 1998).

Use of a Corpus

A corpus is a large, principled collection of naturally-occurring texts that is stored in electronic form (accessible on computer). Corpora can include both written and transcribed spoken texts.

Corpus design is crucial to reliable and generalizable results. Although a full discussion of issues in corpus design is beyond the scope of this paper, it is important to note that the size of the corpus, the types of texts included, the number of texts, the sampling procedure, and the size of each sample are all important considerations. In general, corpora are designed following principles for representing demographic characteristics and recognized types of texts (e. g., see Aston & Burnard, 1998; Biber, Johansson, Leech, Conrad, & Finegan, 1999, chapter l; Granger, 1998, chapter l; Hennoste, Koit, Roosmaa, & Saluveer, 1998; McCarthy, 1998; and the websites listed in the annotated bibliography). Advances in computer technology have made increasingly large corpora possible, but there has unfortunately been relatively little empirical investigation of the size and sampling that are reliable yet efficient for representing all the variation in a language. In the early 1990s, Biber (1990, 1993) found 1, 000 word samples reliable for representing many grammatical features and 10 texts reliable for representing the genre categories in the Lancaster-Oslo/Bergen (LOB) Corpus (e. g., press reportage, official documents, academic prose), and also called for the representation of empirically determined "text types." However, there has been little work published recently that empirically investigates corpus design issues. (One exception is Kilgarriff, in press, on design issues with reference to word frequencies.)

Use of Computer-assisted Analysis Techniques

Corpus linguistics relies on computer-assisted techniques in order to handle the large amount of data in a corpus. Early publications often emphasized concordancing (e. g., Sinclair, 1991). In addition to showing words in context, concordancers calculate frequencies, analyze collocates (words that occur together) and often calculate statistical measures of the strength of word associations. However, much work in discourse analysis requires other kinds of analyses. With knowledge of computer programming, researchers can write specialized programs to analyze more complex aspects of texts, as described in subsequent sections. Such programs can be interactive, asking the researcher to make judgments about ambiguous forms as they are identified and coded. For an example of an interactive program, see Biber, Conrad, and Reppen, 1998, chapter 5.

Emphasis on Empirical Analysis of Patterns in Language Use

Corpus linguistic studies often develop from research questions that grow out of intuition or casual observations about language, and interpretations of corpus findings often include intuitive impressions about the impact of particular language choices. Nevertheless, the primary focus of analysis is empirical, based on what is observed in the corpus. Researchers are concerned with the patterns in language, determining what is typical and unusual in given circumstances. As McCarthy (1998) states, "The particular strength of computerised corpora is that they offer the researcher the potential to check whether something observed in everyday language is a one-off occurrence or a feature that is widespread across a broad sample of speakers" (p. 151).

Use of Ouantitative and Oualitative/Interpretive Techniques

Some corpus studies emphasize either the quantitative or the qualitative aspects of analysis. A recent issue of *TESOL Quarterly* highlights this contrast in methodologies (Biber & Conrad, 2001; McCarthy & Carter, 2001). However, all studies include both aspects of analysis to some extent. Recognizing patterns of language use necessarily entails assessing whether a phenomenon is common or unusual—a quantitative assessment. At the same time, numbers alone give little insight about language. Even the most sophisticated quantitative analyses must be tied to functional interpretations of the language patterns.

With these four characteristics, corpus linguistics has certain analytical strengths. Primary among them is the capacity for analyzing many more variables and data than were previously possible. Corpus linguistics is thus particularly helpful in providing "big picture" perspectives on discourse—determining patterns of language behavior across many texts, identifying typical and unusual choices by users, and describing the interactions among multiple variables. It provides a complementary perspective to more intensive approaches to discourse analysis, such as in conversation analysis (Schegloff, Koshik, Jacoby, & Olsher, this volume).

Four Approaches in Corpus–Based Research

Investigating Characteristics Associated with the Use of a Language Feature

One of the most common approaches taken in corpus studies is to focus on a particular language feature—a word, phrase or grammatical structure—and investigate factors associated with its use. Such investigations offer insight into the factors that shape the choices that language users make for different discourse conditions.

For an example of this type of approach, consider the choice between omission and retention of the complementizer *that* in clausal complements to verbs and adjectives in English, such as

I think [that] he might have gotten false teeth. Or
It was real clear [that] he did that. [1]

Native and nonnative speakers alike usually recognize that, as one popular ESL grammar book puts it, "Frequently [that] is omitted, as in [the example], especially in speaking" (Azar, 1999, P. 248). However, such a statement leaves many questions unanswered: To what extent is that omitted in conversation and in other registers? If omission is common, why is that ever retained?

Analyzing about 20 million words in the Longman Spoken and Written English Corpus, [2] Biber et al. (1999)show how common *that* omission is across registers and under what conditions *that* is retained. (Results reported here are summarized in slightly different form from analyses conducted for Biber et al., 1999, chapter 9.)The study finds that the great majority of the complement clauses in conversation do omit that. The percentage of that omission is striking when compared with three written registers, even a nonexpository written register such as fiction, which often includes dialogue and other informal language(see Figure 1).

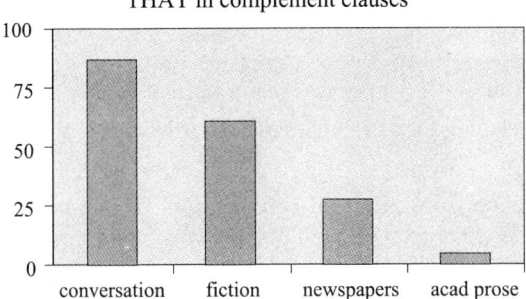

Figure 1: Percent omission of THAT in complement clauses.

The study then goes on to analyze conditions associated with the retention of *that* in conversation. Three conditions are particularly noteworthy:

- virtually all coordinated *that*-clauses retain *that*, for example:

And he said that I looked very good on paper, but that during the interview they felt...

- virtually all *that*-clauses that occur with intervening noun phrases retain *that*, for example:

I think I'll tell him that it's not a good idea right now.

- about 75 % of the clauses that have passive voice main verbs retain *that*, for example:

I was told that it was too expensive.

The full study compares the influence of these conditions across registers and covers many other aspects of that-clause complementation. Yet even this brief piece of the study contributes to our understanding of the characteristics of conversation. Though observers have noticed that *that* is often omitted, the corpus-based study, with over 3, 000 conversations included, shows how widespread that omission is and how strong a relationship exists between particular conditions and retention of that.

In other corpus studies, grammatical features have also been associated with discourse management functions, such as the foregrounding and backgrounding of information. For example, Hughes and McCarthy (1998) analyze the use of past perfect verb forms in cases where other choices of tense or aspect are possible, for example:

> Well yeah I mean Christmas was really for us this time. I mean we'd done a lot of pre-planning for it...(Hughes & McCarthy, 1998, p. 269).

With evidence from informal conversation in one million words of the Cambridge and Nottingham Corpus of Discourse in English (CANCODE; see McCarthy, 1998), they argue that, across a wide range of speakers, the past perfect has a broader and more complex function than is often maintained—i. e., to show that events happened in a past time before another past time. They find that speakers use it in conveying relationships among narrated events, manipulating foregrounding and backgrounding, often as part of explanations and justifications. In other corpus studies, Breivik (1999) finds that factors such as end focus and the grounding of main clauses have important associations with the use of relative clauses in existential sentences.

The expression of ideologies and attitudes have also been addressed with corpus-based techniques, especially in studies of word associations. Partington (1998) uses corpus analyses to argue that attitude is created in a text through the use of semantic prosody—not the connotations of a word, but the word's association with positive or negative contexts (e. g., the verb *commit* is usually used with negative objects such as foul, crime, suicide). Stubbs (1996) uses corpus-based techniques to analyze historical speeches to the Boy Scouts and Girl Guides. Looking at word collocations and grammatical structures, he shows how the speaker's language choices reflect his beliefs about men's and women's roles in society. Even the occurrences of a word such as happy are found to be intricately tied to ideology and sexism. Such a study also demonstrates the applicability of corpus linguistics techniques to critical discourse analysis (Luke, this volume).

Corpus linguistic techniques have also been important for discerning the strong associations that exist between the lexicon and grammatical structures. For example, Biber et al. (1999, chapter 9) also analyze the lexico-grammar of verb complement clauses, comparing different registers. In conversation, *that*-clauses are strongly associated with the verbs *think*, *say* and *know*, corresponding to the typical functions in conversation of reporting the thoughts and ideas of oneself or others (e. g., *I think you need a rest*). In academic prose, on the other hand, there are stronger associations between *that*-clauses and the verbs *show* and *suggest*. These constructions are often used with inanimate subjects, expressing an argument without a personal agent (e. g., *Other models show that...*). Hunston and Francis (2000, especially chapter 8) argue the importance of lexico-grammatical patterns further, based on analyses of the COBUILD corpus (see Sinclair, 1987). They argue that the senses of a word are associated with particular patterns, that discourse is made up of sequences of these patterns, and that different patterns are associated with different genres.

The types of characteristics included in corpus-based studies of language features cover a wide gamut. In addition to variation across registers, studies have included subregisters; for example, Ferguson (2001) analyzes how conditionals are used differently across different types of medical discourse—research articles vs. journal editorials vs. doctor-patient consultations. Other studies have focused on personal characteristics of speakers: Stenström (1999), for instance, considers associations between gender and the choice of intensifiers in a corpus of London teenager language (e. g., *really bad day* vs. *bloody right cow*). Other studies primarily focus on variation between national dialects, such as British and American varieties of English; for example, Leech (1999) compares the use of vocatives. Still others consider change over time as the variable of interest (e. g., see Hundt & Mair, 1999, on the historical development of "agile" vs. "uptight" prose). Of course, many studies include more than one characteristic; Botley and McEnery (2001) cover associations with six characteristics in their study of demonstrative pronoun use. Furthermore, all of these characteristics can be studied in other languages besides English (e. g., Butler, 1998, investigates collocations across spoken and written Spanish; Verhagen, 2000, examines language change in verb use in Dutch).

Examining the Realizations of a Particular Function of Language

In the previous section, studies focused on individual language features, such as words or grammatical constructions. A second approach within corpus linguistics is to focus on a function of language and to determine how it is realized in discourse. Thus, within the investigation of stance, a study of an individual language feature focuses on just stance adverbials (Conrad & Biber, 1999); in contrast, Hunston & Sinclair (1999) address the entire functional system: They use corpus analyses to investigate all the lexico-grammatical patterns whose primary purpose it is to express evaluation, finding patterns that begin with verbs, dummy subject there, pseudoclefts, and nouns.

The advantage of a corpus linguistic approach in studying a function of language is that many interacting characteristics can be examined simultaneously. Biber, Conrad, and Reppen (1998, chapter 5) illustrate this advantage in a study of reference. Six characteristics are included in the study: register (conversation, speeches, newspaper writing, academic prose); pronoun vs. noun forms; given vs. new information status; type of reference (anaphoric, exophoric, or inferable); type of expression for anaphoric reference (synonyms vs. full nouns); and the distance between the referring expression and its antecedent. In the results, there are clear relationships among the characteristics. For example, register, average distance, type of referring expression and given/new information status are interconnected: newspaper writing and academic prose are found to have many full-noun referring expressions that present new information, with a large number of expressions intervening between coreferential nouns. Conversation, on the other hand, shows a preference for pronominal reference, with repeated reference to already-mentioned (given) entities, and as a result, has a much lower average distance between the referring expression and its antecedent. Even with the assistance of a computer, such a study can be very time-consuming because disambiguating references requires a good deal of interactive computer coding before the analysis can take place—but by hand, keeping track of the numerous variables in numerous texts would soon become completely unmanageable.

Corpus linguistics has also been used for the analysis of themes in texts. This area of functional-systemic linguistics has traditionally been studied with intensive analysis of a small number of texts. In contrast, Gómez-González (1998) uses corpus linguistic techniques to include over 4,000 themes in her study. She uses multivariate techniques to investigate the typical ordering of parts within 1,660 extended multiple themes (e.g., those that contain textual or interpersonal items as well as topical themes, e.g., *but of course I...*). Green, Christopher, and Kam Mei (2000) apply corpus-based theme analysis to ESL student writing. They conduct a study of theme choices in native speaker and Chinese-ESL writers'academic texts, showing that differences—and especially the greater frequency of connectors as theme choice (e. g., *besides, furthermore*)—have a negative effect on the coherence of the ESL writers' texts.

Anping and Kennedy (1999) demonstrate that corpus linguistics techniques can be applied even to an interactive discourse function: turn-bidding in conversation. They examine the linguistic devices (e. g., initial words) and pragmatic devices (e. g., types of repetition) that speakers use when they successfully bid for a turn, as well as the prosodic, grammatical, and lexical markers of turn-unit boundaries. Their study also looks at associations with the formality of the situation, the familiarity of the interlocutors, and the speaker's status and gender. With 193 speakers in 83 conversations, Anping and Kennedy have a much wider base from which to draw conclusions than in most previous studies of turn-taking.

Characterizing a Variety of Language

Many studies mentioned in the prior two sections have included register or dialect as a variable. However, a third approach within corpus linguistics makes the language variety the primary focus; these studies have as a goal the characterization of a variety of discourse.

One area in which corpus linguistics has proven useful is in characterizing the vocabulary of a specific domain. The desire to identify an English academic vocabulary—and thereby improve the effectiveness of instruction in English for Academic Purposes—has received attention for many decades (e. g., Ghadessy, 1979; Xue & Nation, 1984). Without corpus linguistics techniques, however, the amount of language that could be included was quite limited. For example, Ghadessy (1979) developed a word list using 20 textbooks from three disciplines, with a total of slightly under 500, 000 words. With corpus-based techniques, Coxhead (2001) bases an academic word list on a corpus that includes over 400 texts and 28 subject areas with a total of about 3. 5 million words. Because Coxhead's goal is a word list representing widespread academic use, the broader coverage of texts and subject areas is a great advantage. (Smaller corpora have also been used to characterize the vocabulary or lexico-grammatical patterns of specialized domains; for example, see Williams, 1998, on plant biology and Gledhill, 2000, on cancer research articles.)

Within corpus linguistics, one methodology was developed specifically for characterizing language varieties: multi-dimensional (MD) analysis, developed by Biber (1988). This method uses factor analysis to analyze the co-occurrence patterns of numerous linguistic features; for example, over 60 linguistic features have been used in the analysis of English, including grammatical, lexical, and some semantic features. The analysis quantitatively determines several continua along which texts vary, and these are then given functional interpretations, such as the expression of overt argumentation or narrative vs. nonnarrative concerns.

One of the strengths of the MD methodology is that it allows complex comparisons to be made among language varieties. To take just two registers and two dimensions, consider conversation and academic prose. As expected, they are very different when compared in their use of features related to involvement and real-time processing (e. g., first and second person pronouns, main verb *be*, contractions, etc.) vs. features of densely packed information (nouns, prepositions, attributive adjectives). However, they are also similar in the frequency of use of features of overt argumentation; neither has a particularly high frequency as newspaper editorials do, nor a particular absence, as broadcasts do. Analyses can also be extended to investigate the amount of variability across texts within a variety, and to compare more specialized subvarieties. (See Conrad & Biber, 2001, for a more complete description of the MD methodology and relationships among registers in English.)

The MD methodology has proved a useful method of analysis for diverse contexts. For example, a recent collection of MD studies covers among other topics: the historical development of scientific discourse (Atkinson, 2001); oral proficiency test validation (Connor-Linton & Shohamy, 2001); the discourse of different academic disciplines (Conrad, 2001); registers of children's speech and writing (Reppen, 2001); gendered language use in *Star Trek* (Rey, 2001); and comparisons of British and American spoken registers (Helt, 2001). In addition, Biber, Conrad, Reppen, Byrd, & Helt (in press) use MD analysis to compare several spoken and written registers used at American universities, and Hoogesteger (cited in de Haan, 1999) adapts the technique in a study of English writing by Dutch students.

Finally, for characterizing a language variety, it is also possible to consider the body of work that has analyzed a specialized corpus, even if independent studies have focused on individual features. For example, spoken academic language is the focus of studies using the Michigan Corpus of Academic Spoken English (e. g.,

Mauranen, 2001; Swales, 2001; Swales & Malczewski, 2001). Results from this corpus can also be compared with results of studies from the spoken section of the TOEFL 2000 Spoken and Written Academic Language Corpus (Biber, Reppen, Clark, & Walter, 2001).

Mapping the Occurrence of a Language Feature through a Text

One additional approach within corpus linguistics is particularly applicable to discourse analysis, though it thus far has received little attention. In this approach, one or more features are tracked through an entire text to determine how the features contribute to some aspect of the discourse development, such as its rhetorical organization, topic progression, or the author's construction of authority. A "map" of the feature through the text is produced, giving a visual representation of its use. Multiple texts are then compared to determine consistent patterns.

Working with institutional memos, Burges (1996) maps writers' reference to participants (e. g., I, *you, faculty*), comparing the patterns for memos written to groups with superior, inferior, and equal hierarchical standing. She finds that the selection of the noun or pronoun and the level of prominence (theme or rheme positioning) give insight into how writers manipulate their writing to construct their authority for writing the memo. A similar technique is exemplified in Biber, Conrad, and Reppen (1998, chapter 5) for the analysis of verb tense and voice throughout science research articles. Areas with numerous shifts—e. g., when occurrences of verbs alternative between active and passive, and past and present—correspond to transition zones that are of particular rhetorical interest. Intensive analysis of the communicative purposes of these transition zones is then possible.

Another mapping technique has been used to track the introduction of new vocabulary into a text, producing a visual display of "vocabulary management profiles" (Youmans, 1991). Csomay (2000) adapts this technique, showing how the profiles of vocabulary correspond to topical and functional structure within oral academic discourse in university classrooms.

Though few studies have used a mapping approach, its potential to contribute to our understanding of discourse is great. In the past, it was usually too time-consuming to track a feature through more than a few complete texts. With corpus linguistics, once a program is written, and especially if it can be run without interactive analyses, it is a simple matter to use it on numerous texts. Studies of patterns in discourse thus have a much firmer basis for generalization than in the past.

Additional Foci Within Corpus Linguistics

In a chapter of this size it is impossible to cover all facets of corpus linguistics, and several other areas may be of interest to discourse analysts. In particular, I have neglected much work with cross-linguistic comparisons, parallel corpora (designed to represent the same varieties in two languages), and the application of corpus linguistics to translation (see, e. g., Botley & Wilson, 2000; Hasselgård & Oksefjell, 1999, section 3; Johansson, 1997; Partington, 1998, chapter 3). Corpus-based studies of recurring word sequences also deserve mention since they have implications for discourse production and processing. Researchers are finding that fixed sequences account for a notable percentage of discourse, and are arguing that these prefabricated units appear to be basic building blocks of discourse (e. g., Barlow, 2000; Biber & Conrad, 1999; McCarthy, 1998). Although their importance was noted in the past, only corpus-based studies have provided quantitative support to show just how common these recurring sequences are over a wide range of texts.

Several studies mentioned above have included comparisons of native speakers with second language learners, but many more such studies of second language learners exist (e. g., de Cock, 1998, and the studies collected in Granger, 1998). Studies of language change also cover diverse topics (see, e. g., the papers in Curzan & Meyer, 2000). Recently, a good deal of attention has also been paid to profitable connections between corpus linguistics and natural language processing, machine translation, and lexical knowledge databases (e. g., Dini & Di Tomaso, 1998; Hoard, 1998; and the collection edited by Nerbonne, 1998).

The role of corpus linguistics in language teaching has become an increasingly popular topic. Several recent publications discuss the role of corpora in classroom pedagogy (see, e. g., Fox, 1998; Gavioli & Aston, 2001; Granger & Tribble, 1998; Thurston & Candlin, 1998; and numerous papers collected in Aston, 2001), and the role corpus-based research should play for developing, adapting, and assessing pedagogical materials (e. g., Conrad, 1999; Kaszubski, 1998; McCarthy, 1998; for a less positive orientation, see Owen, 1996). Within grammar pedagogy, corpus linguists have argued that their work demonstrates the need for new perspectives on grammar, especially related to stronger discourse and lexico-grammar orientations, register comparisons, and considerations of grammar in terms of probabilities and appropriate choices, rather than deterministic rules and notions of correctness (see, e. g., discussions in Biber & Conrad, 2001; Conrad, 2000; Hughes & McCarthy, 1998; Hunston & Francis, 1998; McCarthy, 1998).

Issues concerning the annotation of corpora—such as identifying the grammatical classes of words or functional categories of expressions—are beyond the scope of this chapter. Interested readers will find useful information in Aarts and Oostdyk (1997); Assi and Abdlhosseini (2000, for experience with a language other than English); Hockey (1998); and Meunier (1998, for work with a learner corpus). Powell and Simpson (2001) provide information about developing a web interface for public access to a corpus.

The Future for Corpus Linguistics and Discourse Analysis

As corpus linguistics first developed, it was often thought that it could not be applied to language phenomena that extended beyond clause boundaries. As the field has matured, it has instead become apparent that many studies within corpus linguistics address discourse-level concerns, many showing association patterns or the interactions of variables that would not be apparent without corpus-based techniques.

In the past several years, corpora have become increasingly numerous and accessible (see annotated bibliography) and corpus-based studies have begun to appear more regularly in mainstream venues. It thus seems likely that corpus linguistics will continue to expand. Nevertheless, I believe there are two major challenges that will affect the popularity and acceptance of corpus-based discourse studies in the future.

The first challenge concerns the availability of computer tools that allow discourse-level studies of corpora. Currently, most researchers have, at most, access to a concordancer, which allows only limited investigation of discourse-level features. More software, more adaptable to discourse concerns, needs to become available to more researchers. More computer programming classes specifically for corpus linguistics need to be offered so that researchers can write their own programs.

The second challenge concerns corpus design. Corpora are meant to capture the variation that exists in a language, and our present corpora are clearly capturing a great deal. However, as mentioned above, empirical evidence about how best to represent all language variation is scanty. Further investigations into corpus sizes and sampling techniques are needed, as well as further research into the kinds of variation that exist in language so that we can make sure to capture all kinds of variation in new corpora. In fact, corpus design itself is interwoven with the process of discourse analysis. A better understanding of discourse leads to improvements in corpus design, and research into corpus design increases our understanding of variation in discourse.

Notes

1. Samples of that-clauses have been taken from the Longman Spoken American Corpus.

2. The brevity of this chapter and its purpose—to introduce the discourse research approaches within corpus linguistics—prohibit a full description of the corpora used in each study that I mention. Details can be found in the publications cited.

ANNOTATED BIBLIOGRAPHY

Anping, H., & Kennedy, G. (1999). Successful turn-bidding in English conversation. *International Journal of Corpus Linguistics*, *4*, 1–27.

This article is particularly noteworthy because it applies corpus linguistic techniques to a complex area of interaction—turn-taking. The study not only considers the linguistic and pragmatic devices that turn-bidders use, but also examines the influence of different speech domains, different participant relationships, social status, and gender. The preparation of the corpus and analytical techniques for such a study are clearly described.

Conrad, S., & Biber, S. (Eds.). (2001). *Variation in English: Multi-dimensional studies*. Harlow, Essex: Longman.

This collection begins with an explanation of the technique of Multi-Dimensional Analysis and the model of variation in English developed by Biber (1988), written for readers with no previous background in the methodology. The book then presents diverse studies applying the model in new areas, including the historical evolution of registers, applications to specialized domains and dialect variation. Topics are as diverse as American/Soviet nuclear arms talk, the discourse of different academic disciplines and the language of *Star Trek*. The final section of the book presents three studies that develop new Multi-Dimensional models—for student speech and writing, 18th century discourse, and discourse complexity.

Granger, S. (Ed.). (1998). *Learner English on computer*. London: Longman.

In this edited collection, a number of studies using the International Corpus of Learner English and other learner corpora are presented. Studies cover grammar, lexis, and discourse concerns, and include sub-corpora from learners in a wide variety of (mostly European) countries. The studies present numerous interesting findings about learner language, yet the book is also useful as a resource for the compiling and use of learner corpora generally, with several articles about design and pedagogical applications.

McCarthy, M. (1998). *Spoken language and applied linguistics*. Cambridge: Cambridge University Press.

This book brings together revised versions of papers published by McCarthy over the late 1980s and 1990s, covering much of his work with the CANCODE (Cambridge and Nottingham Corpus of Discourse in English). The first chapter of the book describes the CANCODE project, and subsequent chapters discuss findings about informal spoken English, particularly features which have been overlooked in traditional reference materials and textbooks. McCarthy presents many arguments for the positive effects that corpus linguistics can have on language pedagogy, as well as acknowledging concerns such as the teachability and learnability of features and the appropriate use of corpora in different learner contexts.

Partington, A. (1998). *Patterns and meanings: Using corpora for English language research and teaching*. Amsterdam: John Benjamins.

Each chapter of this book presents a different area of interest within corpus linguistics. Some of these are topics commonly covered, such as lexical studies and collocations, translation, and syntax, but the book is notable for its inclusion of less commonly discussed areas as well, including chapters on metaphor and creative language use. The explanations are accessible for beginners in corpus linguistics, and many teaching applications are exemplified.

Websites

For researchers with computer access, one of the easiest ways to learn about corpora and try some basic concordancing is online. The following is a very short list of sites to illustrate corpora representing varieties of English. The sites are chosen because they clearly describe their design criteria, provide search software on the site, and cover corpora that are available for public (noncommercial) use. Numerous other useful sites also exist.

http: //titania. cobuild. collins. co. uk/boe_info. html—The Bank of English

The Collins-COBUILD project has been growing since the 1980s. Currently, the COBUILD corpus is over 400 million words, and continues to have new texts added. The website describes the corpus and its use for language description and learning. Sample concordance and collocation analyses are easy to conduct from the website.

http: //info. ox. ac. uk/bnc/—The British National Corpus

The BNC is a 100 million word corpus of spoken and written British English from a variety of sources. The website offers simple concordancing searches, as well as information on obtaining more sophisticated analysis programs and all or part of the corpus.

http: //americannationalcorpus. org—The American National Corpus

The American National Corpus project is currently creating a corpus comparable to the British National Corpus, with about 100 million words representing the same registers. This corpus will be distributed free for noncommercial research purposes. The site describes the design and current status of the project.

http: //www. ucl. ac. uk/english-usage/ice/—The International Corpus of English

Approximately 20 varieties of English from around the world will be represented in this corpus. The comparative study of Englishes will be facilitated by the common design for each sub-corpus. Parts of the ICE are now available, as is a demonstration of software to use with the corpus.

http: //www. lsa. umich. edu/eli/micase/micase. htm—The Michigan Corpus of Academic Spoken English

The current phrase of the MICASE is near completion, with about 1. 5 million words of text recorded in academic contexts across the University of Michigan. Almost 1 million words is available on the web, along with easy-to-use concordancing software that allows users to search the corpus using a variety of specifications.

Additional useful sites:

http : //www. ruf. rice. edu/-barlow/corpus. html

Michael Barlow's website about corpus linguistics offers many useful links to other sites, including corpora in over 20 languages.

http : //www. ldc. upenn. edu and http : //www. hit. uib. no/icame. html

Information and many corpora are also available through these websites of the Linguistic Data Consortium and ICAME (International Computer Archive of Modern and Medieval English)

OTHER REFERENCES

Aarts, J., & Oostdyk, N. (1997). Handling discourse elements in syntax. In U. Fries, V. Müller, & P. Schneider (Eds.), *From AElfric to the New York Times: Studies in English corpus linguistics* (pp. 107–124). Amsterdam: Rodopi.

Assi, S. M., & Abdlhosseini, M. H. (2000). Grammatical tagging of a Persian corpus. *International Journal of Corpus Linguistics, 5*, 69–81.

Aston, G. (Ed.). (2001). *Learning with corpora*. Houston, TX: Athelstan.

Aston, G., & Burnard, L. (1998). *The BNC handbook: Exploring the British National Corpus with SARA*. Edinburgh: Edinburgh University Press.

Atkinson, D. (2001). Scientific discourse across history: A combined multi-dimensional/ rhetorical analysis of *The Philosophical Transactions of the Royal Society of London*. In S. Conrad & D. Biber (Eds.), *Variation in English: Multi-dimensional studies* (pp. 45–65).

Harlow, Essex: Longman.

Azar, B. (1999). *Understanding and using English grammar* (3rd ed.). White Plains, NY: Longman.

Barlow, M. (2000). Usage, blends and grammar. In M. Barlow & S. Kemmer (Eds.), *Usage-based models of language* (pp. 315–346). Stanford, CA: Center for the Study of Language and Information.

Biber, D. (1988). *Variation across speech and writing*. Cambridge: Cambridge University Press.

Biber, D. (1990). Methodological issues regarding corpus-based analyses of linguistic variation. *Literary and Linguistic Computing, 5*, 257–269.

Biber, D. (1993). Representativeness in corpus design. *Literacy and Linguistic Computing, 8*, 243–257.

Biber, D., & Conrad, S. (1999). Lexical bundles in conversation and academic prose. In H. Hasselgård & S. Oksefjell (Eds.), *Out of corpora: Studies in honour of Stig Johansson* (pp. 182–190). Amsterdam: Rodopi.

Biber, D., & Conrad, S. (2001). Quantitative corpus-based research: Much more than bean counting. *TESOL Quarterly, 35*, 331–336.

Biber, D., Conrad, S., & Reppen, R. (1996). Corpus-based investigations of language use. *Annual Review of Applied Linguistics, 16*, 115–136.

Biber, D., Conrad, S., & Reppen, R. (1998). *Corpus linguistics: Investigating language structure and use*. Cambridge: Cambridge University Press.

Biber, D., Conrad, S., Reppen, R., Byrd, P., & Helt, M. (in press). Speaking and writing in the university: A multi-dimensional comparison. *TESOL Quarterly*.

Biber, D., Johansson, S., Leech, G., Conrad, S., & Finegan, E. (1999). *The Longman grammar of spoken and written English*. Harlow, Essex: Pearson Education.

Biber, D., Reppen, R., Clark, V., & Walter, J. (2001). Representing spoken language in university settings: The design and construction of the spoken component of the T2K-SWAL Corpus. In R. Simpson & J. Swales (Eds.), *Corpus linguistics in North America: Selections from the 1999 Symposium* (pp. 48–57). Ann Arbor, MI: University of Michigan Press.

Botley, S., & McEnery, T. (2001). Demonstratives in English: A corpus-based study. *Journal of English Linguistics, 29*, 7–33.

Botley, S., & Wilson, A. (Eds.). (2000). *Multilingual corpora in teaching and research*. Atlanta, GA: Rodopi.

Breivik, L. E. (1999). On the pragmatic function of relative clauses and locative expressions in existential sentences in the LOB corpus. In H. Hasselgård & S. Oksefjell (Eds.), *Out of corpora: Studies in honour of Stig Johansson* (pp. 121–135). Amsterdam: Rodopi.

Burges, J. (1996). Hierarchical influences on language use in memos. Unpublished doctoral dissertation. Flagstaff, AZ: Northern Arizona University.

Butler, C. (1998). Collocational frameworks in Spanish. *International Journal of Corpus Linguistics, 3,* 1–32.

Connor-Linton, J., & Shohamy, E. (2001). Register variation, oral proficiency sampling, and the promise of multi-dimensional analysis. In S. Conrad & D. Biber (Eds.), *Variation in English: Multi-dimensional studies* (pp. 124–137). Harlow, Essex: Longman.

Conrad, S. (1999). The importance of corpus-based research for language teachers. *System, 27,* 1–18.

Conrad, S. (2000). Will corpus linguistics revolutionize grammar teaching in the 21st century? *TESOL Quarterly, 34,* 548–560.

Conrad, S. (2001). Variation among disciplinary texts: A comparison of textbooks and journal articles in biology and history. In S. Conrad & D. Biber (Eds.), *Variation in English: Multi-dimensional studies* (pp. 94–107). Harlow, Essex: Longman.

Conrad, S., & Biber, D. (1999). Adverbial marking of stance in speech and writing. In S. Hunston & G. Thompson (Eds.), *Evaluation in text: Authorial stance and the construction of discourse* (pp. 56–73). Oxford: Oxford University Press.

Coxhead, A. (2001). A new academic word list. *TESOL Quarterly, 34,* 213–238.

Csomay, E. (2000). Episodes and the vocabulary management profile. Unpublished manuscript. Flagstaff, AZ: Northern Arizona University.

Curzan, A., & Meyer, C. (Eds.). (2000). Special issue on historical corpora. *Journal of English Linguistics, 28* (3).

de Cock, S. (1998). A recurrent word combination approach to the study of formulae in the speech of native and non-native speakers of English. *International Journal of Corpus Linguistics, 3,* 59–80.

de Haan, P. (1999). English writing by Dutch-speaking students. In H. Hasselgård & S. Oksefjell (Eds.), *Out of corpora: Studies in honour of Stig Johansson* (pp. 203–212). Amsterdam: Rodopi.

Dini, L., & Di Tomaso, V. (1998). Corpus linguistics for application development. *International Journal of Corpus Linguistics, 3,* 305–311.

Ferguson, G. (2001). If you pop over there: A corpus-based study of conditionals in medical discourse. *English for Specific Purposes, 20,* 61–82.

Fox, G. (1998). Using corpus data in the classroom. In B. Tomlinson (Ed.), *Materials development in language teaching* (pp. 25–43). Cambridge: Cambridge University Press.

Gavioli, L., & Aston, G. (2001). Enriching reality: Language corpora in language pedagogy. *ELT Journal, 55,* 238–246.

Ghadessy, P. (1979). Frequency counts, word lists, and materials preparation: A new approach. *English Teaching Forum, 17,* 24–27.

Gledhill, C. (2000). The discourse function of collocation in research article introductions. *English for Specific Purposes, 19*, 115–135.

Gómez-González, M. A. (1998). A corpus-based analysis of extended multiple themes in PresE. *International Journal of Corpus Linguistics, 3*, 81–113.

Granger, S., & Tribble, C. (1998). Learner corpus data in the foreign language classroom: Form-focused instruction and data-driven learning. In S. Granger (Ed.), *Learner English on computer* (pp. 199–209). London: Longman.

Green, C. F., Christopher, E. R., & Kam Mei, J. L. K. (2000). The incidence and effects on coherence of marked themes in interlanguage texts: A corpus-based enquiry. *English for Specific Purposes, 19*, 99–113.

Hasselgård, H., & Oksefjell, S. (Eds.). (1999). *Out of corpora: Studies in honour of Stig Johansson.* Amsterdam: Rodopi.

Helt, M. (2001). A multi-dimensional comparison of British and American spoken English. In S. Conrad & D. Biber (Eds.), *Variation in English: Multi-dimensional studies* (pp. 171–183). Harlow, Essex: Longman.

Hennoste, T., Koit, M., Roosmaa, T., & Saluveer, M. (1998). Structure and usage of the Tartu University corpus of written Estonian. *International Journal of Corpus Linguistics, 3*, 279–304.

Hoard, J. (1998). Language understanding and the emerging alignment of linguistics and natural language processing. In J. Lawler & H. A. Dry (Eds.), *Using computers in linguistics: A practical guide* (pp. 197–230). London: Routledge.

Hockey, S. (1998). Textual databases. In J. Lawler & H. A. Dry (Eds.), *Using computers in linguistics: A practical guide* (pp. 101–133). London: Routledge.

Hughes, R., & McCarthy, M. (1998). From sentence to discourse: Discourse grammar and English language teaching. *TESOL Quarterly, 32*, 263–287.

Hundt, M., & Mair, C. (1999). "Agile" and "uptight" genres: The corpus-based approach to language change in progress. *International Journal of Corpus Linguistics, 4*, 221–242.

Hunston, S., & Francis, G. (1998). Verbs observed: A corpus-driven pedagogic grammar of English. *Applied Linguistics, 19*, 45–72.

Hunston, S., & Francis, G. (2000). *Pattern grammar: A corpus-driven approach to the lexical grammar of English.* Amsterdam: John Benjamins.

Hunston, S., & Sinclair, J. (1999). A local grammar of evaluation. In S. Hunston & G. Thompson (Eds.), *Evaluation in text: Authorial stance and the construction of discourse* (pp. 74–101). Oxford: Oxford University Press.

Johansson, S. (1997). In search of the missing *not*: Some notes on negation in English and Norwegian. In U. Fries, V. Müller, & P. Schneider (Eds.), *From AElfric to the New York Times: Studies in English corpus linguistics* (pp. 197–214). Amsterdam: Rodopi.

Kaszubski, P. (1998). Enhancing a writing textbook: A national perspective. In S. Granger (Ed.), *Learner English on computer* (pp. 172–185). London: Longman.

Kennedy, G. (1998). *An introduction to corpus linguistics*. London: Longman.

Kilgarriff, A. (in press). Comparing corpora. *International Journal of Corpus Linguistics, 6,* 1–37.

Leech, G. (1999). The distribution and function of vocatives in American and British English conversation. In H. Hasselgärd & S. Oksefjell (Eds.), *Out of corpora: Studies in honour of Stig Johansson* (pp. 107–118). Amsterdam: Rodopi.

Luke, A. (this volume). Beyond science and ideology critique: Developments in critical discourse analysis.

Mauranen, A. (2001). Reflexive academic talk: Observations from MICASE. In R. Simpson & J. Swales (Eds.), *Corpus linguistics in North America: Selections from the 1999 Symposium* (pp. 165–178). Ann Arbor, MI: University of Michigan Press.

McCarthy, M., & Carter, R. (2001). Size isn't everything: Spoken English, corpus, and the classroom. *TESOL Quarterly, 35,* 337–340.

McEnery, T., & Wilson, A. (1996). *Corpus linguistics*. Edinburgh: Edinburgh University Press.

Meunier, F. (1998). Computer tools for the analysis of learner corpora. In S. Granger (Ed.), *Learner English on computer* (pp. 19–37). London: Longman.

Nerbonne, J. (Ed.). (1998). *Linguistic databases*. Stanford, CA: Center for the Study of Language and Information.

Oakes, M. (1998). *Statistics for corpus linguistics*. Edinburgh: Edinburgh University Press.

Owen, C. (1996). Do concordances require to be consulted? *ELT Journal, 50,* 219–224.

Powell, C., & Simpson, R. (2001). Collaboration between corpus linguists and digital librarians for the MICASE web search interface. In R. Simpson & J. Swales (Eds.), *Corpus linguistics in North America: Selections from the 1999 Symposium* (pp. 32–47). Ann Arbor, MI: University of Michigan Press.

Reppen, R. (2001). Register variation in student and adult speech and writing. In S. Conrad & D. Biber (Eds.), *Variation in English: Multi-dimensional studies* (pp. 187–199). Harlow, Essex: Longman.

Rey, J. (2001). Changing gender roles in popular culture: Dialog in *Star Trek* episodes from 1966 to 1993. In S. Conrad & D. Biber (Eds.), *Variation in English: Multi-dimensional studies* (pp. 138–156). Harlow, Essex: Longman.

Schegloff, E. A., Koshik, I., Jacoby, S., & Olsher, D. (this volume). Conversation analysis and applied linguistics.

Sinclair, J. (1987). *Looking up: An account of the COBUILD project in lexical computing*. London: Collins ELT.

Sinclair, J. (1991). *Corpus, concordance, collocation*. Oxford: Oxford University Press.

Stenström, A. (1999). He was really gormless—She's bloody crap: Girls, boys, and intensifiers. In H. Hasselgärd & S. Oksefjell (Eds.), *Out of corpora: Studies in honour of Stig Johansson* (pp. 69–78). Amsterdam: Rodopi.

Stubbs, M. (1996). *Text and corpus analysis*. Oxford: Blackwell.

Svartvik, J. (Ed.). (1992). *Directions in corpus linguistics: Proceedings of the Nobel symposium*. Berlin: Mouton de Gruyter.

Swales, J. (2001). Metatalk in American academic talk: The cases of *point* and *thing*. *Journal of English Linguistics, 29*, 34–54.

Swales, J., & Malczewski, B. (2001). Discourse management and new-episode flags in MICASE. In R. Simpson & J. Swales (Eds.), *Corpus linguistics in North America: Selections from the 1999 Symposium* (pp. 145–164). Ann Arbor, MI: University of Michigan Press.

Thomas, J., & Short, M. (Eds.). (1996). *Using corpora for language research*. London: Longman.

Thurston, J., & Candlin, C. (1998). Concordancing and the teaching of the vocabulary of academic English. *English for Specific Purposes, 17*, 267–280.

Verhagen, A. (2000). Interpreting usage: Construing the history of Dutch causal verbs. In M. Barlow & S. Kemmer (Eds.), *Usage-based models of language* (pp. 261–286). Stanford, CA: Center for the Study of Language and Information.

Williams, G. C. (1998). Collocational networks: Interlocking patterns of lexis in a corpus of plant biology research articles. *International Journal of Corpus Linguistics, 3*, 151–171.

Youmans, G. (1991). A new tool for discourse analysis: The vocabulary management profile. *Language, 67*, 763–789.

Xue, G., & Nation, I. S. P. (1984). A university word list. *Language Learning and Communication, 3*, 215–229.

5. BEYOND SCIENCE AND IDEOLOGY CRITIQUE: DEVELOPMENTS IN CRITICAL DISCOURSE ANALYSIS[1]

Allan Luke

Critical discourse analysis (CDA) is an explicitly normative analysis of how texts and discourses work in ideological interests with powerful political consequences. This chapter provides an historical overview of CDA, placing it in the long lineage of attempts to develop a normative political linguistics beginning with Voloshinov. Recent approaches and procedures are discussed. These attempt to bring together text analysis with contemporary social, political, and cultural theory. The case is made that new conditions of economic and cultural globalization have created theoretical and empirical challenges for CDA and, more generally, for a critical applied linguistics. It is argued that these will require that CDA augment its strong focus on ideology critique with the study of texts that model the productive uses of power and discourse in new conditions.

A Genealogy of the Critical

Critical discourse analysis isn't new. But it is at a crucial point in its formation as method, as field, and as intellectual and political project. My purpose here is neither to recount or recant its procedures and methods for novices, nor to take sides on disputes between particular approaches for those who presently are using and refining it. Nor is my task to convince and convert the skeptical. There are numerous textbooks and key works in the field that do the job quite adequately, some cited here. My aim in this review is to historically and theoretically resituate critical discourse analysis, reviewing its key principles, current dilemmas, and possible futures.

Questions about the emergence and stability of a discipline are crucial for applied linguistics, with its impure history and practices, contested institutional position, and aspirations. There are many ways to explain the rise and fall of discourses and disciplines. These include now classical Kuhnian explanations of change of natural sciences that focus on paradigm crisis, unresolved anomalies in the field, and the formation of new theory. Such explanations concentrate on the internal dynamics of scientific discovery, and on the generative relationship of method and theory in the identification and solution of problems. By contrast, studies in the sociology of science stress political, cultural, and economic forces that historically shape the force of fields.

Turning to the state of critical discourse analysis (hereafter, CDA, having won its own acronym): What are we to make of a field that ties itself in word and deed, theory and method, to a normative, explicitly political inquiry into social, economic, and cultural power? How do we appraise research that sets out to disrupt and interrupt ideological common sense, everyday language use, and the codification of discourse power by dominant groups and interests? One answer, of course, is to treat it as an aberration in an otherwise unblemished march of linguistics *qua* normal science. This would be to argue that CDA doesn't stand directly in the lineage of a proper scientific, empirical linguistics and that it needlessly biases work on the pressing, practical tasks facing applied linguistics: the formation of language planning and policy and the teaching and learning of language and literacy in social institutions.

To do so would ignore a distinguished if incomplete history of attempts at a normative political linguistics, from the Voloshinov/Bakhtin circle to the more recent work of Michel Pecheux, Jacob Mey, and others. It also would fail to engage with the late-twentieth century acknowledgment among social scientists of the constitutive force of language and discourse in social formation and discipline, economic exploitation and power. CDA thus stands in *this* sustainable counter-tradition in linguistics, as against the technical, scientific projects of Humboldt, Saussure, and Chomsky. It is overtly skeptical of the claims of those postwar interactional and sociolinguistic approaches to the 'social' that are premised on liberal and neoliberal theories of the individual and society. Nor should it be surprising that we find its earliest 'revoicings' in early twentieth century European attempts to generate a neoMarxist analysis of language, linguistics, and signs that would seek to critique and transform material relations and conditions.

To treat CDA as a formalized corpus of analytic and methodological techniques thus might be to miss the point altogether. Critical discourse analysis is more akin to a repertoire of political, epistemic stances: principled reading positions and practices for the critical analysis of the place and force of language, discourse, text, and image in changing contemporary social, economic, and cultural conditions (Luke, 1997; van Dijk, 1993).

A more constructive approach might be to treat it as discourse itself, contingent upon particular historical conditions, agents and possibilities. It is a field of force, power, and relations in formation. New forms of social life in advanced capitalist societies turn on text and discourse. If indeed the emergence of the modern European nation-state, with all of its achievements and foibles, was driven by "print capitalism" (Anderson, 1991), it is clear that conditions of globalized capitalism are enabled by discourse-saturated technology and environments. We might term these *semiotic economies*, where language, text, and discourse become the principal modes of social relations, civic and political life, economic behavior and activity, where means of production and modes of information become intertwined in analytically complex ways.

The stances, positions, and techniques of CDA vary. There have been major attempts to formalize and codify approaches (Fairclough, 1992; Wodak, 1996). These synthesize a corpus of text analytic techniques drawn from a number of related areas: systemic linguistics, sociolinguistics and the ethnography of communications, ethnomethodology, pragmatics and speech act analysis, and narrative text grammar analysis. In turn, approaches to text analysis are integrated with concepts from contemporary social and cultural theory drawn, variously, from Frankfurt School critical theory, neoMarxist, poststructuralist and feminist cultural studies, Bourdieuian sociology, and, most recently, postcolonial and multiculturalist theory. How we stitch these together into an intellectual, explicitly political project is the task at hand. This is complicated given the predilections of some of the aforementioned models, both linguistic and social, toward comprehensive, rational grand theory, and the penchant of others for radical skepticism toward system and structure.

CDA, like all social inquiry, faces fundamental dilemmas: changing objects of study, as blended life-worlds and identities, transnational institutions and social formations, new forms of exploitation and oppression, and persistently troubling material and discourse conditions emerge. I will make the case here that, despite the articulation of canonical principles and regularized procedures and approaches, CDA and 'the critical' more generally cannot sit *in media res*. The next generation of CDA research must contend with blended and hybrid forms of representation and identity, and new spatial and temporal relations generated by the technologically enhanced 'flows' of bodies, capital, and discourse that characterize economic and cultural globalization. These are likely to require new, hybrid blends of analytic techniques and social theories. Part of this challenge, I argue here, is for CDA to move beyond a focus on ideology critique and to document 'other' forms of text and discourse—subaltern, diasporic, emancipatory, local, minority, call them what we may—that may mark the productive use of power in the face of economic and cultural globalization.

Like many other forms of contemporary social theory, the generational basis of CDA can be traced to the political events of 1968. This would include neoMarxist theories of interpellation and hegemony, as in the Birmingham Centre for Cultural Studies interpretations of Gramsci and Althusser (e. g., Hall, 1996). But it also explains the emergence of anti-essentialist, post-Marxist philosophies of discourse and society generated by Foucault and Derrida, and, more recently, Lyotard and Baudrillard's versions of postmodernity. Directly and indirectly, whether in response or reaction, much of this work was spurred by the student movements, especially the rise and perceived failure of the Marxist project in 1968. A *de facto* effect was a generational politicization of scholarship and research in Western academic work in social sciences and humanities. While the student revolution as political force may have met with varying degrees of success and failure, it succeeded in changing the character of university scholarship and life. The resultant work has been extremely intellectually generative and, as might have been expected, shifted the then emergent "linguistic turn" in the social sciences to another epistemological and political level: an understanding of the centrality of language, text, and discourse in the constitution of not just human subjectivity and social relations, but also social control and surveillance, the governance of polity and nation-state, and attendant modes of domination and marginalization, lived desire and pleasure.

With historical prototypes in the admixtures of political linguistics, pragmatics and neoMarxist theory by Jacob Mey, Michel Pecheaux, and colleagues over two decades ago; the powerful adaptation of systemic functional linguistics by Gunther Kress, Robert Hodge, Roger Fowler, and colleagues (see Kress & Hodge, 1979); and finally, its mature theoretical engagement with Foucault, Bourdieu, and Gramsci by Norman Fairclough and colleagues in the last decade, it would hardly be appropriate to define CDA as a newcomer, as an outsider to the formalized fields of linguistic-based discourse analysis, or to view it as a kind of radical chic moment that is likely to fade with shifts in partisan politics. But why is CDA still considered a fringe dweller in mainstream analysis? Relatedly, if it is to remain a sustainable field of inquiry and, indeed, a productive mode of sociopolitical intervention, what are its millennial theoretical and empirical challenges?

To survey the field: Through the editorial advocacy of Teun van Dijk in the journal *Discourse and Society*, CDA has achieved some degree of stability, canonicity, and, indeed, conventionality. Contemporary work in CDA has produced different, innovative analyses of a range of texts, some of which went unnoticed in conventional linguistic analysis. These include: violent and conflictual face-to-face exchanges in institutional settings; political speeches and parliamentary proceedings; advertising and mass media texts of all types; textbooks and other official pedagogic texts; different views of the political and economic dimensions of clinical, legal and service encounters; and, more recently, analysis of digitalized communications including online exchanges, mobile phone exchanges, and webpages. Graduate student theses openly declare CDA as a method and supervisors needn't look far for paradigmatically sympathetic examiners. Undergraduate and masters-level courses in CDA in education, cultural and literary studies, and linguistics are more common, with a host of 'how to' textbooks available from major publishers. Specific journals and publishers have staked their claims on the field; indeed, major encyclopedias and annual reviews such as this volume routinely assemble chapters on the topic. Its spread is uneven. It proliferates in the United Kingdom, Europe, and Australia in part because of the very different historical attitudes toward applied political analysis within the academy. But United States scholarship in such fields as feminist studies, critical legal studies, communications and media, multiculturalism, and critical race studies has applied

CDA to study matters of identity, control, and power.

Taken together, these are all signs that CDA is showing some signs of maturity, if not late adolescence. If indeed this is the case, and particularly for an analytic activity that is premised less on scientism than its own normative status as intervention, we can ask, first, how and to what extent CDA has moved from an emergent, marginal approach in applied linguistics and the host of affiliated fields noted above, and to what extent its key shared assumptions and approaches require critical self-inspection. That is, putting aside for a moment the debate over whether discourse analysis should be political, the question is how, with what analytic tools, and with what effects.

Method or Standpoint?

There have been significant attempts at taxonomies of analytic categories, most notably the continuing work of Fairclough (1989, 1992), Chouliaraki and Fairclough (1999) in the United Kingdom, European work by van Dijk (1997), Wodak (1996), and related work in the United States by Gee (1999). Though they vary considerably in technical specification, there share a common strategy. CDA involves a principled and transparent shunting back and forth between the microanalysis of texts using varied tools of linguistic, semiotic, and literary analysis and the macroanalysis of social formations, institutions, and power relations that these texts index and construct.

If there is a generalizable approach to CDA, then, it is this orchestrated and recursive analytic movement between text and context. But what differentiates it from previous attempts at socially-based linguistics is that it does not work from liberal and neoliberal, structural functionalist, and symbolic interactionist social theory. CDA sets out to capture the dynamic relationships between discourse and society, between the micropolitics of everyday texts and the macropolitical landscape of ideological forces and power relations, capital exchange, and material historical conditions. This sets CDA apart from the ubiquitous forms of social constructionist and interactionist analysis, particularly in educational studies, that draw liberally upon Vygotsky and Foucault *sans* materialist or micropolitical analysis. Consequently, attempts to systematize CDA draw, on the one hand, from theories and models of text analysis and, on the other, from contemporary social, political, and cultural theories.

For the former, text analysis, there are of course rich technical resources for 'doing' the classical work of discourse analysis; that is, for the parsing of text according to systematic and replicable rewrite rules. In instances, we can extract techniques directly from text linguistics more or less intact. For example, Kress and Hodge's (1979) and Fairclough's (1989) early descriptions of CDA are based upon Hallidayan analysis of formal properties of text, beginning with systematic analysis of lexical resources and categories, moving through a targeted analysis of syntactic functions (e. g., transitivity, modality), building toward the analysis of genre and text metafunction (e. g., macropropositional analysis, exchange structure). Consequently, like others who begin from a systemic functional perspective, these prototypes have a comprehensive focus on the *text qua intentional code*, a position that is theoretically compatible with a neoMarxist focus on ideology and hegemony.

In his organization of the field more generally, van Dijk (1997) offers a programmatic approach based on four categories: action, context, power, and ideology.[2] Within each of these he identifies guiding concepts, many of which are derived not from linguistics but variously from the ethnography of communication, Marxist theories of ideology, schema theoretic models of cognitive processing, and speech act theory. While not purporting to be a formal approach to critical discourse analysis, Gee's (1999) recent model involves methodological heuristics for six categories of discourse resources that subjects use to build representations. He calls these "semiotic building," "world building," "activity building," "identity and relationship building," "political building," and "connection building."

In contrast with Fairclough's approach, van Dijk (1997) and Gee (1999) both develop more theoretically eclectic toolkits, less oriented toward lexicosyntactic features of texts and more focused on the variable cultural and social resources and contexts required of text construction and comprehension. In this regard, both are able to move beyond a reliance on theories of ideology to engage with cognitive and connectionist theories of meaning and cognition, and social psychological work on identity. Their approaches balance an emphasis on the code with an emphasis on the agentive practices of text participation, comprehension, and use. This move matches work in cultural studies that shifts from a strong neoMarxist emphasis on ideological code to the ethnographic analysis of the variable, idiosyncratic uptake of text and discourse by audiences (Ang, 1991).

What sets CDA analyses apart is their attempt to inform text analyses with broader social theory. If, as I suggested earlier, the methodological tactic is to move back and forth from analysis of text to analysis of social formation and institution, then the text can only be made sense out of if we have sufficiently theorized power, political relations, material and historical change, and the social institutions under scrutiny. What this means is that the text analysis can only be explicitly normative and political if it explicates how "discourse does ideological work" (Wodak, 1996, p. 17), and (unlike, most overtly, ethnomethodology) if it has a strongly theorized reading of the social world.

But CDA equally needs to move beyond text analysis to the critical analysis of the visible practices of text interpretation and use. To build such a bridge, Fairclough's (1989) widely cited model of text and context draws from political economy: context is defined in terms of conditions of production and conditions of interpretation. These, in turn, are historically contested sites for ideological social relations and delimited by the availability of what Fairclough (1992) calls "members' resources" and van Dijk (1993) refers to as "social cognitions." These contexts could equally be construed as "social fields" for the agentive exchange of symbolic and cultural capital (Bourdieu, 1998). In such a model, the text becomes commodity and artifact subject to forces of production, alienation, appropriation, control, and so forth (cf. Mey, 1985). This is a programmatic way of defining context politically, and thereby avoids the kinds of individualist and depoliticized interactionist approaches to context that have characterized applied linguistics (Pennycook, 2000). However, it only partially resolves the problem of which social theory to select.

Fairclough (1992), Gee (1996), and Chouliaraki and Fairclough (1999) are the strongest attempts to engage with a range of major social theories. These works variously review neoMarxist and Frankfurtian theory, poststructuralist theory, Bourdieuian and Durkheimian sociology, postcolonial theory, and other sources with text analysis, focusing, variously, on contested definitions of discourse, ideology, hegemony, power, identity, and capital and adding their own specialized terminologies. Fairclough (1992) distinguishes between "discursive practice" and "social practice," discourse and "orders of discourse." Gee (1996) differentiates between what he terms "big 'D' discourse" from "little 'd' discourses" arguing for the primacy of the latter when acquired in the contexts of primary socialization. In so doing, this work builds a 'meso' analytic vocabulary around these terms that has the potential to open out readings of texts to more sophisticated institutional and political analysis. Alternately, it can, in weaker applications, simply act as a stand-in for a more rigorous sociological and cultural, or political and economic, analysis of the contexts and consequences of discourse.

My point is that a linguistic and text analytic metalanguage, no matter how comprehensive, cannot 'do' CDA in and of itself. It requires the overlay of a social theoretic discourses for explaining and explicating the social contexts, concomitants, contingencies and consequences of any given text or discourse. That is, what texts 'do' in the world cannot be explained solely through text analysis or text analytic language (Pennycook, 2000). To reiterate, the actual power of the text, its material and discourse consequences, can only be described by reference to broader social theoretic models of the world. In what we might term the logocentric fallacy, we run the risk of fetishizing the power of the text, preempting its local uptake, and presupposing the systematicity and consequences of its discourses. Let us take this as Foucault's cautionary and promissory note and return to it momentarily.

To summarize: CDA involves a principled shunting back and forth between analyses of the text and the social, between cultural sign and institutional formation, between semiotic/discourse analysis and the analysis of local institutional sites, between a normative reading of texts and a normative reading of the social world. In this way, where each analysis falls on these binary continua reenacts a central unresolved theoretical issue facing discourse theory and social theory alike: the contingent relationship between discourse change and changes in corporeal, spatialized, and material conditions; the relative power of social structure and human agency; the dynamics of bids at centralized state and corporate control versus local appropriation and resistance.

After two decades of discourse analysis and cultural studies, the poststructuralist axiom that "everything is discourse," or that "discourse talks things into existence" has become almost facile. While these are profound and potentially productively disruptive claims, they only take us so far toward a political and social analysis (Luke, 1997). It is a far more difficult task to trace, politically, which discourses have which material and discursive effects and consequences for communities, cultures, and human subjects. In this way, the methodological decisions facing us when we undertake any specific critical discourse analysis inevitably lead us back to the theoretical anomalies of its host theories.

Techniques in Search of a Theory

Reviewing key journals and collections in the field, it would appear that there are three common CDA genres of research: (1) traditional sociolinguistic, ethnomethodological, pragmatic, and systemic linguistic analyses that focus on social and political issues as their objects of study (e. g., racism, sexism, violence and oppression, political policies); (2) interactional and ethnomethodological analyses that graft Foucauldian concepts of power into data analysis; and (3) applications of approaches outlined by Fairclough, Wodak, and colleagues that aim to integrate detailed text analysis and depth engagement with recent social theory. What therefore differentiates the field are degrees and levels of explicit politicization, ranging from: (1) a content politicization called for by Wodak (1996) and van Dijk (1993), to (2) a relabeling of conventional analysis by the grafting of social theoretic lexicon, to (3) an explicit politicization of both theory and method.

We began this chapter by noting the binary tension within critical discourse analysis between linguistic formalism and ideology critique between science and politics. This may no longer be the central issue. Despite the ostensive tensions between text and social analysis, the shunting between them is tenable and coherent as long as it stays within the domains of particular rationalist, structuralist species of social theory. That is, linguistic formalism, historical materialism, and Frankfurtian ideology critique share a common focus on rationality, systematicity, and logical coherence. Linguistic structuralism, in its Hallidayan and other variants, views discourse and text as a meaning-producing microphysics, a network of systematically linked propositions, coherent and organized ideas. In a legacy that leads from Hegel through Althussarian determinism, Frankfurt School social theory and neoMarxist cultural studies hold that ideology is coherent, that there is a "logic" to capital, and a systematicity of intent and consequence to the texts and discourses of mass capitalism, whether state or multinational.

By contrast, the Foucauldian tradition is antistructuralist and post-Marxist, attempting to capture the almost Dionysian character of discourse in local sites. For our present purposes, we can begin from Foucault's (1982) definition of discourse as "systematically recurrent statements." The contribution of philosophical and literary poststructuralism to CDA is not simply the oft-cited recognition of the constitutive force of discourse in the formation of social and psychological identity, social, economic and political position. The insight that discourse systematically constructs human subjects, versions of 'reality,' relations of power and knowledge, as contestable as it may be to empiricists and positivists, is but our starting point. Foucault consistently warns his readers not to privilege or presuppose structure, not to suppose coherence, intention, systematicity. Discourse might be acting arbitrarily, randomly, and idiosyncratically for, he argues, it tends to take on a life of its own, autonomous from its historical authors, conditions of production, and so forth. This work marks the shift from a strong focus on the central and hegemonic production of discourse and its illocutionary and perlocutionary political intents to the unpredictable lateral and recursive traverse of discourse across institutions and social fields, and the idiosyncrasy and unpredictability of the local exchange and uptake of discourse.

The second, and equally profound, lesson from poststructuralism is based on Derrida's (1980) insights into absence and silence. For Derrida, the absent signifier, the 'unsaid' and the 'unwritten,' can be as significant as what is said. Because CDA has been more or less tied to linguistic modes of analysis, it has had great difficulties dealing not only with multimodal texts, issues of embodiment, place, and those things experienced corporeally and physically. It has even greater difficulty dealing with the unsaid and the unspeakable, that which is not present in visible linguistic traces. Even for an ideology critique, the silent and the absent, represented in terms of euphemism and implied intertextual references, can have powerful political effects.

This isn't to deny that discourse can have what classical ideological critiques call oppressive intents and effects, the patterns framed by van Dijk's (1993) important introduction to CDA. Nor should it distract us from the continuing need for ideology critique, particularly in semiotic economies where the boundaries between work and leisure, production and consumption, and private and civic lifeworlds are blurred and transgressed by media discourse and representation. In current conditions, new technologically mediated modes of surveillance and control sit alongside the forms of face-to-face symbolic violence and print-culture hegemony well documented in current work in CDA.

But discourse and its attendant knowledge/power configurations can be both positive and negative. In this regard they are not necessarily 'ideological' in the classical Marxist sense of deliberate distortion in the service of specific class interests. The fundamental challenge to ideology critique raised as early as Voloshinov's work remains: If all discourse is ideological, refractive, and distorting in the interests of dominant classes (and patriarchies), is it possible to have a nonideological text?

Answers may be found both in the work of Habermas (1984) and Freire and Macedo (1987). I refer here not just to the philosophic construct of "ideal speech situation" as a "counterfactual ideal" —the dialogic, democratic exchange recognised by Fairclough and Wodak as normative ideals. As well, I refer to the possibility of what Freire and colleagues term "emancipatory" discourses: those forms of talk, writing, and representation that are counter-ideological and act to articulate and configure collective interests in transformative ways.

Returning to its original aims: if CDA is a normative form of social science and political action, it must be able to demonstrate what 'should be' as well as what is problematic with text and discourse in the world. I am arguing that a key task facing an effectively normative CDA is to:

- identify and document, in neoMarxist terms, preferred modes of emancipatory discourse; and/or to
- analytically deconstruct, in poststructuralist terms, positive and productive configurations of power/knowledge in discourse.

Without such work, CDA risks becoming entrenched in a neo-Althussarian paradigm operating under the assumption that all media are forms of centrally controlled interpellation, and further assuming that the general populace are victims and objects of this ideological interpellation; then holding that the principal role of CDA practitioners is to act as Gramscian transformative intellectuals in the task of unveiling, countering, and consciousness-raising around dominant ideologies, with the aim of mobilizing opinion and action against them and their classes of producers.

The tension in CDA therefore is not solely between the micro/text analytic and macro/social analysis. I have here argued that the prevailing project of CDA is that of ideology critique, which shares with most forms of textual analysis the presupposition of order, systematicity, and logic. CDA has the productive potential to capture, describe, and critique a broader range of normative orders of discourse, including those that construct and transform knowledge and power relations in productive, equitable, and enfranchising ways. It would appear that, regardless of which initial philosophic turn in linguistic and political analysis we make—by starting from Hegel or Nietzsche—we return to issues of power.

CDA, Applied Linguistics, and New Times

Many current accounts treat CDA as a radical, 'alternative' field in formation, on the fringes of applied linguistics and sociolinguistics more generally. CDA is bound to be troubling to those who view linguistics as an archetypal disinterested science. Yet given the degree to which applied linguistics is indeed applied (with direct engagement with normative, politically charged fields for the commodification of knowledge and language; proscription of face-to-face educational intervention; the shaping of second language policy and pedagogy; and governmental language policy), the notion of a neutral, 'uncritical' applied linguistics itself is problematic. This is precisely the point of Pennycook's (2000) proposal for a "critical applied linguistics," an extension of his previous work on the implication of language education, planning, and policy in the practices of colonialism, neocolonialism, and, indeed, economic and cultural globalization.

I have argued that to move beyond a strong focus on ideology critique, CDA would need to begin to develop a strong positive thesis about discourse and the productive uses of power. To paraphrase Marcuse (1971), we would need to begin to capture an affirmative character of culture where discourse is used aesthetically, productively, and for emancipatory purposes. Yet it would appear that applied linguistics has progressed little in terms of the building of an analytic stance on the normative goals of discourse beyond Hymes' (1996) prototypical statements on "linguistic inequality."

Particularly in the case of education, the affirmative character of discourse can take many forms (Luke, 1995). The purview of CDA could include the documentation of:

1. minority discourses, diasporic voices, texts, and statements that are 'written out' and over by dominant institutions;
2. emergent discourses of hybrid identity generated by learners counter to dominant pedagogic discourses;
3. idiosyncratic local uptakes—Fairclough's conditions of interpretation—where human subjects take centrally broadcast or dominant texts and discourses and reinterpret, recycle, and revoice them in particular ways that serve their local political interests; and
4. those micropolitical strategies of interruption, resistance, and counter-discourse undertaken by speakers in face-to-face institutional and interpersonal settings.

What forms does productive, liberatory political speech take? What are the textual shapes and practices of 'open' and locally enabling social policies? What would a critical or normatively preferable representation of history in a textbook look like? If CDA is avowedly normative and explicitly political, than it must have the courage to say what is to be done with texts and discourse.

Much of this work is underway, but it is scattered across fields, disciplines, and journals. This renewed agenda would have the potential of pushing CDA through some of the epistemological impasses that I have described above. It might move CDA through generative and necessary, but ultimately self-limiting thresholds: a preoccupation with centrally broadcast texts as modes of ideology, balanced by politically undertheorized analyses of face-to-face exchanges. Perhaps rather than seek a theoretical consensus on what might count as CDA, we should seek out and engage with new objects of study and new theories of the social. I conclude with some comments on possible directions.

Theories of discourse momentarily aside, the empirical, phenomenal reality facing applied linguists and critical discourse analysts is that, for better and worse, semiotic systems have become the engines of globalization and of the new economies. In a now classical description of the new 'scapes' of cultural, economic and political globalization, Appadurai (1996) introduces the multilayered descriptive metaphor of "flows." We can describe the impacts of globalization in terms of the variably regulated and unregulated, systematic and chaotic, organized and disorganized, intentional and accidental flows of bodies, capital, and discourse across what historically were constrained and regulated geographic, geopolitical, and cultural borders and boundaries. The result is that many of the constants of postwar social formation—systems of government and regulation, economic exchange, and even place and displacement—have been disrupted, or, in instances, are morphing into different formations.

I have here described the strong reliance both by CDA, and by its more conventional predecessors and kin in linguistics and applied linguistics, on theories and models of the social that were devised to explain both traditional monopoly "print capitalism," and inter-and postwar nation-state governmentality. The result is that both CDA and current approaches to applied linguistics remain caught up very much in the dialectical analysis of economic and cultural disparity, political oppression, and repression. To date, this has led CDA to a successful focus on tracking changes in state, media, and corporate systems of representation, and on the public representation and repression of diversity and difference. Yet new times may require an expanded research agenda, one that focuses not just on the suppression of diasporic identities by dominant classes. Needed is one that engages with new textual configurations, one that de-reifies concepts of culture, and explores new definitions not only of discourse, but as well of language as necessarily blended, multiglossic, and transcultural. This will require that linguists and sociologists alike question the essentialist symmetries between language, culture, and nation that we continue to take for granted. It also indicates that a nonessentialist focus on blended forms of local "social cognition" (van Dijk, 1993), "cultural models" (Gee, 1999), and "members' resources" (Fairclough, 1992) may offer key insights into the "glocalized" (Robertson, 1992) uptake and use of transnational flows of discourses, images, and texts.

Our very approaches as 'liberal' and 'radical' applied linguists to addressing issues of state policies toward multilingualism and multiculturalism, issues of educational access and opportunity, and, indeed, to redressing matters of historical marginalization remain captured by the dialectics and Manichean allegories of oppressor/oppressed, mainstream/minority, privileged/deficit, center/margin, indeed, and North/South and Eastf/West. These include debates over whether the purposes of a redressive language and literacy education are, indeed, to ensure more equal access, to recognize and (repressively) tolerate linguistic diversity and new forms of identity, to enable direct access to mainstream "cultural capital" , or to teach various versions of the "critical," including CDA to students as a means of "empowerment" (Muspratt, Luke, & Freebody, 1997).

The challenges of economic and cultural globalization have already generated quite productive explorations of new social theory, including new materialist analyses (Comaroff & Comaroff, 2000) of transnational capital, theories of new geographical and social spaces (Soja, 1999), discussions of new forms of blended cosmopolitan identity (Cheah & Robbins, 1998), and, in educational studies, analyses of transnational youth and corporate culture. Taken together, these suggest that CDA and a project of "critical applied linguistics" forwarded by Pennycook (2000) may need new tools to describe new textual formations, new configurations of discourse, and, indeed, blended forms of governmentality and identity. Whether disinterested linguistic science and ideology critique in and of themselves are up to these complex methodological and theoretical challenges is moot.

Notes

1. The author wishes to thank Mary McGroarty for editorial assistance and advice; Carmen Luke and Alaister Pennycook for resources and ideas; Salla Lahdesmaki of the University of Helsinki, Yonjg Bing Liu, Katie Weir, and Margaret Kettle for rich discussion in the ongoing doctoral seminar on CDA at the University of Queensland.

2. Thanks to Katie Weir for drawing this work to my attention as part of her CDA research on curriculum and educational policy.

REFERENCES

Anderson, B. (1991). *Imagined communities: Reflections on the origin and spread of nationalism.* London: Verso.

Ang, I. (1991). *Desperately seeking an audience.* New York: Routledge.

Appadurai, A. (1996). *Modernity at large: Cultural dimensions of globalization.* Minneapolis: University of Minnesota Press.

Bourdieu, P. (1998). *Practical reason: On the theory of action.* Cambridge: Polity Press.

Cheah, P., & Robbins, B. (Eds.) (1998). *Cosmopolitics: Thinking and feeling beyond the nation.* Minneapolis: University of Minnesota Press.

Chouliaraki, L., & Fairclough, N. (1999). *Discourse in late modernity: Rethinking critical discourse analysis*. Edinburgh: Edinburgh University Press.

Comaroff, J., & Comaroff, J. F. (2000). Millennial capitalism: First thoughts on a second coming. *Public Culture, 12*(2), 291–343.

Derrida, J. (1980). *Writing and difference*. Chicago: University of Chicago Press.

Foucault, M. (1982). *The archaeology of knowledge*. New York: Pantheon.

Fairclough, N. (1989). *Language and power*. London: Longman.

Fairclough, N. (1992). *Discourse and social change*. Cambridge: Polity Press.

Freire, P., & Macedo, D. (1987). *Literacy: Reading the world and the world*. South Hadley, MA: Bergin & Garvey.

Gee, J. P. (1996). *Social linguistics and literacies* (2nd ed.). London: Taylor & Francis.

Gee, J. P. (1999). *An introduction to discourse analysis: Theory and method*. London: Routledge.

Habermas, J. (1984). *A theory of communicative action*. Boston: Beacon Press.

Hall, S. (1996). The meaning of new times. In D. Morley&K. Chen (Eds.), *Stuart Hall: Critical dialogues in cultural studies* (pp. 223–238). London Routledge.

Hymes, D. (1996). *Ethnography, linguistics and narrative inequality*. London: Taylor & Francis.

Kress, G., & Hodge, R. (1979). *Language as ideology*. London: Routledge.

Luke, A. (1995). Text and discourse in education: An introduction to critical discourse analysis. In M. W. Apple(Ed.), *Review of Research in Education, 21* (pp. 3–48). Washington, DC: American Educational Research Association.

Luke, A. (1997). The material effects of the world: Apologies, 'stolen children' and public discourse. *Discourse, 18*, 343–368.

Marcuse, H. (1971). *Negations: Essays in critical theory*. Boston: Beacon Press.

Mey, J. L. (1985). *Whose language? A study in linguistic pragmatics*. Amsterdam: John Benjamins.

Muspratt, S., Luke, A., & Freebody, P. (Eds.). (1997). *Constructing critical literacies*. Creskill, NJ: Hampton.

Pennycook, A. (2000). *Critical applied linguistics*. Mahwah, NJ: Lawrence Erlbaum.

Robertson, R. (1992). *Globalization: Social theory and global culture*. London: Sage.

Soja, E. (1999). *Third space*. London: Verso.

van Dijk, T. A. (1993). Principles of critical discourse analysis. *Discourse and Society, 4*, 249–283.

van Dijk, T. A. (Ed.) (1997). *Discourse studies: A multidisciplinary introduction, Vol. 2, Discourse as social interaction*. London: Sage.

Wodak, R. (1996). *Disorders of discourse*. London: Longman.

APPLICATIONS OF DISCOURSE ANALYSIS

6. GENRE: LANGUAGE, CONTEXT, AND LITERACY[1]

Ken Hyland

In the last decade genre approaches have had a considerable impact on the ways we understand discourse and in transforming literacy education in different contexts around the world. This chapter reviews the main directions of recent literature in both these areas, showing how the concept of genre is beginning to offer applied linguists a socially informed theory of language and an authoritative pedagogy grounded in research on texts and contexts. In terms of language description, I describe recent studies which seek to elaborate our understanding of generic integrity and variation, the ways that genres are seen as similar and different in terms of their internal structures and as systems of social processes. This research focuses on the contexts, lexi—grammatical features, and rhetorical patterns of genres. In terms of pedagogy, the chapter considers how genre approaches address central issues of language education and critical literacy and the ways that genre is applied in classrooms.

The last decade has seen increasing attention given to the notion of genre and its application in language teaching and learning. This interest has been driven by a dual purpose. The first is a desire to understand the relationship between language and its contexts of use. That is, how individuals use language to orient to and interpret particular communicative situations and the ways these uses change over time. The second is to employ this knowledge in the service of language and literacy education. This second purpose both complements research in New Literacy Studies, which regards literacy as social practice (Barton & Hamilton, 1998; Gee, 1996), and encourages us to explore language and pedagogies in ways that move beyond narrowly conceived formal and cognitivist paradigms.

Genre approaches have therefore had a considerable impact on the ways we see language use and on literacy education around the world by developing a socially informed theory of language and an authoritative pedagogy grounded in research of texts and contexts. The purpose of this article is to review some of the recent genre literature in both these areas, although the breadth of this work means I can make no claims to completeness. This review therefore covers those areas that seem most interesting and which offer the most for both research and teaching.

Some Background: The Situatedness of Genre Theories

Genres are abstract, socially recognized ways of using language. Genre analysis is based on two central assumptions: that the features of a similar group of texts depend on the social context of their creation and use, and that those features can be described in a way that relates a text to others like it and to the choices and constraints acting on text producers. Language is seen as embedded in (and constitutive of) social realities, since it is through recurrent use and typification of conventionalized forms that individuals develop relationships, establish communities, and get things done. So genre theorists locate participant relationships at the heart of language use and assume that every successful text will display the writer's awareness of its context and the readers which form part of that context. Genres are then, "the effects of the action of individual social agents acting both within the bounds of their history and the constraints of particular contexts, *and* with a knowledge of existing generic types" (Kress, 1989, p. 49).

Despite this general agreement on the nature of genre, analysts differ in the emphasis they give to either context or text; whether they focus on the roles of texts in social communities, or the ways that texts are organized to reflect and construct these communities. It is customary to identify three broad schools of genre theory (Hyon, 1996; Johns, in press). While it is possible to overemphasize the differences between what are essentially overlapping approaches, genre theories are themselves highly situated and this is a useful way of distinguishing different conceptions of genre in terms of the research and pedagogies they encourage.

First is the New Rhetoric group, consisting mainly of North Americans working within a rhetorical tradition and influenced by their work in universities and first language composition. This orientation draws on the seminal paper by

Miller (1984) and is represented in the work of Bazerman (1988), Freedman and Medway (1994), and Berkenkotter and Huckin (1995). Genre is regarded as "a socially standard strategy, embodied in a typical form of discourse, that has evolved for responding to a recurring type of rhetorical situation" (Coe & Freedman, 1998, p. 137). This orientation therefore principally concerns itself with investigating contexts, studying genre "as the motivated, functional relationship between text type and rhetorical situation" (Coe, 2002, p. 195). Methodologies tend to be ethnographic, rather than text analytic, with the aim of uncovering something of the attitudes, values, and beliefs of the communities of text users that genres imply and construct. The approach has not tended to address itself to the classroom, generally regarding it as an inauthentic environment lacking the conditions for complex negotiation and multiple audiences. Some recent contributions however have suggested pedagogic applications for academic writing (Adam & Artemeva, 2002; Coe, 2002).

A second orientation, based on the theoretical work of Michael Halliday's (1994) Systemic Functional Linguistics (SFL) and known in the United States as the 'Sydney School,' has stressed the importance of the social purposes of genres and of describing the schematic (rhetorical structures that have evolved to serve these purposes. Genre is seen as a staged, goal-oriented social process (Martin, 1992), emphasizing the purposeful, interactive, and sequential character of different genres and the ways that language is systematically linked to context. Work in this area has sought to explicate the distinctive stages, or moves, of genres together with the patterns of lexical, grammatical, and cohesive choices which "construct the function of the stages of the genres" (Rothery, 1996, p. 93). Significant contributions to this approach are Cope and Kalantzis (1993), Martin (1992, 1997), and Christie and Martin (1997). This approach is motivated by a commitment to language and literacy education, particularly in the context of schools and adult migrant programs (see Feez, 2001). A rich and sophisticated pedagogy has developed to provide the historically disadvantaged with access to the cultural capital of socially valued genres through an explicit grammar of linguistic choices.

The final perspective, generally referred to as the ESP approach, steers between these two views. Like the New Rhetoricians, it employs Bakhtinian notions of intertextuality and dialogism, but it also draws heavily on Systemic Functional understandings of text structure and, more sparingly, on Vygotskian principles of pedagogy. In fact, with its emphasis on communicative purpose and the formal properties of texts, the ESP approach might be seen as an application of SFL (Bloor, 1998), although it lacks a systematic model of language and does not make extensive use of a stratified, metafunctional grammar. Genre here comprises a class of structured communicative events employed by specific discourse communities whose members share broad communicative purposes (Swales, 1990). These purposes are the rationale of a genre and help to shape the ways it is structured and the choices of content and style it makes available. Those working in this tradition, such as Swales (1990, 1993), Bhatia (1993, 1999), and Johns (1997), like the Australians, are motivated by pedagogical applications. Much of their activity has thus focused on translating research findings into materials for both L1 and L2 tertiary students and professionals (Master, 2000; Swales & Feak, 1994, 2000).

Uniting these approaches is a common attempt to describe and explain regularities of purpose, form, and situated social action. For the Australian and ESP schools, there is an additional determination to render these understandings usable for teachers. In the following sections I will briefly review some of the directions that this work has taken in the last five years.

Generic Integrity: Moves and Beyond

Genres are rhetorical actions that we draw on to respond to perceived repeated situations; we recognize certain patterns of language/meaning choices as representing effective ways of getting things done in familiar contexts. As a result, one fruitful line of research has been to explore the lexico-grammatical and discursive patterns of particular genres to identify their recognizable structural identity, or what Bhatia (1999, p. 22) calls "generic integrity." Analyzing this kind of patterning is the staple of much ESP and SFL research, and has yielded useful information about the ways texts are constructed and the rhetorical contexts in which they are used, as well as providing valuable input for genre-based teaching.

Some of this research has followed the move analysis work pioneered by Bhatia (1993), Hopkins and Dudley-Evans (1988) and, most famously, Swales's (1990) description of the research article introduction. Recent work has focused on academic genres such as grant proposals (Connor, 2000; Connor & Mauranen, 1999), sections of the research article (Dubois, 1997; Holmes, 1997), and abstracts

(Hyland, 2000). Studies have also explored business genres such as direct mail letters (Upton, 2001), application letters (Henry & Roseberry, 2001), and business faxes (Akar & Louhiala-Salminen, 1999). Move analyses have also interested those working within an SFL framework, and recent work here has described various macro-genres such as narrative, recount, argument, and report, both in school and university contexts, in terms of their *stages* (or rhetorical structures) and the constraints on typical move sequences (Butt, Fahey, Feez, Spinks, & Yallop, 2000; Lock & Lockhart, 1999).

While analyzing schematic structures has proved an invaluable way of looking at texts, analysts are increasingly aware of the dangers of oversimplifying by assuming blocks of texts to be mono-functional and ignoring writers' complex purposes and "private intentions" (Bhatia, 1999). There is also the problem raised by Crookes (1986) many years ago, of validating analyses to ensure they are not simply products of the analyst's intuitions. Move shifts are, of course, always motivated outside the text as writers respond to their social context, but analysts have not always been convincingly able to identify the ways these shifts are explicitly signalled by lexico-grammatical patterning.

Increasingly, then, mainstream research has moved away from simple constituency representations of genre staging to examine clusters of register, style, lexis, and other rhetorical features which might distinguish particular genres. An important feature of much recent work has been a growing interest in the interpersonal dimensions of academic and technical writing. This research has sought to reveal how persuasion in various genres is not only accomplished through the representation of ideas, but also by the construction of an appropriate authorial self and the negotiation of accepted participant relationships. Once again, academic articles have attracted considerable attention in this regard, with recent work looking at, for example, imperatives (Swales, Ahmad, Chang, Chavez, Dressen, & Seymour, 1998), personal pronouns (Kuo, 1999), and hedges (Hyland, 1998). This work has also addressed theme choices in engineering reports (McKenna, 1997), grammatical sentence types in e-mail memos (Price, 1997), mitigation in teacher written feedback (Hyland & Hyland, 2001), and reader-oriented features of functional healthcare texts such as medicine-bottle labels (Wright, 1999).

One important feature of this research has been the adoption of more varied and triangulated methodologies. Recent work has increasingly extended analyses beyond the page to the sites where relationships, and the rules which order them, can facilitate and constrain composing (Gollin, 1999), and to the communities in which texts will be used and judged (Hyland, 2000). Thus research has explored ethnographic case studies (Prior, 1995), reader responses (Locker, 1999), group composition and revising (Pogner, 1999), and interviews with insider informants (Hyland, 2000). Such approaches promise to infuse text analyses with greater validity and to offer richer understandings about the production and use of genres in different contexts.

Genre theorists have also recently begun to turn their attention to longer and more complexly structured genres. Addressing Stubbs's (1996) criticism that analysts have largely concentrated on conveniently short texts, writers have explored texts such as Stephen Jay Gould's popular science books (Fuller, 1998), school textbooks (Coffin, 1997; Veel, 1998), and Ph. D. dissertations (Bunton, 1999). Bunton, for instance, shows how writers use metatextual signals to orient and guide their readers through Ph. D. theses, employing devices which vary in terms of their scope and distance to structure texts which may be as long as 500 pages.

Eggins and Slade's (1997) *Analysing casual conversation* is also interesting in this regard, not only because of the relative paucity of work on spoken genres, but because of the uncertain status of conversation as a genre (e. g., Swales, 1990). Drawing on the analytical tools of both SFL and Conversation Analysis, Eggins and Slade argue that casual conversations are used to negotiate social identity and interpersonal relationships, and that they have clear structures beyond simple openings, closings, and adjacency, giving examples of narrative, anecdote, recount, and opinion as text types within conversational interactions. Further insights into spoken genres are likely to emerge when analyses of data such as that held in the British Academic Spoken English (BASE) corpus, at the Universities of Warwick and Reading, and the Michigan Corpus of Academic Spoken English (http: //www. hti. umich. edu/micase/) become available.

Finally in this section, research has also begun to explore the complex interactions between verbal and nonverbal features of texts, building on the seminal work of Kress and van Leeuwen (1996). Much of this work has explored text-visual interrelations in academic genres, particularly as visual elements in science textbooks and papers have increased in both size and importance over the years (e. g., Bazerman, 1988; Berkenkotter & Huckin, 1995). Myers (1997), for example, looks at the ways textbook diagrams refer and express certainty while Miller (1998) uses an SFL analysis to show the genre variation of visual elements in *Science* and *Newsweek*; noting how in one they function as argument and in the other as explanation. Lemke (1998) examines a number of science genres to show how scientific communication works by the "joint co-deployment" of two or more semiotic modalities. Characterizing science writing as primitive forms of hypertext, where readers typically jump between text, diagrams, and tables, he argues that "joint visual-verbal thematic formation" provides the basis for contextualizing and understanding multimedia texts.

Generic Resources and Functional Variation

All theories of genre rest on notions that groups of texts are similar or different, that texts can be classified as one genre or another. In addition to the research on specific genres, there is a growing body of work which examines language variation across genres and the resources available for creating meanings in a culture. This research is valuable in that it is beginning to reveal how the patterns of rhetorical features of specific genres construe different contexts. That is, how genres reflect the different personal and institutional purposes of writers, the different assumptions they make about their audiences, and the different kinds of interactions they create with their readers.

Examples of this research include Burgess's (2000) comparison of the rhetorical move structures of online and print academic book reviews in linguistics, Ferguson's (2001) examination of the ways conditionals are used across different genres of medical discourse, and Hyland's studies of the different frequency and purposes of metadiscourse in different sections of company annual reports (1998) and between textbooks and research papers (Hyland, 1999b). These last two analyses illustrate how metadiscourse comprises a range of linguistic resources for constructing an appropriately authoritative and persuasive rhetorical persona, allowing writers in different genres to convey their personality, credibility, reader sensitivity, and evaluation of propositional matter.

Bondi's (1999) monograph length study of a variety of key genres from economics is a good example of what detailed analyses of genre variation can tell us about similarities and differences in the contexts created by discourse. Using functional and rhetorical analyses, Bondi explores the dialogic features of academic argument in both the expert-expert discourses of research papers and abstracting journals and the 'dissemination' genres of textbooks and newspaper articles. Her analyses show how argument is always dialogic, "not only because it presupposes the active role of an addressee, but because it involves a plurality of voices" (p. 5) Focusing on a range of features such as argument forms, voice, patterns of quantifiers, the use of hypotheticality and analogy, theme choices, and speech act verbs, the author suggests some of the ways that writers construct both expert and novice audiences and shows how this construction offers a representation of the discipline of economics.

The social dependency of genre practices can also be clearly seen in their variability across time. Historically, research papers looked much like the argument forms of theology and philosophy until the mid-17th century when Boyle and his colleagues laid down verification procedures which encouraged a rhetoric which gave primacy to the constructive role of the observer. In their notable studies of the evolution of scientific discourse, both Valle (1999) and Atkinson (1999) employ detailed textual analyses to show how changing social conditions, particularly the growing professionalism and specialization of academic disciplines, have gradually transformed textual practices. Research genres have become less affectively and 'narratively' focused and more 'informational' and abstract. They have increasingly displayed an emphasis on discussion and the embedding of texts in codified frames of knowledge at the expense of descriptions of experiments and results. Although they focus on the progressively greater anchoring of research papers in discourse communities, these studies also clearly demonstrate the wider importance of understanding genres as dynamic and socially situated.

From the SFL perspective, the relationship between language and context is also seen in the varied uses to which language is put, with genres being particular configurations of field (what is going on), tenor (who is involved), and mode (what the role of language is). Genres are patterns of discourse for expressing meanings in context, and the basic components of meaning, or macro-functions, are called ideational, interpersonal, and textual (see Martin, this volume). Researchers have therefore explored the linguistic resources for expressing these macrofunctions, modeling the ways that writers and speakers represent the world, interact with each other, and control textual flow, that can be used in different genres.

One example of this work is Halliday's (1998) continuing interest in *grammatical metaphor* in physics writing. This explores how scientists reconstrue human experience by presenting processes as things, packaging complex phenomena as a single element of clause structure. Grammatical metaphor freezes an event, such as atoms bond rapidly, and repackages it as an object, Rapid atom bonding. Adverbs become adjectives, processes become nouns, and nouns become adjectival, creating a noun phrase. Turning processes into objects in this way embodies scientific epistemologies that seek to show relationships between entities. Grammatical metaphor is also central to physics because it allows writers to thematize processes in order to say something about them and to manage the information flow of a text more effectively. But while grammatical metaphor has developed with modern science, the pressure to organize ever more, and more technical, information into written texts has also seen its emergence in many contemporary bureaucratic and institutional genres (Iedema, 1997; Rose, 1998).

In addition to this focus on ideational resources, writers have also recently started to explore interpersonal uses of language, particularly evaluative language (Coffin, 1997; Hunston & Thompson, 2001). Evaluation refers to a speaker/writer's attitudes and values, often termed 'stance,' 'affect,' or 'appraisal,' and it is important both as a system of organizing discourse and a means by which individuals express their value systems and those of their communities. Building on his earlier work, Martin (2001) characterises the resources of appraisal as affect (for expressing emotion), judgment (evaluating behavior in ethical terms), and appreciation (for valuing objects aesthetically), with additional resources for amplification and engagement. The appraisal system is often used in tandem with the separate system of involvement, including naming, slang, technical, or taboo terms, etc., which is designed to negotiate solidarity. Clearly these kinds of typologies can reveal patternings of interpersonal meanings across genres, and work has already begun to show how these resources work in fictional narrative (Martin, 1997), biography (Martin, 2000), and school history textbooks (Coffin, 1997).

Generic Variation and Cultural Contexts

While analysts regard genre as ensuring a degree of inherent rhetorical stability, they also recognize that it implies variability. A single genre can differ in relation to culture, historical period, social community, and communicative setting because users are always aware of their contexts and draw on other texts they are familiar with. The notion of generic integrity is therefore seen in terms of constraints on allowable configurations rather than the identical reproduction of features. Swales's (1990) notion of prototypes and Hasan's (1989) concept of generic structure potential are useful here, suggesting that texts spread along a continuum of approximation to core genre examples with varying options and restrictions operating in particular cases. Our ability to recognize the resemblance of any text to a genre prototype is thus a consequence of exposure to these genres and our experience of using them in specific contexts. In this section I will look at some of the work which reveals this variation.

Although analyses of English language texts dominate the literature, a flourishing field of research has begun to address the ways that preferred patterns of exposition, argument, and interaction differ across cultures and languages (see Connor, 1996, in press). Recent research includes comparisons of move structures ve structures of sales letters in English and Chinese (Zhu, 2000), letters of recommendation by writers in Germany, Eastern Europe, the United Kingdom, and the United States (Precht, 1998), and the rhetorical choices of the same news stories in the Chinese and English language press in Hong Kong (Scollon, 2000). Contrastive rhetoric has lately been criticized for often characterizing groups as static and homogenous (Spack, 1997), for dichotomizing the rhetorical practices of East and West (Kubota, 1999), and for the ideological implication that all English users should conform to Anglo-American genre patterns (Kachru, 1999). However, there is little doubt that cultural contexts influence writing in important ways, and to ignore these differences is to ignore the pluricentricity of genre construction and perhaps the chance to use such knowledge to develop cross-cultural understandings and teaching materials.

In addition to the ways that national or linguistic cultures influence writing, research in ESP has increasingly begun to explore the impact of corporate, institutional, and disciplinary cultures on genres. Berkenkotter and Huckin once famously observed that "genre conventions signal a discourse community's norms, epistemology, ideology, and social ontology" (1995, p. 21), and research into the relationships among textual form, social action, and cultural expectations has revealed the inherently social nature of genres and their power to shape both our individual perceptions and social institutions. Recent work here includes the edited collections by Bargiela-Chiappini and Nickerson (1999a) and Gunnarson, Linell, and Nordberg (1997) on professional genres, and by Samraj (2000) and Hyland (1998, 1999b, 2000, 2001) on academic disciplines. This research suggests that argument, content, structure, and interactions are community defined and that genres are often the means by which institutions are constructed and maintained. It shows that by focusing on the distinctive rhetorical practices of different communities, we can more clearly see how language is used and how the social, cultural, and epistemological characteristics of different disciplines and professions are made real.

Clearly this work draws on the rather contested, yet powerful, metaphor of discourse community to join writers, texts, and readers in a particular discursive space. Often criticized as altogether too structuralist, static, abstract, and deterministic, the notion of discourse community nevertheless foregrounds the socially situated nature of genre and helps illuminate something of what writers and readers bring to a text, implying a certain degree of intercommunity diversity and a degree of intra-community homogeneity in generic forms. For the most part, recent research has sought to capture the explanatory and predictive authority of the concept without framing communities as sociological utopias of shared and agreed upon values and conventions. Instead we find attempts to re-evaluate, and rehabilitate, the idea of discourse community, replacing the idea of an overarching force that determines behavior, with that of systems in which multiple beliefs and practices overlap and intersect (Bargiela-Chiappini & Nickerson, 1999b; Hyland, 2000; Swales, 1998).

Interdiscursivity, Genre Mixing, and Genre Sets

While early genre studies may have set out to identify genre-specific language, the use of corpora has shown this to be a more complex task than first realized (e. g. Biber, Johansson, Leech, Conrad, & Finegan, 1999). The research sketched above therefore seeks to characterize and show relationships among particular genres rather than define their immanent properties. In this regard genre analysis has been considerably influenced by the concepts of intertextuality and interdiscursivity (Bakhtin, 1986) and the processes by which texts and events are mediated through relationships with other texts. Sometimes these relationships involve the mixing of genres in ways that blur clear distinctions, perhaps to the extent that new genres become recognized in a community's nomenclature (e. g., *infotainment, advertorial,* and *docudrama*).

The notion of genre mixing has been widely discussed by Bhatia (1997). He notes that while a genre is identified by reference to the typical communicative purpose that it tends to enact, many professional genres serve a variety of purposes associated with novel and changing contexts. Like Fairclough (1995), Bhatia sees the increasing intrusion of promotional elements into information-giving genres as diverse as news editorials, academic book introductions, legal documents, and bureaucratic reports. In addition, however, he also identifies a tendency of professional genres to mix not only a variety of communicative purposes, but also private intentions within the context of socially recognized communicative contexts (Bhatia, 1997).

However, while genres are dynamic and subject to manipulation (Berkenkotter & Huckin, 1995), genres typically respond significantly to contextual changes only over relatively long periods. How then can we determine the degree of flexibility that is possible within generic constraints? The extent to which we can identify particular features as 'borrowing' from other genres is uncertain because the notion of 'mixing' presupposes the possibility of 'pure' and independent generic forms. It assumes that academic introductions, for instance, were once neutral informational texts that became infected with persuasive or promotional features. To describe certain genres as hybrid, then, we need to establish what an actual 'homogenous' text looks like and come up with a model of how mixing is accomplished (Hyland, 2000). This is an important area that is only likely to be clarified when we have more research evidence to sharpen our theories about genre variation and change.

The Systemic writers view this issue rather differently, preferring to look at genre features in terms of the co-occurrence of linguistic patterns which relate them to their contexts, rather than to vague notions of 'promotional' or 'informational' elements. One approach to genre blends is to distinguish the categories of genre and text-type (Paltridge, 2002), enabling a genre to include more than one 'text type.' Thus rhetorical components can combine serially rather than mix together so that an editorial might be composed of an exposition, a discussion, and a rebuttal. Equally, more than one genre may share the same text type, allowing us to see how scientific lab reports, instruction manuals, recipes, and directions for self-assembly furniture all consist of a sequence of commands optionally prefaced by a list of ingredients or apparatus (Rose, 1998).

Mainstream SFL does not make a theoretical distinction between genre and text type, although political debates in Australia have led to the latter term being used in teacher education, instructional materials, syllabus documents, and so forth. Instead, Martin (1995) has proposed the term macro genre for texts which combine more fundamental elemental genres such as recounts, narratives, explanations, and so on. He further suggests (Martin, 1997) a number of complex structuring principles to describe how interpersonal, ideational, and textual features can range over an entire text. These he calls *partitioning*, where the text unfolds segmentally in various ways, typically through layout, headings, etc. ; staging, where layers of theme and new elements help scaffold a text; and phasing, whereby a text is organized with more or less abrupt transitions (Martin & Rose, in press).

There is, then, clearly enormous potential for internal heterogeneity and feature-blending of genres which raises important issues of unity and identity. This obviously forces us to examine how we see and use genres and suggests that our understanding of discourse is itself socially constructed by the ways we see and act in the world. Genres help unite the social and the cognitive because they are central to how we understand, construct, and reproduce our social realities. But while we need a shared sense of genre to accomplish understanding, genre research increasingly shows that we do not need to assume that genres are fixed, monolithic, discrete, and unchanging.

Related to this growing interest in the ways texts are produced and connected to other texts is the concept of 'genre sets' or 'systems,' originally discussed by Devitt (1991) and Bazerman (1994). While this concept has yet to be fully explored and elaborated, it is clear that genre sets may be an important way of conceptualizing social contexts and understanding the ways texts cluster to constitute particular social and cultural practices. Genres may be networked in a constrained linear sequence, for example, as in the case of those contributing to a formal job offer (Paltridge, in press), or the progress of an academic paper from submission to publication. Alternatively, they may more loosely cohere as a 'repertoire' of options in a particular context, such as the choice of a formal letter, a brief e-mail, or a social chat as a means of finding some information (Swales,

2000), each mode selection requiring different genre options. Systemists talk here of 'genre agnation' (Martin, 1997) and seek to model systems of genres through a topological perspective which locates texts on a cline of functional similarity and difference. These systems can then be used to identify learner pathways for teaching about texts and provide students with a means of making sense of non-prototypical cases.

Equally, the notion of genre sets and systems is likely to play an increasingly important role in the ways we understand and study connections between the structural properties of institutions and individual communicative actions. Further research here will not only reveal how genres evolve, but perhaps reveal more about how disciplines and professions are organized and orchestrated through their systems of genres. The implications of this for teaching also need to be elaborated, but there would seem to be obvious advantages in describing the systems of genres relevant to our students (Christie & Martin, 1997, Paltridge, 1995).

Genre, Literacies, and Ideology

A central principle of genre theory is that genres are ideological. This is true in both the sense that no texts are free of the values and beliefs of their users and the sense that some genres are more dominant and hegemonic within a community. Genres are systems of meaning which help construct the social realities within which we live, and so this advantages those who have access and control of valued genres and disadvantages others who do not. Conceptions of genre thus have a close affinity with current work in literacy studies. They reinforce the view that all uses of written language are socially situated and indicative of broader social practices (Barton & Hamilton, 1998; Barton, Hamilton & Ivanic, 2000), and bring an important text-analytic dimension to literacy studies.

The New Rhetoric perspective, with its emphasis on the socially constructed nature of genre and on unpacking the complex relations between texts and contexts, provides important insights and support for ideological views of genre. Research here has helped to reveal the social, cultural, ideological, and political foundations of texts; the ways they evolve and change in response to their contexts; and how this also works to reshape those contexts (Berkenkotter & Huckin, 1995; Coe, 2002). It thus opens up the possibility of challenge and resistance. But while this perspective underlines the position that literacy is not the single set of technical skills or a monolithic competence it is often perceived to be, this orientation has not directly engaged with the central issues of ideology and literacy education. These issues include the most effective ways of providing students with both access to the powerful discourses and genres of particular communities and the means to critique these textual and cultural practices.

The goals of Australian and ESP genre pedagogies, however, have been to intervene in the process of literacy development, providing students with an explicit knowledge of relevant genres so they can act effectively in their target contexts. The teaching of key genres is seen as a means of helping learners gain access to ways of communicating that have accrued cultural capital in particular communities. In ESP this represents demystification and control of the academic and professional genres that will enhance or determine learners' career opportunities; in Australia it constitutes access to the complete range of life choices for marginalized social groups (Feez, 2001; Macken-Horarik, 2002; Martin, 2000). The central notion here is that students stand more chance of success in a transparent curriculum which makes the genres of power visible and attainable through explicit induction.

For critical literacy theorists, however, this commitment to a redistribution of literacy resources is not enough (e. g., Benesch, 2001). Providing access to the dominant genres of our culture does nothing to change the power structures that erect and support these prestigious practices, nor to challenge the social inequalities which are maintained through exclusion from them. This, of course, is a charge that could be leveled at most other approaches to literacy—but surprisingly rarely is. U. S. process pedagogies, for instance, have not been noted for their impact on sociopolitical consciousness-raising. Indeed, by failing to provide students with better access to powerful genres, such pedagogies simply perpetuate inequalities. Typically, valued genres are abstract, technical, and metaphorical, increasingly infiltrated by valorized scientific and bureaucratic discourses (Rose, 1998), and sharply differentiated from vernacular genres of the home and neighborhood (Barton & Hamilton, 1998). Without the resources to understand these genres, students will continue to find their own writing practices regarded as failed attempts to approximate prestigious forms (Christie, 1996; Johns, 1997; Lea & Street, 1999).

Genre approaches, in fact, seem to offer the most effective means for learners to both access and critique cultural and linguistic resources (Hammond &

Macken-Horarik, 1999). The provision of a rhetorical understanding of texts and a metalanguage to analyze them allows students to see texts as artifacts that can be explicitly questioned, compared, and deconstructed, so revealing the assumptions and ideologies that underlie them (Fairclough, 1995). Moreover, because genre theories take a social view of language use, they show that literacy varies with context and cannot be distilled down to a set of cognitive or technical abilities. Literacy is revealed as a relative term, representing a wide variety of practices appropriate for particular times, places, participants, and purposes. By focusing on the literacy practices they encounter at school, at work, and at university, genre pedagogies help learners to distinguish these differences and provide them with a means of conceptualizing their varied experiential frameworks. Highlighting variability thus helps undermine a deficit view which sees writing difficulties as learner weaknesses and which misrepresents writing as a universal, naturalized, self-evident, and noncontestable way of participating in communities (Barton et al., 2000; Candlin & Plum, 1999).

Genre-based Pedagogies

Genre-based pedagogies rest on the idea that literacies are community resources which are realized in social relationships, rather than the property of individual writers struggling with personal expression. This recognition, however, has been applied in a variety of different ways and educational contexts.

The New Rhetoricians' emphasis on situated learning theories (Chaiklin & Lave, 1996) and their reservations about the value of explicit genre teaching have largely restricted their pedagogic contribution to providing a 'facilitative environment' for engaging with academic or workplace writing. In ESP and SFL pedagogic contexts, however, teachers cannot take learners' motivation for granted, nor rely on them having the appropriate cultural, social, and linguistic background to effectively 'engage' with genres. Instead, pedagogies begin with the assumption that students' current norms and literacy abilities are widely different from those that they need, and that clear, research-grounded, genre descriptions are required to bridge this gap. Learning to write thus involves acquiring an ability to exercise appropriate linguistic choices, both within and beyond the sentence, and teachers can assist this by providing students with an explicit functionally-oriented grammar and models of effective texts.

The SFL pedagogic model typically conceives of the teaching and learning process as a cycle, allowing students different points of entry and enabling teachers to gradually and systematically expand the meanings students can create through increasingly sophisticated understanding of how texts work (e. g., Rothery, 1996). This methodology draws on Vygotsky's notion of a scaffolding to support the learner through an interactive process of contextualization, analysis, discussion, and joint negotiation of texts. An excellent example of this approach can be explored online in the New South Wales, Australia, K-6 English syllabus (http: // www. boardofstudies. nsw. edu. au/k6/k6english. html), and recent elaborations can be found in Feez (2001), Hammond and Macken-Horarik (1999), and Macken-Horarik (2002). In addition, classroom ideas have lately been proposed for modeling theme (Fries, 1997), focusing on genre and text-types (Paltridge, 2002), exploiting genre sets (Paltridge, in press), and establishing text-based syllabuses (Feez, 1998).

ESP has tended to adopt a more eclectic set of pedagogies, united by a commitment to needs analysis, contextual analysis, and genre description (see Johns, 1997, in press). These pedagogies, however, are becoming increasingly explicit and coherent as a number of recent notable contributions have begun to spell out procedures, materials, and rationales more clearly and to ground them in both sound theory and solid research. Johns (1997), for instance, recommends teaching genres using methods that require students to reflect on their genre practices, investigate the texts and contexts of their disciplines, and produce mixed-genre portfolios. Dudley-Evans and St. John (1998) emphasize the importance of cooperative pedagogies, Swales and Lindemann (2002) address themselves to teaching the literature review, and Flowerdew (2000) shows how the problem-solution pattern can be taught in engineering reports. A textbook by Swales and Feak (2000) employs a genre-based approach which has a strong focus on rhetorical consciousness-raising through student analyses of the practices and discourse in their fields. Benesch (2001) takes a critical perspective to reveal how the teaching of genres can be related to the ability to critique them.

Finally, research has also recently turned to evaluating the effectiveness of genre teaching in ESP contexts, with positive benefits noted for both reading (Hyon, 2002; Sengupta, 1999) and writing (Henry & Roseberry, 1998). Some experienced teachers, however, remain cautious and recommend careful planning to avoid prescriptivism and ensure appropriate attention to context (Kay & Dudley-Evans, 1998). Doubtless these teachers will be reassured, encouraged, and greatly assisted by two new books. Johns (2002) and Paltridge (in press) offer practical, accessible, and theoretically grounded approaches to genre pedagogy and include many sensible suggestions for classroom practice.

Conclusion

While I have attempted to cover some core areas of current research and practice in genre. I am aware of huge gaps. There is, for example, little here on work in languages other than English, on new electronic genres, on the constraints of composing contexts, or on genre and reading research. These omissions are partly due to limits of space and awareness, but also highlight areas of relative neglect in genre work. Nevertheless, I hope to have shown something of the range, dynamism, and potential of genre theories to research and pedagogy. Genre approaches have their flaws and exclusions, but through their attempts to unite language, purpose, and context, they continue to refine our conceptions of discourse, literacy, and community and to extend the ways we practice applied linguistics.

Notes

1. My thanks are due to Ann Johns and Brian Paltridge for prepublication copies of their new books, to Fiona Hyland for comments on my draft, and to my Sydney Sisters, Susan Feez, Sue Hood, and Bev Derewianka, for their suggestions and patient efforts to initiate me into the mysteries of SFL.

ANNOTATED BIBLIOGRAPHY

Bargiela-Chiappini, F., & Nickerson, C. (Eds.) (1999a). *Writing business: Genres. media and discourses.* London: Longman.

   A wide-ranging, well-written and strongly interdisciplinary collection concerned with the analysis of business genres in commercial settings, particularly those using electronic media.

Christie, F. & Martin, J. R. (Eds.) (1997). *Genre and institutions: Social processes in the workplace and school.* London: Continuum.

An excellent showcase of current SFL work in genre. The collection shows how genres enact social practices and facilitate apprenticeship in a variety of institutional contexts. In so doing it presents a coherent theory of genre in constructing experience.

Hyland, K. (2000) *Disciplinary discourses: Social interactions in academic writing.* London: Longman.

This book takes a broadly social constructionist perspective focusing on the interactional rhetorical elements of various key academic genres. Using corpus analysis and insider interviews the author attempts to show how genre choices reflect and construct the epistemological and social realities of the disciplines.

Johns, A. (Ed.) (2002). *Genre in the classroom: Multiple perspectives.* Mahwah, NJ: Lawrence Erlbaum.

An outstanding collection of articles providing a clear and readable understanding of the issues and problems of applying genre-based pedagogies. The papers draw on theory, research, and practical experience to illustrate what each of the three schools of genre can offer teachers.

Paltridge, B. (in press). *Genre and the language learning classroom.* Ann Arbor: University of Michigan Press.

A well-written, informative, hands-on book for teachers. The book provides both a clear and comprehensive overview of the main theoretical and practical issues of genre-based teaching for newcomers together with sensible and imaginative advice for applying genre in the classroom.

OTHER REFERENCES

Adam, C., & Artemeva, N. (2002). Writing instruction in English for Academic Purposes (EAP) classes: Introducing second language learning to the academic community. In A. M. Johns (Ed.), *Genre in the classroom* (pp. 175–194). Mahwah, NJ: Lawrence Erlbaum.

Akar, D., & Louhiala-Salminen, 1. (1999). Towards a new genre: A comparative study of business faxes. In F. Bargiela-Chiappini & C. Nickerson (Eds.), *Writing business: Genres, media and discourses* (pp. 207–226). London: Longman.

Atkinson, D. (1999). *Scientific discourse in sociohistorical context: The philosophical transactions of the Royal Society of London, 1675–1975*. Mahwah, NJ: Lawrence Erlbaum.

Bakhtin, M. (1986). *Speech genres and other late essays*. Austin: University of Texas Press.

Bargiela-Chiappini, F., & Nickerson, F. (1999b). Business writing as social action. in F. Bargiela-Chiappini, & F. Nickerson (Eds.), *Writing business: Genres, media and discourses*. (pp. 207–226.). London: Longman.

Barton, D., & Hamilton, M. (1998). *Local literacies*. London: Routledge.

Barton, D., Hamilton, M., & Ivanic, R. (Eds.). (2000). *Situated literacies: Reading and writing in context*. London: Routledge.

Bazerman, C. (1988). *Shaping written knowledge*. Madison: University of Wisconsin Press.

Bazerman, C. (1994). Systems of genres and the enactment of social intentions. In A. Freedman & B. Medway (Eds.), *Genre and the new rhetoric* (pp. 79–101). London: Taylor and Francis.

Benesch, S. (2001). *Critical English for academic purposes: Theory, politics and practice*. Mahwah, NJ: Lawrence Erlbaum.

Berkenkotter, C., & Huckin, T. (1995). *Genre knowledge in disciplinary communication*. Hillsdale, NJ: Lawrence Erlbaum.

Bhatia, V. K. (1993). *Analysing genre: Language use in professional settings*. London: Longman.

Bhatia, V. K. (1997). The power and politics of genre. *World Englishes, 17*, 359–371.

Bhatia, V. K. (1999). Integrating products, processes, processes and participants in professional writing. In C. N. Candlin, & K. Hyland (Eds.), *Writing: Texts, processes and practices* (pp. 21–39). London: Longman.

Biber, D., Johansson, S., Leech, G., Conrad, S., & Finegan, E. (1999). *Longman grammar of spoken and written English*. Harlow: Pearson.

Bloor, M. (1998). English for Specific Purposes: The preservation of the species (Some notes on a recently evolved species and on the contribution of John Swales to its preservation and protection). *English for Specific Purposes, 17*, 47–66.

Bondi, M. (1999). *English across genres: Language variation in the discourse of economics*. Modena: Edizioni Il Fiorino.

Bunton, D. (1999). The use of higher level metatext in Ph. D. theses. *English for Specific Purposes, 18*, S41–S56.

Burgess, S. (2000, November). 'Books for review' and reviewers for books: A genre analysis of print and electronic reviews in linguistics. Paper presented at Research and Practice in Professional Discourse Conference. City University of Hong Kong.

Butt, D., Fahey, R., Feez, S., Spinks, S. & Yallop, C. (2000). *Using functional grammar: An explorer's guide*, 2nd. ed. Sydney: National Centre for English Language Teaching and Research (NCELTR).

Candlin, C. N., & Plum, G. A. (1999). Engaging with challenges of interdiscursivity in academic writing: researchers, students and teachers. In C. N. Candlin, & K. Hyland (Eds), *Writing: texts, processes and practices* (pp. 193–217). London: Longman.

Chaiklin, S., & Lave, J. (Eds.). (1996). Understanding practice: Perspectives on activity and context. Cambridge: Cambridge University Press.

Christie, F. (1996). The role of functional grammar in development of a critical literacy. In G. Bull, & M. Anstey (Eds.), *The literacy lexicon* (pp. 46–57). Sydney: Prentice Hall.

Coe, R. M. (2002). The new rhetoric of genre: Writing political briefs. In A. M. Johns (Ed.), *Genre in the classroom* (pp. 195–205). Mahwah, NJ: Lawrence Erlbaum.

Coe, R. M., & Freedman, A. (1998). Genre theory: Australian and North American approaches. In M. Kennedy (Ed.), *Theorizing composition* (pp. 136–147). Westport, CT: Greenwood Publishing Company.

Coffin, C. (1997). Constructing and giving value to the past: An investigation into secondary school history. In F. Christie & J. Martin (Eds.). *Genre and institutions* (pp. 196–230). London: Continuum.

Connor, U. (1996). *Contrastive rhetoric*. Cambridge: Cambridge University Press.

Connor, U. (2000). Variations in rhetorical moves in grant proposals of US humanists and scientists. Text, *20*, 1–28.

Connor, U. (in press). Changing currents in contrastive rhetoric: Implications for teaching and research. In B. Kroll (Ed.), *Exploring the dynamics of second language writing*. New York: Cambridge University Press.

Connor, U., & Mauranen, A. (1999). Linguistic analysis of grant proposals: European Union research grants. *English for Specific Purposes, 18*, 47–62.

Cope, B., & Kalantzis, M. (Eds). (1993). *The powers of literacy: A genre approach to teaching writing*. Bristol, PA: Falmer Press.

Crookes, G. (1986). Towards a validated analysis of scientific text structure. *Applied Linguistics, 7*, 57–70.

Devitt, A. (1991). Intertextuality in tax accounting. In C. Bazerman, & J. Paradisi (Eds.), *Textual dynamics of the professions* (pp. 336–357). Madison, WI: University of Wisconsin Press.

Dubois, B. L. (1997). *The biomedical discussion section in context*. Greenwich, CT: Ablex.

Dudley-Evans, T., & St. John, M. J. (1998). *Developments in English for Specific Purposes*. Cambridge: Cambridge University Press.

Eggins, S., & Slade, D. (1997). *Analyzing casual conversation*. London: Cassell.

Fairclough, N. (1995). *Critical discourse analysis*. Harlow: Longman.

Feez, S. (1998). *Text-based syllabus design*. Sydney: National Centre for English Language Teaching and Research/Adult Migrant English Service.

Feez, S. (2001). Heritage and innovation in second language education. In A. M. Johns (Ed.),

Genre in the classroom (pp. 47–68). Mahwah, NJ: Lawrence Erlbaum.

Ferguson, G. (2001). If you pop over there: A corpus study of conditionals in medical discourse. *English for Specific Purposes, 20*, 61–82.

Flowerdew, 1. (2000). Using a genre-based framework to teach organisational structure in academic writing. *ELT Journal, 54*, 369–376.

Freedman, A., & Medway, P. (1994). *Genre and the New Rhetoric*. London: Taylor & Francis.

Fries, P. (1997). Theme and New in written English. In T. Miller (Ed.), *Functional approaches to written text: Classroom applications* (pp. 230–241). Washington, DC: United States Information Agency.

Fuller, G. (1998). Cultivating science: Negotiating discourse in the popular texts of Stephen Jay Gould. In J. R. Martin, & R. Veel (Eds.), *Reading science: Critical and functional perspectives on discourses of science* (pp. 35–62). London: Routledge.

Gee, J. (1996). *Social linguistics and literacy*, 2nd ed. London: Taylor & Francis.

Gollin, S. (1999). 'Why? I thought we'd talked about it before' : Collaborative writing in a professional workplace setting. In C. N. Candlin & K. Hyland (Eds.), *Writing: Texts, processes and practices* (pp. 267–290). London: Longman.

Gunnarson, B. L., Linell, P., & Nordberg. B. (Eds.). (1997). The construction of professional discourse. London: Longman.

Halliday, M. A. K. (1994). *An introduction to functional grammar* (2nd ed.). London: Edward Arnold.

Halliday, M. A. K. (1998). Things and relations: Regrammaticising experience as technical knowledge. In J. R. Martin, & R. Veel (Eds.), *Reading science* (pp. 185–235). London: Routledge.

Hammond, J., & Macken-Horarik, M. (1999). Critical literacy: Challenges and questions for ESL classrooms. *TESOL Quarterly, 33*, 528–544.

Hasan, R. (1989). The structure of a text. In M. A. K. Halliday, & R. Hasan (Eds.), *Language, context and text: Aspects of language in a social semiotic perspective* (pp. 52–69). Oxford: Oxford University Press.

Henry, A., & Roseberry, R. (1998). An evaluation of a genre-based approach to the teaching of EAP/ESP writing. *TESOL Quarterly, 32*, 147–156.

Henry, A., & Roseberry, R. (2001). A narrow-angled corpus analysis of moves and strategies of the genre: 'letter of application.' *English for Specific Purposes, 20*, 153–167.

Holmes, R. (1997). Genre analysis and the social sciences: An investigation of the structure of research article discussion sections in three disciplines. *English for Specific Purposes, 16*, 321–337.

Hopkins, T., & Dudley-Evans, T. (1988). A genre-based investigation of the discussion section in articles and dissertations. *English for Specific Purposes, 7*, 113–122.

Hunston, S., & Thompson, G. (Eds.). (2001). *Evaluation in text: Authorial stance in the construction of discourse.* Oxford: Oxford University Press.

Hyland, F., & Hyland K. (2001). Sugaring the pill: Praise and criticism in written feedback. *Journal of Second Language Writing, 9.*

Hyland, K. (1998). *Hedging in scientific research articles.* Amsterdam: John Benjamins.

Hyland, K. (1999a). Disciplinary discourses: Writer stance in research articles. In C. Candlin & K. Hyland (Eds.), *Writing: texts, processes and practices* (pp. 99–121). London: Longman.

Hyland, K. (1999b). Talking to students: Metadiscourse in introductory textbooks. *English for Specific Purposes, 18,* 3–26.

Hyland, K. (2001). Humble servants of the discipline? Self mention in research articles. *English for Specific Purposes, 20,* 207–226.

Hyon, S. (1996). Genre in three traditions: Implications for ESL. *TESOL Quarterly, 30,* 693–722.

Hyon, S. (2002). Genre and ESL reading: A classroom study. In A. M. Johns (Ed.), *Genre in the classroom* (pp. 119–139). Mahwah, NJ: Lawrence Erlbaum.

Iedema, R. (1997). The language of administration: Organizing human activity in formal institutions. In F. Christie, & J. Martin (Eds.), *Genre and institutions* (pp. 73–100). London: Continuum.

Johns, A. M. (1997). *Text, role and context: developing academic literacies.* Cambridge: Cambridge University Press.

Johns, A. M. (in press). Genre and ESL/EFL composition instruction. In B. Kroll (Ed.), *Exploring the dynamics of second language writing.* New York: Cambridge University Press.

Kachru, Y. (1999). Culture, context and writing. In E. Hinkel (Ed.), *Culture in second language teaching and learning* (pp. 75–89). Cambridge: Cambridge University Press.

Kay, H., & Dudley-Evans, T. (1998). Genre: What teachers think. *ELT Journal, 52*(4), 308–314.

Kress, G. (1989). *Linguistic processes in sociocultural practice.* Oxford: Oxford University Press.

Kress, G., & Van Leeuwen, T. (1996). *Reading images: The grammar of visual design.* London: Routledge.

Kubota, R. (1999). Japanese culture constructed by discourses: Implications for applied linguistics research and ELT. *TESOL Quarterly, 33,* 9–64.

Kuo, C. H. (1999). The use of personal pronouns: Role relationships in scientific journal articles. *English for Specific Purposes, 18,* 121–138.

Lea, M., & Street, B. (1999). Writing as academic literacies: Understanding textual practices in higher education. In C. N. Candlin, & K. Hyland (Eds), *Writing: texts, processes and practices* (pp. 62–81). London: Longman.

Lemke, J. (1998). Multiplying meaning: Visual and verbal semiotics in scientific text. In

J. Martin, & R. Veel (Eds.), *Reading science: Critical and functional perspectives on discourses of science* (pp. 87–113). New York: Routledge.

Lock, G., & Lockhart, C. (1999). Genres in an academic writing class. *Hong Kong Journal of Applied Linguistics, 3,* 47–64.

Locker, K. O. (1999). Factors in reader response to negative letters: Experimental evidence for changing what we teach. *Journal of Business and Technical Communication, 13,* 5–48.

Macken-Horarik, M. (2002). 'Something to shoot for' : A systemic functional approach to teaching genre in secondary school science. In A. M. Johns (Ed.), *Genre in the classroom* (pp. 21–46). Mahwah, NJ: Lawrence Erlbaum.

Martin, J. R. (1992). *English text: System and structure.* Amsterdam: John Benjamins.

Martin, J. R. (1995). Text and clause: Fractal resonance. *Text, 15,* 5–42.

Martin, J. R. (1997). Analyzing genre: functional parameters. In F. Christie, & J. R. Martin (Eds.), *Genre and institutions* (pp. 3–39). London: Continuum.

Martin, J. R. (2000). Design and practice: Enacting functional linguistics. *Annual Review of Applied Linguistics, 20,* 116–126.

Martin, J. R. (2001). Beyond exchange: Appraisal systems in English. In S. Hunston, & G. Thompson (Eds.), *Evaluation in texts* (pp. 142–175). Oxford: Oxford University Press.

Martin, J. R. (this volume). Meaning beyond the clause: SFL perspectives.

Martin, J. R., & Rose, D. (in press). *Working with discourse: Through context, beyond the clause.* London: Continuum.

Master, P. (Ed.) (2000). Responses to English for Specific Purposes. Washington, DC: Bureau of Educational and Cultural Affairs, United States Information Agency.

McKenna, B. (1997). How engineers write: An empirical study of engineering report writing. *Applied Linguistics, 18,* 189–211.

Miller, C. (1984). Genre as social action. *Quarterly Journal of Speech, 70,* 157–178.

Miller, T. (1998). Visual persuasion: A comparison of visuals in academic texts and the popular press. *English for Specific Purposes, 17,* 29–46.

Myers, G. (1997). Words and pictures in a biology textbook. In T. Miller (Ed.), *Functional approaches to written text: Classroom applications* (pp. 93–104). Washington, DC: United States Information Agency.

Paltridge, B. (1995). Working with genre: A pragmatic perspective. *Journal of Pragmatics, 24,* 393–406.

Paltridge, B. (2002). Genre, text type and the English for Academic Purposes (EAP) classroom. In A. M. Johns (Ed.), *Genre in the classroom* (pp. 69–88). Mahwah, NJ: Lawrence Erlbaum.

Pogner, K. H. (1999). Discourse community, culture and interaction: On writing by consulting engineers. In F. Bargiela-Chiappini & F. Nickerson (Eds.), *Writing business; Genres, media and discourses* (pp. 101–128). London: Longman.

Precht, K. (1998). A cross-cultural comparison of letters of recommendation. *English for Specific Purposes, 17,* 241–266.

Price, R. (1997). An analysis of stylistic variables in electronic mail. *Journal of Business and Technical Communication, 11,* 5–23.

Prior, 1995. Tracing authoritative and internally persuasive discourses: A case study of response, revision, and disciplinary enculturation. *Research in the Teaching of English, 29*(3), 288–325.

Rose, D. (1998). Science discourse and industrial hierarchy. In J. R. Martin & R. Veel (Eds.), *Reading science: Critical and functional perspectives on discourses of science* (pp. 236–265). London: Routledge.

Rothery, J. (1996). Making changes: Developing an educational linguistics. In R. Hasan & G. Williams (Eds.), *Literacy in society* (pp. 86–123). London: Longman.

Samraj, B. (2000). Discursive practices in graduate level content courses: the case of environmental science. *Text, 20,* 347–372.

Scollon, R. (2000). Generic variability in news stories in Chinese and English: a contrastive discourse study of five days newspapers. *Journal of Pragmatics, 32,* 761–791.

Sengupta, S. (1999). Rhetorical consciousness raising in the L2 reading class. *Journal of Second Language Writing, 8,* 291–319.

Spack, R. (1997). The rhetorical construction of multilingual students. *TESOL Quarterly, 31,* 765–774.

Stubbs, M. (1996). *Text and corpus analysis.* Oxford: Blackwell.

Swales, J. (1990). *Genre analysis: English in academic and research settings.* Cambridge: Cambridge University Press.

Swales, J. (1993). Genre and engagement. *Revue Belge de Philologie et d'Histoire, 71,* 689–698.

Swales, J. (1998). *Other floors, other voices: A textography of a small university building.* Mahwah, NJ: Lawrence Erlbaum.

Swales, J. (2000). Languages for Specific Purposes. *Annual Review of Applied Linguistics, 20,* 59–76.

Swales, J., Ahmad, U., Chang, Y. Y., Chavez , D., Dressen, D., & Seymour, R. (1998). Consider this: The role of imperatives in scholarly writing. *Applied Linguistics, 19,* 97–121.

Swales, J., & Feak, C. (1994). *Academic writing for graduate students: Essential tasks and skills.* Ann Arbor, MI: University of Michigan Press.

Swales, J., & Feak, C. (2000). *English in today's research world: A writing guide.* Ann Arbor, MI: University of Michigan Press.

Swales, J., & Lindemann, S. (2002). Teaching the literature review to international graduate students. In A. M. Johns (Ed.), *Genre in the classroom* (pp. 101–118). Mahwah, NJ:

Lawrence Erlbaum.

Upton, T. (2001, February). Understanding direct mail letters as a genre: A moves analysis. Paper presented at American Association Applied Linguistics Conference, St Louis, MO.

Valle, E. (1999). *A collective intelligence: The life sciences in the Royal Society as a scientific discourse community.* Turku, Finland: University of Turku.

Veel, R. (1998). The greening of school science: Ecogenesis in secondary classrooms. In J. R. Martin & R. Veel (Eds.), *Reading science: Critical and functional perspectives on discourses of science* (pp. 114–151). London: Routledge.

Wright, P. (1999). Writing and information design of healthcare materials. In C. N. Candlin & K. Hyland (Eds.), *Writing: Texts, processes and practices* (pp. 85–98). London: Longman.

Zhu, Y. (2000). Structural moves reflected in English and Chinese sales letters. *Discourse Studies, 2,* 525–548.

7. DISCOURSE ANALYSIS AND STYLISTICS

Paul Simpson and Geoff Hall

This review focuses on contemporary work in discourse stylistics, defined here as that designated branch of stylistics which draws specifically on the techniques and methods of discourse analysis. The review acknowledges a key assumption in modern discourse stylistic research, namely that the distinction between 'literary' and 'nonliterary' discourse, if tenable at all, is drawn not on a purely linguistic basis but in terms of multiple intersections among texts, readers, institutions, and sociocultural contexts. In spanning studies of both literary and nonliterary discourse, therefore, the coverage of the present review is intended to reflect this axiom. It also attempts to foreground the diversity of method and approach in contemporary discourse stylistics. Given that the techniques of discourse analysis are themselves many and various, the survey seeks to cover stylistic work that offers productive applications of the many available models in pragmatics, conversation analysis, cognitive linguistics, speech act theory, and discourse psychology. Finally, in covering a selection of important monographs, articles, and book chapters, the review seeks both to highlight some of the critical, cultural, and ideological frameworks currently employed by discourse stylisticians and to demarcate, in more general terms, the current state-of-play in this research tradition.

A recurrent issue in modern discourse stylistic research has been the problematic literary/nonliterary divide, with a general consensus emerging that any divisions made are not effected on a purely linguistic basis. Rather, discourse stylistics views literary texts as instances of naturally occurring language use in a social context, where discourse analysis should reveal as much about the contexts as about the text, and where readers, audiences, and institutions will form a key component of characterizations of these contexts (compare Carter & Simpson, 1989; Coupland, 1988). Discourse stylistics at its best will necessarily be a thoroughgoing interdisciplinary, even transdisciplinary, endeavor. These are stringent demands, and have unsurprisingly not always been fully achieved in published discourse stylistic work. The publications reviewed here are characteristically conservative, tending to focus more on text explication and interpretation than on social and institutional explanations and implications. Nevertheless, the issues broached, if not always explored in depth, are at the heart of social theory, and the validity of dynamic and grounded discourse analytic approaches to these large and sometimes overly abstract topics is well illustrated in considerations of identity and individuality, politeness and power relations, or storytelling and mediatized social interaction. As in so many other disciplines at present, Bakhtin is a salient name in much of this research, but areas such as conversation analysis, pragmatics, speech act theory, and discourse psychology have also importantly influenced researchers and research agendas. We turn first to significant book-length approaches to discourse and dialogue in and around literary texts.

Recent Books Drawing on Stylistics

Magnusson's monograph, *Shakespeare and Social Dialogue* (1999) offers a valuable rapprochement of poetics and linguistics, specifically New Historicism (e. g., Greenblatt, 1984, 1988) and pragmatics, especially politeness theory (Brown & Levinson, 1987). The study of Shakespeare's language is historicized by contextualizing verbal interaction in the plays through a study of Elizabethan letter writing and etiquette and letter-writing manuals for courtiers, merchants, and others. The textuality of documents formerly treated as mere contexts for literary works becomes an object of attention in itself. The boundaries between the literary and the nonliterary are problematized. Dominant approaches to studies of Shakespeare's dramatic language are criticized for New Critical-inspired formalism (valorization of intricacies, images, ambiguities, and puns out of context) and "a focus on the speech rather than the exchange as the unit of dramatic discourse" (Magnusson, 1999, p. 4). Speech, moreover, is traditionally studied as issuing from an individual 'character' with an 'essential nature,' expressed through his or her words, rather than in the conversation analysis tradition proposed by Magnusson, where self is viewed as an online, contingent, and provisional co-construction requiring continual 'repair' and maintenance (see chap. 6 especially). This perception of conversation as self maintenance in everyday interaction views identity as a leakier vessel than, for example, that posited by Greenblatt in *Renaissance Self-Fashioning* (1984). It is a view of identity as always undergoing maintenance and repair, always being patched even in the making, and a view of that patchwork and maintenance of selves as a cooperative or collaborative activity. 'Character effects' (chap. 1) will accordingly derive from speakers' relative social positions and speech patterns. Social position and 'subjectivity' are determinants of style to a greater degree than any posited individual personal identity.

In line with both New Historicism as well as studies in discourse analysis, Magnusson analyzes verbal negotiations as social and political interaction through which power relations such as 'service' or 'friendship' are co-constructed. In a hierarchical society, 'negative politeness' (see Brown & Levinson, 1987) is traced in letters and the interactions of Shakespearean characters, though the solidarity constructed through 'positive politeness' is much in evidence too (as, for example, in Iago's apparently undue familiarity with Othello as they discuss his errant wife) (Ch. 7). Against the old dictum 'style is the man,' Magnusson argues, after Bakhtin (1984), "style is at least two persons" (p. 24).

The book falls into three sections: Part I. The rhetoric of politeness; Part II, Eloquent relations in letters; and Part III, A prosaics of conversation. The careful work of the earlier sections most obviously bears fruit in Chapter 6, The pragmatics of repair in *King Lear* and *Much Ado About Nothing*; and Chapter 7, 'Voice potential: ' Language and symbolic capital in *Othello*. In *Much Ado*, for example, Magnusson usefully traces the pervasiveness of miscommunication and concerns about miscommunication. But where some deconstructive readings stop at this point, Magnussson shows the workings of repair mechanisms in characters' dialogues, and careful anticipations of possible misunderstandings (compare Bakhtin's anticipatory poetics), so that the play's "concern is not only with how language fails but with how language works" (p. 158). The study of Othello in the following chapter explores the relevance of Bourdieu's (1979) notion that the social position of a speaker affects the meaning and value of what is said more than the content of the utterance in itself. Desdemona is used to being listened to and understood. Her reception by Othello is increasingly problematic and distressing. Iago's mastery of politeness is studied not as 'polite eloquence,' since he makes a point of bluff speaking, but as a deep and sophisticated understanding of the 'social logic' of social interaction (p. 179), when and how to speak. The workings of Bourdieu's (1979) 'habitus' and subjectification are shown to be relevant in observing Cordelia (Ch. 6) as an instance of "history turned into nature," the speaker "endlessly overtaken by [his] own words" (Bourdieu, 1979, as cited in Magnusson, pp. 151-153). Where commentators on *King Lear* have frequently noted and examined the 'recognition' scenes, Magnusson offers a new perspective on these instances of the importance of 'reciprocal acknowledgment' (or not: dying Lear-Kent; Kent-Oswald) as enacted in dialogue. Here again her intersubjective theory of identity stresses "the role of talk both in generating social identities and shared realities and in negotiating social change" (p. 142).

Magnusson could be criticized for a certain eclecticism in her borrowings from conversation analysis (hereafter CA) and discourse analysis (hereafter DA), and even in the use of Brown and Levinson (1987). At times readers may wish to see more analysis of Shakespeare and less quotation of Elizabethan letters. Some of her work has of course been anticipated as her own generous notes fully acknowledge. Nevertheless, the bringing together of a linguistics of social interaction with the demands of literary theory in the form of New Historicism makes this book one of the more important contributions to the study of dialogue and discourse in the field of stylistics in recent years. In his influential 1989 essay, Montrose proposes that the linguistic and the social are not opposed, and instead emphasizes "their reciprocity and mutual constitution" (p. 6), but offers no further examples of discussion. Greenblatt (1988), on the other hand, castigates formalist linguistics as "textual analyses...[which] convey almost nothing of the social dimension of literature's power" (p. 5). *Shakespeare and Social Dialogue* is an important response to these criticisms and should be followed up by more such studies not restricted to the Renaissance.

A monograph that complements Magnusson in a number of useful ways is Culpeper's *Language and Characterisation: People in Plays and Other Texts* (2001). The points of intersection between the two volumes are indeed multiple. Both are interested in how characterization is mediated through structures of dialogue and discourse, both draw on stylistic and pragmatic models of analysis (and notably on Brown and Levinson's model of politeness), and both place a strong emphasis on the language of Shakespearean plays. Where Culpeper's study differs principally from Magnusson's is in his greater reliance on the insights offered to stylistics by, in particular, schema theory and theories of discourse processing (such as that exemplified by van Dijk and Kintsch's 1983 model of text comprehension). However, many other stylistic models are brought into play here, as well as a body of sociolinguistic research on variation and speech styles, making Culpeper's monograph highly eclectic.

Implicit in much of Culpeper's central thesis is the assumption that if literary critics insist on talking about characterization in literature, then they should do so with a firm grasp of relevant aspects of social psychology or with, at least, a solid grounding in stylistic research on dialogue and discourse. Culpeper casts his position rather more diplomatically than we have done by identifying and critiquing, early in the book, two traditional approaches to characterization in literary criticism. The first is the 'humanizing' tradition, wherein fictional characters are judged as if they were real people in the real world. The second, the 'dehumanizing' tradition, is where characters are resolutely divorced from real life and seen purely as agents for, and reflexes of, plot development. Culpeper suggests that in their purer forms each tradition is manifestly flawed, and that the process of inferring character from text is rather more complex. His own aim is to show "how the cognitive structures and inferential mechanisms that readers have already developed for real-life people might be used in their comprehension of characters" (p. 10). Further, he sees his task as describing "both the textual factors and the cognitive factors that jointly lead a reader to have a particular impression of a character" (p. 11). Later in the book, Culpeper looks at structuralist approaches to characterization in the vein of Propp's folk-tale morphology, although he highlights problems in these models as well. The main problem is that structuralist models fail to discriminate between psychological and textual aspects of characterization. As Culpeper puts it, "our conception of a particular character arises as a result of a complex interaction between the contents of our heads and the incoming textual information" (2001, p. 56).

In addition to the special emphasis on Shakespeare noted earlier, which includes a chapter devoted exclusively to characterization in *The Taming of the Shrew*, there is a chapter which applies Brown and Levinson's (1987) model of politeness specifically. In a sense, Culpeper subverts the Brown and Levinson model, preferring to recast their strategies of politeness as strategies of *impoliteness*; in other words, he isolates a specific set of strategies which speakers use consciously to attack the face of the interlocutor. It is not clear to what extent this marks a genuine departure from the Brown and Levinson framework (given that their original model offers a full account of face threatening acts) nor it is clear how much descriptive benefit can be derived from designing a set of parallel categories which invert the original ones, though this observation marks a theoretical debate which is perhaps best conducted elsewhere. What is important here is the way in which Culpeper, working principally from discourse patterns in John Osborne's play *The Entenainer*, traces the intersection between politeness strategies (or impoliteness as he would see it) and the manner by which verbal conflict and opposition impact the development of both character and plot.

Culpeper ultimately seeks to present a model that accounts for how categories of characterization are realized both cognitively and sociolinguistically. Indeed, relatively early in the book, he offers a diagrammatic representation of this composite, heterogeneous model which embodies the theoretical eclecticism noted above. The extent to which this model will become part of contemporary stylistics' methodological stock-in-trade is still too early to assess, but this is undoubtedly a lively and cogent book which, moreover, demonstrates considerable skill in its synthesis of such a diverse array of material.

Person's short monograph *Structure and Meaning in Conversation and Literature* (1999) examines the ways in which conversational structures are represented in literary discourse and the ways in which the reading process is guided by these structures. Person synthesizes two broad strands of research in conversation analysis (CA) and in reader response theory, although only the first of these is given significant prominence in his analytic framework. While Person quite properly acknowledges the existing body of work in stylistics that draws on CA and DA frameworks for dialogue analysis, the principal impetus for his own study comes from not from the stylisticians but from scholars working on non-literary discourse. Lakoff and Tannen (1984), in particular, argue that the formal analysis of naturalistic conversations can be enriched by the study of dialogue in plays and novels and that, moreover, "artificial dialog may represent an internalized model or schema for the production of conversation—a competence model that speakers have access to" (1984, p. 323). In developing further the rationale for his study,

Person argues that his work differs from that of other stylisticians in terms of its coverage. Whereas previous stylistic work has suffered from an over reliance on the mechanisms of turn taking and preference organization, Person's remit is broader, adopting Harvey Sacks' axiom that a properly exhaustive study must examine 'order at all points' in conversation. To the author's credit, he takes his study of discourse features beyond the familiar territory of turn-taking and preference organization and to a level of analytic detail that is refreshing. That said, the first two chapters of Person's book cover familiar terrain, looking respectively at how conversations between fictional characters are presented and at how preference organization is negotiated in literary dialogue. The material on speech presentation includes a critique of the influential work of Short and his coresearchers on 'hypothetical' speech presentation (see, for example, Short, Semino, & Wynne, 1997). This phenomenon, in the context of natural occurring conversation, is where a speaker projects what another participant might have said or might typically be assumed to say. It is their contention that literary speech presentation assumes a nonhypothetical, *verbatim* reproduction of what another character said, because in fiction the 'original' piece of speech has no independent existence and is only accessible via the report itself (Short et al., 1997, p. 222).

Person disagrees and argues that reported speech *can* be hypothetical in literary discourse. He provides this example: in an E. Annie Proulx short story, a female character "reports" the written text of another character in the following way: "She shuffled a deck of envelopes. 'Here sheriff writes blah, blah, vandals broke in. Threw chairs and furniture over the ledge...' " (Person, 1999, p. 26). It is obvious that the putative antecedent discourse (the sheriff's report) does not literally contain a 'blah blah' sequence. Rather, the female character's rendition creates a discoursal space for which the reader must hypothesize about the nature of the anterior discourse. Person's observations on this and related issues of speech presentation promise a rich debate for contemporary stylistic theory, although his critique concludes rather abruptly at the end of the chapter which houses it and it is not clear how this fits into the overall direction of the book.

As the book develops, Person examines literary realizations of a number of discourse features that do not come under the traditional compass of stylistic work in this area. These features include nonlexical items such as 'mm hm,' 'uh huh,' 'sort of, ' and 'y' know—features referred to variously by discourse analysts as hedges, particles, fillers, discourse markers, pragmatic devices, and so on. He uncovers many instances of such items in literary dialogue, and in a variety of discourse functions, although something might have been made of the fact that all the exponents identified were in twentieth century fiction. This may suggest a possible diachronic shift in writing styles towards greater sociolinguistic realism in the representation of speech.

Person does indeed take the traditional remit of CA-influenced stylistic work on dialogue and discourse a step further, with later chapters of the book encompassing prosody, restarts, interruptions, body movement and gaze, mimicry across speaker turns, and even a survey of the interactive consequences of the reporting of good and bad news. What is intriguing is just how many instances of these features turn up in his corpus of 77 fictional works. However, the level of analytic rigor promised in the earlier chapters is not always sustained, with the discussion of prosody, in particular, becoming a little speculative and self-evident. For instance, on basis of the reporting verb in the sequence " 'You helped Soha with her box. I saw you,' Mama Bisi accused," Person concludes that 'accused' suggests an "accusatory tone of voice" (1999, p. 84). To be fair, certain paralinguistic features of discourse are hard to accommodate in the linear, graphological medium that constitutes literature, which is why certain of the interpretations on offer here tend toward the anodyne.

The basic conclusion of Person's study, although not articulated in quite these terms, is that readers' communicative competence, derived from the everyday routines of naturally occurring social interaction, acts as a conceptual template for the processing of dialogue in fiction. Over the course of the development of a fictional dialogue, readers may align themselves synchronously with different viewpoints within the literary situation. According to Person, there is no aspect of naturally occurring conversation that is not found in literary dialogue. This is only one of many conclusions drawn in the book that would sustain future investigation in contemporary stylistics.

Narration and narrative continue to receive much attention at the interface of literary, linguistic, and cultural studies. Norrick (2000) is intended as a book-length contribution to conversation analysis as well as to narrative studies. He is suspicious of large claims or characterizations concerning narrative, preferring to look at narratives arising in ordinary everyday conversations. (Compare, in this respect, Fludemik, 1996). Such narratives tend to be diffuse, multiauthored, and in general more 'polyphonic' (Norrick, following Bakhtin, 1984) than the narratives described in Labov's classic studies or by Linde (1993). This, then, is a pragmatic study out of which certain recurrent features are highlighted: repetition patterns; the use of dialogue, tense shifts, and formulaicity to focus interlocutors' attention; segmentation of stories into memorable chunks; and evaluation construction. The focus is always firmly on what the narratives are doing in the ongoing conversational interaction. The data are interesting, the analyses penetrating, and there are plentiful further references for the curious. A bonus for literary stylisticians is a literature chapter (Ch. 7) exploring the relevance of consonances and differences between Norrick's 'natural narratives' and narrative in Shakespeare's *Romeo and Juliet* and Beckett's *Endgame*. In keeping with several of the other scholars whose work is reviewed in this section, Norrick uses stylistics as an illustration of "how linguistic analysis of everyday conversation can inform our study of meaning in literary texts" (2000, p. 189).

Recent Articles on Discourse Analysis and Stylistics

Turning now to article-length treatments of the interplay between discourse analysis and stylistics, Piazza (1999) applies conversation analysis to literary dialogue, looking at examples of exchanges and speeches in modern drama from the point of view of repairs in particular, as self-initiated, other-initiated, self-performed, or other-performed. Piazza takes account of the context of repairs in drama scripts and in performance so that they are recognized even when not purely linguistic in form. The dominance of a type of repair is taken to reveal important features of relations between characters in these plays as well as contributing to characterization itself, if not to wider thematic meanings of the plays. Less realistic characters and scenes in Hayes's play, for example, are found to lack self-repair, the unmarked preference, CA tells us, in everyday conversation. Other characters are found to prefer indirection or mitigation, or more aggressive conversational styles, from which playgoers are likely to form impressions of personality. A sense of lack of meaningful interaction, a struggle to communicate in Pinter's plays, is related to a high proportion of self-initiated self-repairs. In some ways, what Piazza does is simply to recast an ordinary reader's or spectator's responses into the CA jargon, thus adding little to our understanding of the play. The stylistic claim would have to be that seeing these exchanges within a CA framework adds to our understanding of how conversations work (or do not work) both on and off the stage.

In a study in narrative stylistics, Toolan (2000) argues that there has been a shift in recent fiction in English away from detached third-person narration in Standard English toward novels written in first-person vernacular English. Moreover, represented speech in contemporary fiction—whether it be from first-person 'voiced' narrators or even from the characters portrayed in third-person narratives—is marked by an increased use of the dysfluencies, hesitations, and repetitions that characterize everyday spoken language (cf. discussion of Person, 1999, above). This trend suggests a 'quasi-autobiographical turn' in modern writing, which Toolan finds most in evidence in first-person narratives focalized by a speaker or thinker and developed in the form of extended monologue. One of the clearest recent exponents of this pattern, according to Toolan, is Don de Lillo's novel *Libra*, although examples are provided of similar narrative strategies in works by James Kelman and Roddy Doyle who use, respectively, Glaswegian and Dublin vernacular speech in their novels. Toolan's broad thesis, worth quoting here, is that

> as a part of a widespread contemporary understanding of "how to render characters" —thus as part of the contemporary aesthetics of narrative fiction (in English, at least)—it has become accepted that it may be appropriate for "direct speech" in fiction to contain ungrammaticality, repetition, structurally-fractured sentences and so on to an unprecedented extent…it is possible that this is in part is due to a contemporary literary antipathy for anything that might imply omniscience or essentialist foundations (pp. 169–171).

Toolan concludes that this sort of 'quasi-transcnptional' direct speech may be related to the explosion of film and televisual forms of narrative during the twentieth century. He adds that the current range of contrasting methods for creating narratives has consequences for the particular effects sought in, and the particular techniques developed by, each competing format within that range.

Two articles which focus on nonliterary discourse, but which nevertheless draw on the methods, techniques and principles of stylistics, are Günthner's

1999 study of prosodic devices in everyday reported speech and Cülpeper and Semino's 2000 study of the use of speech act verbs in Early Modem English witchcraft narratives. Günthner takes the idea of a 'layering of voices' from Bakhtin (1981) to capture the behavior of interactants in her German language everyday conversational data. She contends that the interactants use 'poetic devices and polphonic strategies' in recognizably Bakhtinian ways as they perform past dialogues reported in the present for the benefit of interlocutors: 'double voiced discourse,' in short. Günthner's critical point here is that these performative-poetic devices (voice quality and prosodic techniques such as exaggeration or changed pitch) are used to offer an evaluation in the very moment of apparently simply 'reporting' past utterances of another speaker:

> In real life we hear speech about speakers and their discourse at every step. We can go so far as to say that in real life people talk most of all about what others talk about—they transmit, recall, weigh, and pass judgement on other people's words, opinions, assertions, information; people are upset by others' words, or agree with them, contest them, refer to them and so forth (Bakhtin, 1981, pp. 337–338,) as cited in Günthner, 1999, p. 686).

We hear two voices: the voice reported and the reporter's evaluation of it—often, in this dataset, exaggerated mimicry which can only be taken ironically or parodically. 'Stylization' (Bakhtin, 1984, pp. 185ff.) may also of course be non-linguistic (e. g., facial expression), though this is not Günthner's interest in the article. Nevertheless, Günthner claims that the performed reported utterances she highlights are characteristically 'recontextualized' for present interactional purposes, and that this is a pervasive device in everyday interaction. Here is an altogether neat illustration of what some of us have argued for many years: that the 'literary' and the 'everyday' are not so easily distinguished at the purely linguistic level (compare also Magnusson, 1999, reviewed above) : in this case hybridity (including code mixing) and 'polyphony' deconstruct any simplistic notions of register or genre.

Culpeper and Semino's (2000) intriguing account of the witchcraft narratives is driven theoretically by work in speech act theory (most notably that of Austin, 1962, and Searle, 1979) and by the work of Levinson on activity types

(Levinson, 1992). Using a corpus of late sixteenth and early seventeenth century courtroom witness depositions, they chart the shift in illocutionary status of the class of verbs that include 'curse' and 'wish (harm/evil upon).' Whereas in contemporary English usage, a verb like 'curse' falls neatly into Austin's category of 'behabitive' or into Searle's category of 'expressive,' in early modern usage it had stronger institutional status such that it could be only be weakly aligned with Austin's category of 'exercitive' or, slightly better, with Searle's category of 'expressive.' Working from the special pragmatic function of the earlier use, Culpeper and Semino develop first a set of prototypical felicity conditions for the 'performing' of a witch's curse and then, using Levinson's model, draw up a set of clustered speech act types which represent the various stages in the discursive practice of witchcraft (right up to the trial of 'witches' in the courtroom). What is chilling about the culturally legitimized aspects of witchcraft is just how little it takes to instantiate a witchcraft 'activity type' : the occurrence of some negative event (such as someone falling ill would in itself suffice as proof of a successful curse. Given that anyone uttering the alleged curse could be assumed to have a pact with the devil, and that the testimony of accused witches is in any case unreliable, the prospects were indeed bleak for the hundreds of invariably poor, old, and marginalized women who were accused and eventually executed as witches around that period.

Interest among stylisticians in the public and media construction of discourse continues to be strong. In 1999 two articles were published (independently of one another) which examine specifically the various discourse representations of Diana, Princess of Wales. In the first of these, Abell and Stokoe (1999) argue that involved speakers routinely allocate and avoid blame, or construct accountability' in everyday talk. In this case, Princess Diana's well-known *Panorama* BBC television interview is explicated as a set of narratives and descriptions of events which cumulatively portray herself and her actions, in her separation from Prince Charles and after, in a favorable light. 'The media,' 'Charles,' and 'the royal household' are presented as making her life difficult despite her own best intentions and interventions. Abell and Stokoe represent these strategies as 'resources for blame management.' The title of their article('I take full responsibility, I take some responsibility, I'll take half of it but no more than that') summarizes Abell and Stokoe's argument (and is not, as might be inferred, a direct quotation from Diana herself). In fact, only limited, brief extracts from the interview transcript itself are used. However, the relation of this formal interview to ordinary everyday talk is defended because, it is argued, royalty and the British royal family are increasingly viewed as ordinary people 'really,' with ordinary problems. However, since the royals' lives are up for scrutiny on TV, there are elements of soap opera too. The intellectual context of the study is conversation analysis and discursive psychology, above all, Billig's work (1998). Diana constructs herself as 'reasonable' where others are obstructive and unreasonable. Just one more way in which she shows her ordinariness then—though most of us will not generally be invited to the *Panorama* television studio.

Montgomery's article on the discursive representation of Princess Diana complements that of Abell and Stokoe in several respects, although Montgomery's principal focus is on the mediatized public reactions to her death in 1997 (Montgomery, 1999). More specifically, Montgomery examines, in the first instance, the linguistic properties of the tributes paid to Diana by Tony Blair, by the Queen, and by Diana's brother, Earl Spencer, and, in the second, the manner by which these tributes are assessed by the media and the public. The conceptual framework which informs this study is drawn from Jürgen Habermas's model of 'Universal Pragmatics' (Habermas, 1979). Montgomery highlights the different means by which speech in the public sphere (as in, for example, the tributes offered to Diana) projects itself as valid in context in determinate ways: it can be seen as true, sincere or appropriate. Furthermore, it is often the case that only one of these validity claims will be foregrounded in media judgments on public speech at any one time. Montgomery argues persuasively that of the three Habermasian parameters, it is sincerity that in the main becomes the touchstone against which the behavior of the tribute-paying public figures is measured; he notes as a significant exception that in some of mediatized reception of the Queen's tribute, the shift is toward the validity claim of appropriateness.

As the survey of these last two articles suggests, contemporary discourse stylistic research tends to straddle the literary—nonliterary divide in terms of both its focus and its coverage. Indeed, our introduction touched upon this issue, where we noted the consensus view in discourse stylistics that the literary/nonliterary division is drawn not on a purely linguistic basis, but in terms of its constitution as a reflex of text and social context. What contributes further to this generally broad remit is the manner by which, within this research paradigm, the application of techniques in discourse analysis serves as a channel to a number of other aspects of text processing and textual understanding. For instance, in a book whose relevance is more implicitly than explicitly related to the compass of the present review, Hidalgo-Downing (2000) draws upon logical, philosophical, and semantic concepts of negation in her investigation of the generation of humor in fictional writing. The bulk of the data used for her study is taken from Joseph Heller's novel *Catch 22*, with much of her analysis concentrated specifically on modelling the humorous aspects used in the dialogue of the novel. Similarly, the Jucker, Fritz, and Lebsanft (1999) volume is a highly diffuse collection of papers on the analysis of dialogue in its historical context. Although manifestly historical-linguistic, as opposed to discourse-stylistic, in orientation, there are nonetheless significant elements in this book's interplay between dialogue and discourse which stylisticians will find interesting. And finally, a book which narrowly misses the publication cycle covered in the present review but which again has relevance to discourse stylistics is Culpeper, Short, and Verdonk (1998). This is a collection of papers specifically devoted to the analysis of drama dialogue, and its twelve chapters, by scholars from around the world, are written at introductory level. With a selection of exercises and activities appended to each contribution, this makes for a useful introductory textbook for the teaching of stylistics and discourse analysis to undergraduate students.

Conclusion

Recent work in discourse stylistics of the sort reviewed here suggests that this particular branch of applied linguistics is becoming progressively more interdisciplinary in scope. Our review has highlighted some of the critical, cultural, and ideological frameworks currently employed by stylisticians. When those frameworks are married with the many available models of analysis in pragmatics, conversation analysis, cognitive linguistics, speech act theory, and discourse psychology, the research paradigm becomes heterogeneous indeed in terms of its variety of approaches and methods of analysis. In consequence, the boundaries of discourse stylistics are sometimes fuzzy: Our conclusion has cited just two works (Hidalgo-Downing, 2000; Jucker et al., 1999) whose relationship is more tangential than direct, although these are only two of many possible candidates that straddle the boundaries. Nevertheless, there is no doubt that discourse stylistics has now its own rich history of established, seminal work and that interest in this subject area, if not all-consuming, is sufficient to guarantee continued, steady output for the foreseeable future.

ANNOTATED BIBLIOGRAPHY

Culpeper, J. (2001). *Language and characterisation: People in plays and other texts.* Harlow: Longman.

An eclectically driven stylistic analysis of how characterization is developed in fictional dialogue, with particular emphasis on the plays of Shakespeare.

Magnusson, L. (1999). *Shakespeare and social dialogue: Dramatic language and Elizabethan letters.* Cambridge: Cambridge University Press.

This study brings together the historical pragmatic study of politeness and etiquette in Shakespeare's plays and sonnets with letters and other contemporary writings on the subject. An important attempt to speak equally to both literary criticism and the study of discourse and conversation in everyday and literary language.

Montgomery, M. (1999). Speaking sincerely: Public reactions to the death of Diana, Princess of Wales. *Language and Literature, 8* (1), 5–33.

An intriguing study which uses the ideas of Jürgen Habermas to explore the discursive construction of public and media tributes in the aftermath of the death of Diana, Princess of Wales.

Person, R., Jr. (1999). *Structure and meaning in conversation and literature.* Lanham, MD: University Press of America.

Working from a substantial corpus of texts, this compact study probes dialogue in fiction using models in ethnomethodology and conversation analysis.

OTHER REFERENCES

Abell, J., & Stokoe, E. (1999). 'I take full responsibility, I take some responsibility, I'll take half of it but no more than that:' Princess Diana and the 'Panorama' interview. *Discourse Studies, 1,* 297–319.

Austin, J. L. (1962). *How to do things with words.* Oxford: Clarendon Press.
Bakhtin, M. M. (1981). *The dialogic imagination: Four essays by M. M. Bakhtin* (M. Holquist, Ed. ; C. Emerson & M. Holquist, Trans.). Austin: University of Texas Press.
Bakhtin, M. M. (1984). *Problems of Dostoevsky's poetics.* (C. Emerson, Ed. & Trans.). Minneapolis: University of Minnesota Press.
Bakhtin, M. M., & Voloshinov, V. N. (1983). Discourse in life and discourse in poetry. In A. Shukman (Ed.), *Bakhtin School Papers: Russian Poetics in Translation, Vol. 10* (pp. 5–30). Oxford: RPT Publications.
Billig, M. (1998). *Talking of the royal family.* London: Routledge.
Bourdieu, P. (1979). *Language and symbolic power.* Cambridge: Polity Press.
Brown, P., & Levinson, S. C. (1987). *Politeness: Some universals in language usage.* Cambridge: Cambridge University Press.
Carter, R., & Simpson, P. (1989). Introduction. In R. Carter & P. Simpson (Eds.), *Language, discourse and literature. An introductory reader in discourse stylistics* (pp. 1–20). London: Unwin Hyman.
Coupland, N. (1988). Introduction: Towards a stylistics of discourse. In N. Coupland (Ed.), *Styles of discourse* (pp. 1–19). London: Croom Helm.
Culpeper, J., & Semino, E. (2000). Constructing witches and spells: Speech acts and activity types in early modern England. *Journal of Historical Pragmatics, 1,* 197–216.
Culpeper, J., Short, M., & Verdonk, P. (Eds.) (1998). *Exploring the language of drama: From text to context.* London: Routledge.
Fludernik, M. (1996). *Natural narratives.* London: Routledge.
Greenblatt, S. (1984). *Renaissance self-fashioning: From More to Shakespeare.* Chicago: University of Chicago Press.
Greenblatt, S. (1988). *Shakespearean negotiations: The circulation of social energy in Renaissance England.* Berkeley: University of California Press.
Günthner, S. (1999). Polyphony and the 'Layering of voices' in reported dialogues: An analysis of the use of prosodic devices in everyday reported speech. *Journal of Pragmatics, 31,* 685–708.
Habermas, J. (1979). Universal pragmatics. In *Communication and the evolution of society* (pp. 1–68). Boston: Beacon Press.
Hidalgo-Downing, L. (2000). *Negation, text worlds, and discourse: The pragmatics of fiction.* Stamford, CT: Ablex.
Jucker, A., Fritz, G., & Lebsanft. F. (Eds.) (1999). *Historical dialogue analysis.* Amsterdam: John Benjamins.
Lakoff, R., & Tannen, D. (1984). Conversational strategy and metastrategy in a pragmatic theory: The example of *Scene from a Marriage. Semiotica, 49,* 323–346.

Levinson, S. L. (1992). Activity types and language. In P. Drew & J. Heritage (Eds.), *Talk at work* (pp. 66–100). Cambridge: Cambridge University Press.

Linde, C. (1993). *Life stories: The creation of coherence.* New York: Oxford University Press.

Montrose, L. (1989). Professing the Renaissance: The poetics and politics of culture. In H. Aram Veeser (Ed.), *The New Historicism* (pp. 15–36). London: Routledge.

Norrick, N. (2000). *Conversational narrative.* Amsterdam: John Benjamins.

Piazza, R. (1999). Dramatic discourse approached from a conversational analysis perspective: Catherine Hayes's *Skirmishes* and other contemporary plays. *Journal of Pragmatics, 31,* 1001–1023.

Searle, J. (1979). *Expression and meaning.* Cambridge: Cambridge University Press.

Short, M., Semino, E., & Wynne, M. (1997). A (free direct) reply to Paul Simpson's discourse. *Journal of Literary Semantics, 26,* 219–228.

Toolan, M. (2000). Quasi-transcriptional speech: A compensatory spokenness in Anglo-Irish literary fiction. In A. Bex, M. Burke, & P. Stockwell (Eds.), *Contextualized stylistics* (pp. 153–172). Amsterdam: Rodopi.

van Dijk, T., & Kintsch, W. (1983). *Strategies of discourse comprehension.* London: Academic Press.

8. DISCOURSE ISSUES IN CROSS-CULTURAL PRAGMATICS

Diana Boxer

This chapter focuses on recent research in cross-cultural pragmatics (CCP) as distinct from interlanguage pragmatics (IP). The essential difference between the two lies in the perspective from which each views cross-cultural communication. CCP takes the point of view that individuals from different societies or communities interact according to their own pragmatic norms, often resulting in a clash of expectations and, ultimately, misperceptions about the other group. The misperceptions are typically two-way; that is, each group misperceives the other. In an age in which cross-cultural interaction is the norm not only across societies but also within them, different rules of speaking have the potential to cause stereotypes, prejudice, and discrimination against entire groups of people. Research in the area of CCP can greatly aid in ameliorating these consequences. Recent studies that view CCP from this two-way perspective are the focus of this chapter. The overview of this body of research demonstrates the potential contribution of the field of applied linguistics to mutual understanding through the study of discourse issues in cross-cultural pragmatics.

The study of cross-cultural discourse represents an especially important endeavor in modern times. The reason for its importance lies in the great potential for miscommunication and misperceptions based upon differing norms of interaction across societies and speech conununities. In a world that grows ever smaller when peoples from different societies interact with greater and greater frequency, felicitous cross-cultural interaction is essential. This part of applied linguistics is usually termed "cross-cultural pragmatics," or "interlanguage pragmatics." (Clyne, 1994, draws even finer distinctions. with not two but three types, also including "contrastive pragmatics" among relevant areas of study.) These two research foci differ from each other in essential ways: interlanguage pragmatics(IP) forms a part of the subfield of applied linguistics that focuses on second language acquisition; in contrast, cross-cultural pragmatics (CCP) is applied sociolinguistics. CCP does not assume that the nonnative speaker is progressing along an interlanguage continuum toward some target language norm. The distinction is a fuzzy one, and involves subtle differences in perspective. The essential difference between the two lies in how they view cross-cultural communication: (1) from a either a one-way perspective (interlanguage pragmatics), or (2) a two-way perspective (cross-cultural pragmatics).

Interlanguage pragmatics typically takes the perspective that it is the task of the language learner or newcomer to acquire the norms of the host community. This focus is logical, since it deals with individuals engaged in formal or informal development of a second or foreign language. The assumption is that these learners, especially those living in a second language context, are acquiring the rules and norms of interaction of the host society along with the phonology, morphology, syntax, and semantics of the L2. Thus, it is reasonable to learn the norms of the community. Until quite recently there has been little effort to teach the pragmatic level in formal classroom L2 instruction. Indeed, it is only in the past two decades that any effort at all has been exerted to make learners aware of pragmatic differences between L1 and L2. Because of this, the field of interlanguage pragmatics is still in its infancy. A host of research studies have contributed greatly to our knowledge of IP issues (see, for example, work by authors such as Beebe, Takahashi, & Uliss-Weltz, 1985; Blum-Kulka, 1982; Blum-Kulka, House-Edmondson & Kasper, 1989; Cohen & Olshtain, 1981; Eisenstein & Bodman, 1986; Hartford & Bardovi-Harlig, 1992; Kasper & Dahl, 1991; Kasper & Rose, 1999; and Olshtain & Cohen, 1983, to name but a few studies in the realm of IP). There has been considerable recent attention paid to IP issues in the applied linguistics literature. Kasper and Rose's overview of pragmatics and SLA in *ARAL* 1999 gives a detailed outline of recent IP research.

Cross-cultural pragmatics takes the point of view that individuals from two societies or communities carry out their interactions (whether spoken or written) according to their own rules or norms, often resulting in a clash in expectations and, ultimately, misperceptions about the other group. The misperceptions are typically two-way; that is, each group misperceives the other (cf. Singh, Lele, & Martohardjono, 1988). Notwithstanding, the consequences of such a situation are scarcely two-way, because inevitably one group wields societal power at the expense of the other. The early work of Gumperz and his colleagues on "crosstalk" (Twitchen, Gumperz, Jupp, & Roberts, 1979) aptly illustrates how speakers of English from two different societies, British vs. South Asian, had different sets of expectations for how to talk to each other. In this British setting, it was the South Asian group that got into trouble by not following the interactional norms of the host society (see, for example, Cook-Gumperz & Gumperz, 1997). The contextualization cues at work led the British speakers to perceive the South Asian speakers as inappropriate and even rude. While it may be true that this perception went the other way as well, with the South Asians perceiving the British negatively also, the consequences in terms of societal power were felt only by the minority group. These repercussions are most notable in the domains of workplace interaction—including service encounters—and in educational domains. Access to the goods and services inherent in such interactions renders successful CCP critical. Without a basis to understand the norms of "the other," power is wielded in insidious ways. Thus, in a certain sense, the old adage of "When in Rome, do as the Romans do" does not fit many modern pluralistic societies. Because cross-cultural interactions have the potential to cause stereotypes, prejudice, and discrimination against entire groups of people, research in CCP has the potential to ameliorate these consequences. The present review focuses principally on CCP research. The bidirectional view of CCP gives us a good sense of applying findings from discourse research to solve real communication problems in a shrinking planet.

Methodological Issues

Most CCP research takes the perspective that in order to fully understand miscommunication from a two-way perspective, it is optimal to take an ethnographic or interactional sociolinguistic approach to the collection and analysis of data. That is to say, microanalytic analyses of the subtleties of miscues are captured in taped interactions. These data are often triangulated via ethnographic-type interviews in which participants view/listen and comment on their perceptions of the miscommunication (for a full explanation of this methodology, see Erickson &

Schultz, 1982).

This approach contrasts with much IP research. With some exceptions (e. g., Bardovi-Harlig & Hartford, 1993), studies carried out by IP researchers focusing on speech act realization have by and large *not* used spontaneous face-to-face data, preferring instead to elicit large amounts of data through role-plays or Discourse Completion Tasks (DCT). This is not surprising, given the difficult task of collecting natural data on speech act realizations. There is a debate on this issue in the literature, begun by the late Nessa Wolfson (cf. Wolfson, Marmor, & Jones, 1989) and thoroughly outlined in Beebe and Cummings (1985, 1996). One can see by the first and second dates of these papers that discussion initiated in the mid-1980s on this methodological debate has continued over the years. The fact remains that there are relatively few IP studies using data from spontaneous face-to-face interaction.

While Wolfson asserted that the only good data is that captured in natural communication, her own work on speech act realization was not specifically interlanguage data, but baseline data on how speech acts were realized among native speakers, in her case native speakers of American English. Thus, her studies on the speech acts of complimenting and inviting, for example, were not specifically cross-cultural studies, and they were definitely not interlanguage studies. They were descriptive analyses of speech act usage among native speakers of U. S. English. These types of studies are indeed important for IP as well as CCP research, since they provide necessary information on just how certain groups of native speakers realize speech acts. They do not, nevertheless, offer information that gives clues to potential communication pitfalls. In order to obtain this sort of information, we also need to have baseline data on how these same speech acts are realized in other languages. In other words, baseline studies on NS speech behavior in one language must be coupled with data on the same speech behavior in other languages and speech communities. For example, if we are studying the cross-cultural realizations of apologies between U. S. English and Japanese, we would need to collect data in a U. S. speech community and also in a Japanese speech community and then compare these two sets of data to ascertain where the differences occur. This type of contrastive pragmatics (Clyne, 1994) can then help us avoid miscommunication. Without using a DCT instrument, collecting relevant data can be a very cumbersome process. For CCP research, in contrast, close ethnographic or interactional sociolinguistic analysis allows for pinpointing instances of two-way miscommunication. For this reason, it is the predominant method in doing such research.

Recent Research in CCP

A decade or so ago, Bourdieu (1991) put forth a new notion of 'practice' that has now been widely adopted in discourse analysis, substantiating the role that communicative or discursive practice plays in all sociolinguistic analysis. This notion is particularly useful in cross-cultural pragmatics. It seems clear that specific situations and discursive practices are best analyzed vis à vis the spheres of activity in everyday action. Following this line of reasoning, as I have done in Boxer (in press), I proceed here to follow Fishman's (1972) categorization of day-to-day language use into "domains." concentrating on those used in Greenfield (1968): family, friendship, religion, education, and employment. In sociolinguistics, a domain refers to a sphere of life in which verbal and nonverbal interactions occur:

> Domains are defined, regardless of their number, in terms of *institutional contexts or socio-ecological co-occurrences*...Domains enable us to understand that language choice and topic, appropriate though they may be for analyses of individual behavior at the level of face-to-face verbal encounters, are...related to widespread socio-cultural norms and expectations (Fishman, 1972, p. 441).

The three domains most relevant to cross-cultural pragmatics are the spheres of social interaction, educational encounters, and work life. There is little if any extant literature that examines the discourse of religious life at all, and cross-cultural religious discourse studies are, to my knowledge, nonexistent. The case is similar for family interactions.

Cross-cultural discourse in social interactions is of primary importance in that social encounters set the stage for perceptions (and misperceptions) of peoples from societies whose norms of speaking differ from one's own. As for educational life, this sphere of interaction is the locus of many gatekeeping encounters, and thus is an important domain for examining discourse issues in cross-cultural pragmatics. Perhaps no domain is currently as important as the workplace. Work life encompasses service and institutional encounters (e. g., Bailey, 2000), cross-cultural business interactions (e. g., Neimeier, Campbell, & Dirven, 1998), and communication in pluralistic workplaces (e. g., Davis & Henze, 1998). These phenomena are not temporary but are enduring. For these very reasons, the study of cross-cultural pragmatics in these three domains is critical.

Cross-Cultural Pragmatics in Social Life

The importance of CCP in social interactions stems from the danger of misperceptions of entire groups of people due to differences in world view. Corson (1995) aptly outlines the basic general concepts of world view and its consequences. He asserts that on the surface we may see cross-cultural communication as relatively easy and therefore overlook the repercussions of its lack of success on more complex levels:

> If the two languages, along with the two cultural domains of which they speak, are not kept separate in a complex intercultural exchange, then the weaker of the two cultures in that contact setting may have its unique values and concepts watered down when they are rendered into the words and expressions of the more dominant language. This is a thorny problem for intercultural relations...(Corson, 1995, p. 186).

Corson uses examples from the area of the South Pacific to illustrate the visibility of world view when using culturally specific rules of speaking to mediate between these concepts and languages. The consequences of world view differences can be serious for minority groups whose world views are devalued, resulting in their own loss of self-esteem and group esteem. Moreover, it can have serious repercussions in situations of world conflict and striving toward peace.

Perhaps the most striking examples of world view differences are illustrated in studies centered on Japanese/U. S. cross-cultural pragmatics. The vast differences in norms of social interaction between the two societies make for fertile ground for CCP research. Indeed, sociolinguistic norms differ so dramatically between Japanese and U. S. English as to make cross-cultural communication a true challenge (see, for example early work of Barnlund, 1975; Boxer, 1993; Lebra, 1984; Maynard, 1986; Ueda, 1974; Wetzel, 1988).

Ide (1998) is a recent example of a pragmatic analysis in Japanese of a linguistic phenomenon that has repercussions for cross-cultural discourse. She ethnographically analyzed the Japanese expression *sumimasen*, an expression of thanks and apology simultaneously, to explicate its social and metapragmatic functions. The analysis indicated that *sumimasen* connotes ritualistic functions that exceed the expression of regret or gratitude. Expressions such as *sumimasen* thus have great potential for pragmatic transfer, since they encapsulate a worldview phenomenon. Because of this, the use of these terms tends to lead to misinterpretations in intercultural interactions.

That apologies and thanks can be expressed by the same term is a result of how languages encode world view. Similarly, world view differences have the potential to lead members of distinct societies to perceive context differentially. This phenomenon is analyzed in recent CCP research by Connor-Linton (1999), a study of Americans and Soviets in televised "spacebridge" discussions. While this speech event is somewhat anomalous, it has parallels to social interaction. Connor-Linton aptly demonstrated how crosstalk (Gumperz, 1982) caused miscommunication between the Russian and U. S. participants stemming from differing conceptualizations of the context, leading to serious misperceptions by each group of the other (see Annotated Bibliography for further details).

Connor-Linton's study illustrates a quintessential lesson: CCP differences in the social domain are important because they are apt to interfere with the establishment of a sense of solidarity between interlocutors from societies with different norms of speech behavior. Without a sense of commonality with the "other", the establishment of friendships is prevented. Without friendship, global harmony is constrained.

It is perhaps true that CCP problems are more immediately interpreted as critical in the workplace and educational domains, where access to goods and services is impeded as a result of different norms for face-to-face encounters. Because of this, we tend to overlook the importance of personal relationships as a critical first tier of cross-cultural face-to-face interactional satisfaction. The goods and services exchanged in the social domain may not be as easily identified and quantified; nonetheless, the establishment of personal relationships and equalization is of paramount importance in establishing harmony between people of different societies and speech communities.

Cross-Cultural Pragmatics in Education

The issue of access is especially important in the domain of education. Because of this, and because most applied linguists interact in this domain daily, there has been a considerable amount of research on cross-cultural pragmatics in education on all levels, from early childhood to higher education. Heath's *Ways With Words* (1983) is perhaps the quintessential CCP study, focusing on the *intra*-cultural interactions of three groups of people living in the same community whose norms differed widely. What sets this work apart is precisely the bidirectionality of the focus: Teachers and school personnel as well as parents and students were eventually brought to an awareness of the mismatch of interactional norms between home and school in order to empower children to succeed.

A similar approach has been taken by Chick in his work on intercultural communication between whites and blacks in South Africa. Chick's research (e. g., 1985, 1989, 1996), much like Heath's, illustrates the serious consequences of cross-cultural pragmatic differences for powerless groups. Most of his work focuses on the domains of education and workplace interaction, illustrating the mismatch of cultural frames and schema that lead to discrimination against and stereotyping of South African blacks. The aim of such research is not to have the powerless group conform to a target set of pragmatic norms, but to educate whites and blacks alike about what happens, on a micro level, when norms clash. Indeed, in a society such as South Africa where the vestiges of apartheid are still felt, such research is critical.

Higher education in the U. S. is a good example of a setting in which individuals from all parts of the world interact, often demonstrating the consequences of misperceptions due to pragmatic differences. Salient examples of the importance of knowing what is appropriate language and behavior in higher education are interactions between NNS teachers or teaching assistants with their NS students. In many cases where NNSs are in the role of teacher, it is the student who has the pragmatic power, simply because the teacher is not a native speaker. This was the subject for a research project that I carried out in collaboration with colleague

Andrea Tyler (Boxer & Tyler, 1996; Tyler & Boxer, 1996;). Tyler's work with international teaching assistants (ITAs) over several years and my own interest in gender and language sparked a series of discussions about incidents in which ITAs said certain things to undergraduates of the opposite sex that were construed by the undergraduates as inappropriate. These discussions led us to design a project that focused specifically on what types of verbal and nonverbal behavior might have sexual implications and therefore what type of teacher behavior might be perceived as sexual harassment.

We wondered whether there was language and behavior that could be construed as sexual in U. S. contexts but not in other societies, and we also wanted to ascertain if certain sexually-tinged language might be more willingly tolerated in societies other than the U. S. Given the heightened state of awareness of sexual harassment in the U. S., understanding this issue seemed (and continues to seem) critical for the success of international graduate students teaching on U. S. campuses. While we realized that some men from cultures outside the United States bring with them negative attitudes toward women in universities and the workplace, we also suspected that some of these negative perceptions might result from cross-cultural misunderstanding.

In order to systematically investigate potential differences in interpretation of appropriateness and sexual intent in various teacher-student interactions, we sought the reactions of both undergraduates and ITAs to twelve scenarios of naturally occurring (and potentially problematic) interactions. A sample scenario follows:

You have a class that meets three times per week. The TA borrowed a book from you two weeks ago. During the last class, which met on Friday, you asked if the TA happened to have brought the book to class When the TA said, "No," you responded with, "OK, no problem." At 9: 30 p. m. Saturday night, the TA dropped by your apartment to return your book. The TA asked what you were doing. When you said you were just reading, the TA said, "I'm not doing anything either."

Our research participants responded to the twelve scenarios, in each case indicating whether they thought it was appropriate or inappropriate. The first study (Tyler & Boxer, 1996) had the subjects respond to the scenarios presented in written form. The second study (Boxer & Tyler, 1996) used videotaped reenactments of the scenarios. In both studies, we carried out in-depth ethnographic interviews with ITAs and students of both sexes to triangulate the data and obtain more in-depth information about perceptions on both sides.

The issue of cross-cultural perceptions of sexual intent is multifaceted and many-layered. The interpretations derived from these studies reflect culturally specific schemata of expectations for teacher-student relationships. For instance, while most U. S. undergraduates found it inappropriate for an ITA to stop by a student's apartment unannounced, many ITAs found this scenario quite acceptable. Some of the narrative comments indicated that this would be normal and neutral in their own cultures. The key notion here is the bidirectional nature of differences in interpretations. Clearly, miscommunication involving conflicting cultural assumptions and linguistic cues is subtle and enduring. Forewarned, ITAs can make informed decisions about how they might avoid being misinterpreted and avoid cross-cultural misunderstandings concerning sexual intent.

We see how role expectations determine the context of just where the burden of pragmatic competence falls. Despite the fact that ITAs are university teachers, it incumbent upon them as NNSs to understand the sociolinguistic norms of the society in which they are teaching and work within them. Undergraduates who pay hefty tuition fees complain to their parents about their inability to understand teachers from other countries. Far worse are complaints about what are construed as violations of pragmatic norms.

Thus the issue of power here is turned on its head. While it is true that teachers are typically the more powerful group vis à vis their students, holding in their power rewards and punishments, the power is diminished where the teacher is an ITA. First, it is diminished by the fact of not being a native speaker of the language of instruction; second, it is diminished by parental pressure on the institution to provide teachers who are both "comprehensible" and appropriately prepared to teach subject matter. Thus, while cross-cultural understanding ought to be a two-way issue, we clearly see here that this is not always the case. Invariably, the NNS, despite playing a role that is traditionally more powerful in the institution of higher education, is cast in a less powerful position, and thus needs to understand more completely the rules and norms of the NS students.

For this reason, and given that higher education is now a very important export for the U. S., there has been a steady increase in empirical research on ITA discourse. A recent example of such research, Jenkins (2000), is a study aimed at investigating the mismatch in communicative behavior of Chinese teaching assistants with faculty members, as opposed to undergraduates, in an academic department. Jenkins sought to ascertain the source of negative perceptions of each group about the other, noting that NS faculty members doubted the motivations of the ITAs due to what faulty members perceived as their lack of cooperation. The Chinese graduate students followed Confucian ideals of silence and avoidance with faculty, both socially and in class (e. g., not seeking clarification of points not understood; not attending office hours for needed explanations). For these reasons, faculty perceived these graduate students as capable in their field, mathematics, but lacking in their teaching abilities and English abilities. On the other hand, the ITAs perceived the faculty as giving them mixed messages as to the importance of their scholarly work in math vs. their English language development and pedagogical skill development. These latter two areas were perceived to conflict with emphasis on math. This qualitative study enabled the two groups to see each other through different lenses, and thus begin to understand the obstacles as well as the expectations.

In addition to research on ITAs, the interaction during academic advising sessions in higher education has been the theme of a body of work by several scholars in cross-cultural pragmatics. This research stems from the early work of Erickson and Schultz (1982), in which the authors documented in microethnographic detail the consequences of pragmatic mismatches between students and academic advisors in advising sessions. Their findings indicated that miscommunication due to linguistic, paralinguistic, and extralinguistic differences between students and advisors who play the role of gatekeepers could have life-altering consequences for the students. In other words, students who came from ethnic and racial speech communities with interactional rules that differed from those of their advisors ran the risk of not gaining the help required in order to succeed in their education. Advising sessions in the context of higher education are clear gatekeeping encounters. The advisors, as representatives of the department and institution, have the power to give or deny access to the student. This is a clear-cut case of the burden of pragmatic competence falling on the less powerful interlocutor, the student. Whether the desired goal is gaining entrance into a needed course, getting a good grade, becoming a ratified member of the discourse community, or obtaining a stellar reference for a future job, the consequences are far-reaching. In the educational domain, the repercussions of not knowing the appropriate norms for verbal interaction are serious indeed.

Since the publication of Erickson and Schultz's groundbreaking work on gatekeeping encounters in higher education, others have followed suit in studying similar gatekeeping contexts. While some focus generally on advising encounters (He, 1998), others explicate CCP as well as IP issues. An excellent example is the work of Bardovi-Harlig and Hartford (e. g., Bardovi-Harlig & Hartford, 1993; Hartford & Bardovi-Harlig, 1992) carried out over a number of years and published mainly in the early 1990s. These researchers studied the interactions of graduate students with their academic advisors, comparing the pragmatic competence of NS students with NNS students. This sort of comparison sheds light on the communicative competence needed on the part of foreign students to successfully participate in such gatekeeping encounters. The research also aptly illustrates the fuzzy line that I have drawn between what falls into the category of cross-cultural pragmatics as opposed to interlanguage pragmatics.

Cross-Cultural Pragmatics in the Workplace

Similar to the setting of higher education, workplace interactions have the potential to provide access or deny access to important goods and services, whether in service, institutional, culturally pluralistic workplace encounters, or business negotiations. The study of cross-cultural workplace discourse is increasing in importance given (1) the current emphasis on a global market; and (2) the fact that workplaces around the world are increasingly diverse.

Michael Clyne's 1994 volume on intercultural communication in Australian workplaces set the stage for more recent research along these lines. With so many immigrant workers (e. g., Turks, Slavs, Vietnamese, Italians, Greeks) interacting with Australian English speakers as well as with each other communicative features such as speech acts, turn-taking, and negotiation are important in achieving success at work. For example, one of Clyne's findings was that South East Asians were disadvantaged communicatively due to their self-effacing language and the fact that their turns tended to be appropriated by others. While they placed a high value on harmony, respect, and restraint, this got them into trouble in the workplace, where they were expected to be more assertive. Understanding such differences in communicative conventions can be a critical first step in equalization between groups that come into contact at work.

Indeed, the view that cross-cultural pragmatics is a two-way communication phenomenon with the burden of understanding falling on *both* sides has been increasingly explored in recent studies of cross-cultural discourse in the workplace. An excellent article by Davis and Henze (1998) provides a thoughtful rationale for the role that ethnographic analysis can play in the study of CCP. In their view, ethnographers do precisely this kind of descriptive analysis in order to adjust the power differential so that it is not only the powerless who must acquire the norms of the powerful. In other words, in this sort of ethnographic perspective it is incumbent upon both interlocutors or sets of interlocutors to come to an understanding of each others' norms. Davis and Henze's discussion does a fine job of explicating just how CCP views pragmatic differences as an area for interlocutors to critically examine:

> In terms of applications, some might favor teaching [the interlocutors] a way to communicate agreement to a task according to middle class white American norms. This approach is based on assimilationist ideology, which sees mainstream norms as the 'target culture.' Ethnographers would lean more toward making all parties aware of the miscommunication and seeking a shared understanding of why it happened (1998, p. 416).

Thus we see that CCP research deals with issues of cultural/linguistic mismatches between societies *and* within societies. Modern pluralistic societies with diverse groups that interact daily in all domains must look within to examine potential CCP pitfalls.

From this perspective derives a study in cross-cultural impression management that sets an example for two-way understanding. Bilbow (1997) examined the multicultural workplace that is present-day Hong Kong. His study specifically investigated a large airline with work teams comprised of both ethnic Chinese and those he terms "expatriates," which include English speakers from Australia, the United States, and England, for example. Employing interactional sociolinguistic methodology, Bilbow studied cross-cultural styles of interaction through the use of directives and suggestions as speech acts leading to impressions of authoritativeness. The study was designed to address existing problems with the two groups' stereotypes of each other (e. g., the Chinese viewed the expatriates as aggressive and rude while expatriates often viewed the Chinese as 'reserved,' 'evasive,' or 'reticent' (Bilbow, 1997, p. 462). Westerners interpreted the Chinese directives and suggestions as lacking in emotional expression. Such discoursal differences, including circumlocution used by Chinese but not by Westerners, led both groups to misperceive each other. The training component that derived from the analysis focused on presentation of the findings of the study with subsequent discussion in which both groups could bring forth issues of concern. Thus, the study's application to this workplace was direct and immediate: to aid each group in understanding how differential use of speech behavior created certain impressions that may have been unwarranted and that have the potential of stereotyping.

Bilbow's research is a good example of applied cross-cultural pragmatics. In a multicultural workplace such as Hong Kong, where English is the medium used but not the Ll of many workers, we need to examine what it means to have felicitous face-to-face interaction. Without raising the consciousness of cultural differences in speech behavior in such a context, the dangers of possible miscommunication are salient indeed. This line of research can thus be viewed in much the way that Davis and Henze (1998) advocate; that is, cross-cultural pragmatics needs to be used to stimulate a two-way understanding. Bilbow eloquently states:

> This approach, I believe, places an appropriate emphasis on the empowerment of those groups that have traditionally been seen as deviating from the 'norm' in discourse, and the development of enabling skills on the part of all parties present in intercultural encounters (1997, p. 466).

The issue of interlanguage pragmatics is not relevant here, as Cantonese is the national language, while English is the official language. It is therefore a situation in which cross-cultural pragmatics is key, calling for the necessity of two-way understanding.

Here we must return once again to the crucial issue of power: Why is it that the burden of understanding falls on the Chinese here, when Hong Kong is a Chinese-speaking city? It seems clear from studies such as Bilbow's that power resides with the westerners in this situation as well as on their own linguistic turf. Perhaps this is a remaining vestige of colonialism. Perhaps this is related to the inherent power of the native English-speaker as "owner" of the world's current lingua franca.

The study of cross-cultural pragmatics in the workplace has great potential to rectify power injustices. By making both groups aware of the other's norms, issues of power and dominance can be brought to the level of consciousness. This is a critical first step in equalization. In the workplace domain this equalization has serious repercussions for access to means of livelihood.

Conclusion

Nowhere are discourse issues in pragmatics more important than in cross cultural encounters, where interlocutors may possess vastly divergent norms and rules of interaction. Cross-cultural interactional competence is increasingly critical in societies where neighbors, coworkers, and colleagues are likely to come from distinct linguistic and cultural backgrounds. To ignore cross-cultural pragmatics entails running the risk of prejudice, stereotyping, and ultimately alienation. Understanding these differences opens doors, not only for those who are in less powerful status, but for all of us.

Anthropologists have long understood that cultural traditions are passed down for many generations, even when migration has been completed and social groups exist in a diaspora. Vestiges of communication styles persist long after migration and settlement in new places. Because of this, we cannot merely hope to "educate" the newcomer into a new set of norms. We have seen this time and time again, starting with subcultures living in same region, to different racial groups interacting in schools and communities. The goal of striving toward homogenization results in serious consequences of in-group/out-group miscommunication and prejudice.

Cross-cultural understanding ought to start in our very families, neighborhoods, and communities. We may find that the people next door, our colleagues or coworkers, our teachers or fellow students, have very different ways of speaking. Without understanding these differences, we may fail to recognize opportunities to establish the social, educational, and workplace networks that support successful communication, thus hindering development of respect and harmony.

ANNOTATED BIBLIOGRAPHY

Bailey, B. (2000). Communicative behavior and conflict between African-American customers and Korean immigrant retailers in Los Angeles. *Discourse and Society*, *11*, 86–108.

Bailey studied face-to-face interactional conflict between Korean shopkeepers and African-American customers in Los Angeles. This context has been frought with racial tensions. Through recorded interactions and interviews, Bailey was able to ascertain the sources of the tensions as two-fold: (1) contrast in communicative expectations for the speech event of service encounter; and (2) circularity of the pre-existing social conflict context of these interactions. The Korean shopkeepers and the African-American customers attributed negative characteristics to each other as a result of the communicative practices of the other group as well as prior schema of negative associations with the other group. Storekeepers perceived the customers as speaking loudly and with profanity, while customers perceive storekeepers as unfriendly, restrained, taciturn, and thereby racist. That which African Americans considered sociable was considered by the Korean shopkeepers as "poorly educated" (not refined). Bailey explicated three important components of this type of service encounter: greetings, negotiation of the business exchange, and closings. African Americans tended to elaborate the greetings and closings with personal talk, which reinforced intimacy. For example, they often finished turns at talk and continued talk when no reply was imminent, and, according to the Koreans, were more voluble than expected, indicating inappropriacy to the Koreans.

Connor-Linton, J. (1999). Competing communicative styles and crosstalk: A multi-feature analysis. *Language in Society*, *28*, 25–56.

The author carried out a quantitative analysis of lexico-semantic features that characterize speech styles of Americans and Soviets in televised "spacebridge" discussions over six hours. Connor-Linton showed that crosstalk, or miscommunication due to different contextualization cues, could be caused not only by suprasegmental features of the talk (cf. Gumperz, 1982) but also by lexico-semantic features of the discourse. Factor analysis indicated that each group's use of these features led to divergent styles that in turn instantiated differing conceptualizations of the context and thus the speech event itself. The American discourse, by and large characteristic of unplanned speech (Ochs, 1979), indicated an informal view of the interaction that was highly interactive. The Soviets, on the other hand, used a style that was much more indicative of their view of the context as a formal one, "oriented toward the exchange of particular information about specific referents" (p. 45). This is an unusual study of cross-cultural pragmatics in that it utilized factor analysis to validate more qualitative conclusions about cross-cultural miscommunication.

Cook-Gumperz, J., & Gumperz, J. J. (1997). Narrative explanations: Accounting for past experience in interviews. *Journal of Narrative and Life History*, 7(1-4), 291-298.

The authors explicate the consequences of cross-cultural miscommunication when nonnative speakers of English (here South Asians in Britain) utilized differing narrative styles in recounting past accomplishments in face-to-face interviews. In this case, the Pakistani workers were applying for traineeships in a governmental education program. The successful recounting of past experiences relevant to getting the post reflected a certain institutional self that is congruent with the program. It was thus necessary for the candidates to recognize cues presented to them by the interviewers, and these were more difficult to identify for the South Asians. Examples from unsuccessful interviews showed that, while interviewees may have provided all the necessary information, they nonetheless failed to follow expected temporal sequences in the narrative. The NNE speakers clearly did not offer satisfactory explanations in response to interviewers' questions. For example, orientation phases typical of such narratives were aborted; successful beginnings of exploratory accounts were not adequately negotiated. The authors demonstrate how different conceptions and expectations accounted for failure on the part of the NNE interviewees, with the consequences of real life loss in terms of not being chosen for the paid traineeships.

Davis, K., & Henze, R. (1998). Applying ethnographic perspectives to issues in cross-cultural pragmatics. *Journal of Pragmatics*, 30, 399-419.

The article describes a situation of cross-cultural miscommunication between three ethnically different interlocutors in a U. S. workplace setting. The interlocutors were a European-American team director, a Spanish-English bilingual team member, and a Chinese-English bilingual team member working in a nonprofit organization. The director typically took a nonimposing stance when it came to task allocation, offering the task as up for grabs rather than assigning it to a specific person. The pattern that evolved was the following: the Chinese-American team member would defer to the Spanish-English bilingual, thinking that perhaps the latter needed the pay that came with putting the hours for the particular case. The Spanish-English bilingual cheerfully agreed to take on the tasks, eventually overloading herself. Since the three had been classmates in graduate school in applied linguistics, they were tuned into the pitfalls of miscommunication and thus engaged in a metalinguistic discussion of their communicative styles. In so doing, they became aware of some linguistic/cultural differences that led them to certain routine behaviors. First, the Chinese-American noted that in her culture excuses were typically made before taking on a task just in case she would be unable to successfully complete it. The Spanish-English bilingual, on the other hand, took on a linguistic style of making light of each task and thus took on more and more. Her style was to resort to excuses/explanations only when the task was overwhelmingly difficult to complete.

Neimeier, S., Campbell, C. P., & Dirven, R. (Eds.). (1998). *The cultural context in business communication*. Amsterdam: John Benjamins.

The volume presents the proceedings of a symposium on the cultural context in international business communication. It contains basic articles on culture (e. g., T. Hall on "Three domains of culture and the triune brain") as well as sections on interculturality; the cultural context; linguistic perspectives; and a final section on training. Two pieces relevant to this review are "Power and distance as cultural and contextual elements in Finnish and English business writing" by Yli-Jokipii, and "Cultural keywords in Chinese-Dutch business negotiations" by Li and Koole. Yli-Jokipii's article demonstrates how the Finnish and English cultures encode social power and social distance differently in written business communication, causing miscommunication. Finnish people employ linguistic devices that encode distance, resembling something more akin to legal writing in English. Interpreting this transfer may inadvertently lead to attributing of avoidance on the part of the Finnish. Li and Koole's piece studies such cultural keywords as *support* in business negotiations between Dutch and Chinese. They show the distinct underlying forces at work. For the Chinese, a request for support indicates a basic Chinese value of humility and respect; the Dutch interpreted such requests as displays of distrust. This lack of shared meaning can lead to trouble in the important area of crosscultural business dealings.

OTHER REFERENCES

Bardovi-Harlig, K., &. Hartford, B. (1993). Learning the rules of academic talk: A longitudinal study of pragmatic development. *Studies in Second Language Acquisition*, *15*, 279–304.

Barnlund, C. C. (1975). *Public and private self in Japan and the U. S.* Tokyo: Simul Press.

Beebe, L., &. Cummings, M. (1985, April). *Speech act performance: A function of the data collection procedure ?* Paper presented at the TESOL Convention, New York.

Beebe, L., & Cummings, M. (1996). Natural speech act data versus written questionnaire data: How data collection method affects speech act performance. In S. Gass & J. Neu (Eds.), *Speech acts across cultures* (pp. 65–86). Berlin: Mouton de Gruyter.

Beebe, L., Takahashi, T., & Uliss-Weltz, R. (1985). Pragmatic transfer in ESL refusals. In R. Scarcella, E. Andersen, & S. Krashen (Eds.), *On the development of communicative competence* (pp. 55–73). Rowley, MA: Newbury House.

Bilbow, G. T. (1997). Cross-cultural impression management in the multicultural workplace: The special case of Hong Kong. *Journal of Pragmatics*, *28*, 461–487.

Blum-Kulka, S. (1982). Learning to say what you mean in a second language: A study of speech act performance of learners of Hebrew as a second language. *Applied Linguistics*, *3*, 29–59.

Blum-Kulka, S., House-Edmondson, J., & Kasper, G. (1989). *Cross-cultural pragmatics: Requests and apologies*. Norwood, NJ: Ablex.

Bourdieu, P. (1991). *Language and symbolic power*. London: Polity Press.

Boxer, D. (1993). Complaints as positive strategies: What the learner needs to know. *TESOL Quarterly*, *27*, 277–299.

Boxer, D. (in press). *Applying sociolinguistics: Domains and face-to-face interaction*. Amsterdam: John Benjamins.

Boxer, D., & Tyler, A. (1996). A cross-linguistic view of sexual harassment. In N. Warner, J. Ahlers, L. Bilmes, M. Oliver, & S. Wertheim (Eds.), *Gender and belief systems*, Proceedings of the 1996 Berkeley Women and Language Group Conference (pp. 85–97). Berkeley, CA: Women and Language Group.

Chick, K. (1985). The interactional accomplishment of discrimination in South Africa. *Language in Society, 14,* 299–326.

Chick, K. (1989). Intercultural communication as a source of friction in the workplace and in educational settings in South Africa. In O. Garcia & R. Otheguy (Eds.), *English across cultures, cultures across English* (pp. 139–160). Berlin: Mouton de Gruyter.

Chick, K. (1996). Intercultural communication. In S. McKay & N. Hornberger (Eds.), *Sociolinguistics and language teaching* (pp. 329–348). Cambridge: Cambridge University Press.

Clyne, M. (1994). *Intercultural communication at work.* Cambridge: Cambridge University Press.

Cohen, A., & Olshtain, E. (1981). Developing a measure of sociolinguistic competence: The case of apology. *Language Learning, 31,* 113–134.

Corson, D. (1995). World view, cultural values and discourse norms: The cycle of cultural reproduction. *International Journal of Intercultural Relations, 19,* 183–195.

Eisenstein, M., & Bodman, J. (1986). "I very appreciate:" Expressions of gratitude by native and nonnative speakers of English. *Applied Linguistics, 7,* 167–185.

Erickson, F., & Schultz, J. (1982). *The counselor as gatekeeper.* New York: Academic Press.

Fishman, J. (1972). Domains and the relationship between micro and macrosociolinguistics. In J. Gumperz & D. Hymes (Eds.), *Directions in sociolinguistics* (pp. 435–453). Oxford: Blackwell.

Greenfield, L. (1968). Spanish and English usage self-ratings in various situational contexts. In J. Fishman, R. Cooper, & R. Ma (Eds.), *Bilingualism in the barrio,* Final report to DHEW under contract no. OEC-1-7-062817-0297. New York: Yeshiva University.

Gumperz, J. (1982). *Discourse strategies.* Cambridge: Cambridge University Press.

Hartford, B., & Bardovi-Harlig, K. (1992). Closing the conversation: Evidence from the academic advising session. *Discourse Processes, 15,* 93–116.

He, A. W. (1998). *Reconstructing institutions: Language use in academic counseling encounters.* Greenwich, CT: Ablex.

Heath, S. B. (1983). *Ways with words: Language, life and work in communities and classrooms.* Cambridge: Cambridge University Press.

Ide, R. (1998). 'Sorry for your kindness' : Japanese interactional ritual in public discourse. *Journal of Pragmatics, 29,* 509–529.

Jenkins, S. (2000). Cultural and linguistic miscues: A case study of international teaching assistant and academic faculty miscommunication. *International Journal of Intercultural Relations, 24,* 477–501.

Kasper, G., & Dahl. M. (1991). Research methods in interlanguage pragmatics. *Studies in Second Language Acquisition, 13,* 215–247.

Kasper, G., & Rose, K. (1999). Pragmatics and SLA. *Annual Review of Applied Linguistics, 19,* 81–104.

Lebra, T. (1984). *Japanese women: Constraint and fulfillment.* Honolulu: University of Hawaii Press.

Maynard, S. (1986). On backchannel behavior in Japanese and English casual conversation. *Linguistics, 24,* 1079–1108.

Ochs, E. (1979). Planned and unplanned discourse. In T. Givon (Ed.), *Syntax and semantics, Vol. 12: Discourse and semantics* (pp. 51–80). New York: Academic Press.

Olshtain, E., & Cohen, A. D. (1983). Apology: A speech act set. In N. Wolfson & E. Judd (Eds.), *Sociolinguistics and language acquistion* (pp. 18–35). Rowley, MA: Newbury House.

Singh, R., Lele, J., & Martohardjono, G. (1988). Communication in a multilingual society: Some missed opporturuties. *Language in Society, 17,* 43–59.

Twitchen, J., Gumperz, J., Jupp, T. C., & Roberts, C. (Producers). (1979). *Crosstalk* [videotape]. London: British Broadcasting Corporation.

Tyler, A., & Boxer, D. (1996). Sexual harassment? Cross-cultural/cross-linguistic perspectives. *Discourse and Society, 7,* 107–133.

Ueda, K. (1974). Sixteen ways to avoid saying 'no' in Japan. In J. Condon & M. Saito (Eds.), *Intercultural encounters with Japan* (pp. 185–192). Tokyo: Simul Press.

Wetzel, P. (1988). Are powerless communication strategies the Japanese norm? *Language in Society,* 17, 555–564.

Wolfson, N., Marmor, T., & Jones, S. (1989). Problems in the comparison of speech acts across cultures. In S. Blum-Kulka, J. House-Edmondson, & G. Kasper (Eds.), *Cross-cultural pragmatics: Requests and apologies* (pp. 174–196). Norwood, NJ: Ablex.

DISCOURSE IN THE CLASSROOM

9. PEER-PEER DIALOGUE AS A MEANS OF SECOND LANGUAGE LEARNING[1]

Merrill Swain, Lindsay Brooks,
and Agustina Tocalli-Beller

From the theoretical perspective of a sociocultural theory of mind, cognition and knowledge are dialogically constructed. Embedded in this theoretical framework, this chapter reviews research studies in which peer-peer dialogue is linked to second language learning as students engage in writing, speaking, listening and reading activities. The review takes the stance that the type of dialogue of particular significance in the language learning process is collaborative dialogue, or that which occurs when learners encounter linguistic problems and attempt to solve them together. In such conditions language is used both as a communicative and cognitive tool. From the studies reviewed, we conclude that peer-peer collaborative dialogue mediates second language learning. We also conclude that although the studies reported few adverse effects of peer collaboration, teaching learners how and why to collaborate may be important to enhance peer-mediated learning. The chapter calls for more research which provides clear evidence of the connections between peer-peer dialogue and second language learning and more studies which investigate longer term learning. Such studies linking peer-peer dialogue to language learning can be instructive for teachers, researchers, and learners, and make us all more aware of the process of learning a second language.

This review article considers recent research in which peer-peer dialogue has been examined with the purpose of understanding its impact on second language (L2) learning. The dialogue may occur while the learners are involved in writing, speaking, listening and reading activities. We review the research from the perspective of a sociocultural theory of mind which claims that cognition and knowledge are dialogically constructed (e. g., Vygotsky, 1997; Wertsch, 1980; 1985). For this reason we have limited our review to those studies in which one can link peer-peer dialogue to a particular aspect of L2 learning.

Theoretical Orientation

The main premise of a sociocultural theory of mind is that cognitive functions such as attention, problem solving and voluntary memory are mediated mental activities (Vygotsky, 1978). The sources of these cognitive functions are social. That is, activities which are external to the learner but in which he or she participates (interpsychological) are transformed into mental ones (intrapsychological). "Psychological processes emerge first in collective behaviour, in co-operation with other people, and only subsequently become internalized as the individual's own 'possessions'" (Stetsenko & Arievitch, 1997, p. 161). The process of internalization is mediated by semiotic tools, language being one of the most important. Applying this premise to the learning of an L2 means that language that has been learned serves to mediate further language learning(Swain, 2000). This is accomplished interpsychologically through dialogic interaction (Donato & Lantolf, 1990; Lantolf, 2000), and intrapsychologically through private speech (Lantolf, 2001). In this paper we focus on the former.

The type of dialogic interaction explored in the studies we review can be regarded as collaborative dialogue(Swain, 1997). In collaborative dialogue, learners work together to solve linguistic problems and/or co-construct language or knowledge about language. Language mediates this process—as a cognitive tool to process and manage meaning making; as a social tool to communicate with others. This means, as Wells (2000) has suggested, that an utterance can be looked at simultaneously as process and product: as "saying" and as "what was said." In the example provided in the next section, the speakers are engaged in the cognitive act of making meaning; yet, once they have spoken, "what they said" becomes an object. As an object, it can be explored further by the speaker or others present. Through such exploration, content and linguistic knowledge are co-constructed, and may serve later as a resource for use by participating individuals.

Vygotsky (1987) argued that what was needed for learning to occur was the presence of a more knowledgeable person who would help the learner to move from being able do something only with the help of that expert to being able to do it independently. This "space," in which support is provided contingent upon the learner's developmental level, Vygotsky called the "zone of proximal development" (ZPD). Because Vygotsky's ideas have mostly been applied within developmental psychology, the more knowledgeable other—the expert in an expert/ novice pair—has typically been conceived of as an adult (e. g., parent, teacher) (e. g., Wertsch, 1985). However in recent years, the idea that peer-peer interaction may also foster learning has been advanced (e. g., Tudge, 1990; Wells, 1999). This idea has been extended within sociocultural SLA by suggesting that in peer-peer interaction, peers can be concurrently experts and novices (Brooks & Swain, 2001; Kowal &Swain, 1997). Furthermore, peers working within the ZPD of each other can support learning through, for example, questioning, proposing possible solutions, disagreeing, repeating, and managing activities and behaviors (social and cognitive) (e. g. DiCamilla & Anton, 1997; Donato, 1994; Ohta, 2001; Swain & Lapkin, 1998; Tocalli-Beller, 2001). A detailed (micro-genetic) analysis of the way new linguistic forms and meanings evolve leads to an understanding of what occurs in the ZPD—how acquisition occurs *in* interaction, not *as a result of* interaction (Swain, 2000). In the following sections, we review the research according to the main skill focus of the activity students were asked to do: writing, speaking, listening, or reading.

Writing

Collaborative writing and peer feedback as an aid to revision in L2 writing have proven to be an effective means of improving L2 learners' writing skills (see Cumming, in press). For us, collaborative writing and peer revision warrant attention because the collaborative dialogue that emerges in the writing process mediates language learning. Attending to the talk generated during the co-construction or revision of a piece of writing has allowed some researchers not only to access the cognitive processes learners deploy (Lantolf, 2000) but also to keep track of the impact of that talk on language learning, as reflected in the students' writing(Swain, 1998).

Swain and Lapkin (1998) conducted a microgenetic analysis of the dialogue of two grade 8 French immersion students as they jointly wrote a story. Swain and Lapkin used "language-related episodes" (LREs) as their unit of analysis. LREs are instances of collaborative dialogue in which students talk about the language they are producing, question their language use, or other- or self-correct their language production. An example is given below.

> Rick: ...*et brosse.*
> (...and brushes)
> Kim: *Et SE brosse les dents...les ch-*. No, wait a second. Isn't it *elle se brosse les dents*? And it's *SE peigne. Elle se peigne.*
> (And brushes [emphasizes the reflexive] her teeth...her hair. No, wait a second. Isn't it she brushes her teeth? And it's combs [again emphasizes the reflexive]. She combs her hair.)

Swain and Lapkin argued that LREs provide opportunities for language learning, and were able to demonstrate, using pre- and posttest data, that some LREs were in fact the site of learning.

In another study conducted by Swain and Lapkin (2001), two grade 7 French immersion students were involved in a multistage activity involving the joint writing of a story, noticing differences between their story and a reformulation of it (done by a native speaker of French), talking about what they noticed during a stimulated recall session, and revising their story. The original story the students wrote and their final revised story were considered as pre- and posttests, respectively. In this study, Swain and Lapkin traced LREs related to the same particular aspect of language (e. g., *souvenir* vs. *se souvenir*) through each stage of the activity in an attempt to understand what was learned and why. They found that the feedback inherent in the reformulation provided an important resource for the students and generated considerable talk between them. The students did not unconditionally accept a particular reformulation. Sometimes they rejected a reformulation because it changed the meaning of what they had been trying to write, and sometimes because they perceived that "it was not necessary." As the students talked their way through the stages of the activity, they came to understand why the changes were made and incorporated those that they accepted into their stories.

Spielman Davidson (2000) carried out a classroom-based study in which a grade 8 French immersion class was taught the form and meaning of the present conditional. Spielman Davidson observed, tape-recorded, and tested the learning of the conditional by four pairs of students who worked together throughout four weeks (16 hours) of an instructional intervention that focussed on planning a space colony. All activities required writing: writing a draft of the plan, editing and revising it, as well as doing and correcting a content-related dictogloss. The pre- and post-tests included a cloze test, a paragraph writing exercise and interviews. Additionally, the posttests included tailor-made test items based on the content of the peer-peer dialogues of each of the four pairs of students (see also Swain, 1998; and Swain & Lapkin, 1998, 2001). The posttests were given at the end of the four weeks and again 11 weeks later. The study group made statistically significant progress in their learning of the conditional during the intervention and maintained the gains in the written measures. Results from the tailor-made test items also indicated that gains were maintained long after the students were involved in the formal unit. This doctoral dissertation is particularly interesting for the detailed analyses provided of the LREs related to the conditional which demonstrate the immense complexity of language learning.

De Guerrero and Villamil explored collaborative peer revision of writing as part of a series of studies with adult learners of Spanish as a L2 (de Guerrero & Villamil, 1994, 2000; Villamil & de Guerrero, 1996, 1998). Their 1998 study assessed the nature and impact of peer mediation on writers' final version of two types of rhetorical modes of writing: narration and persuasion. An analysis of the audiotaped pair interactions showed that the majority of the revisions (74 %) worked on during peer-revision sessions were incorporated into the final drafts of the writers. When revising the narrative mode, the students paid almost equal attention to grammar and content (31% and 27% of the total revisions, respectively), whereas when revising the persuasive mode, the greatest percentage of revisions (38%) were focused on grammar. Moreover, assistance through dialogue prompted further revisions and self-revisions after the sessions, indicating that peer learning was conducive to self-regulated behavior.

De Guerrero and Villamil (2000) adopted a microgenetic approach to analyze 16 episodes of interaction between a "reader" and a "writer" of their previous data set on peer revision. The student who was "the reader" provided other-regulation by instructing or giving mini-lessons, which is a type of scaffolding mechanism by which students exteriorize their expertise and offer each other knowledge about language. The writer incorporated the majority of the changes discussed with his partner and, in some cases, further revised on his own. The "reader" also made progress in aspects of L2 writing and revising as well as in being able to provide peer assistance. As the researchers noted, the opportunity to talk and discuss language and writing issues with each other "allowed both reader and writer to consolidate and reorganize knowledge of the second language in structural and rhetorical aspects and to make this knowledge explicit for each other's benefit" (2000, p. 65).

Concerning the impact of peer feedback on students' writing and language learning, further studies are worth considering. Tang and Tithecott (1999) explored the value of peer-response groups. in ESL writing classes in a university college and noted that students tended to be positive about peer feedback but had some concerns (for example, they did not feel comfortable or know how to criticize somebody else's work). However, many students improved while participating in the sessions because they engaged in socio-cognitive activities that enabled them to become aware of deficiencies in their texts and, in turn, to make revisions. Both less and more proficient students benefited from the peer response sessions and increased their language awareness and self-confidence.

In a number of papers based on her doctoral dissertation concerning the collaborative performance of tertiary ESL learners of intermediate and advanced proficiency, Storch (1999, 2000, 2001a, 2001b) compared individual work to collaborative work and studied the nature of peer assistance and its impact on students' language learning. Storch (1999) found that collaboration and the metatalk it generated had a positive effect on overall grammatical accuracy when students completed a series of grammar-focused exercises (a cloze exercise, a text reconstruction, and a short composition). There were two isomorphic versions to these exercises (i. e., they featured the same theme, the same genre and were the same length and had approximately the same number of similar grammatical items to attend to). The first version was completed individually and the other version was done in pairs (or small groups). In the cloze exercise, accuracy improved in verb tense/aspect choice (up from 58% to 78%) and particularly in morphology (up from 35% to 84%). In the text reconstruction exercise, a greater proportion of items were detected and correctly amended when working collaboratively than when working individually (72% vs. 63%) and fewer were left undetected (10% vs. 17%). With regard to the composition, those written in collaboration with peers demonstrated a lower average number of errors than compositions written individually (7. 75 vs. 13. 6) and a greater proportion of error-free clauses (61% vs. 47%). Storch indicated that pairs spent more time on task as they discussed the changes, which clearly resulted in more accurate performance.

Storch (2000, 2001a, 2001b) noted that the nature of peer assistance is an important factor to consider in terms of the impact collaborative work can have on learning. Detailed analyses distinguished two dimensions of dyadic interactions: equality (i. e., authority over the task) and mutuality (i. e., level of engagement with each other's contribution). From these, Storch (2000, 2001b) derived four distinct patterns. In the collaborative pattern, both students contribute to the task, assisting each other (i. e., the expert role is fluid) and reaching co-constructed solutions acceptable to both of them. The dominant/dominant pattern is one in which, though both students contribute to the task and thus the expert role is also fluid, assistance is often rejected as there is an attempt of control and domination on the part of both students. In the case of the dominant/passive pair there is one dominant student who appropriates the task and who directs his/her partner and allows little or no contribution. The fourth pattern, expert/novice, describes the interaction that takes place when assistance is provided predominantly by one of the participants (expert), which is generally accepted by the novice. Like the dominant/passive pattern, one participant seems to be more in control of the task but unlike the dominant/passive scenario, the expert participant acknowledges the novice and encourages participation.

Analyses which linked interactions to evidence of language development in the students' writing showed that in collaborative and expert/novice dyads there were more instances suggesting evidence of a transfer of knowledge (22 and 15, respectively) than in dominant/dominant or dominant/passive pairs (six in each). Furthermore, these latter pairs produced a larger number of instances showing either no transfer or lost opportunities (due lack to involvement or challenge) than the former pairs (Storch, 2000). Adopting a collaborative orientation resulted in evidence of co-construction, more LREs, extension of knowledge, provision of scaffolded assistance, and language development (grammatical accuracy and new lexical knowledge).

Similarly, DiCamilla and Anton's (1997) analyses of the discourse of five dyads of Spanish L2 learners collaborating on a writing assignment emphasized the importance of co-constructed scaffolded support and guidance through peer dialogue. In particular, they pointed out how repetition allowed students to recognize features of the language and to provide the necessary mediation to solve certain problems (of lexis, spelling, verb form, etc.). Repetition was also used to appropriate the new forms and/or to help peers appropriate the provided forms.

Paulus (1999) analyzed the audiotaped interactions of 11 ESL students who participated in peer review sessions to give each other feedback on their writing. She compared the student revisions to three drafts of a persuasive essay and compared them to modifications resulting from teacher feedback. The results showed that students used both the peer and teacher feedback to revise their drafts. Fourteen percent of total revisions were made as a result of the peer feedback. The majority of the revisions (52%) were influenced neither by the peer nor the teacher feedback but by some other unknown source, including the self. Nevertheless, peer and teacher feedback accounted for more meaning-level revisions than those resulting from the other sources. Notably, 32% of the changes made to the second draft of the essay, written immediately after the peer revision session, were a result of peer feedback. Furthermore, the majority of these changes (63%) were meaning changes, which points to the fact, as Paulus noted, that "not only do students take their classmates' advice seriously, but they also use it to make meaning-level changes to their writing" (p. 281). That is, students find their peers' advice useful. However, the overall result of Paulus' study indicated that teacher feedback was used more often than peer feedback (see also Nelson & Carson, 1998; Tsui & Ng, 2000). Such a result can indicate that there may be a need to help and train students in how to provide peer feedback.

As Tang and Tithecott (1999) conclude about the study we reviewed above, students should be given intensive training to enable them to participate fully in the process of collaboration. Berg (1999) compared the performance of two classes in a university-based Intensive English Program that were trained in how to provide peer response (the treatment group) to two classes in the same program that received no such training. No difference between the pretreatment writing had been found between the two groups. The training provided students with the language and rationale for using peer response in the classroom. Trained peer response then resulted in a significantly greater number of meaning changes in the revised drafts as well as in significantly higher writing scores. Berg noted that peer response can teach students about academic writing because, in discussing each other's essays, they have to apply knowledge about their thesis statements, the development of ideas and the types of text organization. Furthermore, this discussion of ideas (content) and language can help students "discover viable text alternatives to unclear aspects of their writing" (Berg, 1999, p. 232).

Sometimes writing becomes a tool to generate discussion about unclear issues of other aspects of the L2 such as discourse/pragmatics. Recently, language teachers have begun to use interactive computer networks to help students collaborate in their learning process as in the case of the students in Kinginger's (2000) study. Kinginger analyzed classroom interaction between language learners in the United States and France using email exchange and video-conferencing. Involvement and correspondence with French peers encouraged learners to appropriate forms of the language that are adequate for the expression of solidarity, especially the mutual use of the *tu* form of address in student-student interactions. Key-pals provided both explicit instruction and direct assistance (sometimes without being requested) to their partners to help them understand how and why the social context of solidarity is constructed in French. Students acknowledged this assistance and in later exchanges used the form *tu* correctly and appropriately. The videoconference and approximately 350 e-mails showed that these types of exchange can broaden peer-peer discourse options in the foreign language classroom. The peer-peer relationships that were nurtured in the classroom communities engendered positive emotional energy, active interest in learning, and learning itself (i. e., the appropriation of the correct form of addressivity among peers). However, as Kinginger noted, it is not technology itself that is beneficial but "the vagaries, perils and delights of making sense in the company of other human beings who interest them" (2000, p. 44).

Speaking

Face-to-face interaction in speaking activities also can assist learners along the interlanguage continuum. Lynch and Maclean (2001) explored the effects on learners' performance of successive cycles of a "poster carousel" (see also Lynch

& Maclean, 1994). Pairs of learners within a specialist group of 14 oncologists and radiation therapists in an English for Special Purposes (ESP) course each prepared a poster based on a research article. One member of the pair ("the host") then interacted with six other learners who visited their posters in different cycles. Rather than give a mini-lecture, the host at each poster responded to questions posed by "the visitors" so that each performance was unique but may have been shaped by previous cycles. What Lynch and Maclean explored was whether this task "recycling," or the learners' drawing on responses given in previous cycles, resulted in gains in their language development. While the higher proficiency students did not incorporate any language from their interlocutors, their language use did improve over successive cycles as a result of the opportunity to repeat or recycle their performance in front of different listeners. The less proficient learners, however, showed improvements in phonology, syntax, and lexis as a result of the interaction over the six cycles of the poster carousel. These changes were linked directly to the co-constructed performances between the hosts and the visitors. Although Lynch and Maclean could not conclude from the data whether these changes represented long-term acquisition, what is clear is that the peer-peer dialogue resulted in improved language performance.

In another study of peer-peer interaction, Lynch (2001) asked four pairs of students to transcribe a 90–20 second recorded extract of a role play they had performed in front of the class. After initially transcribing the role play verbatim, the learners could make changes to their original scripts. At this stage, through peer-peer negotiation, 81 out of 112 of the changes the learners made were improvements on the original oral performance (11 changes were for the worse, and 20 changes were neither better nor worse). The teacher then reformulated the revised scripts, correcting grammar and lexis, editing out redundancies, and making changes to improve precision and clarify meaning. As a final step in this multistage activity, the learners compared their own revised scripts with the reformulated version and discussed the differences between the two transcripts with each other and with the teacher. Feedback in the form of self-correction, teacher intervention, and peer correction all supported students' language learning. Currently Lynch is studying whether the transcribing and the resulting discussion in such activities result in long-term acquisition and whether they would be feasible in a classroom setting.

In a classroom corpus of seven adult students learning Japanese, Ohta (2001) also investigated peer-peer interaction and, in particular, demonstrated how the social interaction occurring "during second language interactive language learning tasks constitutes learning" (p. 125). The corpus was collected over an academic year as the learners participated in their Japanese classes and thus represents a longitudinal study of classroom language learning. Working within a sociocognitive framework, Ohta examined the corpus for examples of how peers working within their ZPD can assist each other's performance in the classroom and thereby promote language development through scaffolding. Her findings support previous findings (e. g., Kowal &Swain, 1997) that even less proficient peers are able to provide assistance to more proficient peers. Through dialogue, learners can construct utterances that are beyond what each could produce individually. Ohta's analysis of the corpus revealed that the assisted performance comes in the form of peers' waiting for each other to finish their utterances, prompting, or through co-constructions. Peers also provided assistance in the form of recasts which are incorporated in later utterances. Not all of the peer interaction was error-free, but Ohta found, contrary to a previous study by Mackey, McDonough and Kim (1999, cited in Ohta, 2001), that incorporation rates of incorrect utterances were very low. According to Ohta, the benefits of peer interaction outweigh any negative effects, as through scaffolding, learners build "bridges to proficiency" (2001, p. 125). This scaffolding, together with the internalization of the language occurring in social interaction, supports L2 development.

Listening

Other studies in the literature show how peer-peer dialogue after listening activities can also result in L2 learning. He and Ellis (1999) compared the effect of teacher-controlled exchanges and peer-peer interaction following a listening activity on vocabulary acquisition. Six classes in an Intensive English Program in Japan were divided into three groups. The first two groups either involved no interaction or interaction with the teacher only. Only in the third group could the learners interact and negotiate meaning with each other in order to complete a picture labelling activity. Students in the peer-peer interaction group outperformed the other two groups in terms of comprehension and in posttests measuring recognition of the lexical items given one week, three weeks, and four weeks after the activity.

The peer-peer interaction group also performed better on both of the production posttests given two and four weeks respectively after the initial picture labelling activity. He and Ellis attributed gains in performance to the interaction as students wrote, read and if necessary, negotiated meaning with each other. They concluded that interaction in "dialogically symmetrical discourse" (1999, p. 131) between peers was more conducive to incidental vocabulary acquisition than the controlled teacher-learner exchanges. Although the learners did benefit from the teacher-controlled exchanges, they had more opportunities for language learning with their peers.

In another study involving peer-peer interaction after a listening activity, Garcia and Asención (2001) investigated 39 first-semester Spanish students at an American university. Their research examined the effects of interaction on the participants' performance on a post-listening text reconstruction task and a comprehension test. Both the comparison group and the experimental group took notes as they listened to a mini-lecture. After the lecture, the comparison group in the study did not interact while the participants in the experimental group shared their notes for five minutes in small groups. Garcia and Asención found that while the groups did not differ in the text reconstruction task, the experimental group scored significantly higher on the listening comprehension posttest. They therefore concluded that interaction can help improve listening comprehension. Qualitative analysis of the taped interactions corroborated other research on interaction (e. g., Ohta, 1995; Swain & Lapkin, 1998, 2001) that illustrated how the students use language as a cognitive tool. The participants in the experimental group provided scaffolding for each other and through interaction with their peers, students questioned language use and repaired grammatical forms. Garcia and Asención also identified confirming and code-switching as two other features of the students' interaction in which language was used as a tool in language learning.

Reading

Peer-peer dialogue has also been shown to help students apply comprehension strategies and co-construct knowledge while reading. Klingner and Vaughn (2000) investigated how a group of Spanish-English bilingual elementary school students collaborated to build their own reading comprehension and that of their limited English proficient (LEP) peers. Through a classroom technique known as collaborative strategic reading (CSR) (see also Klingner, Vaughn, & Schumm, 1998), the 37 participants in the study were taught four reading strategies to aid their reading comprehension of a content-based text. The text was in English but students discussed the content of the text in both English and Spanish. Qualitative analysis of the students' discourse showed that through interacting in their CSR groups, the fifth-grade students assisted one another in vocabulary comprehension, finding the main idea and asking and answering questions about their text. Klingner and Vaughn reported that in each of the six cooperative learning groups, the students taught concepts and vocabulary to their peers. In some cases bilingual students provided translations for the LEP students. The authors concluded that in their groups, the students provided scaffolding for each other and that even the higher achieving students benefited from the group interaction. According to Klingner and Vaughn, for scaffolding to occur, the important factor is not expertise but rather whether students are instructed in how to provide assistance to their peers, as they had been in this study. Pre-and post-test measures of vocabulary indicated that the students made gains in their language learning. While the LEP students appeared to demonstrate little improvement as measured in the tests, they were able to provide closer approximations to the correct answers than they had in the pretests. However, due to the scoring criteria used, these gains were not quantified.

Conclusions

We conclude from the studies presented in this review that the collaborative dialogue in which peers engage as they work together on writing, speaking, listening and reading activities mediates second language learning. We found that many of these studies center around writing activities, perhaps because one can more directly examine the product of the dialogic process. Although not considered in this review, it is to be noted that both within and across each of these skill areas, the particular activities and tasks used will affect the nature of the dialogue and therefore the language learned. More studies which investigate the transfer of knowledge to new contexts and longer term effects are called for. We also found that few adverse effects of working collaboratively were noted. However, possible effects such as greater reliance on teacher feedback than on peer feedback, students' lack of confidence about knowing how to provide useful feedback, and conflicts amongst collaborating students were noted; these suggest that instructing students both how and why to collaborate may be important.

We believe that a thorough examination of peer-peer dialogue is instructive for teachers, researchers and the learners themselves as a means of understanding how learning is happening, and what is going right or wrong with the process. Relating this dialogue to learning outcomes is, of course, an additional but important step in enriching this understanding.

Notes

1. We wish to thank the following people for reading an earlier draft of this paper at short notice: Carole Bracco, Alister Cumming, Jim Lantolf, Sharon Lapkin, Tony Lynch, Neomy Storch, and Miles Turnbull.

REFERENCES

Berg, E. C. (1999). The effects of trained peer response on ESL students' revision types and writing quality. *Journal of Second Language Writing, 8*, 215–241.

Brooks, L., &Swain, M. (2001). *Collaborative writing and sources of feedback: How they support second language learning.* OISE/UT manuscript.

Cumming, A. (in press). Writing in the L2 classroom: Issues in research and pedagogy. In R. Manchon (Ed.), *International Journal of English Studies, 1*, 2 [special issue].

de Guerrero, M. C. M., & Villamil, O. S. (1994). Social-cognitive dimensions of interaction in L2 peer revisions. *The Modern Language Journal, 78*, 484–496.

de Guerrero, M. C. M., & Villamil, O. S. (2000). Activating the ZPD: Mutual scaffolding in L2 peer revision. *The Modern Language Journal, 84*, 51–68.

DiCamilla, F. J., & Anton, M. (1997). Repetition in the collaborative discourse of L2 learners: A Vygotskian perspective. *The Canadian Modern Language Review, 53*, 609–633.

Donato, R. (1994). Collective scaffolding in second language learning. In J. P. Lantolf & G. Appel (Eds.), *Vygotskian approaches to second language research* (pp. 33–56). Norwood, NJ: Ablex.

Donato, R., & Lantolf, J. P. (1990). The dialogic origins of L2 monitoring. *Pragmatics and Language Learning, 1*, 83–98.

Garcia, P., & Asencion, Y. (2001). Interlanguage development of Spanish learners: Comprehension, production, and interaction. *The Canadian Modern Language Review, 57*,

377–401.

He, X., & Ellis, R. (1999). Modified output and the acquisition of word meanings. In R. Ellis (Ed.), *Learning a second language through interaction* (pp. 115–132). Amsterdam: John Benjamins Publishing Company.

Kinginger, C. (2000). Learning the pragmatics of solidarity in the networked foreign classroom. In J. K. Hall & L. S. Verplaetse (Eds.), *Second and foreign language learning through classroom interaction* (pp. 23–46). Mahwah, NJ: Lawrence Erlbaum.

Klingner, J. K., & Vaughn, S. (2000). The helping behaviors of fifth graders while using collaborative strategic reading during ESL content classes. *TESOL Quarterly, 34*, 69–98.

Klingner, J. K., Vaughn, S., & Schumm, J. S. (1998). Collaborative strategic reading during social studies in heterogeneous fourth-grade classroom. *The Elementary School Journal, 99*, 3–22.

Kowal, M., &Swain, M. (1997). From semantic to syntactic processing: How can we promote it in the immersion classroom? In K. Johnson & M. Swain (Eds.), *Immersion education: International perspectives* (pp. 284–309). Cambridge: Cambridge University Press.

Lantolf, J. P. (2000). Second language learning as a mediated process. *Language Teaching: The International Abstracting journal for Language Teachers and Applied Linguistics, 33*, 79–96.

Lantolf, J. P. (2001, September 28–30). *Private speech and internalization in second language learning: A theoretical argument with some empirical evidence.* Paper presented at the 8th Annual Sociocultural Theory and Second Language Learning Research Working Group. Ontario Institute for Studies in Education of the University of Toronto.

Lynch, T., & Maclean, J. (1994). Poster carousel. In K. Bailey & L. Savage (Eds.), *New ways of teaching speaking* (pp. 108–109). Washington, D. C: TESOL.

Lynch, T., & Maclean, J. (2001). "A case of exercising" : Effects of immediate task repetition on learner's performance. In M. Bygate, P. Skehan, & M. Swain (Eds.), *Researching pedagogical tasks: Second language learning, teaching and testing* (pp. 141–162). London: Longman.

Lynch, T. (2001). Seeing what they meant: Transcribing as a route to noticing. *ELT Journal, 55*, 124–132.

Nelson, G., & Carson, J. (1998). ESL students' perceptions of effectiveness in peer response groups. *Journal of Second Language Writing, 7*, 113–131.

Ohta, A. S. (1995). Applying sociocultural theory to an analysis of learner discourse: Learner-learner collaborative interaction in the zone of proximal development. *Issues in Applied Linguistics, 6*, 93–121.

Ohta, A. S. (2001). Peer interactive tasks and assisted performance in classroom language learning. In A. S. Ohta, *Second language acquisition processes in the classroom: Learning*

Japanese (pp. 73–128). Mahwah, NJ: Lawrence Erlbaum.

Paulus, T. M. (1999). The effect of peer and teacher feedback on student writing. *Journal of Second Language Writing, 8,* 265–289.

Spielman Davidson, S. J. (2000). *Collaborative dialogues in the zone proximal development: Grade eight French immersion students learning the conditional tense.* Unpublished doctoral dissertation, Ontario Institute for Studies in Education of the University of Toronto.

Stetsenko, A., & Arievitch, I. (1997). Constructing and deconstructing the self: Comparing post-Vygotskian and discourse-based versions of social construction. *Mind, Culture, and Activity: An International Journal, 4,* 159–172.

Storch, N. (1999). Are two heads better than one? Pair work and grammatical accuracy. *System, 27,* 363–374.

Storch, N. (2000, December). *Is pair work conducive to language learning? The nature of assistance in adult ESL pair work and its effect on language development.* Paper presented at the conference on Scaffolding and Language Learning in Educational Contexts: Sociocultural Approaches to Theory and Practice. Centre for Language and Literacy, University of Technology, Sydney.

Storch, N. (200la). How collaborative is pair work? ESL tertiary students composing in pairs. *Language Teaching Research, 5,* 29–53.

Storch, N. (200lb). *An investigation into the nature of pair work in an ESL classroom and its effect on grammatical devetopment.* Unpublished doctoral dissertation, University of Melbourne.

Swain, M. (1997). Collaborative dialogue: Its contribution to second language learning. *Revista Canaria de Estudios Ingleses, 34,* 115–132.

Swain, M. (1998). Focus on form through conscious reflection. In C. Doughty & J. Williams (Eds.), *Focus on form in classroom second language acquisition* (pp. 64–81). Cambridge: Cambridge University Press.

Swain, M. (2000). The output hypothesis and beyond: Mediating acquisition through collaborative dialogue. In J. Lantolf (Ed.), *Sociocultural theory and second language learning* (pp. 97–114). Oxford: Oxford University Press.

Swain, M., & Lapkin, S. (1998). Interaction and second language learning: Two adolescent French immersion students working together. *The Modern Language Journal, 82,* 320–337.

Swain, M., & Lapkin, S. (2001, February). *What two learners notice in their reformulated writing, what they learn from it, and their insights into the process.* Paper presented at the American Association of Applied Linguistics, St. Louis, MO.

Tang, G. M., & Tithecott, J. (1999). Peer Response in ESL Writing. *TESL Canada Journal, 16,* 20–38.

Tocalli-Beller, A. (2001). *Cognitive conflict, disagreement and repetition in collaborative groups: Insights into the affective and social dimensions.* OISE/UT manuscript.

Tsui, A. B. M., & Ng, M. (2000). Do secondary L2 writers benefit from peer comments? *Journal of Second Language Writing, 9,* 147–170.

Tudge, J. (1990). Vygotsky, the zone of proximal development, and peer collaboration: Implications for classroom practice. In L. C. Moll (Ed.), *Vygotsky and education: Instructional implications and applications of sociohistorical psychology* (pp. 155–172). Cambridge: Cambridge University Press.

Villamil, O. S., & de Guerrero, M. C. M. (1996). Peer revision in the L2 classroom: Social-cognitive activities, mediating strategies, and aspects of social behavior. *Journal of Second Language Writing, 5,* 51–75.

Villamil, O. S., & de Guerrero, M. C. M. (1998). Assessing the impact of peer revision on L2 writing. *Applied Linguistics, 19,* 491–514.

Vygtosky, L. S. (1978). Mind in society. Cambridge, MA: MIT Press.

Vygotsky, L. S. (1987). Problems of general psychology (including the volume *Thinking and speech, Vol. 1 of The collected works of L. S. Vygotsky*). New York: Plenum.

Vygotsky, L. S. (1997). *Educational psychology.* Boca Raton, FL: St. Lucie Press.

Wells, G. (1999). *Dialogic inquiry: Toward a sociocultural practice and theory of education.* Cambridge: Cambridge University Press.

Wells, G. (2000). Dialogic inquiry in education: Building on the legacy of Vygotsky. In C. D. Lee & P. Smagorinsky (Eds.), *Vygotskian perspectives on literaol research* (pp. 51–85). New York: Cambridge University Press.

Wertsch, J. V. (1980). The significance of dialogue in Vygotsky's account of social, egocentric, and inner speech. *Contemporary Educational Psychology, 5,* 150–162.

Wertsch, J. V. (1985). *Vygotsky and the social formation of mind.* Cambridge, MA: Harvard University Press.

10. TEACHER-STUDENT INTERACTION AND LANGUAGE LEARNING

Joan Kelly Hall and Meghan Walsh

This chapter reviews literature on recent developments in teacher-student interaction and language learning. Based on a sociocultural perspective of language and learning, the studies are drawn from three types of classrooms : first language classrooms; second language classrooms, which include contexts in which the language being learned in the classroom is also the language of the community; and foreign language classrooms. Foreign language learning contexts are those in which exposure to and opportunities for target language interaction are restricted for the most part to the language classroom. Across these three areas, attention is given to studies that investigate the specific means used in teacher-student interaction to promote language learning.

Recent theoretical insights and research on classroom interaction have broadened, and in many ways transformed, our understanding of its link to language learning. Current understandings are based on the premise that much of our linguistic, social, and cognitive knowledge is intimately tied to our extended participation and active apprenticeship in sociocultural events and activities considered significant to our everyday worlds. Because schools are important sociocultural contexts, their classrooms, and more specifically, their discursively-formed instructional environments created through teacher-student interaction, are consequential in the creation of effectual learning environments and ultimately in the shaping of individual learners' language development.

The purpose of this review is to examine recent developments in research on classroom interaction and language learning that draws on this perspective.

Due to space and topic constraints, we limit the main review to studies on teacher-whole-group face-to-face interaction in language classrooms. Before discussing current research, we provide a brief overview of some of the major premises of a sociocultural perspective on language learning and the significance of classroom interaction. We conclude with a brief discussion of recommendations for future research.

Sociocultural Perspective on Language Learning

A sociocultural perspective on language learning is based on theoretical considerations and empirical investigations of learning drawn from a variety of disciplines including human development (e. g., Berman & Slobin, 1994; Ninio & Snow, 1996; Reed, 1996), cultural psychology (e. g., Cole, 1996; Tomasello, 1999; Vygotsky, 1986; Wertsch, 1991, 1994), linguistic anthropology (Ochs, 1988; Schieffelin & Ochs, 1986), and social theory (e. g., Gergen, 1994; Shotter, 1996, 1997). According to this perspective, language development begins in our social worlds, constituted by a varied mix of regularly occurring goal-directed intellectual and practical activities. Through our repeated participation in these activities with others who are more knowledgeable or expert, we transform the specific means for realizing them into individual knowledge and abilities. That is, we learn not only the structural components of our language; we also acquire the communicative intentions and specific perspectives on the world that are embedded in them, and thus learn how to take actions with our words (Tomasello, 1999). It is our eventual internalization or self-regulation of the specific means for realizing our activities, including the particular world views embodied in them, that characterizes psychological growth.

From this perspective, learning is considered not the internal assimilation of structural components of language systems. Rather, it is a process of "changing patterns of participation in specific social practices within communities of practice" (Gee & Green, 1998, p. 147). Because schools are important social institutions, the activities constituting their classrooms are considered fundamental sites of learning. Because most learning opportunities are accomplished through face-to-face interaction, its role is considered especially consequential in the creation of effectual learning environments and ultimately in the shaping of individual learners' development. The next section provides a brief overview of the nature of classroom interaction and its links to learning. Because the review is concerned solely with teacher-student interaction, the discussion will address only that facet of classroom talk.

Classroom Interaction

Classroom interaction is one of the primary means by which learning is accomplished in classrooms. In language classrooms, it takes on an especially significant role in that it is both the medium through which learning is realized and an object of pedagogical attention. Through their interactions with each other, teachers and students construct a common body of knowledge. They also create mutual understandings of their roles and relationships, and the norms and expectations of their involvement as members in their classrooms. That is to say, through interactions with their teachers, students are socialized into particular understandings of what counts as the official curriculum and of themselves as learners of that subject matter. The patterns of interaction also help define the norms by which individual student achievement is assessed. Students draw upon these patterns and norms to participate in subsequent classroom activities and thus they are consequential in terms of not only what students ultimately learn, but also, more broadly, their participation in future educational events and the roles and group memberships that they hold within these events.

Initiation-Response-Evaluation(IRE)

Earlier research on teacher-student interaction focused on describing the patterns typical of interaction found in classrooms (Barnes, 1992; Cazden, 1988; Mehan, 1979). Findings from these studies revealed that although student populations may vary from classroom to classroom and school to school, one particular pattern of interaction, the teacher-led three-part sequence of Initiation-Response-Evaluation (IRE), typifies the discourse of western schooling, from kindergarten to the university. Commonly referred to as the recitation script, or triadic dialogue (Lemke, 1990), the pattern involves the teacher posing a question to a student to which he or she usually already knows the answer. Students are expected to provide a brief but correct response to the question, which is then evaluated by the teacher with such phrases as "Good," "That's right," or "No, that's not right." Each round of interaction typically involves one student at a time with the teacher moving on to ask a question of another student once he or she has evaluated the prior student's response.

In the IRE pattern of interaction, the teacher plays the role of expert, whose primary instructional task is to elicit information from the students in order to ascertain whether they know the material. He or she also serves as gatekeeper to learning opportunities. It is the teacher who decides who will participate, when students can take a turn, how much they can contribute, and whether their contributions are worthy and appropriate. It has been argued that extended use of the recitation script severely limits students' opportunities to talk through their understandings and try out their ideas in relation to the topic-at-hand, and, more generally, to become more proficient in use of intellectually and practically complex language.

Using data from her own and others' classrooms, Cazden (1988), for example, revealed how the use of this pattern more often facilitated teacher control of the interaction rather than student learning of the content of the lesson. Similarly, in his examination of teacher-student interaction from several classrooms, Barnes (1992) found that the frequent use of the IRE sequence did not allow for complex ways of communicating between the teacher and students. As a final example, in her study of 'journal sharing' in language arts classrooms, Gutierrez (1994) found that in classrooms in which the activity was based on a strict use of the IRE, the teacher did most of the talking, commenting or elaborating on individual student's journal entries, while the students were limited to brief responses to the teacher's questions.

While many of the earlier studies on classroom interaction have argued that prolonged participation in the recitation script provides limited learning opportunities, few have actually documented links between long-term participation and achievement. One recent investigation is a notable exception. In one of the most comprehensive studies of teacher-student interaction, Nystrand and his colleagues (Nystrand, 1997) examined 112 eighth and ninth grade language arts and English classrooms. He found that the overwhelming majority of teachers used the recitation script almost exclusively in their classrooms and that its use was negatively correlated with learning. More specifically, it was found that students in classrooms whose interaction was limited primarily to the IRE script were less able to recall and understand the topical content than were students who were involved in more topically-related, participatory discussions. Because the use of the recitation script was more prevalent in lower-track classes, Nystrand argued that such teacher-student interaction was a significant factor in creating inequalities in student opportunities to develop intellectually complex language knowledge and skills.

Although most of the studies on classroom interaction have occurred in first language classrooms, a few recent studies have confirmed the ubiquity of the IRE pattern of interaction in second and foreign language classrooms as well. In her recent examination of junior form (comparable to junior high school in the U. S.) English language classrooms in Hong Kong, for example, Lin (1999a, 1999b, 2000) found that with one exception the recitation script was the common pattern of interaction. And, like Nystrand, she found that it most often occurred in classrooms comprised primarily of students from socioeconomically disadvantaged backgrounds. Lin extended her examination to looking at how students acted to resist what she argued was a stifling, alienating form of learning. In one classroom, for example, Lin reveals how one student attempted to provide a linguistically playful rendition of the expected contribution in response to a teacher question. However, rather than respond to this playfulness, the teacher kept to the narrow confines of the IRE, and reiterated his demand for a response based on factual information drawn from the story they were reading together. Lin argues that while such play can reveal students' language creativity, it also serves to alienate them even further from the official instructional purpose, if such contributions are constructed as unruly or uncooperative. By holding to the strict IRE pattern of interaction, the teacher in this classroom, Lin argued, pushed students "further away from any possibility of developing an interest in English as a language and culture that they can appropriate for their own communicative and sociocultural purposes" (2000, p. 75).

IRF and Dialogic Interaction

In an attempt to tease apart some of the intricacies of teacher-student interaction, some have begun to take a closer look at the IRE. In an early paper, Wells (1993) proposed a reconceptualization of the IRE pattern. His proposal came about from having spent extensive time in a number of science classrooms with teachers he considered expert. His observations revealed enthusiastic, extended student participation in class discussions, although initial analysis of transcriptions of the interactions revealed what looked to be a healthy number of IRE sequences. Upon closer inspection, however, he found subtle changes to the standard pattern, primarily in the third part. While the teachers Wells observed often asked questions of students, instead of closing down the sequence with a narrow evaluation of their responses in the third part of the three-part sequence, the teachers more often followed up on them, asking students to elaborate or clarify, and in other ways treated their responses as valuable contributions to the ongoing discussion. Wells concluded that when the third part of the IRE sequence contained a teacher evaluation (E) of a student response, it severely constrained students' learning opportunities. However, if, instead of evaluating student responses, the teacher followed up on their responses (F) by asking them to expand on their thinking, justify or clarify their opinions, or make connections to their own experiences, the teacher-directed pattern of interaction enhanced opportunities for learning. Thus, he concluded that the typical three-part interaction exchange found in classrooms is neither wholly good nor wholly bad. Instead, it can only be evaluated by looking at how it unfolds moment-to-moment on particular occasions in particular classroom contexts.

Hall (1998) confirmed these subtle differences in the ways teachers directed the classroom interaction. In her study of a high school Spanish-as-a-foreign language classroom, it was found that just a slight variation to the third part of the standard three-part IRE exchange made a subtle but significant difference in student participation in whole group interactions with the teacher. One group of students received more interactional attention from the teacher in that in addition to evaluating their responses, she often followed up with additional questions, or asked them to elaborate. The teacher also sometimes handed the interactional floor to this group of students, allowing them to initiate an exchange or take over other students' turns. In contrast, she provided subtly different opportunities for participation to students in the other group. While these students were called on by the teacher to respond to her inquires almost as often as the other group participants were, the teacher's response was most often an evaluation of the students' contributions. In some cases, student responses were completely ignored. That is, the teacher sometimes did not even acknowledge the student's response and instead moved on to ask a question of another student. Moreover, these students were not given many chances to initiate exchanges. And, when they tried to, their initiations were not taken up by the teacher as frequently as those of the other group were.

These subtle differences in the third part of the triadic exchange, Hall argued, resulted in the formation of two groups of students, a primary group and a secondary group, each with distinct participatory rights and responsibilities. These differences, in turn, were used by the teacher as a partial basis for her evaluation of the learners' midyear performances. When asked to discuss individual learners' performances in the class in an interview with the researcher, the students the teacher considered active, creative, and successful users of Spanish happened to be those to whom she gave more interactional attention. Like Wells (1993), Hall concluded that subtle changes to the standard pattern of interaction, primarily to the third part of the triadic dialogue, can create significantly different language learning environments.

Nassaji and Wells (2000) provide a more comprehensive discussion of various options for the follow-up move in the triadic dialogue. The data on which their discussion is based come from a six-year collaborative action research project involving nine elementary and middle school teachers and three university researchers. Their focus in the project was on teacher use of follow-up moves and the contexts in which they occurred. They were specifically interested in examining the links between the types of initiating moves and the kinds of follow-up moves they called forth. In addition to finding that follow-ups to student responses served a wide range of functions, Nassaji and Wells found that the choice of follow-up move determined to a large extent the direction of subsequent talk. Just as suspected, teacher contributions that evaluated rather than encouraged tended to suppress student participation. Conversely, teacher follow-ups that invited students to expand upon or qualify their initial responses opened the door to further discussion, and provided more opportunities for learning.

The potential value of the IRF has been confirmed in other recent studies as well. For example, in the study of language arts classrooms noted above, Nystrand (1997) found a subtly different pattern of interaction in higher-tracked classes. Here, the teacher's third part contribution to the pattern was comprised of what Nystrand regarded as high-level evaluation. In addition to ratifying the student's response, the teacher incorporated it into the discourse of the class usually in the form of either an elaboration or a follow-up question. In so doing, Nystrand argued, the teachers affirmed student participation in the process of knowledge building, challenged them to extend their thinking and engagement with the subject matter, and provided opportunities for them to take ownership of the ideas. These strategies, in turn, helped to create an inclusive classroom culture that valued participation and learning, and ultimately enhanced students' academic performances in the language arts classroom.

Rex and McEachen (1999) found similar interaction patterns in their study of a high school English literature class. Earlier studies of the same class by Rex and her colleagues (Rex, 1997; Rex, Green, & Dixon, 1997) had revealed that the English teacher interacted with the students in a way that was quite similar to the teachers marked as effective in Nystrand's study. The attempt in the 1999 study was to move beyond describing the teacher-student interactions to documenting the strategies used by the teacher to build an effective community of learners. Analysis of the classroom interactions revealed that the dominant way of talking about the class texts was what the teacher referred to as 'making a case.' This involved posing hypotheses about why the students considered something they found in the text boring, odd, or confusing, and then supporting the claims, linking them to specific pieces of evidence. During the beginning weeks of the academic year, the teacher assumed most of the responsibility for helping the students make a claim by asking leading questions and directing student responses. Like Wells, the researchers found that on the surface the early exchanges appeared to be standard IREs. However, closer inspection revealed that in addition to brief affirmations of student responses, the teacher elaborated on them or further probed students' understandings by asking additional questions. Moreover, when student interpretations were considered inappropriate or unwarranted, the teacher did not overtly challenge or evaluate them with statements like "That's not right." Rather, he acknowledged the students' contributions, and then offered his own interpretation along with evidence from the text. As he did, he directed his talk to all the students, rather than to the one student who had responded, and in so doing, helped to build an inclusive community of learning.

As the academic year unfolded, the teacher handed over his role as leader in 'making a case' to the students. Not only were the students encouraged to question and probe each other's interpretations, but they were also encouraged to question the teacher's readings of specific passages. From end-of-term survey assessments, Rex and McEachen found that nearly all of the students believed they had learned a great deal from this teacher's class and identified the class discussions as "the most valuable arena of their learning" (Rex & McEachen, 1999, p. 76).

The benefits of the IRF for supporting and promoting student interaction have been confirmed in recent studies of two university English-as-a-second-language classrooms (Boxer & Cortés-Conde, 2000; Boyd & Maloof, 2000). It was found that teachers who were effective in stimulating student involvement repeated or recast student utterances in such a way as to affirm their contributions and make them available to the full class for their consideration. In this way, individual student utterances were linked together and woven into the larger classroom discourse. This, in turn, helped to maintain topical coherence by building a collective knowledge base upon which all students could draw for subsequent contributions. The authors of both studies argued that through students' extended participation in their classroom interactions, student appropriation of new words and ideas was facilitated.

These findings have been corroborated in studies of foreign language classrooms as well. In his examination of the interaction of nine English language classrooms in Brazil, for example, Consolo (2000) found that in classrooms characterized by ample student participation, teachers more often followed up on student responses in ways that validated student contributions and helped to create topical connections among them. Likewise, Duff's (2000) study of a high school English immersion classroom in Hungary revealed that, in interactions promoting student participation, the teacher often followed up student responses by repeating or paraphrasing their contributions, and offering them back to the class for further discussion. Such follow-ups, Duff argues, served as an important means of encouraging learners' attempts to express their own thoughts and opinions on the topics, validate the concepts and ideas initiated by students, and draw their attention to key concepts or linguistic forms.

Sullivan's (2000) examination of a university English-as-a-foreign-language classroom in Vietnam led to similar conclusions. Here Sullivan revealed how the teacher nurtured student participation in the building of a shared base of knowledge through his frequent affirmations, elaborations, and other kinds of follow-ups to student contributions. In addition to the cognitive benefits of such interaction, Sullivan argued that such building of extended networks of talk among the class members also lent a humorous, light-hearted side to learning in that both the teacher and students could use their collectively constructed knowledge to play on each other's words and ideas. This use of humor heightened the students' enjoyment of their classroom interactions and motivated them to continue participation. This, in turn, provided them with extensive opportunities not only to become more affiliated with the subject but to build on and sustain their interpersonal relationships as a community of English language learners as well. The following excerpt illustrates a round of playful, collaborative repartee engaged in by the teacher and learners in the study. According to Sullivan, the researcher unknowingly triggered the game by commenting that the question asked by the teacher is a "major" one (line 3). This is picked up by the teacher with the words "very big," and followed by students who expand it to "huge," "gigantic," "enormous," and finally, from the teacher, "titanic."

1. Teacher: Uh huh? Right. Now 14. "What problems do you think a developing country may face in its social and economic development?"
2. Students: ((*Several repeat the question in Vietnamese*)).
3. Researcher: A major question. h-h-h-h.
4. Teacher: Yes. A very big question uh
5. Student 1: A huge question.
6. Teacher: Huge question. OK.
7. Students: [It's very big]
8. Students: [A gigantic question]
9. Teacher: ((*laugh*)) A gigantic question. OK.
10. Student: ( )
11. Teacher: OK.
12. Student 2: An enormous question
13. Teacher: A titanic question. OK.

Such play, Sullivan argued, not only helped to draw learners' attention to the language itself, but also helped to create a meaningful and motivating context for language use. This, in turn, enhanced the learners' interest in continuing to use the target language in their interactions, helping them reinforce and expand their vocabulary knowledge as they did. These findings on the value of interactional playfulness colloborate those by Wong Fillmore, Ammon, McLaughlin, and Ammon (1985) who, in their examination of successful language-learning lessons for children learning English as a second language, noted the use of such playfulness and its role in bringing learners' attention to forms. They state, "The final characteristic of the language used in successful lessons is that of richness and occasional playfulness as well...the teachers in successful classes tended to use language in ways that called attention to the language itself" (p. 42).

In all of the studies previously noted, a motivating learning environment was characterized by teacher contributions that encouraged students to participate by asking them to elaborate on their responses, comment on the responses of others, and propose topics for discussion. Moreover, the classroom was characterized by teacher actions that treated student responses as valuable and legitimate regardless of whether they were 'right, ' and attempted to understand the learners' expressed thoughts from the learners' particular perspectives rather than impose their own views on what the students were attempting to say. In the questions they posed to students, their responses to student-posed questions and comments, and their own reflections and musing on the topics, the teachers in these different studies not only maintained a cognitively and socially rich interactional environment and provided models of appropriate academic and social discourse for the students. Importantly, regardless of the level of students' linguistic and intellectual abilities, the issue being addressed, or, as shown in Consolo's (2000) study, the native speaker status of the teacher, in all cases classroom interactions promoting student involvement in intellectually engaging ways were topically coherent, cognitively and linguistically complex, and meaningful to the learners.

Links Between Discourse Patterns and Epistemologies

Recent efforts to probe more deeply the connections between patterns of classroom interaction and learning have turned to examining the links between interaction and teacher beliefs. Earlier research argued that the use of particular patters of teacher-student talk reflected certain pedagogical epistemologies (e. g., Barnes, 1992; Cazden, 1988; Gutierrez, 1994; Wells, 1993). Wells (1993), for example, maintained that the choices teachers make about the kinds of interactional patterns they use in their classrooms are linked to their pedagogical beliefs. Teachers who view themselves as leaders of communities of learners, and who view students as active agents in the learning process and thus take student involvement seriously, are more likely to use follow-ups to student responses that promote intellectually challenging interactions and actively engage students in them. Conversely, teachers who perceive themselves as authorities and transmitters of knowledge, and students as passive recipients of their knowledge, are more likely to use the more constraining IRE pattern of interaction. Few studies, however, have actually provided empirical evidence linking the discursive conditions of language classrooms to teachers' epistemologies.

The recent study by Johnston, Woodside-Jiron, and Day (2000) is a notable exception in that a primary focus of the study was on tracing the empirical connections among the discourse patterns found in fourth-grade language arts classrooms and teachers' epistemological stances. The authors based their analysis on data gathered from classrooms whose teachers were considered capable by their peers and supervisors. The means used to collect data included classroom observations, field notes, audio-and video-tapings, and both teacher and student interviews. Their findings provide empirical support for earlier assertions on the links between the kinds of interactions teachers promote in their classrooms and their beliefs about teaching and learning. However, they also found that while some classrooms maintained a dominant pattern of discourse and that these discourse patterns were consistently linked to one particular stance, many more classrooms reflected a mixture of patterns and teacher beliefs. These findings raise interesting questions for future research on the developmental consequences arising from classrooms typified by an assortment of patterns and epistemologies rather than one dominant paradigm.

Conclusions and Implications for Future Research

Several conclusions about classroom interaction and language learning can be drawn from this review. First, we can state with certainty that at least two versions of the triadic dialogue are used with great frequency in teacher-whole group instruction and that the versions give rise to qualitatively different language learning environments. The versions are similar in that they each contain teacher initiations and student responses to these initiations. Where they vary is in follow-ups to student contributions. In one version, the teacher most often assesses the quality of student responses with short evaluative responses such as "Good," or "Well done." The three-part interactions usually occur between the teacher and individual students and few attempts are made to extend the sequence, unless the student response is inaccurate or in some way inappropriate. In that case, the teacher usually seeks a response to her question from another student. Consistent use of this pattern provides very limited opportunities for student participation in learning.

In the second version, the teacher follow-ups include a range of functions. Evaluations of student responses still take place, since they can provide opportunities for teachers to check students' understandings and make adjustments to the instructional activities as needed. However, they are not the sole or primary follow-up. Rather, the repertoire of teacher contributions include response affirmations, reformulations, comments, and requests for justification, clarification, or elaboration. Together these serve to promote student involvement, highlight key concepts and ideas, build a shared base of knowledge, and, more generally, evoke feelings of inclusivity. As we have seen, the use of a full range of patterns is essential to creating effective language learning communities. This is so not just in first language classrooms, but in second and foreign language classrooms as well. Moreover, these patterns signal effective teaching in a variety of grades, from elementary to university levels, and a host of national and international contexts, including the United States, Canada, Brazil, Vietnam, and Hungary. Future research can add to our understanding by continuing to look more closely at the linguistic resources effective teachers use to create stimulating learning environments. In addition to the frameworks used in many of the studies reviewed here, the analytic frameworks of Nassaji and Wells (2000), Hellerman, Cole and Zuengler (2001), and Rojas-Drummond (2000) could prove useful in future explorations of teacher-student interaction in language classrooms.

A second conclusion that can be drawn has to do with the underlying epistemologies connected to the patterns of interaction. Based on the studies reviewed here, it is reasonably clear that consistent use of each version of the triadic dialogue is tied to a particular epistemological stance. Teachers who consistently use the IRE view teaching as a process of transmission. They see themselves as institutional authorities whose primary role is to pass down information to students, whose sole responsibility is to receive and internalize the information, and, when called upon, to extract and accurately display it. On the other hand, teachers who use a fuller range of follow-up moves in their interactions with students, incorporating student contributions into the ongoing dialogue, holding students responsible for monitoring and expanding on their own and each other's contributions, and in other ways sharing the responsibility for learning, lead to higher levels of student achievement. Teachers who consistently employ such actions have more of an inquiry-based understanding of learning, which values the activities of exploration, hypothesis testing, and problem-solving. They see both themselves and their students as responsible partners in what is considered a fundamentally jointly constructed social process.

Given these connections between actions and beliefs, the concern becomes how to bring about awareness and change in teacher practices and beliefs. The long-term action research project on which Wells (1999; Nassaji & Wells, 2000) and his colleagues have collaborated offers one possible means for doing so. We also need to look at the larger sociocultural contexts of classrooms to see how teacher beliefs and practices serve to reinforce or undermine those larger activities, values, and beliefs embedded in them. Here, the framework for conducting a critical classroom discourse analysis offered by Kumaravadivelu (1999) may be helpful in conceptualizing future research studies.

A final conclusion has to do with language learning and interaction. While many studies have asserted links between them, only recently have researchers begun gathering empirical evidence for these assertions. Clearly, a more complete understanding of the developmental consequences arising from the discursive practices of a classroom requires following the paths along which the varied patterns of interaction lead. This, in turn, requires more longitudinal studies, and more studies that include a full range of data sources (see Ford, Zuengler, & Fassnacht, 1998) in addition to transcriptions of interaction and that incorporate both qualitative and quantitative methods of analysis, as, for example, Nassaji and Wells (2000), Nystrand and Gamoran (1997), and Rojas-Drummond (2000) have done in their research. Incorporating methodologies that make use of the latest technologies for data collection and analysis may also help. Using digital tools for gathering classroom discourse data, for example, can provide instant links to other data sources, and support the electronic sharing and analysis of data across space and time. The use of such tools can transform the representation of our findings. Visually representing the path of a language learner's development through representative video clips, for example, can reveal the remarkable complexity of the process of language development in a way that pages of written text cannot. Moreover, the rich empirical base of findings engendered by such electronic collaborations not only will enhance our theoretical understandings of language learning. Such endeavors will also help advance our understanding of and ability to sustain effective language learning environments.

ANNOTATED BIBLIOGRAPHY

Ford, C., Zuengler, J., & Fassnacht, C. (1998). Analyst eyes and camera eyes: Theoretical and technological considerations in "seeing" the details of classroom interaction. *CELA Report Series 2. 40*. Albany, NY: National Research Center on English Learning and Achievement.

This report provides a useful discussion on the benefits and potential drawbacks of the various methods such as field notes, videotapes, and audiotapes used to study classroom discourse and learning. Based on a view of language learning as a dynamic and socially grounded practice, the discussion includes descriptions of actual data collection procedures used in a study of interaction in a senior-level physics class to illustrate the advantages and disadvantages to using different methodologies. The researchers argue, for example, that using two cameras allows for the best access to the classroom's communicative events, including both verbal and nonverbal exchanges between teacher and students. Although the focus of the study used to illustrate the various points made in the report is not on language learning per se, the discussion of the different methods for collecting interaction data is useful.

Gee, J., & Green, J. (1998) Discourse analysis, learning, and social practice: A methodological study. *Review of Educational Research, 23*, 119–169.

The authors present a conceptual and methodological framework for the investigation of learning in social settings. Emphasizing the relationship between theory and method in research design, their approach is a combination of various discourse analytic and ethnographic perspectives. The first part of the article describes the socioculturally-based theoretical perspectives on language and discourse on which the framework is based. The second part is an application of the proposed framework. Samples of actual classroom discourse are provided to illustrate the need for different analytic approaches to study the dynamics of moment-to-moment interaction and to link the complex patterns of language use that build up over time to actual learning. The paper concludes with suggestions for future research on learning in social settings.

Hall, J. K., & Verplaetse, L. S. (Eds.). (2000). *Second and foreign language learning through classroom interaction*. Mahwah, NJ: Lawrence Erlbaum.

This collection of studies on classroom interaction and second and foreign language learning emphasizes particular aspects of interactive environments that promote language learning. While there is variation among the studies in terms of the learning context and issues addressed, they each share certain elements. For example, each provides evidence that supports a sociocultural perspective on language development. In addition, each breaks from traditional studies of second language acquisition in that ethnographic and discourse analytic methods are used to investigate the dynamic, moment-to-moment interactions characteristic of classroom talk. Findings show that certain interaction patterns used by teachers and certain interaction exchanges between classroom participants can foster the construction of a collaborative classroom community and simultaneously promote language learning. The volume concludes with a discussion of future research possibilities and suggestions for organizing instruction in order to optimize meaningful language learning opportunities in both second and foreign language classrooms.

Hellerman, J., Cole, K., & Zuengler, J. (2001). Developing thinking communities through talk: Two case studies from science class. *CELA Research Report Series 14001*. Albany, NY: National Research Center on English Learning and Achievement.

This study looks at the interaction of two linguistically and culturally diverse high school science classrooms. While not concerned specifically with language classrooms, it is included here because the researchers' analytic focus on particular linguistic means used by teachers to socialize students into particular kinds of learning communities during interaction and their attempts to connect these uses of language to the teachers' pedagogical philosophies are useful additions to research on teacher-student interaction. In their analysis of audio-and videotaped data collected from one classroom over a five-year period, the researchers found that the teacher consistently used the first-person singular pronoun 'I' when introducing conceptual information. She also used the pronouns 'you' and 'we/us' but for different purposes. The frrst-person plural was used when the teacher wanted to point out student deficiencies or weaknesses and change their behavior or thinking. The second-person singular and plural pronouns were used to distinguish student responsibility for learning from the teacher's for teaching as in T: "You're adult now, you decide where the voids are." (p. 9). The authors argue that the teacher's distinctive use of these pronouns over time served to socialize the students into particular understandings of the role of the teacher and their role as students. The findings point to the significant role that teacher actions and beliefs play in socializing students into particular communities of learners.

Kumaravadivelu, B. (1999). Critical classroom discourse analysis. *TESOL Quarterly*, 33, 453–483.

In this article, Kumaravadivelu offers a framework for conducting what he terms *critical classroom discourse analysis* (CCDA). He begins by reviewing two approaches commonly used to analyze classroom interaction in L2 classrooms, the interaction approach and the discourse approach. While both approaches have provided useful insights into classroom learning, the author argues that their limited focus has produced "only a fragmented picture of classroom reality" (p. 456). To construct his framework, he draws on ideas and concepts from two current schools of thought, Foucauldian poststructuralism and Saidian postcolonialism, and from educational applications of this work. These ideas are then integrated into a three-dimensional perspective on discourse: the sociolinguistic, the sociocultural, and the sociopolitical, which he uses to review some recent classroom studies that provide "glimpses of the possibilities and potential of CCDA" (p. 472). He concludes with suggestions for conducting critical discourse analysis and a list of research questions for further explorations into classroom-based L2 learning.

Rojas-Drummond, S. (2000). Guided participation, discourse and the construction of knowledge in Mexican classrooms. In H. Cowie & G. van der Aalsvoort (Eds.), *Social interaction in learning and instruction: The meaning of discourse for the construction of knowledge* (pp. 193–213). Amsterdam: Pergamon.

Although the research reported on here is concerned with interaction and learning in math classrooms, the methodologies used to analyze the data in addition to the findings have something to offer those interested in documenting links between interaction and language learning. Rojas-Drummond and her colleagues investigated the particular discursive strategies teachers used to guide students' participation in instructional activities and then compared the use of these patterns across classrooms. Standard discourse analytic methods were used to examine their transcriptions of videotaped data. The interactions were examined on three levels and then characterized according to five dimensions describing the teaching-learning process. Once they characterized the classrooms, Rojas-Drummond and her colleagues compared students' performance from two fairly different learning environments, as defined by the typical patterns of teacher-student interaction, on two dynamic assessment arithmetic tests. They found that those in a classroom typified by an inquiry-based IRF outperformed their peers whose classroom interactions were dominated by the IRE recitation script. Teacher actions in the higher performing classroom that were found to differ significantly from the other group included using complex actions in the third part of the IRF that affirmed student responses, probed students' understandings, elicited student elaborations, and modeled desired actions, strategies and outcomes. The framework outlined in Table 1 (pp. 198–199) detailing particular teacher and student behaviors indicative of each teaching-learning dimension could be usefully employed in research on interaction found other kinds of classrooms.

Wells, G. (1999). *Dialogic inquiry: Toward a sociocultural practice and theory of education*. Cambridge, MA: Cambridge University Press.

Dialogic Inquiry is a three-part analysis of sociocultural theory and practice in the classroom. Wells first compares the theoretical insights of Vygotsky and M. A. K. Halliday on language learning and development. Despite their different orientations, Wells finds them compatible; both, for example, believe that language development is a process of making meaning with others. Wells builds upon these ideas in the construction of a conceptual framework for understanding the role of discourse in learning. In the second part of the book, Wells gives examples from classroom interaction to illustrate the co-construction of knowledge among teacher and students and the functions that different dialogic exchanges serve in the process. A case study is included as an example of a collaborative community in which scaffolding is an important part of knowledge building. In the third part of the book, Wells discusses the importance of the zone of proximal development (ZPD) using examples taken from his own research on classroom interaction.

OTHER REFERENCES

Barnes, D. (1992). *From communication to curriculum*. Portsmouth, NH: Boynton/Cook.

Berman, R., & Slobin, D. (1994). *Relating events in narratives: A crosslinguistic developmental study*. Hillsdale, NJ: Lawrence Erlbaum.

Boxer, D., & Cortés-Conde, F. (2000). Identity and ideology: Culture and pragmatics in content-based ESL. In J. K. Hall & L. S. Verplaetse (Eds.), *Second and foreign language learning through classroom interaction* (pp. 203–220). Mahwah, NJ: Lawrence Erlbaum.

Boyd, M., & Maloof, V. M. (2000). How teachers can build upon student-proposed intertextual links to facilitate student talk in the ESL classroom. In J. K. Hall & L. S. Verplaetse (Eds.), *Second and foreign language learning through classroom interaction* (pp. 163–182). Mahwah, NJ: Lawrence Erlbaum.

Cazden, C. (1988). *Classroom discourse: The language of teaching and learning*. Portsmouth, NH: Heinemann.

Cole, M. (1996). *Cultural psychology*. Cambridge, MA: Harvard University Press.

Consolo, D. (2000). Teachers' action and student oral participation in classroom interaction. In J. K. Hall & L. S. Verplaetse (Eds.), *Second and foreign language learning through classroom interaction* (pp. 91–108). Mahwah, NJ: Lawrence Erlbaum.

Duff, P. (2000). Repetition in foreign language classroom interaction. In J. K. Hall & L. S. Verplaetse (Eds.), *Second and foreign language learning through classroom interaction*. (pp. 109–138). Mahwah, NJ: Lawrence Erlbaum.

Gergen, K. J. (1994). *Reality and relationships: Soundings in social construction*. Cambridge, MA: Harvard University Press.

Gutierrez, K. (1994). How talk, context, and script shape contexts for learning: A cross-case comparison of journal sharing. *Linguistics and Education, 5*, 335–365.

Hall, J. K. (1998). Differential teacher attention to student utterances: The construction of different opportunities for learning in the IRF. *Linguistics and Education, 9*, 287–311.

Johnston, P., Woodside-Jiron, H., & Day, J. (2000). Teaching and learning literate epistemologies. *CELA Research Report Series 13009*. Albany, NY: National Research Center on English Learning and Achievement.

Lemke, J. L. (1990). *Talking science: Language, learning and values*. Norwood, NJ: Ablex Publishing Company.

Lin, A. (1999a). Doing-English-Lessons in the reproduction or transformation of social worlds? *TESOL Quarterly*, 33, 393–412.

Lin, A. (1999b). Resistance and creativity in English reading lessons in Hong Kong. *Language, Culture and Curriculum*, 12, 285–296.

Lin, A. (2000). Lively children trapped in an island of disadvantage: Verbal play of Cantonese working-class schoolboys in Hong Kong. *International Journal of the Sociology of Language*, 143, 63–83.

Mehan, H. (1979). *Learning lessons*. Cambridge, MA: Harvard University Press.

Nassaji, H., & Wells, G. (2000). What's the use of 'triadic dialogue' ?: An investigation of teacher-student interaction. *Applied Linguistics*, 21, 376–406.

Ninio, A., & Snow, C. (1996). *Pragmatic development*. Boulder, CO: Westview.

Nystrand, M. (1997). Dialogic instruction: When recitation becomes conversation. In M. Nystrand, A. Gamoran, R. Kachur, & C. Prendergast (Eds.), *Opening dialogue: Understanding the dynamics of language learning and teaching in the English classroom* (pp. 1–29). New York: Teachers College Press.

Nystrand, M., & Gamoran, A. (1997). The big picture: Language and learning in hundreds of English lessons. In M. Nystrand, A. Gamoran, R. Kachur, & C. Prendergast (Eds.), *Opening dialogue* (pp. 30–74). New York: Teachers College Press.

Ochs, E. (1988). *Culture and language development: Language acquisition and language socialization in a Samoan village*. Cambridge, MA: Cambridge University Press.

Reed, E. (1996). *Encountering the world: Toward an ecological psychology*. New York: Oxford University Press.

Rex, L. (1997). *Making a case: A study of the classroom construction of academic literacy*. Unpublished doctoral dissertation, University of California, Santa Barbara.

Rex, L., Green, J., & Dixon, C. (1997). Making a case from evidence: Constructing opportunities for learning academic literacy practices. *Interpretations*, 30 (2), 78–104.

Rex, L., & McEachen, D. (1999). "If anything is odd, inappropriate, confusing, or boring, it's probably important" : The emergence of inclusive academic literacy through English classroom discourse practices. *Research in the Teaching of English*, 34, 65–127.

Schieffelin, B., & Ochs, E. (1986). Language socialization. *Annual Review of Anthropology*, 15, 163–191.

Shotter, J. (1996). Living in a Wittgensteinian world: Beyond theory to a poetics of practices. *Journal for the Theory of Social Behaviour*, 26, 292–311.

Shotter, J. (1997). Dialogical realities: The ordinary, the everyday and other strange new words. *Journal for the Theory of Social Behaviour, 27*, 245–357.

Sullivan, P. (2000). Spoken artistry: Performance in a foreign language classroom. In J. K. Hall & L. S. Verplaetse (Eds.), *Second and foreign language learning through classroom interaction* (pp. 73–90). Mahwah, NJ: Lawrence Erlbaum.

Tomasello, M. (1999). *The cultural origins of human mind*, Cambridge, MA: Harvard University Press.

Vygotsky, L. S. (1986). *Thought and language.* Cambridge, MA: MIT Press.

Wells, G. (1993). Reevaluating the IRF sequence: A proposal for the articulation of theories of activity and discourse for the analysis of teaching and learning in the classroom. *Linguistics and Education, 5*, 1–17.

Wertsch, J. (1991). *Voices of the mind.* Cambridge, MA: Harvard University Press.

Wertsch, J. (1994). The primacy of mediated action in sociocultural studies. *Mind, Culture, and Activity, 1*, 202–208.

Wong Fillmore, L., Ammon, P., McLaughlin, B., & Ammon, M. S. (1985). *Final report for learning English through bilingual instruction.* Berkeley, CA: University of California at Berkeley.

11. TEACHERS' USES OF THE TARGET AND FIRST LANGUAGES IN SECOND AND FOREIGN LANGUAGE CLASSROOMS[1]

Miles Turnbull and Katy Arnett

This chapter reviews recent theoretical and empirical literature regarding teachers' uses of the target (TL) and first (L1) languages in second (SL) and foreign (FL) language classrooms. Theoretically, the article explores several issues related to teachers' use of the L1 and the TL in the classroom: exposure to TL input, student motivation, cognitive considerations, code-switching, and appropriate teacher use of the L1. A review of recent discourse analysis studies examines how much, when, and why FL and SL teachers use the L1 and TL in their pedagogy. The article also presents findings from studies that have considered teachers' self-reports and teachers' and learners' beliefs and attitudes regarding the use of the L1 and the TL in FL and SL classrooms. The paper concludes with recommendations for future research.

This chapter reviews both recent and earlier research related to teachers' use of the target language (TL) and first language (L1) in second (SL) and foreign language (FL) teaching contexts.[2] The chapter is divided into three main sections. Drawing on theoretical perspectives and empirical work, the first section examines teachers' use of the TL and L1 in the classroom from a theoretical perspective. The second section reviews recent quantitative and qualitative studies that have used discourse analysis to examine how much, when, and why teachers use the TL and the L1 in SL and FL classrooms. Studies that have focussed on teachers' and learners' beliefs and attitudes toward TL and L1 use are also reviewed. The final section in the article proposes future research directions on this topic.

Theoretical Perspectives

Research has examined several issues related to teachers' use of the L1 and TL in the classroom: exposure to TL input, student motivation, ways in which teacher use of the L1 can promote TL learning at cognitive levels, code-switching, and when it is appropriate for teachers to introduce the L1 into their pedagogies.

Exposure to Target Language Input

Carroll (1975) and others (e. g. Burstall, 1968, 1970; Burstall, Jamieson, Cohen, & Hargreaves, 1974; Carroll, Clark, Edwards, & Handrick, 1967; Wolf, 1977) found a direct correlation between FL achievement and teacher use of the TL; some regard this as the most persuasive theoretical rationale for maximizing the teacher's use of the TL in the classroom (Turnbull, 2001b). Since teachers are often the students' primary source of linguistic input in the TL, it is therefore reasonable to argue that maximizing the TL in the classroom is a favorable practice.[3]

However, Turnbull (2001b) and others (e. g., Macaro, 1997; Polio & Duff, 1994; van Lier, 1995) question what "maximize" means in terms of "optimal" L1 and TL use. Most SL and FL educators agree that students need to be exposed to input in the TL if they are expected to learn (Krashen, 1982), but how much exposure to TL input is optimal from a theoretical and pedagogical standpoint? Ellis (1994) and Sharwood-Smith (1985) suggest that mere exposure to the TL input does not entirely guarantee that it becomes internalized as intake (see, e. g., Chaudron, 1985; Ellis, 1994; Gass, 1988). Long (1996) argues that learners internalize the TL input once they have been given the opportunity to interact with and negotiate the meaning of the input. Swain (1985, 1993, 1995) argues that learners need to be provided not only with the opportunity to interact with the TL input, but also with the opportunity to produce written or spoken output related to the input, because she contends (1995) that producing the TL is an important aspect of the learning process.

Cook (2001) and van Lier (1995) observe that the idea of maximizing the TL in the classroom has been interpreted by most teachers to mean that they should avoid the L1 altogether or restrict its use to grammar lessons or classroom management. Cook (2001) contends that the long-held tradition of discouraging the integration of the Ll in the TL classroom has sharply limited the "possibilities of language teaching" (p. 405). Even though he agrees that using considerable amounts of the TL is critical, he believes that the Ll deserves a place in the TL classroom. Based undoubtedly on his experiences as an English as a foreign language educator, he argues that treating the students' Ll as a resource instead of a hindrance to successful learning will help to create more authentic users of the TL. Van Lier (1995) agrees, contending that teachers' use of the learners' Ll helps to create more salient input for the learner, hence promoting intake. In his view, (1995), the quality of the input is more important than the quantity of the input when it comes to intake, and introducing the Ll can enhance the quality of the input. Turnbull (2001b) agrees that the first language can be used "judiciously" to help facilitate the intake process, allowing input to more readily become intake (p. 533). The teacher's use of the Ll thus provides an enhanced form of input that is more salient for the learner, more easily processed, and consequently results in a greater understanding of the TL (see also Dickson, 1992; Py, 1996).

Motivation

Second language educators and researchers have long acknowledged the influence of student motivation on TL learning (e. g., Crookes & Schmidt, 1991; Dörnyei, 1994; Gardner & Lambert, 1972). MacDonald (1993) argues that the teacher's maximized use of the TL in the classroom has an impact on student motivation, as the learners can see how knowledge of the TL will be immediately useful to them. Turnbull (2001a) offers anecdotal support of this argument, adding that his students felt that they had learned more by the end of the year because of his insistence on maximizing his own use of French in the classroom. Macaro (1997) found that students were more likely to learn French as a means of furthering personal goals (instrumental goals) than learn the language because they were genuinely interested in the TL and its culture (integrative goals); he argues that if teachers use the TL exclusively in the classroom, the students are more likely to set instrumental goals (Gardner & Lambert, 1972), thus enhancing learning. MacDonald (1993) also contends that relying too much on the Ll can lead to student de-motivation; if the teacher overuses the Ll to convey meaningful information, the students have no immediate need to further their understanding in the TL.

Cognitive Issues Related to L1 Use in the Classroom

Drawing on the ideas of Vygotsky (1978), Antón and DiCamilla (1998) contend that when a teacher uses the Ll in the TL classroom, the learner uses the Ll as a cognitive tool to help "scaffold" his/her learning. Brooks and Donato (1994) argue that learners sometimes use the Ll to negotiate meaning. They propose that using the Ll helps learners produce the TL and to sustain interactions in the TL, thus making it reasonable to argue that teachers' use of the Ll may prove to be beneficial to the students' TL acquisition.[3]

Swain and Lapkin (2000) report that student use of the Ll during collaborative tasks occurred for three primary reasons—increasing efficiency, focusing attention, and facilitating interpersonal interactions. They contend that student access to the Ll input possibly enabled students to accomplish their tasks more successfully. Therefore, it would be possible to extend the argument that teachers can facilitate student learning by making the Ll available to them. However, Ellis (1984) argues that when a teacher chooses to use the Ll as part of the usual pedagogy, he/she is depriving learners of input in the TL; Swain and Lapkin (2000) suggest that denying students access to the Ll deprives them of an invaluable cognitive tool.

Code-Switching

Alternating rapidly between two languages in either oral or written expression is known as "code-switching" (Coste, 1997). Cook (2001) contends that teaching methods that enable the teacher to use the Ll and the TL concurrently (e. g., incorporate some form of code-switching) create particularly authentic learning environments, as they acknowledge the influence of the Ll on the TL. Furthermore, Cook argues that code-switching is a natural phenomenon in settings in which the speakers share two languages, so teachers should not necessarily discourage it. Castellotti and Moore (1997) agree that code-switching can be an effective teaching strategy, as they acknowledge the Ll of the students to be an important pedagogical tool, but encourage teachers to make conscious decisions about when they introduce the Ll into their pedagogy. They believe that code-switching should be deliberate if it is to benefit the students' TL proficiency; teachers should decide before a lesson when they are going to use the Ll (e. g., to clarify vocabulary). Coste (1997) also concurs that code-switching can be used to help further student proficiency in the

TL by using the L1 as a reference point. However, he stipulates that the L1 should only be used to help construct knowledge in the target language and should not be accorded the same status and role as the TL in the classroom.

When Teachers Should Use the L1

Both Cook (2001) and Turnbull (2001b) agree that the L1 can be used as a resource in the TL classroom, but to varying degrees. Cook describes several scenarios in which teachers should consider introducing the L1 into their pedagogy. He argues that teachers should resort to the L1 if it is apparent that using the TL would be inefficient and/or problematic for the learner. He encourages teachers to use the L1 when explaining grammar, organizing tasks, disciplining students, and implementing tests; Cook believes teachers should use the L1 when "the cost of the TL is too great" —whenever it is too difficult or time-consuming for the students to process and understand the TL (2001, p. 418).

Turnbull (2001b) agrees that using the L1 to help ensure that students understand a particular grammatical concept or vocabulary term can be an efficient practice, but he cautions against teachers relying too much on the L1. Teachers should use the TL as much as possible in their teaching, especially in "contexts in which students spend only short periods of time in class on a daily basis, and when they have little contact with the TL outside of class," such as core French programs in Canada and Spanish programs on the U. S. northeastern coast (Turnbull, 2001b, p. 535). (Core French is defined by LeBlanc as "a basic program in French as a second language where French is the subject being studied and the language is taught in periods that vary between 20 and 50 minutes a day" [1990, p. 2]). Turnbull argues that if teachers are "licensed" (Cook, 2001, p. 410) to use the L1 in their teaching, it will result in an overuse of the L1. Furthermore, Turnbull questions Cook's suggestions about which classroom functions should be implemented in the TL, contending that Cook's suggestions leave "few classroom functions left to be conducted in the TL" (2001b, p. 537). Therefore, the question then becomes how and when teachers should use the first language in their pedagogy and what impact this has on the students' learning.

Empirical Studies

Since the early 1980s, considerable research has examined how much and in which contexts teachers use the TL and the Ll in SL and FL classrooms (e. g., Aston, 1983; Duff & Polio, 1990; Fleming, 1994; Franklin, 1990; Kharma & Hajjaj, 1989; Macaro, 1995; MacDonald, 1993; Mitchell, 1988; Papaefthymiou-Lytra, 1990; Polio & Duff, 1994).

Recent work has continued to address similar questions in different teaching contexts, using similar discourse analysis techniques, but a variety of units of analysis. Two recent studies have also attempted to understand teachers' beliefs and attitudes towards their use of the TL and Ll in their SL and FL classes. Learners' perspectives on the teacher's use of the TL and Ll use have also been explored in one recent study.

Analysis of Classroom Discourse: Teachers' Uses of TL and L1

Three recent studies[4] have drawn on the sociolinguistic notion of code-switching to examine teachers' uses of the TL and Ll. Rolin-Ianziti and Brownlie (in press) analyzed transcripts of four university-level French instructors' language use recorded over five class periods. Two of the instructors were native speakers of French and two were nonnative, but highly proficient speakers of the TL. Using a word-count approach, the authors determined how much French and English each instructor used. Qualitative analyses of the recordings used the utterance as unit of analysis. The researchers used prosodic features of the teachers' speech to help determine the beginning and end of utterances. The data were coded into three main functional categories (translation, metalinguistic uses, communicative uses) and either intersentential or intrasentential code-switching. Unlike most other studies, all four teachers used the Ll relatively infrequently and the range of Ll use among these teachers was also quite low (from 0% to 18. 2%). No notable differences were observed according to the instructor's Ll. Intrasentential translation and language contrast were the most common reasons for code-switching. The authors hypothesize that teachers who code-switch within the same sentence to contrast the TL and the Ll may help avoid negative transfer. Strategic translation may contribute to enhanced input, drawing learners' attention to specific features of the TL and hence promoting vocabulary uptake.

Gearon (1997) used Myers-Scotton's (1993) Matrix Language-Frame model to describe the code-switching identified in six secondary French teachers' discourse. Gearon examined intrasentential and intersentential code-switching, relating it to language dominance, based on frequency of words in a sentence, and to the morphosyntax of the code-switched sentences. Gearon found that most code-switching occurred within the same sentence, wherein English (the students' L1) was considered the dominant language by four of six teachers and the TL was used to talk about French. All teachers reported in follow-up retrospective interviews that they were generally not aware of the extent of their code-switching They reported being aware that they used the Ll to help students understand when they see puzzled looks on their faces. They also felt that using the Ll allowed them to move through the curriculum more quickly.

Castellotti (1997) analyzed recordings from four secondary foreign language classes, Spanish and English, in order to promote conscious and principled code-switching in SL and FL classes. Using examples drawn from her corpus, she argues that it is beneficial for teachers to switch from TL to Ll as a way of enhancing the input to which students are exposed. She refers to code-switches to help students understand, as a way to check comprehension, to highlight important points or salient vocabulary, to draw students' attention to what they already know or have studied, and to help students make the transition from unilingualism to bi-or plurilingualism.

Three more recent studies have examined teachers' TL and Ll uses within a pedagogical, functional framework. For example, Tumbull (2000) conducted exploratory analyses of four secondary level French second language teachers' uses of English (L1) and French (TL). The teachers' discourse was coded by dividing the teacher talk into units of analysis corresponding to their communicative or pedagogical function. The functional units were first coded as one of three macro-categories (social, academic, managerial), then on a microlevel, and then according to language (L1, L2, or mixed). The four teachers differed in the amount of Ll and L2 used (e. g., from 24% to 72% of L2 functional units). The qualitative functional analyses revealed considerable variation and few commonalties among the four teachers.

Macaro (1997) used surveys, semistructured interviews, and classroom observation to explore TL and Ll use amongst experienced, beginning, and student teachers of foreign languages at the secondary level in England and Wales. Classroom observations revealed that teachers resorted to the Ll most often to give and clarify instructions for classroom activities, to give feedback to students, for translating, and for checking comprehension.

In a study to examine how a grade 9 teacher accommodated the needs of students with learning disabilities in a core French classroom, Arnett (2001) found the most prevalent modification strategy to be 'use English to clarify.' Through classroom observation and transcript analysis, Arnett determined that the teacher used English to clarify difficult points of the TL (e. g., grammatical concepts and vocabulary) in 44. 9% of the episodes in which French was the primary language of instruction. Arnett also reports that, during a semistructured interview, the participating teacher stated that she felt that she needed to use the L1 as a reference point to help the students, especially those with learning disabilities, process the TL information more easily and more readily.

Teachers' Beliefs and Self-Reports about TL and L1 Use

Macaro's 1997 study also included a focus on the teachers' beliefs and attitudes about TL and L1 use. In general, most of Macaro's participants reported in the survey component of the study that it was impossible and undesirable to use the TL exclusively with all but the most motivated classes. A majority of teachers felt, however, that using the TL was an important component of good FL pedagogy. A majority of teachers reported that the TL was useful and important for giving basic instructions and giving feedback and a near majority (47%) indicated the same for organizing classroom activities. However, these teachers preferred the L1 for disciplining, socializing, or relationship building and for explaining difficult grammar. During the interview component of Macaro's study, most teachers indicated that students' ability in the TL, regardless of age, most consistently affected the amount of TL teachers could use. The teachers also reported that it was much easier to use the TL with younger as compared to older learners.

The Center for Applied Linguistics (CAL) reported the results of a national survey completed by more than 3,000 elementary and secondary school principals and foreign language teachers in the United States (see Rhodes & Branaman, 1997). The survey was designed to provide a national and state-by-state profile of foreign language education in the United States. The survey also replicated CAL's 1987 survey, thus enabling researchers to make comparisons with the 1997 results and to show trends in FL education over the preceding decade. A range of topics was covered by the survey, including use of the TL in secondary classrooms. Just over a fifth of respondents indicated that teachers used the TL most of the time (defined as 75% to 100% of the time). This represents a slight increase since 1987 when 18% of respondents indicated using the TL most of the time.

Turnbull (2001a) and Turnbull and Lamoureux (2001) investigated preservice teacher candidates' second and foreign language experiences before beginning their preservice program, as well as these students' beliefs and attitudes about the use of the TL and the Ll in second language teaching, before and after their practicum in a SL classroom. Results from surveys and interviews completed before the students' practicum experiences revealed that the participants seemed to have clearly formed notions about the teacher's TL use. Most of them felt it is desirable for a teacher to use the TL, many referring to a belief that immersing oneself in the TL is the most effective way to learn a language. This belief did not change over time. However, before the practicum, the participants were not as certain about how realistic it would be to implement their beliefs in the classroom. Many perceived that the Ll might be useful, especially for teaching grammar, disciplining and interacting informally and joking with students. After the practicum, about 40% of participants perceived the Ll to be either necessary or very useful for disciplining students. Otherwise, these participants did not see the Ll as necessary or very useful for any other pedagogical activity. The most notable shift was for teaching grammar—at survey 1, 78% of these participants believed that the Ll was useful for teaching grammar, whereas only 28% said the same at survey 2—in fact, 61% said that the Ll was not necessary for teaching grammar. This exploratory study is part of a larger project, framed within Azjen's (1988) theory of planned behavior, that aims to explain the factors that are most influential in filtering and shaping a new teacher's belief systems and intended and actual classroom practice related to TL and Ll use.

Learners' Perspectives

Few studies have focused on what learners feel about their teachers' TL and Ll use. In their 1990 study, Duff and Polio found that a large majority of the university-level learners from the 13 classes they observed were satisfied with the amount of Ll their teachers used, whether their teacher spoke a high percentage of Ll or not. Most learners also reported that they understood most of their teacher's TL use.

More recently, Macaro (1997) used questionnaires and focus group interviews to examine learners' perspectives on their teachers' TL and Ll use. Although a small group of learners, mostly academically-inclined girls, reported that they preferred their teachers to speak the TL exclusively, most students reported that they needed their teachers to speak the Ll sometimes to understand; many indicated that they could not learn if they could not understand their teacher.

Future Research

Important advances have been made to better understand when and why SL and FL teachers use the TL and Ll. There seems to be near consensus that teachers should aim to make maximum use of the TL. However, future research must determine what this really means in terms of the quantity and qualities of TL and Ll use and in terms of when it is acceptable and/or effective for teachers to draw on the students' L1.

Future discourse analysis studies could profitably aim to consider whether TL input might become intake more readily if teachers use the Ll judiciously to catalyze the intake process in some way. More research is also needed to understand what factors, including the teacher's TL proficiency level and teaching context, prompt SL and FL teachers to speak the students' L1 when guidelines clearly prescribe the opposite and how and why curriculum guidelines may influence teachers' TL and Ll use. Finally, and perhaps most importantly, more process-product studies are also needed to determine the relationship between teachers' TL and Ll use and students' TL proficiency and achievements more clearly than the existing small-scale studies (Fleming, 1994; Kaneko, 1992; Sparks, Ganschow, Pohlman, Skinner, & Artzer, 1992; Turnbull, 1998, 1999a, 1999b) or outdated investigations (Burstall, 1968, 1970; Burstall, Jamieson, Cohen, & Hargreaves, 1974; Carroll, 1975; Carroll, Clark, Edwards, & Handrick, 1967; Wolf, 1977) have been able to do.

Notes

1. We are very grateful to Alister Cumming, Sharon Lapkin, Charlene Polio and Merrill Swain for useful feedback on an earlier version of this paper.

2. Due to space limitations, we will not include literature from bilingual

education contexts, and we will not focus on the "English only" debates in ESL teaching in the United States.

3. Researchers examining the classroom experience of students with foreign language learning difficulties have also argued for maximized use of the TL in the classroom (for a review of literature on foreign language learning difficulties. see Ganschow, Sparks, & Javorsky, 1998). Sparks, Ganschow, Pohlman, Skinner, & Artzer (1992) argue that teachers should use the TL as much as possible in classes with students with foreign language learning difficulties or learning disabilities as it helps the students bolster their typically lower phonological processing skills.

4. There have been other studies that have examined teacher code-switching, but were excluded from this review because they were smaller scale and did not provide any new insights (Causa, 1997; Pochard, 1997; Simon, 1997).

ANNOTATED BIBLIOGRAPHY

Cook, V. (2001). Using the first language in the classroom. *Canadian Modern Language Review, 57,* 402–423.

Turnbull, M. (2001b). There is a role for the L1 in second and foreign language teaching, but...*Canadian Modern Language Review, 57,* 531–540.

These two articles, published in consecutive issues of the *Canadian Modern Language Review*, renewed the debate on the role of the L1 in the TL classroom. Cook argues that foreign/second language teachers should incorporate the L1 into their pedagogies, as it helps to create more "authentic" users of the TL. He contends that the argument for maximizing TL use has been misinterpreted to mean that the L1 cannot be a useful classroom resource. Cook believes that teachers can use the L1 to explain difficult grammar points, clarify new vocabulary, and manage the classroom. In response to Cook, Turnbull argues that teachers can indeed use the students' L1 as a resource in order to further student proficiency in the TL; Turnbull agrees that the L1 can be helpful in clarifying grammar and/or vocabulary. However, he questions what the notion of maximal TL usage means in relation to optimal and acceptable levels of L1 and TL usage in the classroom.

Castellotti, V., & Moore, D. (Eds). (1997). Alternances des langues et apprentissages [Special issue]. *Etudes de Linguistique Appliquée, 108,* 389–509.

The entire issue of this journal examines the roles of the L1 and the TL in the

TL classroom from a myriad of sociolinguistic perspectives. All of the contributors agree that the Ll plays a crucial role in TL learning, but they differ as to when, why, and how the Ll should be used in teachers' pedagogies. Theoretical articles examine the variety of ways in which teachers can use code-switching in their teaching, differentiate between the various types of code-switches, and explain the impact code-switching can have on communication. Several articles address empirical issues: the function of the teacher's code-switching, how the role and prevalence of teacher uses of the Ll change depending on learner's proficiency level, how teachers translate theory related to Ll usage into practice, and the limitations of code-switching as it relates to linguistic and cultural competencies.

Rolin-Ianziti, J., & Brownlie, S. (in press). Teacher use of the learners' native language in the foreign language classroom. *Canadian Modern Language Review / La Revue canadiennes des langues vivantes, 58* (3).

This article presents the findings of a pilot study undertaken at an Australian university to examine four professors usage of the students' L1, English, in their introductory French courses. The researchers recorded five class sessions taught amongst the four instructors and analyzed the transcribed data to determine how much, when, and why the teachers incorporated the students' L1 into their pedagogies. The researchers found that English usage varied between 0 and 18% among the four professors. The findings of the study also indicate that there were two primary purposes for using the Ll: to clarify unknown vocabulary and to compare the structures of the Ll and TL. In most cases, the Ll word or phrase was incorporated into a sentence in the TL (i. e., intrasentential code-switching). The researchers also found that the professors' decisions to introduce the Ll were influenced by the type of activity being implemented. The teachers also used the Ll for classroom management and social interactions with the students.

Sparks, R., Ganschow, L., Pohlman, J., Skinner, S., & Artzer (1992). The effects of multisensory structured language instruction on native language and foreign language aptitude skills of at-risk high school foreign language learners. *Annals of Dyslexia, 42,* 25–53.

The authors examined the role of the Ll in relation to a student population that has not been considered in much of the mainstream literature. They endeavored to determine how a multisensory, structured approach to language teaching impacted the phonological processing skills and foreign language aptitude of three groups of first-year high school Spanish students with language-based difficulties. Two groups of the students were instructed using the multisensory approach, while the remaining group was taught using a more traditional second language methodology. In one of the two groups taught in the multisensory approach, the teacher was allowed to incorporate English into her pedagogy, while the other teacher could only use Spanish. The results of the study indicate that the students in the group who were instructed using a multisensory approach that incorporated English outperformed all other students on measures of native language phonological processing abilities, and on all short and long forms of the Modern Language Aptitude Test and its subtests.

OTHER REFERENCES

Ajzen, 1. (1988). *Attitudes, personality and behaviour*. Milton Keynes, UK: Open University Press.

Antón, M., & DiCamilla, F. (1998). Socio-cognitive functions of L1 collaborative interaction in the L2 classroom. *Canadian Modern Language Review, 54,* 314–342.

Aston, G. (1983). The use of English and Italian in classroom management. In S. Holden (Ed.), *Focus on the learner* (pp. 101–105). London: ELT Publications.

Arnett, K. (2001). *The accommodation of grade 9 students with learning disabilities in the applied core French classroom*. Unpublished master's thesis, The Ontario Institute for Studies in Education of the University of Toronto.

Brooks, F., & Donato, R. (1994). Vygotskian approaches to understanding foreign language learner discourse during communicative tasks. *Hispania, 77,* 262–274.

Burstall, C. (1968). *French from eight: A national experiment*. Windsor, Berks, UK: National Foundation for Educational Research.

Burstall. C. (1970). *French in the primary school: Attitudes and achievement*. Windsor, Berks, UK: National Foundation for Educational Research.

Burstall, C., Jamieson, M., Cohen, S., & Hargreaves, M. (1974). *Primary French in the balance*. Windsor, Berks, UK: National Foundation for Educational Research.

Carroll, J. B. (1975). *The teaching of French as a foreign language in 8 countries*. Stockholm: Almqvist & Wiksell Tryckeri AB.

Carroll, J. B., Clark, J. L. D., Edwards, T. M., & Handrick, F. A. (1967). *The foreign language attainments of language majors in the senior years: A survey conducted in US colleges and universities*. Cambridge, MA: Harvard University Press.

Castellotti, V. (1997). Langue étrangère et français en milieu scolaire: didactiser l'alternance? In V. Castellotti & D. Moore (Eds.), *Études de Linguistique Appliquée*, *108*, 401–410.

Castellotti, V. & Moore, D. (1997). Alterner pour apprendre, alterner pour enseigner, de nouveaux enjeux pour la classe de langue. In V. Castellotti & D. Moore (Eds.), *Études de Linguistique Appliquée*, *108*, 389–392.

Causa, M. (1997). Maintien, transformation et disparition de l'alternance codique dans le discours de l'enseignant: du niveau débutant au niveau avancé. In V. Castellotti & D. Moore (Eds.), *Études de Linguistique Appliquée*, *108*, 457–467.

Chaudron, C. (1985). A method for examining the input/intake distinction. In S. M. Gass & C. G. Madden (Eds.), *Input in second language acquisition* (pp. 285–302). Rowley, MA: Newbury.

Coste, D. (1997). Alternances didactiques. In V. Castellotti & D. Moore (Eds.), *Études de Linguistique Appliquée*, 108, 393–400.

Crookes, G., & Schmidt, R. (1991). Motivation: Reopening the research agenda. *Language Learning*, *41* , 469–512.

Dickson, P. (1992). *Using the target language in modern foreign language classrooms*. Slough, UK: National Foundation for Educational Research.

Dörnyei, Z. (1994). Motivation and motivating in the foreign language classroom. *Modern Language Journal*, *78*, 273–284.

Duff, P., & Polio, C. (1990). How much foreign language is there in the foreign language classroom? *Modern Language Journal*, *74*, 154–166.

Ellis, R. (1984). *Classroom second language development*. Oxford: Pergamon.

Ellis, R. (1994). *The study of second language acquisition*. Oxford: Oxford University Press.

Fleming, S. (1994). *It takes two to tango*. Unpublished MA project, Monterey Institute of International Studies, Monterey, California.

Franklin, C. E. M. (1990). Teaching in the target language: Problems and prospects, *Language Learning Journal*, *2*, 20–24.

Ganschow, L., Sparks, R., & Javorsky, J. (1998). Foreign language learning difficulties: An historical perspective. *Journal of Learning Disabilities*, *31*, 248–259.

Gardner, R. C., & Lambert, W. E. (1972). *Attitudes and motivation in second language learning*. Rowley, MA: Newbury House.

Gass, S. (1988). Integrating research areas: A framework for second language studies. *Applied Linguistics*, *9*, 190–217.

Gearon, M. (1997). L'alternance entre l'anglais et le français chez les professeurs de FLE en Australie. In V. Castellotti & D. Moore (Eds.), *Études de Linguistique Appliquée*, *108*, 467–474.

Kaneko, T. (1992). *The role of the first language in the foreign language classroom.* Unpublished doctoral dissertation, Temple University, Philadelphia, PA.

Kharma, N. N., & Hajjaj, A. H. (1989). Use of the mother tongue in the ESL classroom. *International Review of Applied Linguistics, 27,* 25–42.

Krashen, S. (1982). *Principles and practice in second language acquisition.* New York: Pergamon Press.

LeBlanc, R. (1990). *National core French study: A synthesis.* Ottawa: The Canadian Association of Second Language Teachers.

Long, M. (1996). The role of the linguistic environment in second language acquisition. In W. Ritchie & T. Bhatia (Eds.), *Handbook of second language acquisition* (pp. 413–468). San Diego: Academic Press.

Macaro, E. (1995). Target language use in Italy. *Language Learning Journal, 11,* 52–54.

Macaro, E. (1997). *Target language, collaborative learning and autonomy.* Clevedon, UK: Multilingual Matters.

MacDonald, C. (1993). *Using the target language.* Cheltenham, UK: Mary Glasgow Publications.

Mitchell, R. (1988). *Communicative language teaching in practice.* London: Centre for Information on Language Teaching and Research (CILT).

Myers-Scotton, C. (1993). *Duelling languages: Grammatical structure in code-switching.* Oxford: Oxford University Press.

Papaefthymiou-Lytra, S. (1990). *Explorations in foreign language classroom discourse.* Athens, Greece: The University of Athens.

Pochard, J-C. (1997). Une classe d'anglais en France: quelle(s) langue(s) y parle-t-on? In V. Castellotti & D. Moore (Eds.), *Études de Linguistique Appliquée, 108,* 411–422.

Polio, C., & Duff, P. (1994). Teachers' language use in university foreign language classrooms: A qualitative analysis of English and target language alternation. *Modern Language Journal, 78,* 313–326.

Py, B. (1996). Reflection, conceptualisation, and exolinguistic interaction: Observations on the role of the first language. *Language Awareness, 5,* 179–187.

Rhodes, N., & Branaman, 1. (1997). *Foreign language instruction in the United States: A national survey of elementary and secondary schools.* Washington, DC: Center for Applied Linguistics (also available from Delta Systems, http: //www. delta-systems. com. Retrieved August 31, 2001).

Sharwood-Smith, M. (1985). From input to intake: On argumentation in second language acquisition. In S. M. Gass & C. G. Madden (Eds.), *Input in second language acquisition* (pp. 394–404). Rowley, MA: Newbury House.

Simon, D. (1997). Alternance codique en classe de langue: rupture de contrat ou survie? In V.

Castellotti & D. Moore (Eds.), *Études de Linguistique Appliquée, 108*, 445–456.

Swain, M. (1985). Communicative competence: Some roles of comprehensible input and comprehensible output in its development. In S. M. Gass & C. G. Madden (Eds.), *Input in second language acquisition* (pp. 235–254). Rowley, MA: Newbury House.

Swain, M. (1993). The output hypothesis: Just reading and writing aren't enough. *Canadian Modern Language Review, 50,* 158–164.

Swain, M. (1995). Three functions of output in second language learning. In G. Cook & B. Seidlhofer (Eds.), *Principles and practice in applied linguistics: Studies in honor of H. G. Widdowson* (pp. 125–144). Oxford: Oxford University Press.

Swain, M., & Lapkin, S. (2000). Task-based second language learning: The uses of the first language. *Language Teaching Research, 4,* 251–274.

Turnbull, M. (1998). *Multidimensional project-based teaching in core French: A case study.* Unpublished Ph. D. dissertation, Ontario Institute for Studies in Education, University of Toronto, Toronto.

Turnbull, M. (1999a). Multidimensional project-based teaching in French Second Language (FSL) : A process-product case study. *Modern Language Journal, 83,* 548–568.

Turnbull, M. (1999b). Multidimensional project-based second language teaching: Observations of four grade 9 core French teachers. In S. Lapkin & M. Turnbull, (Eds.), Research in FSL education: The state of the art [Special issue]. *Canadian Modern Language Review, 56,* 3–35.

Turnbull, M. (2000). Analyses of core French teachers' language use: A summary. Proceedings of Bilingual Child, Global Citizen Colloquium, University of New Brunswick, Fredericton, New Brunswick. Available: http: //www. caslt. org. (Retrieved on August 31, 2001).

Turnbull, M. (2001a, March). L1 and L2 use in French second language teaching: Pre-service students' views and classroom practice. Paper presented at the annual conference of the American Association of Applied Linguistics, St. Louis, MO.

Turnbull, M., & Lamoureux, S. (2001, May). L1 and L2 use in core French: A focus on pre-service students. Paper presented at the annual conference of the Canadian Association of Applied Linguistics, Québec.

van Lier, L. (1995). The use of the Ll in L2 classes. *Babylonia, 2,* 37–43.

Vygotsky, L. S. (1978). *Mind in society: The development of higher psychological processes.* Cambridge, MA: Harvard University Press.

Wolf, R. M. (1977). *Achievement in America: National report of the United States for the international educational achievement project.* New York: Teachers College Press.

DISCOURSE ANALYSIS AND ASSESSMENT

12. DISCOURSE AND ASSESSMENT

Tim McNamara, Kathryn Hill, and Lynette May

Many contemporary currents in applied linguistics have favored discourse studies within assessment; there have been calls for cross-fertilization with other areas within applied linguistics, critiques of the positivist tradition within language testing research, and the growing impact of Conversation Analysis (CA) and sociocultural theory. This chapter focuses on the resulting increase in discourse-based studies of oral proficiency assessment techniques. These studies initially focused on the traditional oral proficiency interview but have since been extended to new test formats, including paired and group interaction. We discuss the research carried out on a number of factors in the assessment setting, including the roles of interlocutor, candidate, and rater, and the impact of tasks, task performance conditions, and rating criteria. Recent research has also concentrated more specifically on the assessment of pragmatic competence and on the applications of technology within the assessment of spoken language, including the comparability of semidirect and direct methods for such assessment and the use of computer corpora.

The Growth of Interest in Discourse Studies in Assessment Research

One of the encouraging features of research in language assessment in the last decade has been the impact of ideas and insights from outside the traditional ambit of language testing. This is no more so than in the area of discourse, particularly spoken discourse. If structural linguistics was the source of the views on language of the formative period of postwar language testing, best represented in the work of Lado (1961), then discourse analysis has taken its place in the assessment of oral language. As the communicative movement has found performance assessment to be its natural accompaniment, a feature first pointed out by Morrow (1979), so interest in the assessment of spoken language has grown. This interest first lighted on the practical, policy-driven tradition of oral language assessment represented by the Oral Proficiency Interview or OPI (Clark & Clifford, 1988). But discourse analysis was soon found to offer discomforting insights into the construct of language proficiency implicit within the OPI, and more generally into the construct of proficiency as a projection of individual competence.

A number of intellectual currents in applied linguistics have favored discourse studies within assessment. The first is a general call for a greater openness to the possibility of cross-fertilization of research in language testing from research in other areas of applied linguistics, including second language acquisition (Bachman & Cohen, 1998; Young, 1995) and, specifically, discourse analysis (Jacoby & McNamara, 1999; McNamara, 1997; Shohamy, 1998; Young & He, 1998). The challenge to the positivist epistemology of applied linguistics generally (Pennycook, 2001) and of language testing in particular (Hamp-Lyons & Lynch, 1998; Lynch, 2001; Lynch & Hamp-Lyons, 1999; Shohamy, 2001) has favored non-quantitative research methodologies including discourse analysis and other interpretative methods (Halvari & Tarnanen, 1996). The increasing influence on applied linguistics of Conversation Analysis, triggered by the intellectual synergy between conversation analysts and applied linguists within the applied linguistics program at UCLA, has been a significant factor (Egbert, 1998; He, 1998; Kim & Suh, 1998; Lazaraton, 1992, 1997, in press; Schegloff, Koshik, Jacoby, & Olsher, this volume; Riggenbach, 1998). The current strong interest in Vygotskyan sociocultural theory and Activity Theory has also been an increasing influence on studies of joint activity in assessment settings, which has tended toward a close examination of the discourse of participants (Coughlan & Duff, 1994; Johnson, 2001; Swain, 2001; Young, 2001). A feature of all these developments has been their critical edge, challenging and disturbing the assumptions underlying current practice.

Discourse Analysis and the Validation of Oral Tests

In this section, research is reported involving various kinds of discourse analysis in the service of the validation of a range of oral tests. We begin where the work on discourse analysis in oral assessment began, with critical work on the familiar Oral Proficiency Interview. The role of discourse analysis in the definition of the construct of speaking in oral tests in general is then considered, including a short section on tests of pragmatics; then we discuss work on the impact of various facets of the assessment setting: interlocutor, task, performance conditions, test takers, and raters. Occasional reference will be made where relevant to the scant research that exists applying discourse analysis techniques to the validation of tests of other skills, especially writing.

The Oral Proficiency Interview (OPI)

Discourse analysis has been an effective and illuminating tool for the analysis of aspects of validity of Language Proficiency Interviews (LPIs), the most well known of which is the ACTFL Oral Proficiency Interview (OPI. Van Lier (1989), in a now classic paper, noted a lack of research pertaining to the kind of speech event an OPI actually constituted, and concluded, "a comparison of OPIs and basic features of conversation reveals significant differences between these two modes of social interaction" (p. 505). Relying on techniques of Conversation Analysis, Lazaraton (1992) found that "the most that can be said about the question 'interview or conversation?' is that the encounters share features with conversations, but they are still characteristically instances of interviews, and interviews of a distinctive kind, for the participants" (p. 383). An important collection of papers on the topic of the OPI from a variety of discourse analytic perspectives appeared in the late 1990s (Young & He, 1998). In their introduction to this volume, He & Young (1998) provide a theoretical introduction to the issues in the volume. They stress the interactional nature of the event, which in some ways masks its institutional character, as participants (perhaps most significantly, test designers and assessors) may be led to think of it as a conversation, or perhaps an interview, without fully appreciating its institutional and culturally specific character. They suggest that a range of possible discourse analytic perspectives may be required to illuminate its nature. Egbert (1998), using CA techniques, compares OPI interactions involving American learners of German and an extensive corpus of naturally occurring conversation in German, and concluded that the OPI differed from conversation in its handling of the organization and means of repair. Moder and Halleck (1998), on the other hand, while conceding that the OPI is not an informal conversation because of its lack of interviewee topic nomination and control, nevertheless find no difference between native and nonnative speaker interviewees in their interpretation of the framing of the interviews. They suggest that the OPI can be viewed as an authentic instance of talk-in-interaction, a point which perhaps was not in dispute. Johnson (2000, 2001) is perhaps the most strident critic of the OPI. She concluded from a study of 35 OPIs conducted over the telephone that the OPI tests speaking ability in the context of a specific type of interview, rather than in the real-life context of a conversation, as claimed by its proponents. Similarly, Johnson and Tyler (1998), who analyzed an interview found on a training tape for OPI assessors, claimed that the OPI handles several important features of everyday conversation in specific ways that are untypical of everyday conversation.

It is not clear what we are to conclude from these findings. Clearly the OPI, as with any other test, is not 'natural'; it is constructed and contrived. The issue is whether the interpretations that we draw from it about ability to perform in nontest situations are sustainable. For this we need evidence. The contribution of the work on the OPI is to problematize the claims for validity it makes. This is in contrast to many of the proponents of the OPI over the years who have assumed it is automatically valid because of its surface resemblance to face-to-face conversational interaction, its 'directness.' The most interesting of the detailed studies reported below address the validity of interpretations of scores from oral assessment tasks, and make practical suggestions about changes—in interviewer behavior, in rating scale development, in interlocutor and assessor training, in candidate preparation—that will improve the relative validity of test scores.

Meanwhile, those wishing to stay with the OPI have also used insights from discourse analysis of test performance to suggest modifications to the wording of its rating scales or accompanying materials. For example, Liskin-Gasparro (1996) analyzed the use of communication (lexical repair) strategies in the OPI by learners of Spanish, and concluded that the statements in the ACTFL Guidelines about communication strategies should be expanded to include strategies other than circumlocution, particularly to assist in defining differences between levels. In an attempt to address long-standing concerns about the validity and reliability of the OPI, Salaberry (2000) proposes a number of changes, including to the development and relative weighting of assessment criteria, based on a more explicit description of the criterion.

Definition of the Construct of Speaking in Oral Tests

Test development begins with the development of a view of the construct being measured. This will draw on current debates about the nature of oral test performance, which in turn are informed by insights from discourse analysis or other fields which themselves use discourse analysis. The revision of major tests such as the Test of Spoken English (TSE) (Douglas & Smith, 1997) and the Test of English as a Foreign Language (TOEFL) (Butler, Eignor, Jones, McNamara, & Suomi, 2000; Chapelle, Grabe, & Berns, 1997; Jamieson, Jones, Kirsch, Mosenthal, & Taylor, 2000) has involved the articulation of relevant constructs, and insights from discourse analysis are a significant influence on the frameworks on which the revisions are based. The field of second language acquisition offers relevant discourse-based viewpoints. For example, Selinker (2001) points to the gap between speaking performance in testing and nontesting contexts to identify a possible 'test taking domain,' which presumably would constitute a problem for the validity of oral tests. Upshur and Turner (1999) argue that the combined insights of second language acquisition and language testing fall short of providing an adequate account of systematic effects in second language performance testing. They propose the need for a new paradigm, one that would consider the effect of test method on discourse, the effect of discourse on ratings and of task on assessment criteria. More generally, McNamara (1997) shows how developments in discourse analysis, particularly Conversation Analysis, provide fundamental challenges to the notion of oral test performance as being essentially a psycholinguistic phenomenon, and instead require us to face the interactive, social and thereby jointly constructed character of the performance. He cites the work of Coughlan and Duff (1994), discussed here, which problematizes the notion of oral test task, this time from the point of view of Activity Theory.

Interlocutor Effects

A greater understanding of the interactive nature of discourse has led to a detailed consideration of the role of the interlocutor in speaking tests and its impact on test validity. This line of research, building on a crucial early paper of van Lier (1989), has been influenced most clearly by Conversation Analysis in the work of graduates of the program at UCLA, particularly Lazaraton (1992, 1996, 1997, in press, this volume) and Ross (1992, 1995, 1996, Berwick & Ross, 1996, Ross & Berwick, 1992). This latter work has focused on the notion of accommodation between interviewer and candidate, including differences among interviewers such as cultural background and level of experience. Lazaraton (1996) conducted detailed discourse analysis of interviews from the Cambridge Assessment of Spoken English (CASE) and identified eight types of linguistic and interactional support offered to candidates by examiners, then speculated on the possible effects of such support on proficiency ratings. Lazaraton (1997) considers the significance of the reception by the interlocutor of self-deprecating remarks by the candidate in a context where the assessment is used to channel students into elective classes, and uses the CA notion of 'preference sequences' to identify the institutional character of the talk. Conversation Analysis has also been influential as a research tool in Australian research on this subject. Filipi (1994) looked at expansion sequences in a high stakes Italian language test for school leavers; Cafarella (1997) used CA techniques to reveal a range of interviewer support strategies in the same test. Brown and Hill (1998) were able to demonstrate that variability in interviewer style does, in fact, impact ratings and used discourse analysis to identify language behaviors which appeared to distinguish the 'easier' from the 'more difficult' interviewers. In an extension of this study Brown (in press) used a discourse analysis of the interaction in two interviews involving the same candidate with two different interviewers in order to investigate the interviewer's role in the construction of candidate proficiency. An analysis of raters' comments about the two test performances indicated that interviewing style led to different impressions of the candidate's ability. Both studies concluded that more emphasis needed to be placed on interviewer training.

One response to the issue of interviewer variability has been to prescribe the behavior of interlocutors more closely, by providing 'scripts' or suggesting a wording for individual prompts. This has been tried in the Cambridge Assessment of Spoken English (CASE). Lazaraton (1996) examined the adherence of interlocutors to such scripts, and found considerable variation among them; she recommends more attention to interlocutor training as part of assessor training (in those cases where the interviewer and assessor roles are combined in the one person).

Mohan (1998) explores a related phenomenon in the use of an interview as part of the assessment of international teaching assistants at a Canadian university.

Lumley and Brown (1996) identified interlocutor behaviors that hindered or helped candidate performance in medically related role-plays in the speaking subtest of the Australian Occupational English Test for immigrant health professionals. Katona (1998) investigated differences in interactions with unknown and familiar interlocutors, an important consideration when, for example, teachers are required to conduct interviews with members of their own classes.

The impact of several different categorical differences among interviewers in relation to candidates has been explored using discourse analytic techniques. Among the most important of these is the impact of gender. Berry (1997) found that personality factors (extraversion/introversion) and gender influenced the discourse produced in dyads of varying composition in terms of these factors in paired oral tasks (see below). However, O'Loughlin (in press) found no significant effect for gender on either discourse or scores, suggesting that multiple factors in the test setting were influencing candidate discourse. Another factor is native speaker status: Richards and Malvern (2000) found that what had previously been discovered about the extent of native speaker interviewer accommodation in oral interviews (e. g., in the work of Ross, cited above) held true in certain respects for nonnative speaking interviewers, although less delicately.

A particularly interesting and seriously underresearched situation arises in the case of a relatively innovative format for oral tests, the paired or group oral. In this type of assessment, candidates interact with each other rather than with a native speaker interlocutor and are observed by one or more assessors. Ikeda (1998) draws on Vygotskian theory to characterize the interaction in paired learner interviews in a Japanese classroom setting. Iwashita (1998) carried out a small-scale study of a paired oral assessment in Japanese, with candidates matched with higher proficiency and lower proficiency candidates, respectively. She found that being matched with a higher proficiency candidate generally led to the production of more talk, but that this did not necessarily have an impact on scores. Egyud and Glover (2001) provide brief examples of candidate discourse in a paired oral test in a secondary school setting in Hungary. The paired oral format is used extensively in the University of Cambridge Local Examinations Syndicate (UCLES) suite of examinations, but to date little of their research on the validity of this format has been published (UCLES, 2000). The research is said to include studies of the discourse generated in the paired interaction. An extension of the paired oral format is the group oral. Among the relatively few studies of this format are Fulcher (1996) and particularly Berry (1995, 1998). Berry (1995) shows that differences between learners in their approach to the task forming the basis of the group discussion influences the discourse they produce, and that raters are affected by these differences, although in ways that raise issues about the validity of the format. Berry (1998) examined the discourse of extravert and introvert students in a group oral, and found that the discourse varied according to this factor. She also discovered that the accommodative features of interaction of native speaker interlocutors found in previous studies were present in the discourse of these learners interacting with each other.

Research on Tasks

Kormos (1999) uses discourse analysis in a comparison of interview and guided role play formats in oral assessments. She finds the role-play to have more of the features of casual conversation than the interview, with greater candidate control of topic introduction, topic maintenance, and topic shift. Riggenbach (1998) uses discourse analysis to suggest the advantages of tasks in which learners choose native speaking interlocutors outside the classroom and record their conversation in an informal setting. However, Spence-Brown (2001) uses interviews to reconstruct the process through which the tape recordings of such conversations are carried out as part of assessment in a university language course, and reveals the artifice and strategic sophistication underlying such apparently artless conversation. Her study will be seen as important for establishing the authenticity of tasks as a research field, with discourse analysis as an important tool in the investigation. In a study of EFL learners in Brazil, Ejzenberg (1995) reports an effect for task variation (cued and uncued dialogues and monologues) on the nature of the discourse produced and resulting fluency measures. Lazaraton and Wagner (1996) used discourse analysis to validate tasks within the Test of Spoken English (TSE) in terms of the functions they were intended to elicit, and found considerable support for the proposed functions in test discourse. Wigglesworth (1997) studied the impact on test discourse of differing types of tasks, particularly those containing an information gap. Tasks with and without an information gap were found to differ significantly in the type of discourse produced and the degree of interactivity.

Task Performance Conditions

An important line of research on tasks used in oral assessments stems from the work of Skehan (1998) on a cognitive approach to the characterization of task demands. This work, which originated in research on task-based learning, proposes that task structure and the conditions under which tasks are carried out can impact task difficulty. Research on this approach in a nontesting context has involved careful analysis of discourse produced with different task types and under varying performance conditions. Skehan (1998) has argued that the approach may be useful in constructing an interpretable scale of performance on oral tasks, based on characterizing performance in terms of task demands. In order to investigate the potential of the approach to help understand the impact of task demands under test conditions, Wigglesworth (1997) investigated the effect of planning time on oral test discourse, and found some impact on discourse measures of complexity and fluency, although not for subjects at all proficiency levels. Iwashita, McNamara, and Elder (2001) in a large scale study of this issue as part of the development of a speaking test for New TOEFL found little support for the impact of the proposed dimensions of task difficulty in discourse on monologic narrative tasks elicited under test conditions. This finding may have implications for the development of the theory of task demands as a whole, and supports the call for increased collaboration between second language acquisition and language testing researchers.

Test Taker Characteristics

The view of oral test performance as interactive, so central to much current work, means that it is difficult to consider the impact of test taker characteristics in isolation from those of interlocutors. For example, the impact of gender in the work of O'Loughlin (in press), cited above, involves consideration of the gender of both participants in an oral assessment. Similarly, investigations of the impact of the cultural and linguistic background of testtakers only makes sense in terms of the match with or divergence from the background of their interlocutors. Some research has begun in this area, although studies comparing matched and unmatched interactions are yet to be done. Morton (1988) demonstrated evidence of cultural and linguistic background in test-taker discourse on a monologic narrative task, although there was no impact on test scores. The cross-cultural character of the encounter in an oral interaction assessment has been investigated by Berwick and Ross (1996), who analyzed the discourse of interactions between Japanese learners of ESL interacting with an American male, and Canadian learners of Japanese as a foreign language interacting with a Japanese male. They found differences in the two cross-cultural settings, and suggest that the issue of second language pragmatic competence as a potential feature of the assessment is raised by the analysis. Ross (1998) emphasizes that the expectations of extended (rather than minimal) candidate responses and of self-disclosure in ESL oral interviews with Japanese speaking subjects runs counter to Japanese cultural norms. Young and Halleck (1998) explore the impact of cultural norms in relation to interviews involving American-Korean, Mexican-American, and Japanese-American dyads. In a study of American students taking an oral exam in Korean, Davies (1998) argues that "the complex cross-cultural context of the face-to-face interaction creates competing role expectations for the participants" (p. 271). Kim and Suh (1998) examine the impact of speaker status on topic development in oral assessments in Korean. He (1998) similarly raises the issue of culture-specific conversational styles as one explanation for the performance of native speakers of Chinese in an English oral proficiency interview used with international teaching assistants.

Rating Criteria

Research on oral assessment has come increasingly to understand the attributes and behavior of raters as affecting test scores, and the way in which rating scales and rating criteria, and their interpretation by raters, act as de facto test constructs in such assessments. Discourse analysis has proved to be a useful tool in investigating rater behavior and in assisting in the development of empirically-based rating scales.

A number of studies have used think-aloud methods used to study rater cognition in the assessment of second language oral performance (Brown, 2000; Brown, McNamara, Iwashita, & O'Hagan, 2001; Meiron, 1998; Pollitt & Murray, 1996). For example, Brown (2000) used protocol analysis to investigate what IELTS raters were paying attention to in the assessment of the IELTS oral interview, and its impact on the scores they gave. Such information can be used in rater training, or in revising or developing the wording of rating scales, and extensions of this work are now informing the development of rating scales for rating performance on cognitively complex speaking tasks as part of the proposed New TOEFL. Further studies on rater cognition in relation to writing scales are relevant here. Lumley (2000) used protocol analysis of raters scoring a test of written English for adult immigrants to Australia to develop insight into the rating process and the use of a rating scale. He demonstrated the fundamentally institutional character of the process, most clearly revealed when the usually automatic process of allocation of scripts to score categories was disturbed in the context of resolving some uncertainty in score allocation because of some particular feature of the script in question. Using retrospective written reports, introspective verbal reports, and group interviews with trained and untrained raters, Milanovic, Saville, and Shen (1996) were able to identify four distinct approaches to marking written compositions as well as a number of linguistic elements that influenced ratings. Turner (2000) explores discourse data from teachers engaged in a process of creating a rating scale for writing ability in Québec, and demonstrates how the actions of the participants and features of sample scripts influenced the criteria included in the scale.

Jacoby and McNamara (1999) draw attention to the significant gap between linguistically based assessment criteria typically used in performance assessments and criteria that are actually used by participants in the target use setting. These latter are often unconsciously held and applied, but can be revealed by close analysis of discourse in real-world settings where judgments of performance occur naturally, for example in oral feedback on performance. Jacoby (1998) refers to such locally motivated assessment occasions as 'indigenous assessment.' Jacoby and McNamara suggest they can be used as the basis for deriving relevant criteria for performance assessments, and give examples from research on feedback in a physics research team involving native and nonnative speaking participants. Interestingly, no clear distinction is made between the criteria used in feedback to the two groups, and linguistic features of performance are rarely commented upon and do not appear to be salient. Douglas (2001) suggests that this issue of assessment criteria has problematic implications for the construct validity of many specific purpose language assessments.

Another approach to rating scale development involves close analysis of test taker discourse. Critical of the a priori, non-empirical basis of rating scales, Fulcher (1996) proposes a data-based approach to rating scale development, using discourse from oral performances on the ELTS test to construct a fluency rating scale.

Indirect Methods and the Investigation of Sociopragmatic Competence

Another site in which the insights of discourse analysis are having an impact of tests, and this time in tests used in research as well as in assessments of individual proficiency, is in the area of the assessment of interlanguage pragmatics. Investigation of interlanguage pragmatics has been conducted primarily with the aid of the Discourse Completion Task (DCT), which is usually presented in written form. A given social situation is presented, and the subject asked to choose what they would say in it. A thorough introduction to the format of these tests is provided in Hudson, Detmer, and Brown (1995). There has been much discussion of this format. Johnston, Kasper, and Ross (1998) demonstrated the sensitivity of data from questionnaires used to elicit subject responses to the format of the questionnaire. Billmyer and Varghese (2000) modified the format of the DCT to achieve different results. Hinkel (1997) cautions about the use of DCT for the investigation of sociopragmatic issues in Chinese. Yuan (2001) goes further: In an investigation of the validity of the written DCT in comparison with an oral version of the DCT, oral interviews, and field notes of actual usage, the written DCT was shown to be the least valid of the approaches.

Bisshop (1996) questions the validity of the DCT from another perspective: She elicited open-ended responses to stem items on apology from native speakers of English and nonnative speakers from Asian first language backgrounds. Then, after removing surface errors of syntax and lexical choice so that the native or nonnative speaker status of the respondents would not be immediately apparent, she presented a combined, randomized list of the responses to a further group of native speaker subjects and asked them to judge their acceptability and to offer reasons for their judgments. While the native speaker responses were reliably judged to be better than the nonnative speaker ones, the reasons given for why they were unsatisfactory entirely failed to support the rationale for the content of the DCT distracter items in the literature. Johnston, Kasper, and Ross (1998) claim their results highlight the need for different types of data and further validation studies. Elsewhere, in a review of different methods of data collection, Kasper (1998) concludes that differential, sequential, or triangulated combinations of data collection methods are usually called for.

Discourse Analysis and Classroom Assessment

Unfortunately, there has been a marked absence of studies using discourse analysis in the context of classroom assessment, a situation that matches the neglect of classroom assessment research in the field more generally. The notable exception, however, is the ongoing work of Rea-Dickins (Gardner & Rea-Dickins, 2001; Rea-Dickins, 2001; Rea-Dickins & Gardner, 2000) on formative assessment in the primary classroom in the context of the implementation of assessment requirements under the National Curriculum in England and Wales. In this work, careful transcription and analysis of classroom discourse is carried out to identify modes and functions of assessment in such classrooms in the immediate context of lessons. This work is exemplary in its extension of the concept of assessment beyond formal assessment occasions and its reconceptualization of the fact of assessment in primary school classrooms.

Discourse Analysis and Technology

This section explores the growing use of technology, both in the delivery of speaking tests, most commonly in semidirect formats such as the Simulated Oral Proficiency Interview or SOPI, and in the analysis of discourse that is used in the development of test material.

Semi-direct Tests of Speaking

The Simulated Oral Proficiency Interview (SOPI has emerged in the last decade as a cheaper and more flexible alternative to the OPI. The equivalence of the two, and more generally the validity of the SOPI, relying as it does on monologic discourse in the absence of a 'live' interlocutor, has been an issue since Shohamy's seminal paper (Shohamy, 1994), which criticized the SOPI largely on discourse grounds. O'Loughlin (1995, 2001) has studied the issue intensively in the context of a different test, the Access test, used to award points for English language proficiency for certain categories of intending immigrants to Australia, where immigration places are allocated on a competitive basis. The test was offered in two formats, face-to-face and tape-mediated, and the insights of the Shohamy study were used at the design stage in an attempt to ensure their equivalence.

Nevertheless, using a range of qualitative and quantitative studies, including analyses of lexical density of candidate discourse, O'Loughlin demonstrates that the two formats are not equivalent, testifying to the indelible impact on discourse of the existence of face-to-face interaction, no matter how muted that interaction is planned to be. O'Loughlin's finding that discourse elicited in semidirect formats is more formal, and more like written language than discourse elicited in face-to-face interaction, is supported by the findings of Koike (1998) on a Spanish SOPI. She found more organized and less conversation-like discourse in this format. Malone (2000) used counts of discourse features to validate levels of performance on an English SOPI based on the ACTFL Guidelines, with mixed results. Luoma (1997) carried out a study similar to that of O'Loughlin in many ways, again using a range of methods, including analysis of test taker discourse, to establish similarities and differences between the direct and semidirect formats of an English test in Finland.

Testing Pragmatics Online

The widespread use of multimedia in the second language classroom has been accompanied by increasing interest in computer-based approaches to language test delivery. Roever (2001a, b) reports on a web-based test of ESL pragmalinguistic knowledge, operationalized in the test as knowledge of implicature, situational routines, and specified speech acts. Both qualitative and quantitative data from ESL/EFL students and a native speaker comparison group were used during the validation process.

The Use of Corpora

The use of corpora, of both spoken and written English, is an increasing feature of the design of language tests, particularly in academic purpose contexts. Biber (2001) describes a corpus of 2.5 million words of spoken and written academic discourse used in the development of the new TOEFL. At the University of Michigan, the MICASE (Michigan Corpus of Academic Spoken English) project constitutes a shared corpus resource for the development of listening and other tests of academic spoken English. The growing interest in the field is attested by the convening of a major symposium at the 2001 Language Testing Research Colloquium entitled *Using language corpora in language testing*. Rapid developments in Natural Language Processing (NLP) offer great promise for automatizing the assessment of spoken language: These developments rely on advances in the application of discourse analysis within the field of computational linguistics. Burstein, Kaplan, Rohen-Wolff, Zuckerman, and Lu (1999) summarize the potential of computer-based speech technology for the development of an assessment of spoken language within the new TOEFL. Applications of such technologies have already been made in some areas of written assessment, using automatic scoring, known as 'e-rater', as a second rater in the scoring of essays at ETS (Burstein, Marcu, Andreyev, & Chodorow, in press).

ANNOTATED BIBLIOGRAPHY

Brown, A., & Hill, K. (1998). Interviewer style and candidate performance in the IELTS oral interview. In S. Wood (Ed.), *IELTS Research Reports, 1*, 1–19.

This study explored the consequences of variation in interviewer style, within the context of IELTS interviews. By separating the role of interviewer and rater and using multiple ratings to remove rater effects, they were able to demonstrate that interviewer style can have a significant impact on candidate performance and hence on ratings of candidate ability Through an analysis of candidate and interviewer discourse, Brown and Hill were able to identify distinct interviewer styles, which could be categorized as "easy" or "difficult." Both this and a subsequent study (Brown, in press) highlighted the need for more comprehensive rater training, and a deeper understanding of the co-constructed nature of interaction within the interview by the test developers.

Coughlan, P., & Duff, P. A. (1994). Same task, different activities: Analysis of an SLA task from an activity theory perspective. In J. P. Lantolf & G. Appel (Eds.), *Vygotskian Approaches to Second Language Research* (pp. 173–193). Norwood, NJ: Ablex.

Though not strictly in the field of language testing, this thought provoking article uses Vygotsky's sociocultural theory of learning to question the belief that tasks can be regarded as a constants in second language acquisition research. The social construction of tasks is explored through discourse analysis, leading to the conclusion that the same task can be conceptualised and realized quite differently by different people. This has important implications for language testing.

Jacoby, S., & McNamara, T. (1999). Locating competence. *English for Specific Purposes*, *18*(3), 213–241.

This paper argues that the criteria used in the assessment of performance in specific purpose contexts should reflect criteria that are actually used in the setting in question. It proposes discourse analysis of naturally occurring instances of feedback on performance in such settings—termed 'indigenous assessment' —as a means of making these implicit criteria available for use in the design of formal assessments.

Johnson, M. (2001). *The art of non-conversation: A re-examination of the validity of the Oral Proficiency Interview*. New Haven, CT: Yale University Press.

Discourse analysis is a key tool for the investigation of the construct validity of the Oral Proficiency Interview (OPI in Johnson's study. Johnson explores the nature of the speech event that constitutes the OPI, and proposes a prototypical model of the OPI communicative event. Her analysis is grounded in Vygotsky's sociocultural theory.

Lazaraton, A. (in press). *A qualitative approach to the validation of oral language tests. Studies in Language Testing 14*. Cambridge: Cambridge University Press/University of Cambridge Local Examination Syndicate.

Lazaraton's research over the last decade represents perhaps the most consistent application of discourse analysis to problems of oral language testing. This new book represents the most complete account of her work to date.

McNamara, T. (1997). 'Interaction' in second language performance assessment: Whose performance? *Applied Linguistics*, *18*, 444–466.

This paper makes the case for the unsettling implications for the validity of oral assessments of views of performance implicit in current work in discourse analysis, particularly Conversation Analysis. The idea that test performance is 'co-constructed' challenges the focus of testing theory on the individual cognitive abilities central to current notions of language proficiency.

O'Loughlin, K. (2001). *The equivalence of direct and semi-direct speaking tests Studies in Language Testing 13*. Cambridge: Cambridge University Press/

University of Cambridge Local Examination Syndicate. This study of two closely parallel versions of an oral test, one version delivered face-to-face and the other delivered on tape, demonstrates the lack of equivalence of the two formats. This has implications for the validity of semidirect tests, and attests to the co-constructed nature of test performance.

Shohamy, E. (1994). The validity of direct versus semi-direct oral tests. *Language Testing, 11* (2), 99–123.

This classic article used discourse analysis as one means through which to explore aspects of the validity of semidirect and direct tests of oral proficiency. Her evidence strongly favors the direct format over the semi-direct one.

Young, R. , &He. A. W. (Eds.). (1998). *Talking and testing: Discourse approaches to the assessment of oral proficiency.* Amsterdam: John Benjamins.

In this collection of fourteen articles, aspects of the validity of Language Proficiency Interviews (LPIs) are examined through discourse analysis. The focus of many of the studies is the extent to which LPIs exhibit the features of natural conversation. The findings of most studies in this volume add to the growing awareness within the field that there may be a specific oral test discourse, giving rise to concerns about validity.

OTHER REFERENCES

Bachman, L., & Cohen, A. (Eds.). (1998). *Interfaces between second language acquisition and language testing research.* Cambridge: Cambridge University Press.

Berry, V. (1995). *A qualitative analysis of factors affecting learner performances in group oral tests.* Paper presented at the 17th Language Testing Research Colloquium. Long Beach, CA.

Berry, V. (1997, March). *Gender and personality as factors of interlocutor variability in oral performance tests.* Paper presented at 19th Language Testing Research Colloquium, Orlando, FL.

Berry, V. (1998, March). *Personality and oral test score variability.* Paper presented at TESOL' 98 Conference, Seattle. WA.

Berwick, R., & Ross, S. (1996). Cross-cultural pragmatics in oral proficiency interview strategies. In M. Milanovic, & N. Saville (Eds.), *Performance testing, cognition and assessment: Selected papers from the 15th Language Testing Research Colloquium, Cambridge and Arnhem* (pp. 34–54). Cambridge: Cambridge University Press and

University of Cambridge Local Examinations Syndicate.

Biber, D. (2001, February). Academic discourse: Corpus-based perspectives. Plenary paper presented at the American Association for Applied Linguistics Annual Conference, St Louis, MO.

Billmyer, K., & Varghese, M. (2000). Investigating instrument-based pragmatic variability: Effects of enhancing discourse completion tests. *Applied Linguistics, 21*, 517–552.

Bisshop, C. (1996). '*I am apologize...*' : *Asian speakers of English saying sorry in the Australian context.* Unpublished master's thesis, University of Melbourne, Australia.

Brown, A. (2000). An investigation of rater's orientation in awarding scores in the IELTS Interview. In R. Tulloch (Ed.), *IELTS Research Reports, 3*, 30–49.

Brown, A. (in press). Interviewer variation and the co-construction of speaking proficiency. *Language Testing.*

Brown, A., McNamara, T., Iwashita, N., & O'Hagan, S. (2001). *Investigating raters' orientations in specific-purpose task-based oral assessment.* Final report to TOEFL 2000 Oversight Committee, Educational Testing Service, Princeton, NJ.

Burstein, J., Marcu, D., Andreyev, S., & Chodorow, M. (in press). Towards automatic classification of discourse elements in essays. *Proceedings of the 39th Annual Meeting of the Association for Computational Linguistics*, Toulouse, France.

Burstein, J., Kaplan, R. B., Rohen-Wolff, S., Zuckerman, L. E., & Lu, C. (1999). *A review of computer-based speech technology for TOEFL 2000. Monograph Series 13*, Princeton, NJ: Educational Testing Service.

Butler, F., Eignor, D., Jones, S., McNamara, T., & Suomi, B. (2000). TOEFL 2000 Speaking Framework: A Working Paper. *Monograph Series 20*, Princeton, NJ: Educational Testing Service.

Cafarella, C. (1997). Assessor accommodation in the V. C. E. Italian Oral Test. *Australian Review of Applied Linguistics, 20* (1), 21–41.

Chapelle, C., Grabe, W., & Berns, M. (1997). Communicative language proficiency: Definition and implications for TOEFL 2000. *Monograph Series 10*, Princeton, NJ: Educational Testing Service.

Clark, J. L., & Clifford, R. T. (1988). The FSI/ILR/ACTFL Proficiency scales and testing techniques: Development, current status, and needed research. *Studies in Second Language Acquisition, 10*, 129–147.

Davies. C. E. (1998). Maintaining American face in the Korean Oral Exam: Reflections on the power of cross-cultural context. In R. Young & A. W. He (Eds.), *Talking and testing: Discourse approaches to the assessment of oral proficiency* (pp. 271–296). Amsterdam: John Benjamins.

Douglas, D. (2001). Language for Specific Purposes assessment criteria: Where do they come from? *Language Testing, 18,* 171–185.

Douglas, D., & Smith, (1997). Theoretical underpinnings of the Test of Spoken English Revision Project. *Monograph Series 9,* Princeton, NJ: Educational Testing Service.

Egbert, M. M. (1998). Miscommunication in language proficiency interviews of first-year German Students: A comparison with natural conversation. In R. Young, & A. W. He (Eds.), *Talking and testing: Discourse approaches to the assessment of oral proficiency* (pp. 147–169). Amsterdam: John Benjamins.

Egyud, G., & Glover, P. (2001). Oral testing in pairs: A secondary school perspective. *ELT Journal* 55(1), 70–76.

Ejzenberg, R. (1995, March). *The role of task structure in oral fluency assessment.* Paper presented at TESOL'94 Conference and at the 17th Annual Meeting of the American Association for Applied Linguistics, Long Beach, CA.

Filipi, A. (1994). Interaction in an Italian oral test: The role of some expansion sequences. *Australian Review of Applied Linguistics, 11,* 119–136.

Fulcher, G. (1996). Testing tasks: Issues in task design and the group oral. *Language Testing, 13,* 23–49.

Gardner, S., & Rea-Dickins, P. (2001). Conglomeration or chameleon? Teachers' representations of language in the assessment of learners with English as an additional language. *Language Awareness, 10,* 2–3.

Halvari, A., & Tarnanen, M. (1996). Qualitative procedures for comparability—experiences from a multi-language, multi-lingual testing system. In A. Huhta, V. Kohonen, L. Kurki-Snonio, & S. Luoma (Eds.), *Current developments and alternatives in language assessment: Proceedings of Language Testing Research Colloquium 1996* (pp. 127–136). Jyväskylä: University of Jyväskylä.

Hamp-Lyons, L., & Lynch, B. K. (1998). Perspectives on validity: A historical analysis of language testing conference abstracts. In A. J. Kunnan (Ed.), *Validation in language assessment: Selected papers from the 17th Language Testing Research Colloquium, Long Beach* (pp. 253–276). Mahwah, NJ: Lawrence Erlbaum.

He, A. W. (1998). Answering questions in LPIs: A case study. In R. Young, & A. W. He (Eds.), *Talking and testing: Discourse approaches to the assessment of oral proficiency* (pp. 101–116). Amsterdam: John Benjamins.

Hinkel, E. (1997). Appropriateness of advice: DCT and multiple choice data. *Applied Linguistics, 18* (1), 1–26.

Hudson, T., Detmer, E., & Brown, J. D. (1995). *Developing prototypic measures of cross-cultural pragmatics.* Technical Report #7, Second Language Teaching and Curriculum Center, University of Hawai'i at Manoa, Honolulu, HI: University of Hawai'i Press.

Ikeda, K. (1998). The paired learner interview: A preliminary investigation applying Vygotskian insights. *Language, Culture and Curriculum, 11*, 71–96.

Iwashita, N. (1998). The validity of the paired interview in oral performance assessment. *Melbourne Papers in Language Testing, 5* (2), 51–65.

Iwashita, N., McNamara, T., & Elder, C. (2001). Can we predict task difficulty in an oral proficiency test? Exploring the potential of an information-processing approach to task design. *Language Learning, 51*, 401–436.

Jacoby, S. (1998). *Science as performance: Socializing scientific discourse through conference talk rehearsals.* Unpublished doctoral dissertation, University of California, Los Angeles.

Jamieson, J., Jones, S., Kirsch, I., Mosenthal, P., & Taylor, C. (2000). TOEFL 2000 Framework: A Working Paper. *Monograph Series 16*, Princeton, NJ: Educational Testing Service.

Johnson, M. (2000). Interaction in the Oral Proficiency Interview: Problems of validity. *Pragmatics, 10*(2), 215–231.

Johnson, M., & Tyler, A. (1998). Re-analyzing the OPI: How much does it look like natural conversation? In R. Young & A. W. He (Eds.), *Talking and testing: Discourse approaches to the assessment of oral proficiency* (pp. 27–51). Amsterdam: John Benjamins.

Johnston, B., Kasper, G., & Ross, S. (1998). Effect of rejoinders in production questionnaires. *Applied Linguistics, 19*, 157–182.

Kasper, G. (1998). Datenerhebungsverfahren in der Lernersprachenpragmatik [Data collection methods in interlanguage pragmatics]. *Zeitschrift fur Fremdsprachenforschung, 9* (1), 85–118.

Katona, L. (1998). Meaning negotiation in the Hungarian Oral Proficiency Examination of English. In R. Young & A. W. He (Eds.), *Talking and testing: Discourse approaches to the assessment of oral proficiency* (pp. 239–267). Amsterdam: John Benjamins.

Kim, K., & Suh, K. (1998). Confirmation sequences as interactional resources in Korean Language Proficiency Interviews. In R. Young & A. W. He (Eds.), *Talking and testing: Discourse approaches to the assessment of oral proficiency* (pp. 297–332). Amsterdam: John Benjamins.

Koike, D. A. (1998). What happens when there's no one to talk to? Spanish Foreign Language discourse in Simulated Oral Proficiency Interviews. In R. Young & A. W. He (Eds.), *Talking and testing: Discourse approaches to the assessment of oral proficiency* (pp. 69–98). Amsterdam: John Benjamins.

Kormos, J. (1999). Simulating conversations in oral-proficiency assessment: a conversation analysis of role plays and non-scripted interviews in language exams. *Language Testing, 16*, 163–188.

Lado, R. (1961). *Language testing.* London: Longman.

Lazaraton, A. (1992). *A conversation analysis of structure and interaction in the language interview.* Unpublished doctoral dissertation, University of California, Los Angeles.

Lazaraton, A. (1996). Interlocutor support in oral proficiency interviews: The case of CASE. *Language Testing, 13,* 151–172.

Lazaraton, A. (1997). Preference organization in Oral Proficiency Interviews: The case of language ability assessments. *Research on Language and Social Interaction, 30,* 53–72.

Lazaraton, A. (this volume). Quantitative and qualitative approaches to discourse analysis.

Lazaraton, A., & Wagner, (1996). The revised test of spoken English: Discourse analysis of native speaker and nonnative speaker data. *Monograph Series 7,* Princeton. NJ: Educational Testing Service.

Liskin-Gasparro, J. E. (1996). Circumlocution, communication strategies, and the ACTFL proficiency guidelines: An analysis of student discourse. *Foreign Language Annals, 29,* 317–330.

Lumley, T. (2000). *The process of the assessment of writing performance: The rater's perspective.* Unpublished doctoral dissertation, The University of Melbourne, Australia.

Lumley, T., & Brown, A. (1996). Specific-purpose language performance tests: Task and interaction. *Australian Review of Applied Linguistics, 13,* 105–136.

Luoma, S. (1997). *Comparability of a tape-mediated and a face-to-face test of speaking: A triangulation study.* Unpublished Licentiate thesis, Centre for Applied Language Studies, University of Jyväskylä, Jyväskylä, Finland.

Lynch, B. K. (2001). Rethinking assessment from a critical perspective. *Language Testing, 18,* 351–372.

Lynch, B. K., & Hamp-Lyons, 1. (1999). Perspectives on research paradigms and validity: Tales from the Language Testing Research Colloquium. *Melbourne Papers in Language Testing, 8,* 57–93.

Malone, M. E. (2000). *The development of the English Speaking Test: An investigation of reliability and validity.* Unpublished doctoral dissertation, University of Michigan, Ann Arbor, MI.

Meiron, B. (1998). *Rating oral proficiency tests: A triangulated study of rater thought processes.* Unpublished master's thesis, University of California, Los Angeles.

MICASE project (Michigan Corpus of Academic Spoken English). http : //directory. umich. edu/dirsvcs-bin/search?search_text =micase

Milanovic, M., Saville, N., & Shen, S. (1996). A study of the decision-making behaviour of composition markers. In M. Milanovic & N. Saville (Eds.), *Performance testing, cognition and assessment: Selected papers from the 15th Language Testing Research Colloquium, Cambridge and Arnhem* (pp. 92–114). Cambridge: Cambridge University Press and University of Cambridge Local Examinations Syndicate.

Moder, C., & Halleck, G. (1998.) Framing the language proficiency interview as a speech event: Native and non-native speakers' questions. In R. Young & A. W. He (Eds.), *Talking* and testing: Discourse approaches to the assessment of oral proficiency (pp. 117–146). Amsterdam: John Benjamins.

Mohan, B. (1998). Knowledge structures in Oral Proficiency Interviews for international teaching assistants. In R. Young & A. W. He (Eds.), *Talking and testing: Discourse approaches to the assessment of oral proficiency* (pp. 173–204). Amsterdam: John Benjamins.

Morrow, K. (1979). Communicative language testing: Revolution or evolution? In C. J. Brumfit & K. Johnson (Eds.), *The communicative approach to language teaching* (pp. 143–157). Oxford: Oxford University Press.

Morton, J. (1988). A cross-cultural study of second language narrative discourse on an oral proficiency test. *Prospect, 13*(2), 20–35.

O'Loughlin, K. (1995). Lexical density in candidate output on direct and semi-direct versions of an oral proficiency test. *Language Testing, 12*, 217–237.

O'Loughlin, K. (in press). The impact of gender in oral proficiency testing. *Language Testing, 19*, 2.

Pennycook, A. (2001). *Critical applied linguistics: A critical introduction*. London: Routledge.

Pollitt, A., & Murray, N. L. (1996). What raters *really* pay attention to. In M. Milanovic & N. Saville (Eds.), *Performance testing. cognition and assessment: Selected papers from the 15th Language Testing Research Colloquium, Cambridge and Arnhem* (pp. 74–91). Cambridge, UK: Cambridge University Press and University of Cambridge Local Examinations Syndicate.

Rea-Dickins, P. (2001). Mirror, mirror, on the wall: Identifying processes of classroom assessment. *Language Testing, 18*, 429–462.

Rea-Dickins, P., & Gardner, S. (2000). Snares or silver bullets: Disentangling the construct of formative assessment. *Language Testing, 17*, 215–241.

Richards, B. J., & Malvern, D. D. (2000). Accommodation in oral interviews between foreign language learners and teachers who are not native speakers. *Studia Linguistica, 54*, 260–271.

Riggenbach, H. (1998). Evaluating learner interactional skills: Conversation at the micro level. In R. Young & A. W. He (Eds.), *Talking and testing: Discourse approaches to the assessment of oral proficiency* (pp. 53–67). Amsterdam: John Benjamins.

Roever, C. (2001a, February). Validation of a web-based test of second language pragmatics. Paper presented at the American Association of Applied Linguistics Conference, St. Louis, MO.

Roever, C. (2001b). *A web-based test of interlanguage pragmalinguistic knowledge: Speech acts, routines, implicatures*. Unpublished doctoral dissertation, University of Hawai'i at Manoa.

Ross, S. (1992). The discourse of accommodation in oral proficiency interviews. *Studies in*

Second Language Acquisition, 14, 159–176.
Ross, S. (1995). Aspects of communicative accommodation in oral proficiency interview discourse. Unpublished doctoral dissertation, University of Hawai'i at Manoa.
Ross, S. (1996). Formulae and inter-interviewer variation in oral proficiency interviewer discourse. *Prospect, 11,* 3–16.
Ross, S. (1998). Divergent frame interpretations in language proficiency interview interaction. In R. Young & A. W. He (Eds.), *Talking and testing: Discourse approaches to the assessment of oral proficiency* (pp. 333–353). Amsterdam: John Benjamins.
Ross, S., & Berwick, R. (1992). The discourse of accommodation in oral proficiency interviews. *Studies in Second Language Acquisition, 14,* 159–176.
Salaberry, R. (2000). Revising the revised format of the ACTFL oral proficiency interview. *Language Testing, 17,* 289–310.
Schegloff, E., Koshik, I., Jacoby, S., & Olsher, D. (this volume). Conversation analysis and applied linguistics.
Selinker, L. (2001, February). Speaking as performance within a discourse domain. Presentation at a joint symposium of Language Testing Research Colloquium and American Association for Applied Linguistics Annual Conference, *The Brahmin and the Elephant: Defining and assessing Speaking Ability.* St Louis, MO.
Shohamy, E. (1998). How can language testing and SLA benefit from each other? The case of discourse analysis. In L. Bachman & A. Cohen (Eds.), *Interfaces between second language acquisition and language testing research* (pp. 156–176). Cambridge: Cambridge University Press.
Shohamy, E. (2001). Democratic assessment as an alternative. *Language Testing, 18,* 373–391.
Skehan, P. (1998). Task-based instruction. *Annual Review of Applied Linguistics, 18.* 268–286.
Spence-Brown, R. (2001). The eye of the beholder: Authenticity in an embedded assessment task. *Language Testing, 18,* 463–481.
Swain, M. (2001). Examining dialogue: Another approach to content specification and to validating inferences drawn form test scores. *Language Testing, 18,* 275–302.
Turner, C. E. (2000). Listening to the voices of rating scale developers: Identifying salient features for second language performance assessment. *Canadian Modern Language Review/ Revue Canadienne des langues vivantes, 56,* 555–584.
University of Cambridge Local Examinations Syndicate (UCLES) 2000: Investigating the paired speaking test format. UCLES research Notes (August 2000). URL: http: //www. cambridge-efl. org/rs_notes2_7. cfm
Upshur, J. A., & Turner, C. E. (1999). Systematic effects in the rating of second-language speaking ability: Test method and learner discourse. *Language Testing, 16,* 82–111.
van Lier, L. (1989). Reeling, writhing, drawling, stretching and fainting in coils: Oral

proficiency interviews as conversations. *TESOL Quarterly, 23,* 480–508.

Wigglesworth, G. (1997). An investigation of planning time and proficiency level on oral test discourse. *Language Testing, 14,* 85–106.

Young, R. (1995). Discontinuous interlanguage development and its implications for oral proficiency rating scales. *Applied Language Learning, 6*(1–2), 13–26.

Young, R. (2001, February). The role of speaking in discursive practice. Presentation at *The Brahmin and the Elephant: Defining and Assessing Speaking Ability,* a joint symposium of Language Testing Research Colloquium and American Association for Applied Linguistics Annual Conference, St Louis, MO.

Young, R., & Halleck, G. (1998). "Let them eat cake!" or how to avoid losing your head in cross-cultural conversations. In R. Young & A. W. He (Eds.), *Talking and testing: Discourse approaches to the assessment of oral proficiency* (pp. 355–382). Amsterdam: John Benjamins.

Yuan, Y. (2001). An inquiry into empirical pragmatics data-gathering methods: Written DCTs, oral DCTs, field notes, and natural conversations. *Journal of Pragmatics, 33,* 271–292.

13. DISCOURSE APPROACHES TO ORAL LANGUAGE ASSESSMENT

Richard F. Young

This chapter begins with a careful look at a sample conversation and examines the many layers of interpretation that different academic traditions have constructed in order to interpret it. These layers of interpretation include linguistic forms, nonverbal communication, linguistic context, situational context, and the embodied histories that participants bring to interaction. All are incorporated into a rich definition of discourse. The chapter then reviews recent studies that have compared the discourse of oral interaction in assessment with oral discourse in contexts outside assessment to show how different they are. The next section discusses studies that have related ways of speaking to the cultural values of communities of speakers with a view to understanding the cultural miscommunication that occurs in assessment of speaking in a second language community. The review concludes by stressing the wholeness of face-to-face interaction, listing the layers of interpretation of interaction that have not thus far been considered in oral testing, and setting out a potentially fertile area for future research.

Oral language is a complex phenomenon and understanding how well a second language learner uses oral language is one of the most challenging issues in language assessment. For more than fifty years now, the technology of recording and reproducing speech has allowed researchers to understand it in greater detail; that technology together with theoretical advances in discourse analysis have created a detailed and nuanced picture of speech. In recent years, language assessment researchers and test developers have begun to utilize the new understanding of oral discourse in order to examine existing means of assessing oral language and to put forward new methods of testing. In this review, I will take as a point of departure a conversation that I will then analyze in order to illustrate some of the properties of oral language that discourse analysts have identified. I will then turn to the concerns of language testers to produce a valid assessment of an individual's oral language ability and review comparisons between the discourse of the assessment task and the discourse of conversation. Finally, I will review the manner in which ways of speaking form part of a culture and are valued accordingly and, consequently, how cross-cultural variation on speaking influences its assessment.

The Discourse of Oral Interaction

In order to understand the phenomenon of oral language, I reproduce here a conversation between a child (C) and his mother (M) published some years ago by Ray Birdwhistell (1960, 1970). In order to demonstrate the complexity of oral interaction, I will provide a layered description of the conversation in which each partial layer of interpretation builds on the layers that precede it. Let us first look at the words of the conversation (Birdwhistell, 1970, pp. 283–285):

C : Mama. I gotta go to the bathroom.
M : [no response]
C : Mama. Donnie's gotta go.
M : Sh-sh.
C : But mama.
M : Later.
C : Ma ma.
M : Wait.
C : Oh mama, mama, mama.
M : Shut up. Will yuh.

By studying only the words of this conversation, there is already much that can be said about the structure of the discourse. The first obvious observation is that there are two speakers and the conversation has a beginning and an end. In this case, oral language is clearly created by more than one person. And although there are words that we attribute to one speaker and not to another, the two speakers are part of one conversation, which we infer from the observation that they take turns and that adjacent turns by C and M appear to be related to one another. The conversation begins with a call from C to which M's response is noticeably absent.

Each of the other adjacent lines forms a pair—a call by C and a response by M. Not only do these adjacent lines form a pair that is topically and functionally related, but the whole conversation from beginning to end is about a single topic: C wants to go to the bathroom. Already, the discourse of this conversation is showing its dialogic nature through orderly turn taking, adjacency pairs, and topical coherence. We can infer from this sample of oral language that doing oral language is about far more than just one person speaking.

Clearly though, the speech patterns of each person in the conversation are important in expressing that individual's meaning; at the same time, interpreting those patterns is important for the other individual in order for both to maintain the orderly dialogic structure that I have shown here. The words that the participants speak are part of what helps them to construct the conversation, but the way in which they say them is also an important ingredient of their meaning. I now reproduce the conversation again, this time indicating the sentence stress, intonation, pausing, and the voice quality of each utterance that Birdwhistell (1970. pp. 293–285) assigns.[1]

1. C: ^{3}Ma^{2}ma((pause))^{3}I ^{2}gotta go to the ^{3}bath^{2}room
2. M: ((pause))
3. C: ^{2}Ma^{3}ma((pause))^{2}Donnie's gotta ^{3}go^1
4. M: ^{2}Sh-^{1}sh
5. C: ^{1}But((pause))^{4}ma^{3}ma
6. M: ((softly))^{3}La^{1}ter
7. C: ((whining))^{3}Ma: ^{1}ma:
8. M: ((rasping voice))^{3}Wait^1
9. C: ^{1}Oh ^{3}ma^{1}ma ^{4}ma^{2}ma ^{3}ma^{3}ma:
10. M: ((loudly))^{3}Shud^{1}dap((softly))^{2}will ^{3}yuh

This second layer of description shows that intonation and voice quality add a further dimension to our understanding of this conversation. Consider how C's intonation on the word "mama" changes as the conversation progresses. In line 1, the tones on the two syllables are "^{3}ma^{2}ma, " a slight fall, but when he receives no response, this tone changes to marked stress and a rise in line 3 "^{2}ma^{3}ma." Then, when M responds with a dispreferred second pair part to C's request, the tone changes to a fall in line 5: "^{4}ma^{3}ma." C persists in this request by increasing his pitch range to a high fall in line 7 accompanied by a change in voice quality to a whine, to which M responds with a change of voice quality to a rasp in line 8, but M's response is still not the one C wishes to hear and he repeats his call with increasing volume in line 9. M's closure of the interaction is done with loud volume on the words "shuddap." Such a close analysis of the way the speech patterns of each participant in the conversation change as the conversation progresses illuminates another aspect of oral language: Language provides a context for itself. In other words, the way that a participant pronounces a word is not fixed but varies according to where that word is used in the sequence of interaction and according to the attitudinal meaning that the participant wishes to convey.

Thus far, the conversation has been abstracted from the situational context in which it occurred, but of course all conversation occurs in a context that is both linguistic and situational, and a discourse approach to the study of language must take situational or extralinguistic context into consideration. Birdwhistell observed the conversation at about 2: 30 p. m., April 14, 1952 on a bus in Arlington, Virginia. The participants were a mother and her son; and Birdwhistell provides the following description of the context in which the conversation occurred:

> Mother and child spoke with a tidewater Virginia accent. The bus route on which the event was recorded leads to a middle-class neighborhood. The way in which the mother and child were dressed was not consistent with the dress of other riders...The little boy was seated next to the window...The child was about four, and his mother seemed to be about twenty-seven to thirty (1970, p. 283).

Birdwhistell's description gives contextual information about what Bourdieu (Bourdieu & Thompson, 1991) has called the *habitus* of the participants: their accents and dress, which distinguish them from the middle-class neighborhood through which they are passing and imply that mother and child are from a lower socioeconomic class than the other riders on the bus. The description of the physical and social context tells us that this conversation between mother and child did not take place in private and the context—on a bus in front of other participants from a higher social class—also allows us to interpret the mother's refusal of her son's request. It is not possible to go to the bathroom on a bus and talking loudly about such things can cause embarrassment if the talk is overheard by people from a higher social class. The mother's nonresponse in line 2 to the child's request is an attempt to avoid the conversation, she then attempts to terminate the conversation in line 4, and then to make the conversation inaudible to other passengers on the bus by her low volume in line 6. None of these attempts succeed until she finally manages with loud volume and informal command in line 10 to terminate what seems for her to be an embarrassing conversation.

The final layer of description that Birdwhistell (1970, pp. 283–285) provides is a line-by-line description of the nonverbal aspects of interaction and an interpretation of the participants' intentions. (The descriptions and interpretations precede the speaker's verbal turns, shown in boldface) :

1. The little boy...seemed tired of looking out of the window, and, after surveying all of the car ads and the passengers, he leaned toward his mother and pulled at her sleeve, pouted and vigorously kicked his legs.
1. **Child: ^{3}Ma^{2}ma ((pause)) ^{3}I ^{2}gotta go to the ^{3}bath^{2}room**
2. His mother had been sitting erectly in her seat, her packages on her lap, and her hands lightly clasped around the packages. She was apparently "lost in thought."
2. **Mother: ((no verbal reply))**
3. When the boy's initial appeal failed to gain the mother's attention, he began to jerk at her sleeve again, each jerk apparently stressing his vocalization.
3. **Child: ^{2}Ma^{3}ma ((pause)) ^{2}Donnie's gotta ^{3}go^1**
5. The mother turned and looked at him, "shushed" him, and placed her right hand firmly across his thighs.
4. **Mother: ^{2}Sh-^{1}sh**
5. The boy protested audibly, clenched both fists, and pulled them with stress against his chest. At the same time he drew his legs up against the restraint of his mother's hand. His mouth was drawn down and his upper face was

pulled into a tight frown.
5. Child: ¹But((pause))⁴ma³ma
6. The mother withdrew her hand from his lap and resettled in her former position with her hands clasped around the packages.
6. Mother:((softly))³La¹ter
7. The boy grasped her upper right arm tightly, continued to frown When no immediate response was forthcoming, he turned and thrust both knees into the lateral aspect of her left thigh.
7. Child:((whining))³Ma: ¹ma:
8. She looked at him, leaned toward him. and slapped him across the anterior portion of his upper legs.
8. Mother:((rasping voice))³Wait¹
9. He began to jerk his clenched fists up and down, vigorously nodding between each inferior-superior movement of his fists.
9. Child: ¹Oh ³ma¹ma ⁴ma²ma ³ma³ma:
10. She turned round, frowning, and with her mouth pursed, she spoke to him through her teeth. Suddenly she looked around, noted that the other passengers were watching, and forced a square smile. At the same time that she finished speaking, she reached her right hand in under her left arm and squeezed the boy's arm. He sat quietly.
10. Mother:((loudly))³Shud¹dap((softly))³will ³yuh

Birdwhistell's line-by-line description shows the coordination of speech and nonverbal communication. In line 3, the child's jerking of his mother's sleeve is in rhythm with his stressed syllables, and in line 7 he digs his knees into his mother's thigh to accentuate his whining call. His mother's verbal response in line 4 is accompanied by a movement to constrain him, and her "wait" in line 8 is accompanied by a slap on his legs, a nonverbal response that follows the child's digging of his knees into her thigh. The participants' facial expressions are also coordinated with their talk; for example, in line 5 the child frowns to complement his protest, and in line 10 his mother frowns and purses her mouth to accompany her "shuddap will yuh." Birdwhistell also confirms the interpretation that there are more than two participants in this interaction by noting that the mother "looked around, noted the other passengers were watching, and forced a square smile." As Bell (1984) has shown, the co-participation of the other participants may result in the mother's designing this interaction (or at least its termination) with this audience in mind.

I have described this conversation in layers in order to give the reader a sense of the procedure that Ryle (1971) and Geertz (1973) have suggested that we use to approach the problem of interpreting interaction in context—what Geertz called "thick description." All these layers contribute to an understanding of the discourse of interaction, which Celce-Murcia and Olshtain define as follows:

> A piece of discourse is as an instance of spoken or written language that has describable internal relationships of form and meaning (e. g., words, structures, cohesion) that relate coherently to an external communicative function or purpose and a given audience/interlocutor. Furthermore, the external function or purpose can only be properly determined if one takes into account the context and participants (i. e., all the relevant situational, social, and cultural factors) in which the piece of discourse occurs (2000, p. 4).

A valid and accurate assessment of oral language must somehow index each of the layers of description that we have seen are part of the complex process of interpreting spoken interaction. Such an assessment indexes the interactional structure of the conversation that has been described by Young (He & Young, 1998; Young, 1999) as a complex configuration of interactional features including boundaries such as openings and closings, participation frameworks, sequential organizations of turns and topics, and semiotic structure (Young & Nguyen, in press). It also indexes the context in which the conversation takes places on at least two dimensions: linguistic and situational. Other language in the conversation contextualizes and thus influences the choice of language at a specific point in the conversation. And at the same time the situational context (including the personal histories of the participants, where the conversation takes place, and the invoked presence of other non-focal participants) influences the language of the focal conversation. And finally, the conversation is not constructed through the single modality of speech. As Birdwhistell's description of the participants' hand gestures, body movements, and facial expressions shows, communication through speech is tightly coordinated with action in the nonverbal channel.

The 20th century tradition of assessing oral language as described by Spolsky

(1990, 2000) has not taken into consideration the layers of interpretation of speech in any systematic way, and indeed some oral assessment procedures specifically exclude any consideration of oral language as interaction (Bernstein, 1999). Instead, two aspects of the discourse of oral language assessment have been studied at some length: their construct validity and cross-cultural variation in speaking. The question of the construct validity of oral tests is the degree to which discourse in oral tests corresponds to a theoretical model of speaking. Variation in ways of speaking across cultures has been studied because oral second language assessment often involves an assessor from the target linguaculture judging the speech of a candidate from a different linguaculture (Agar, 1994). These are the issues that this review will now address. I will first review recent studies of validity, and I will follow that with a review of studies that have addressed questions of cross-cultural variation in oral testing. [2]

Validity in Oral Testing

Cumming (1996) describes a large number of ways in which the concept of validity has been used in language testing and in psychology, citing 16 definitions given by Angoff (1988). Construct validation, according to Cumming, is the type of validity that has been most important in recent years. Several organizations have said that construct validity is "the most important consideration in test evaluation" (American Educational Research Association, American Psychological Association, & National Council on Measurements Used in Education, 1985). This has led to considerable work describing the discrepancies between what a Language Proficiency Interview (LPI is supposed to measure and what it does measure.

The question of whether the discourse of an LPI reproduces the discourse of natural conversation has been asked by several researchers. Van Lier (1989) and Young and Milanovic (1992) questioned the supposedly conversational nature of OPIs and van Lier proposed an alternative modular approach to the existing OPI format so as to transform an OPI into a conversation. Lazaraton (1992, 1996a, 1997) examined the overall structural organization of the LPI as well as examiners' question design and the interactively co-constructed nature of the assessment of the learners' language ability. She showed that, although LPIs import their fundamental structural and interactional features from conversation, they are identifiably instances of interviews for the participants.

One particular LPI, the Oral Proficiency Interview, used extensively by organizations such as the American Council on the Teaching of Foreign Languages (ACTFL) (American Council on the Teaching of Foreign Languages, 2001; Breiner-Sanders, Lowe, Miles, & Swender, 2000), has been critically examined in some detail by Johnson (Johnson, 2000, 2001; Johnson & Tyler, 1998). Johnson (2001) conducted a discourse analysis of 35 LPIs and compared the discursive architecture of this practice with ordinary conversation. One of the major findings that resulted from her comparison was that the distribution and allocation of turns in LPIs differs markedly from the way that turns are distributed and allocated in ordinary conversation. The kind of turn structure that is typical of LPIs is illustrated by the following transcript from an Oral Proficiency Interview conducted by telephone in English as a second language (Johnson, 2001, p. 94). [3]

1. Inter: How long does it take you to get from Salt Lake City to Provo?
2. Cand: I took a bus this morning so it took me about an hour and twenty
3. minutes to get here.
4. Inter: Oh you rode the bus?
5. Cand: Yeah I did.
6. Inter: Did they have a good bus service from between the two cities?
7. Cand: Yeah they have UTA Utah Transit Service and it's real good.
8. Inter: (clears throat) What kind of buses are they uh do they have? Are
9. they big ones?
10. Cand: It's really big one.
11. Inter: Oh I see I see. Interesting! Now, is there any kind of train
12. connection between the two cities?
13. Cand: Uh [c] usually II think they do but I never take a train. They
14. have Amtrak from Provo to Salt Lake and: I don't know how
15. much it costs but they have it a Amtrak [c] from Provo to Salt
16. Lake.
17. Inter: Now, (clears throat) you say that you have lived in Provo for four
18. years now?
19. Cand: Yeah.
20. Inter: Is that the only place in Utah that you've lived?
21. Cand: Yeah, I came I came here in nineteen...ninety.

22. Inter: Oh nineteen ninety. And from where did you come?

As illustrated in this excerpt, Johnson found that interviewers' turns in LPIs most often consisted of a question, while candidates asked questions relatively infrequendy. As Johnson remarked, this one-sided pattem of question and response contradicts the assumption that an LPI represents a conversation because "in conversation, turn unit type (along with turn allocation and turn distribution) is unpredictable" (Johnson, 2001, p. 93). The means by which participants in an LPI allocate the next turn is also illustrated in this excerpt, and in this particular case it is related to the fact that the interviewer's turn consists solely of questions. At transition relevance places (TRPs) in the interviewer's turns, he selects the next speaker (i. e., the candidate). For example, in the interviewer's long turn in line 11 according to Ford, Fox, and Thompson (1996), there are four points at which the syntax indicates a new turn may be taken. A change of speaker is possible after "Oh I see I see," after "Interesting!" after "Now," and at the end of the question about the train. Although after the first three TRPs the candidate may take the floor by selecting herself as the next speaker, she does not in fact take a turn until the interviewer selects her as the next speaker at the end of the question.

Meanwhile at TRPs in the candidate's turns, either the candidate continues her turn or the interviewer self selects. For example, the syntax of the candidate's long turn in lines 13-16 indicates five TRPs: after "uh usually I I think they do," after "but I never take a train," after "they have Amtrak from Provo to Salt Lake," after "and I don't know how much it costs," and after "but they have it a Amtrak from Provo to Salt Lake." At none of these TRPs, however, does the candidate select the interviewer as the next speaker. This happens only when the interviewer selects himself at the end of candidate's turn by introducing a new topic with "Now, you say that you have lived in Provo for four years now?" in lines 17 and 18. There are very few occasions in Johnson's data when the candidate allocates the next turn to the interviewer, and in this way the different and complementary discursive roles of candidate and interviewer contribute to constructing a participation structure of the LPI that differs from ordinary conversation.

Other researchers have criticized the validity of other aspects of the LPI. Using the methods of conversation analysis, Egbert (1998) analyzed 20 LPIs conducted in German as a foreign language with American students and found that the organization of conversational repair was explicitly explained by the interviewer, and that thus the students initiated repair by means of the forms taught to them, which are not found in interaction between native speakers. On the other hand, Moder and Halleck (1998) freely admit that the discourse of the ACTFL oral proficiency interview (OPI does not measure proficiency in an informal conversation, but that in itself does not establish that it is an inadequate measure of communicative competence. Outside the testing situation, nonnative speakers may engage in other speech events having features that are similar to an interview and thus will have to respond to questions intended to seek information, to check information, and to clarify (Schiffrin, 1994). Moder and Halleck (1998) compared OPI interviews of native and nonnative speakers and concluded that the interview frame is interpreted by both groups in a similar way, suggesting that the examination frame does not override the communicative frame of the event. This suggests that the OPI can be viewed as an authentic instance of talk in interaction. It is not an informal conversation, but it does sample the communicative behavior of interviewees in an authentic speech event.

The discourse of other modes of assessing oral interaction besides the ACTFL OPI has been described, including role play, scripted stimulus-response, picture description, and group discussion with another candidate. A role play is part of the Occupational English Test (OET) described by McNamara (Jacoby & McNamara, 1999; Lynch & McNamara, 1998; McNamara & Lumley, 1997; McNamara, 1996, 1997). In the OET role play, an interlocutor plays the role of a member of the public seeking professional help from the nonnative speaking candidate. Lazaraton (1996b) has described the examiners' questions in the Cambridge Assessment of Spoken English as scripted, allowing none of the spontaneous interaction that is found in conversation and modeling more closely the stimulus-response model of interaction described by Silverman (1976). And Riggenbach (1998) has proposed assessment based on an oral language portfolio that includes a range of speech samples: audio or video recordings of the learner engaged in a variety of orally-communicated exchanges, some of which are monologues, some dialogues, some structured (e. g., read-aloud tasks), some semi-structured (e. g., tasks), some rehearsed (e. g., short lectures), and some spontaneous (e. g., role plays). Riggenbach (1998) believes that "this approach to oral skills testing offers a more holistic and comprehensive assessment that could serve as an alternative to more traditional speaking test formats that rely on a single sample and/or a single genre" (p. 65).

Differences between the discourse of interviews and conversation were also noted by Fulcher (1996). Fulcher conducted a comparative study of students taking three different oral assessments: two interviews—one based on picture description, and one discussion on a text—and one non-interview—a group discussion monitored by an examiner. Fulcher discussed the validity of the three tests as perceived by the candidates. He concluded that, "Engaging in a group discussion with a partner gave the students more confidence to speak and say what *they* wanted, rather than having to respond to an examiner" (p. 33). Perhaps for this reason, the group oral "was seen as an enjoyable experience by well over half the students" (p. 34), and students saw the group oral as the most preferable of the three tests.

Apart from the discourse of the conversation itself, the situational context of assessment has also been investigated. Several studies have made comparisons between rating scales used in assessment and intuitive ratings of conversations by nonraters (Milanovic, Saville, Pollitt, & Cook, 1996; Pollitt & Murray, 1996). Pollitt and Murray (1996) found that raters focused on different qualities of talk depending on the overall proficiency level of the candidate. With higher proficiency candidates, raters distinguished among candidates according to stylistic devices the candidates used and according to candidates' content-focused elaboration, creativity, parenthetical statements, and idiomatic expressions. At the lower proficiency level, raters distinguished among candidates according to candidates' grammatical competence; whether candidates were hesitant or staccato; or used form-focused language, set 'textbook' phrases, and rehearsed or stilted speech. In fact, the lack of an empirical basis for rating scales used in the assessment of oral interaction has been criticized by Young (Young, 1995b), and Kenyon (Kenyon, 1998; Stansfield & Kenyon, 1996) has investigated the correspondence between levels of difficulty established *a priori* by rating scales and perceptions of difficulty by students and teachers.

The most fundamental investigation of the wider context of oral assessment is Jacoby's notion of indigenous assessment (Jacoby, 1998; Jacoby & McNamara, 1999). Indigenous assessment, according to Jacoby, differs from the traditional activity of examiners or assessors of oral interaction in a second language, whose aim is to evaluate the performance of candidates according to linguistic criteria. Indigenous assessment involves at least one participant who frames another participant's prior communication as good or bad. The response of the co-present participant and any ensuing discussion is also part of the assessment. Indigenous assessment of communication performance can occur in nontesting situations such as an assessment of a child at the family dinner table in response to something a child just said, and it occurs when scientists critique one another's run-throughs of upcoming conference presentations. An indigenous assessment is accomplished among insider participants in some culturally situated activity for their own local purposes and it is not prompted by or designed to serve the purposes of an outside rater. Indigenous assessment has been applied to the assessment of English for specific purposes by Douglas (Douglas, 2000; Douglas & Myers, 2000).

Cross-Cultural Variation in Oral Testing

Most methods of assessing oral ability in a second language involve an assessor evaluating learners' discourse from the perspective of the cultural norms of oral interaction in the target community. Work on the ethnography of speaking has, however, demonstrated that the ways of speaking of a particular group are in effect reflections of the culture of the group and that these cultural patterns transfer into the speech patterns of a second language even among quite advanced learners. According to Gumperz (1982), in different communities participants in speech activities have specific expectations about thematic progression, turn-taking rules, form, and the outcome of the interaction, as well as constraints on what counts as context. Cross-cultural misunderstanding may result from discourse cues that have a certain meaning in one linguaculture being transferred into the second language and being interpreted differently by an interlocutor from another linguaculture (Agar, 1994; Boxer, this volume; Scollon & Scollon, 2001; Young & Halleck, 1998). The effect of such culture-specific discourse organization on the assessment of speaking has been investigated by a number of researchers including Davies (1998) and Kim and Suh (1998) for Americans speaking Korean; Ross (Berwick & Ross, 1996; Ross, 1998) for Japanese speakers of English; and Young, who compared Mexicans and Japanese speaking English (Young, 1995a; Young & Halleck, 1998).

A clear example of the connection between conversational organization and cultural values is provided by Kim and Suh (1998). In Korean OPIs with American candidates, Kim and Suh observed this recurrent question-answer sequence over five turns. [4]

1st Turn (IR) :   Question
2nd Turn (NNS) :   Answer
3rd Turn (IR) :   Confirmation request
4th Turn (NNS) :   Confirmation
5th Turn (IR) :   Follow-up

According to Kim and Suh, the interviewer's confirmation request in the 3rd turn is a place where "IR claims his/her right to evaluate prior talk and initiates subsequent talk" (1998, p. 316). The Korean interviewer expects the learner to respond by confirming the interviewer's right to evaluate and to wait for IR to initiate a new topic. The learner's close orientation toward and confirmation of the interviewer's third turn "constitutes a crucial aspect of sociolinguistic competence by indexing that NNS treats IR as a socially higher status person whose assessment he or she respects and values" (p. 317). Kim and Suh mention this as one way in which Korean interviewers assess the proficiency of a conversational partner. Less proficient students respond to the interviewer's confirmation request either by silence or by continuing the topic they began in the second turn, thus ignoring the interviewer's confirmation request. Both of these responses by the candidate challenge the positive face of the interviewer because they fail to recognize the need to recognize IR's higher status. Although such discourse may not of itself determine an assessment of low oral proficiency, Kim and Suh show that such patterns are nonetheless characteristic of low proficiency candidates.

Another type of culture-specific oral assessment that is not normally considered in discussions of second language assessment is the oral exams that are often part of university assessments, especially in the humanities. Such assessments are prevalent in Italian universities and have been analyzed by Anderson (1999) and Ciliberti (1999), who show how a student's knowledge of subject matter is co-constructed by the student and by the examining professors.

Conclusions

At the beginning of this review, I showed a conversation between a mother and her child in its entirety, and I argued that the wholeness of the interaction could be best understood by considering the layers of interpretation that different academic traditions had formed around the interaction in order to describe and understand it. In the tradition of language assessment, one layer of this description has been thicker than others: the words spoken, their pronunciation, and prosodic contours. In reviewing more recent work in assessing oral language, I have emphasized the layers of interpretation that have not been previously considered in testing—the linguistic and situational context of the interaction, the outcome that the participants intend, the outcome intended by those who make the assessment, and the close relationship between oral interaction and the culture of the participants.

Finally, one important layer of discourse not yet studied in oral language proficiency tests is the role of nonverbal behavior in those tests and the influence of the nonverbal channel on assessment. As Birdwhistell illustrated in his transcription of the nonverbal channel in the conversation between a mother and her child with which this article began, it is a small step from a linguistic discourse analysis to an analysis of interaction at both the nonverbal and verbal levels. Although this has been done in recent work in interactional sociolinguistics (Egbert, 1996; Erickson, 1992; Goodwin, 1981; Key, 1980a, b; Ochs, Jacoby, & Gonzalez, 1994; Streek, 1995; Wells, 2000), and some attempts have been made to understand the role of nonverbal behavior in cross-cultural communication (Adams, 1998; Ekman, 1973; Houck & Gass, 1997; Kellerman, 1992; Stam, 1999; Young, 1994), no studies have so far been published that analyze nonverbal behavior in oral language assessment. This is a potentially fertile area for future research.

Notes

1. Birdwhistell indicated intonation by using the symbols of Trager and Smith (1957) in which the pitch level of the following syllable is indicated by superscript numbers, with [1] indicating a speaker's lowest pitch and [4] representing the highest pitch in their range. Stresses louder than normal are indicated by underlining the stressed syllable. Pauses and voice quality affecting the following words are indicated between double parentheses.

2. The majority of the research on oral assessment in the language testing community has not in fact addressed the two issues of validity and cross-cultural variation. Most research has instead focused on the systematic ways in which variation in scores can be related to the task, the rater, and the rating scale, in other

words, to the method of oral testing. Upshur and Turner (1999) provide a very clear overview of this research, which I mention here only in passing because the focus of the present review is on the discourse of oral assessment.

3. The native speaking interviewer is identified as 'Inter" and the nonnative speaking candidate as "Cand."

4. IR is the native speaking Korean interviewer; NNS is the American speaker of Korean as a second language.

ANNOTATED BIBLIOGRAPHY

Jacoby, S., & McNamara, T. (1999). Locating competence. *English for Specific Purposes, 18*(3), 213–241.

This article goes into detail about the concept of indigenous assessment. Indigenous criteria for assessment are important in performance tests in which some criterion situation is simulated to a much greater degree than is represented in the usual pencil-and-paper test. The criterion for assessment is usually based on a theoretical (usually psychological) and educationally motivated construct assumed to underlie performance, but ethnographic research can reveal what criteria experts in the given field feel are appropriate for assessment. The article describes the assessment criteria used in the Australian Occupational English Test and compares it with the indigenous assessment criteria used by physicists who evaluate rehearsals of upcoming conference presentations by their colleagues.

Johnson, M. (2001). *The art of non-conversation: A re-examination of the validity of the Oral Proficiency Interview.* New Haven, CT: Yale University Press.

The heart of this book is a detailed discourse analysis of 35 oral proficiency interviews conducted over the phone. Based on a close conversation analysis of the discourse, Johnson challenges the construct validity of the OPI. Johnson rejects the uncontextualized communicative competence model of language ability that underlies the OPI. She concludes by proposing a model of interactional competence in which language ability is considered to reflect the contexts in which it is acquired and used.

Young, R., & He, A. W. (Eds.). (1998). *Talking and testing: Discourse approaches to the assessment of oral proficiency.* Amsterdam: John Benjamins.

This book is a collection of studies on the assessment of oral proficiency in a second language that combine language assessment and discourse analysis. It is introduced by a chapter in which the editors lay out their framework of interactional competence. The following 13 chapters report empirical studies of oral assessment and are all based on close analyses of audio-and/or videotaped discourse. Questions addressed include: How do participants construct identity and competence through interaction? How do interviewers form their judgments about the candidates' interactional abilities? And how does the meaning of an interview change from one speech community to another?

OTHER REFERENCES

Adams, T. W. (1998). *Gesture in foreigner talk*. Unpublished Ph. D. dissertation, University of Pennsylvania, Philadelphia.

Agar, M. (1994). *Language shock: Understanding the culture of conversation*. New York: Morrow.

American Council on the Teaching of Foreign Languages. (2001). *The ACTFL Oral Proficiency Interview (OPI)*. Available: http : //www. actfl. org/public/articles/details. cfm?id= 17. Retrieved October 2, 2001.

American Educational Research Association, American Psychological Association, & National Council on Measurements Used in Education. (1985). *Standards for educational and psychological testing*. Washington, DC: Authors.

Anderson, L. (1999). La co-costruzione di competenza negli esami orali e il ruolo della comunicazione metapragmatica [The co-construction of competence in oral exams and the role of metapragmatic communication]. In A. Ciliberti & L. Anderson (Eds.), *Le forme della communicazione accademica: Ricerche linguistiche sulla didattica universitaria in ambito umanistico* (pp. 192–219). Pavia, Italy: FrancoAngeli.

Angoff, W. (1988). Validity: An evolving concept. In H. Wainer & H. Braun (Eds.), *Test validity* (pp. 19–32). Hillsdale, NJ: Lawrence Erlbaum.

Bell, A. (1984). Language style as audience design. *Language in Society, 13*, 145–204.

Bernstein, J. (1999). *PhonePass^{TM} testing: Structure and construct*. Available: http : //www. ordinate. com/pdf/StructureAndConstruct990826. pdf. Retrieved October 1, 2001.

Berwick, R., & Ross, S. (1996). Cross-cultural pragmatics in oral proficiency interview strategies. In University of Cambridge Local Examinations Syndicate (Ed.), *Performance testing, cognition and assessment: Selected papers from the 15th Language Testing Research Colloquium (LTRC), Cambridge and Arnhem* (pp. 34–54). Cambridge, England: University of Cambridge Press.

Birdwhistell, R. L. (1960). Kinesics and communication. In E. S. Carpenter & M. McLuhan (Eds.), *Explorations in communication: An anthology* (pp. 54–64). Beacon Hill, NC: Beacon Press.

Birdwhistell, R. L. (1970). *Kinesics and context: Essays on body motion communication.* Philadelphia, PA: University of Pennsylvania Press.

Bourdieu, P., & Thompson, J. B. (1991). *Language and symbolic power* (G. Raymondson & M. Adamson, Trans.). Cambridge, MA: Harvard University Press.

Boxer, D. (this volume). Discourse issues in cross-cultural pragmatics.

Breiner-Sanders, K. E., Lowe, P., Jr., Miles, J., & Swender, E. (2000). ACTFL Proficiency guidelines—speaking: Revised 1999. *Foreign Language Annals, 33*(1), 13–18.

Celce-Murcia, M., & Olshtain, E. (2000). *Discourse and context in language teaching: A guide for language teachers.* Cambridge, England: Cambridge University Press.

Ciliberti, A. (1999). Gli esami orali: Tra agentività e dipendenza, tra auto-referenzialità ed etero-referenzialità [Oral exams: Between agency and dependency, between self-referentiality and other-referentiality]. In A. Ciliberti & L. Anderson (Eds.), *Le forme della communicazione accademica: Ricerche linguistiche sulla didattica universitaria in ambito umanistico* (pp. 166–191). Pavia, Italy: FrancoAngeli.

Cumming, A. (1996). Introduction: The concept of validation in language testing. In A. H. Cumming & R. Berwick (Eds.), *Validation in language testing* (pp. 1–14). Clevedon and Philadelphia: Multilingual Matters.

Davies, C. E. (1998). Maintaining American face in the Korean oral exam: Reflections of the power of cross-cultural context. In R. Young & A. W. He (Eds.), *Talking and testing: Discourse approaches to the assessment of oral proficiency* (pp. 271–296). Amsterdam and Philadelphia: John Benjamins.

Douglas, D. (2000). *Assessing languages for specific purposes.* Cambridge, England: Cambridge University Press.

Douglas, D., & Myers, R. (2000). Assessing the communication skills of veterinary students: Whose criteria? In A. J. Kunnan (Ed.), *Fairness and validation in language assessment: Selected papers from the 19th Language Testing Research Colloquium, Orlando, Florida* (pp. 60–81). Cambridge, England: Cambridge University Press.

Egbert, M. M. (1996). Context-sensitivity in conversation: Eye gaze and the German repair initiator *bitte? Language in Sociery, 25*(4), 587–612.

Egbert, M. M. (1998). Miscommunication in language proficiency interviews of first-year German students: A comparison with natural conversation. In R. Young & A. W. He (Eds.), *Talking and testing: Discourse approaches to the assessment of oral proficiency* (pp. 147–169). Amsterdam: John Benjamins.

Ekman, P. (1973). Cross-cultural studies of facial expression. In P. Ekman (Ed.), *Darwin and facial expression* (pp. 169–222). New York: Academic Press.

Erickson, F. (1992). They know all the lines: Rhythmic organization and contextualization in a conversational listing routine. In P. Auer & A. Di Luzio (Eds.), *The contextualization of language* (pp. 365–397). Amsterdam and Philadelphia: John Benjamins.

Ford, C. E., Fox, B. A., & Thompson, S. (1996). Practices in the construction of turns: The "TCU" revisited. *Pragmatics, 6*, 427–454.

Fulcher, G. (1996). Testing tasks: Issues in task design and the group oral. *Language Testing, 13*(1), 23–51.

Geertz, C. (1973). *The interpretation of cultures: Selected essays.* New York: Basic Books.

Goodwin, C. (1981). *Conversational organization: Interaction between speakers and hearers.* New York: Academic Press.

Gumperz, J. J. (1982). *Discourse strategies.* Cambridge, England: Cambridge University Press.

He, A. W., & Young, R. (1998). Language proficiency interviews: A discourse approach. In R. Young & A. W. He (Eds.), *Talking and testing: Discourse approaches to the assessment of oral proficiency* (pp. 1–24). Amsterdam and Philadelphia: John Benjamins.

Houck, N., & Gass, S. M. (1997). Cross-cultural back channels in English refusals: A source of trouble. In A. Jaworski (Ed.), *Silence: Interdisciplinary perspectives* (pp. 285–308). New York: Mouton de Gruyter.

Jacoby, S. W. (1998). *Science as performance: Socializing scientific discourse through the conference talk rehearsal.* Unpublished Ph. D. dissertation, University of California, Los Angeles.

Johnson, M. (2000). Interaction in the oral proficiency interview: Problems of validity. *Pragmatics, 10*(2), 215–231.

Johnson, M., & Tyler, A. (1998). Re-analyzing the context of the OPI: How much does it look like natural conversation? In R. Young & A. W. He (Eds.), *Talking and testing: Discourse approaches to the assessment of oral proficiency* (pp. 27–51). Amsterdam and Philadelphia: John Benjamins.

Kellerman, S. (1992). 'I see what you mean' : The role of kinesic behaviour in listening and implications for foreign and second language learning. *Applied Linguistics, 13*, 239–258.

Kenyon, D. M. (1998). An investigation of the validity of task demands on performance-based tests of oral proficiency. In A. J. Kunnan (Ed.), *Validation in language assessment: Selected papers from the 17th Language Testing Research Colloquium, Long Beach* (pp. 19–40). Mahwah, NJ: Lawrence Erlbaum.

Key, M. R. (1980a). Language and nonverbal behavior as organizers of social systems. In M. R. Key (Ed.), *The relationship of verbal and nonverbal communication* (pp. 3–33). The Hague: Mouton.

Key, M. R. (Ed.). (1980b). *The relationship of verbal and nonverbal communication.* The

Hague: Mouton.
Kim, K., & Suh, K. (1998). Confirmation sequences as interactional resources in Korean language proficiency interviews. In R. Young & A. W. He (Eds.), *Talking and testing: Discourse approaches to the assessment of oral proficiency* (pp. 297–332). Amsterdam: John Benjamins.
Lazaraton, A. (1992). The structural organization of a language interview: A conversation analytic perspective. *System, 20,* 373–386.
Lazaraton, A. (1996a). Interlocutor support in oral proficiency interviews. *Language Testing. 13*(2), 173–190.
Lazaraton, A. (1996b). A qualitative approach to monitoring examiner conduct in the Cambridge assessment of spoken English (CASE), In University of Cambridge Local Examinations Syndicate (Ed.), *Performance testing, cognition and assessment: Selected papers from the 15th Language Testing Research Colloquium (LTRC), Cambridge and Arnhem* (pp. 18–33). Cambridge, England: University of Cambridge Press.
Lazaraton, A. (1997). Preference organization in oral proficiency interviews: The case of language ability assessments. *Research on Language and Social Interaction, 30*(1), 53–72.
Lynch, B. K., & McNamara, T. F. (1998). Using G-theory and many-facet Rasch measurement in the development of performance assessments of the ESL speaking skills of immigrants. *Language Testing, 15*(2), 158–180.
McNamara, T. F. (1996). *Measuring second language performance.* London: Longman.
McNamara, T. F. (1997). 'Interaction' in second language performance assessment: Whose performance? *Applied Linguistics, 18*(4), 446–466.
McNamara, T. F., & Lumley, T. (1997). The effect of interlocutor and assessment mode variables in overseas assessments of speaking skills in occupational settings. *Language Testing, 14*(2), 140–156.
Milanovic, M., Saville, N., Pollitt, A., & Cook, A. (1996). Developing rating scales for CASE: Theoretical concerns and analyses. In A. H. Cumming & R. Berwick (Eds.), *Validation in language testing* (pp. 15–38). Clevedon: Multilingual Matters.
Moder, C. L., & Halleck, G. B. (1998). Framing the language proficiency interview as speech event: Native and nonnative speakers' questions. In R. Young & A. W. He (Eds.), *Talking and testing: Discourse approaches to the assessment of oral proficiency* (pp. 117–146). Amsterdam: John Benjamins.
Ochs, E., Jacoby, S., & Gonzalez, P. (1994). Interpretive journeys: How physicists talk and travel through graphic space. *Configurations, 1,* 151–171.
Pollitt, A., & Murray, N. L. (1996). What raters *really* pay attention to. In University of Cambridge Local Examinations Syndicate (Ed.), *Performance testing, cognition and assessment: Selected papers from the 15th Language Testing Research Colloquium (LTRC),*

Cambridge and Arnhem (pp. 74–91). Cambridge, England: University of Cambridge Press.

Riggenbach, H. (1998). Evaluating learner interactional skills: Conversation at the micro level. In R. Young & A. W. He (Eds.), *Talking and testing: Discourse approaches to the assessment of oral proficiency* (pp. 53–67). Amsterdam: John Benjamins.

Ross, S. (1998). Divergent frame interpretations in language proficiency interview interaction. In R. Young & A. W. He (Eds.), *Talking and testing: Discourse approaches to the assessment of oral proficiency* (pp. 333–353). Amsterdam: John Benjamins.

Ryle, G. (1971). The thinking of thoughts: What is 'Le Penseur' doing? In G. Ryle (Ed.), *Collected papers*, Vol. 2, Collected essays 1929–1968 (pp. 480–496). London: Hutchinson.

Schiffrin, D. (1994). *Approaches to discourse*. Cambridge, MA: Blackwell.

Scollon, R., & Scollon, S. W. (2001). *Intercultural communication: A discourse approach* (2nd ed.). Malden, MA: Blackwell.

Silverman, D. (1976). Interview talk: Bringing off a research instrument. In D. Silverman & J. Jones (Eds.), *Organizational work: The language of grading, the grading of language* (pp. 133–150). London: Collier Macmillan.

Spolsky, B. (1990). Oral examinations: An historical note. *Language Testing, 7*(2), 158–173.

Spolsky, B. (2000). Language testing in The Modern Language Journal. *The Modern Language Journal, 84*(4), 536–552.

Stam, G. (1999, September). *Speech and gesture: What changes first in L2 acquisition?* Paper presented at the 19th annual Second Language Research Forum, University of Minnesota, Twin Cities.

Stansfield, C. W., & Kenyon, D. M. (1996). Comparing the scaling of speaking tasks by language teachers and by the ACTFL Guidelines. In A. H. Cumming & R. Berwick (Eds.), *Validation in language testing* (pp. 124–153). Clevedon: Multilingual Matters.

Streek, J. (1995). On projection. In Wissenschaftskolleg zu Berlin & E. N. Goody (Eds.), *Social intelligence and interaction: Expressions and implications of the social bias in human intelligence* (pp. 87–110). Cambridge, England: Cambridge University Press.

Trager, G. L., & Smith, H. L. (1957). *An outline of English structure*. Washington, DC: American Council of Learned Societies.

Upshur, J. A., & Turner, C. E. (1999). Systematic effects in the rating of second-language speaking ability: Test method and learner discourse. *Language Testing, 16*(1), 82–111.

van Lier, L. (1989). Reeling, writhing, drawling, stretching and fainting in coils: Oral proficiency interviews as conversation. *TESOL Quarterly, 23*(3), 489–508.

Wells, G. (2000). Modes of meaning in a science activity. *Linguistics and Education, 10*(3), 307–334.

Young, L. W. L. (1994). *Crosstalk and culture in Sino-American communication*. Cambridge, England: Cambridge University Press.

Young, R. (1995a). Conversational styles in language proficiency interviews. *Language Learning, 45*, 3–42.

Young, R. (1995b). Discontinuous interlanguage development and its implications for oral proficiency rating scales. *Applied Language Learning, 6*, 13–26.

Young, R. (1999). Sociolinguistic approaches to SLA. *Annual Review of Applied Linguistics, 19*, 105–132.

Young, R., & Halleck, G. B. (1998). "Let them eat cake!" or how to avoid losing your head in cross-cultural conversations. In R. Young & A. W. He (Eds.), *Talking and testing: Discourse approaches to the assessment of oral proficiency* (pp. 355–382). Amsterdam: John Benjamins.

Young, R., & Milanovic, M. (1992). Discourse variation in oral proficiency interviews. *Studies in Second Language Acquisition, 14*(4), 403–424.

Young, R. F, & Nguyen, H. T. (in press). Modes of meaning in high school science. *Applied Linguistics, 23*(3).

14. DISCOURSE APPROACHES TO WRITING ASSESSMENT

Ulla Connor and Aymérou Mbaye

At present, mastery of English for educational and professional purposes contributes significantly to expansion of the role of English as a language of world communication. In this context, the teaching—and, consequently, the assessment—of EFL/ESL writing is receiving more attention than ever before. This chapter argues that, although this renewed interest in the evaluation of writing has resulted in advances in the field of language testing, it has by and large failed to incorporate insights gained from recent developments in text analysis. There is a considerable gap between current practices in writing assessment and criteria suggested by advances in knowledge of discourse structure. We illustrate this gap by contrasting current practices in the scoring of two major EFL/ESL writing tests with knowledge of text characteristics generated from recent developments in text analysis. The review concludes by making the case for bridging the gap and by proposing a model of writing assessment that incorporates both linguistic and discoursal features of texts.

With the phenomenal spread of English as global lingua franca, the need for a mastery of this language for educational and/or professional purposes has heightened. EFL and ESL programs that, before, essentially concerned themselves with developing general language proficiency among students, now emphasize the students' development of literacy skills, especially in advanced L2 English classes. As a consequence, writing instruction is now receiving more attention than it probably ever did. Since, in the context of education, testing strives to bridge up the gap between teaching and learning (White, 1985), the resurgence of interest in the teaching of EFL/ESL writing has translated into a resurgence in attention to issues of assessing writing. A testimony to this resurgence is the many publications in the recent past that have visited or revisited the issue of second language writing assessment (Alderson, Clapham, & Wall, 1995: Bachman & Palmer; 1996; Cohen, 1994; Cumming, 1998; Hamp-Lyons, 1991; Kroll, 1998; Weir, 1993; Yancey & Huot, 1997). This added attention has contributed to noticeable changes in L2 and L1 writing assessment. For instance, performance testing and a shift from exclusive indirect testing of writing to a combination of direct and indirect testing, or even direct testing of writing altogether, now characterize testing practices in many places which, until recently, lived by totally different practices. This added attention to the testing of writing has also paved the way for more awareness among teachers and EFL/ESL professionals of important testing issues such as validity and reliability of testing instruments test types and purposes, specific methods for assessing writing and other skills, and so forth.

However, in the specific domain of writing assessment, second language testing developments and the changes in practices that have come with it do not seem to go much beyond traditional overreliance on linguistic criteria for evaluating writing. Holistic, primary trait, and portfolio approaches to writing assessment fundamentally offer no breakaway from an evaluation of writing based almost exclusively on linguistic criteria. Analytic and multiple-trait scoring guides, although they offer room for the inclusion of other criteria of writing, in practice hardly venture beyond inclusion of the generic criterion of "organization." Even where the term "rhetorical features of text" is used, it often appears be synonymous with "organization."

This is occurring despite the valuable insights that great advances in text analysis can provide into our understanding of writing ability. This chapter addresses the resulting gap in second language writing assessment. It will frrst review the development of current practices in the evaluation of writing, and the state of advances in text analysis. After that, it will examine the scoring philosophy of two representative ESL tests to illustrate the discrepancy between the current testing and text analysis theories. It ends with a proposal for a communicative model of writing that incorporates current thinking in linguistic/rhetorical text analysis.

Recent Developments in Second Language Assessment

"Every [language] test has a theory [of language] behind it" (Alderson, Clapham, & Wall, 1995, p. 16). This theory consists of beliefs of what language is and of how its mastery is reflected. For a considerable period in the modern history of English language teaching (ELT) there did not seem to be explicit awareness of this relationship between theoretical constructs of language and procedures for testing language, probably because the attention of ELT researchers was focused on such areas as the structures of language and, later, language errors. With the spread of ELT, and with the increased need for learners of the language to use it, not only for reading purposes, but for actual communication with other speakers of English, researchers concluded that language should mainly be taught for communication; communicative competence, along with its prerequisite of linguistic competence, became what EFL/ESL teachers strove to equip their linguistic competence, became what EFL/ ESL teachers strove to equip their students with. By proposing an insightful framework for the conceptualization of communicative competence, Canale and Swain (1980) provided the grounds for explicitly relating language tests to the construct of language proficiency and communicative competence.

The model of communicative competence developed by Canale and Swain (1980) and Canale (1983) consists of four components. The first, grammatical competence, covers "knowledge of lexical items and of rules of morphology, syntax, sentence-grammar semantics, and phonology" (Canale &Swain, 1980, p. 29); the second component, discourse competence, covers the ability to combine sentences and to form meaningful stretches of language beyond the sentence level, while sociolinguistic and strategic competencies, the last two components, relate respectively to the sociocultural rules of language and discourse, and to the strategies used to compensate for communication breakdowns. Canale and Swain's model of communicative competence, with some adaptations (Bachman & Palmer, 1996), constitutes a significant factor in the developments in language assessment in the last two decades of the last century. It not only brought about more integration of skills and/or language areas in testing; with its grounding in communicative teaching of English, it ushered in considerations of authenticity and context in language testing. Moreover, the explicit relationship it allowed between the language test and the construct of language and/or communicative competence paved the way for issues of validity that were to be central in the above mentioned developments in language assessment.

The breakthrough in language testing brought about by Canale and Swain's framework did not occur, however, without creating some challenges in testing. Prior to the communicative competence paradigm, instruments for measuring language ability were mostly characterized by discrete-point testing. These tests, despite questionable construct validity, offered the advantage of being scored easily and objectively. Integrative tests of language, especially direct tests of writing, did not present this advantage. Once the definition of communicative competence permitted a reduction in the potential lack of validity of writing tests, the challenge in writing assessment moved to development of scoring procedures that would not jeopardize gains in construct validity.

The challenge here appears to be acute, for, despite the availability of different scoring procedures that can be applied to L2 writing, they have invariably tended to fall short of covering the multiple components of writing ability. Holistic scoring (White, 1985) assigns a single score to a piece of writing based on its quality. Primary-trait scoring (Lloyd-Jones, 1977) bases allotting of a score on a predetermined characteristic feature of the writing task at hand. Both scoring methods present the shortcoming that they allow very limited coverage of the multiple facets of writing ability. A piece of writing in academic contexts may present undisputed clarity without satisfying the criterion of expected length. Likewise, if in a piece of writing to be scored, grammatical accuracy is determined as the primary trait, this piece may receive a good or bad score irrespective of the quality of content. By making possible the determination of subscores or overall scores based on specific features of writing, analytic and multiple-trait scoring schemes seemed to indicate that they would be able to achieve in scoring what holistic and primary-trait guides could not. In practice, however, analytic and multiple-trait scales supported few advances. When they covered rhetorical features of writing, these tended to be broad in nature, and thus prevented the evaluation of writing tasks on the basis of the components of writing the most relevant to the specific purpose of the writing task. An illustration of this claim is to be found in the fact that, too often, a persuasive essay would be evaluated on the basis of the presence of an introduction, body, and conclusion. This evaluation may even go as far as judging whether the piece of writing shows, at the paragraph level, identifiable topic sentences and supporting details. However, it is not the mere presence of an identifiable topic statement and supporting details that ensure the persuasiveness of an essay, let alone adherence to an introduction-body-conclusion structure.

Despite progress in second language writing assessment, then, the scoring of writing seems to present some significant challenges. This paper argues that the solution to these challenges in EFL/ESL writing assessment may come from due attention to developments in text analysis.

Recent Developments in Text Analysis

In the previous section, we indicated the usefulness of Canale and Swain's model for language testing. This usefulness is not limited to the testing of spoken language; their research has strong implications for the field of discourse and text analysis and the testing of writing. It provides a convenient framework for categorizing components of spoken and written discourse.

For a communicative competence model of writing, we argue that all four competencies included in the Canale and Swain model are needed. These competencies should be reflected in the scoring criteria for writing tests. Naturally, grammatical competence is required in writing instruction and assessment. In addition, mastery of discourse, sociolinguistic, and strategic competencies should also be tested. However, we maintain that in current writing assessment, competencies beyond the basic language and writing proficiencies are not tested.

Canale and Swain's model of communicative competence was primarily developed for the purposes of spoken language analysis and teaching. For written communicative competence, mastery of each component needs to reflect the grammatical competence for writing, one must show mastery of spelling and punctuation in addition to mastery of words and structures. To show discourse competence, one must demonstrate knowledge of the discourse organization of genre in addition to cohesion and coherence. To indicate sociolinguistic competence in writing, we consider important such characteristics as written genre appropriacy, audience awareness and appeals to audience, pertinence of claim, and tone. In assessing writing, Canale and Swain's fourth component, strategic competence, will be considered to deal with such interpersonal factors between the reader and writer such as transitions and other metatextual markers, because metatext in writing serves a similar function as do repair strategies in spoken discourse.

The next sections survey empirical research studies that have applied linguistic and rhetorical theories to essay analysis; each study used current theories of texts and text comprehension and operationalized the theoretical concepts for empirical verification of holistic writing quality. We will discuss selected empirical studies that contribute to the understanding related to the mastery of what might be called sociolinguistic aspects of writing, followed by a review of studies concerning discourse competence in writing, and, finally, studies of strategic competence in writing. Grammatical competence in writing is not a concern of this chapter because it deals with within-sentence relations.

Studies of Sociolinguistic Competence

Sociolinguistic aspects of writing deal with the writer's awareness of the audience and purpose of writing. Text analytical studies related to persuasive appeals and strength of claims with impact on writing assessment will be described in this section. In research on persuasive essay writing, Connor and Lauer (1988) produced a linguistic/rhetorical system to describe and evaluate persuasive student writing. Relying on theories of classical rhetoric and Aristotle's notions of audience and appeals, Connor and Lauer show how the teaching of argumentation in England and the U. S. had replaced the teaching of persuasion in the 19th and 20th centuries. A four-component model of discourse was used: description, narration, argumentation, and exposition. According to Connor and Lauer, the neglect of persuasion continued until Kinneavy's (1971) classification, which again distinguished persuasion from exposition. Kinneavy included persuasion in his classification as one of the four major aims of communication: referential, persuasive, literary, and expressive. As major features of persuasion, Kinneavy distinguished rational, ethical, and emotional appeals as different strategies. These three appeals were adapted for composition research by Connor and Lauer, who developed a scale and rubrics for evaluating the quality of persuasive appeals in student essays, shown in Table 1.

Table 1: Scoring Scale for Persuasive Appeals

Rational Appeal *

0 No use of the rational appeal

1 Use of some rational appeals, minimally developed, or use of some inappropriate (in terms of major point) rational appeals

2 Use of a single rational appeal or a series of rational appeals with at least two points of development

3 Exceptionally well developed and appropriate single extended rational appeal or a coherent set of rational appeals

Credibility Appeal

0 No use of credibility appeals

1 No writer credibility but some awareness of audience's values, or some writer credibility (other than general knowledge) but no awareness of audience's values

2 Some writer credibility (other than general knowledge) and some awareness of audience's values

3 Strong writer credibility (personal experience) and sensitivity to audience's values (specific audience for the solution)

Affective Appeal

0 No use of affective appeal

1 Minimal use of concreteness of charged language

2 Adequate use of either picture, charged language, or metaphor to evoke emotion

3 Strong use of either vivid picture, charged language, or metaphor to evoke emotion

*Rational appeals were categorized as (quasi-logical realistic structure example, and analogy).

In empirical research on student persuasive writing using a large data set from the international writing study (Purves, 1988), Connor and Lauer also adopted another rhetorical model of persuasion for the analysis of student persuasive essays, namely, the Toulmin model of argumentative writing (1958). Toulmin (1958) designed his theory of argumentation to justify statements of argument. In the model, the first step is to express an opinion, called "claim." The second feature is the "data," designed to support the claim and to counter any possible challenge to the claim in the form of experience, facts, statistics, or occurrences. The third feature, the "warrant," shows the relation of claim and data. Connor and Lauer operationalized Toulmin's model for a quantifiable, reliable analysis in order to evaluate the level of argumentative strength of the essays. In a series of studies, Connor and Lauer found that Toulmin's model was a powerful predictor of writing quality in the international study of Ll writing in English of students from the U. S., England, and New Zealand. Table 2 includes the Toulmin scale with criteria developed by Connor and Lauer.

Table 2: Criteria for Judging the Quality of Claim, Data, and Warrant

Claim

1 No specific problem stated and/or no consistent point of view. May have one subclaim. No solution offered, or if offered, nonfeasible, unoriginal, and inconsistent with claim.

2 Specific, explicitly stated problem. Somewhat consistent point of view. Relevant to the task. Has two or more subclaims that have been developed. Solution offered with some feasibility with major claim.

3 Specific, explicitly stated problem with consistent point of view. Several well-developed subclaims, explicitly tied to the major claim. Highly relevant to the task. Solution offered that is feasible, original, and consistent with major claim.

Data

1 Minimal use of data. Data of the "everyone knows" type, with little reliance on personal experience or authority. Not directly related to major claim.

2 Some use of data with reliance on personal experience or authority. Some variety in use of data. Data generally related to major claim.

3 Extensive use of specific, well-developed data of a variety of types. Data explicitly connected to major claim.

warrant

1 Minimal use of warrants. Warrants only minimally reliable and relevant to the case. Warrants may inlcude logical fallacies.

2 Some use of warrants. Though warrants allow the writer to make the bridge between data and claim, some distortion and informal fallacies are evident.

3 Extensive use of warrants. Reliable and trustworthy allowing rater to accept the bridge from data to claim. Highly relevant. Evidence of some backing.

In a smaller-scale L2 study of writing with 22 ESL essays, Connor (1991) correlated scores on the Test of Written English (TWE) of the essays with scores on the Toulmin scale. The correlation between the claim and holistic scores was high ($r = .72$). In other words, 52 percent of the variation in the holistic scores could be explained by the score for claim. The correlation between the claim and holistic score was even higher than the correlation between the essay length and the holistic score, often a good predictor. The finding suggests that a feature related to persuasiveness was related to raters' holistic quality assessment even though the TWE Scoring Guidelines do not explicitly mention criteria related to the development of a reasonable argument. The criterion closest to this in the TWE Guidelines is "addressing the writing task," which does not appear at TWE levels 3, 2, and l. It is worth noting that the average holistic score in the sample study was 2. 25; Connor suggested that the TWE Scoring Guidelines might not reflect the kind of communicative competence that research on linguistic/rhetorical features of student essays has found important. It was also recommended that writers and interpreters of tests consult this kind of rhetorical/textlinguistic research for the purposes of test construction. The study implies the need for a revised set of rubrics that will include criteria related to persuasion and level of argument development.

Studies of Discourse Competence

Analyses of written discourse related to the discourse competence category in Canale and Swain's model have been plentiful. They can be organized under three categories: studies of cohesion, studies of coherence, and studies of discourse structure. Detailed discussions of these studies are included in Connor (1990) and Connor (1996). A brief summary of studies with the greatest applicability to writing assessment follows.

A textlinguistic measure of coherence, topical structure analysis, has been used to explain differences among student essays rated high and low. Topical structure analysis measures the semantic unity of a text by analyzing the relationships of sentence topics to the overall discourse topic. In an ESL context, Schneider and Connor (1991) used a sample of essays written for the Test of Written English and found that topical structure analysis correlated well with readers' judgment of writing quality. Topical structure analysis has been recommended as a tool for student writers to check coherence of their own writing. It could also be used as a method to train raters of student essays to evaluate coherence accurately and explicitly.

Other written discourse analyses also have strong potential for making the assessment of essays more valid because they provide explicit textual markers for raters. Studies of superstructures or global text structures can be powerful measures of essay quality. Several top-level discourse structure theories have been advanced in the past decade, including macrostructures of expository and argumentative essays as well as story structures of narratives. Thus, theories of superstructures have been developed for different types of texts such as exposition, argumentation, and narration, and have been applied to student writing for the purpose of evaluating and describing quality. For example, in order to evaluate students' narratives or teach students to write well-formed stories, Martin and Rothery's story grammar analysis (1986) has been found to be effective. Connor (1996) suggests that the role of superstructures in writing analysis is just beginning, and applications of well-known discourse theories of global text structures have been relatively few. The role of superstructure analysis is likely to grow if and when linguists and teachers of writing increase the focus on other genres in addition to the expository essay, the most commonly taught text genre of student writing.

Studies of Strategic Competence

A promising theory of the interpersonal dimension in writing is the theory about the metadiscourse of texts. Metatext refers to the nonpropositional information in the text and allows the writer either to organize what is said or express personal feelings and attitudes and interact with the reader. Vande Kopple (1985) was the first to propose a valid and reliable system to describe and evaluate student texts for their metatextual content. In Vande Kopple's system, there are two categories of metatextual markers: textual and interpersonal. Textual markers include text connectives that help readers recognize how texts are organized (e. g., first, next); code glosses help readers grasp the meanings of words; illocution markers make explicit what speech act is being performed (e. g., to sum up, to give an example); and narrators, which let readers know who said or wrote something. Interpersonal metadiscourse includes validity markers, which assess the truth value of propositions, indicate the attitude of the writer, or include commentaries directed at the reader. An analysis of metadiscourse in student essays in a cross-cultural study involving Finnish and American essays (Crismore, Markkonen, & Steffensen, 1993), provides careful guidance for others wishing to apply the theory to student data. The system developed by Vande Kopple for Ll purposes and further refined by Crismore et al. for L2 purposes is a useful tool for describing and evaluating the strategic competence in ESL student writing.

Examples From Two EFL Writing Tests

The Test of Written English (TWE) is a holistically rated test; the essays are scored for overall effectiveness of the communication. The holistic scoring guide has six levels and includes syntactic and rhetorical criteria. For example, an essay in the highest category, according to the Test of Written English (TWE) Scoring Guidelines (Educational Testing Service, 1989):

- Effectively addresses the writing task
- Is well organized and well developed
- Uses clearly appropriate details to support a thesis or illustrate ideas
- Displays consistent facility in the use of language
- Demonstrates syntactic variety and appropriate word choice

Several researchers have questioned the use of holistically rated direct assessment because little is known about what factors influence the scores students receive (Hamp-Lyons, 1991). A think-aloud study of TWE writers' and raters' interpretation of the rating criteria and interpretation of the task was conducted by Connor and Carrell (1993). The results of the study showed neither the writers nor the raters considered the specific requirements of the task (i. e., addressing the rhetorical requirements of the writing task) important. Instead, fluency of language, infrequency of language errors, and development of ideas were consistently mentioned by both groups. Neither did a content analysis reveal a consistent addressing of the task as it was specified in the prompt.

An examination of the scoring guidelines reveals that "addressing the task" appears in the scoring guide as a criterion at the higher levels (6, 5, 4) but is not mentioned as a criterion for levels 3, 2, and 1. In other words, one could conclude that the rhetorical context is not important at lower levels of writing. Instead, only language proficiency is considered at these levels.

The ESL Composition Profile (Jacobs, Zingraf, Wormuth, Hartfiel, & Hughey, 1981) employs an analytic scale rather than a holistic scale to assess ESL writing. In analytic rating, a separate score is assigned for various aspects of writing (e. g., content, organization, vocabulary, language use, and mechanics) unlike holistic rating where only one score is given for each essay. In the ESL Composition

Profile, the "content" category addresses quality of content with such criteria as development of thesis and relevance to topic. No criteria in the scale apply to the effectiveness of addressing the audience and appeals used.

The scoring rubrics for these two tests—the Test of Written English Guidelines and the ESL Composition Profile—are no doubt useful for the purpose of assessing language proficiency required for general writing skills of heterogeneous ESL writers. Yet, they do not consider constraints specific to writing related to a given purpose.

Conclusion

In this chapter, we have argued for the inclusion of rhetorical and communicative aspects of writing in the assessment of student writing. We have shown that commonly used tests tend to focus on linguistic aspects of texts (i. e., grammar and vocabulary, and discourse organization). They neglect, however, to consider such important aspects of writing effectiveness as strength of argument and appeals to the audience.

An analogy can be drawn with the communicative competence model of language (Canale & Swain, 1980), which includes strategic and sociolinguistic competence in addition to grammatical and discourse competence. In Table 3, we propose a communicative model that is more appropriate for writing instruction and assessment. Components appropriate for writing are listed corresponding to Canale and Swain's four categories.

Table 3: Proposed Writing Competence Model

Communicative Competence Model (Canale & Swain, 1980)	Criteria for Writing Competence Model
Grammatical Competence	Grammar, Vocabulary, Spelling, Punctuation
Discourse Competence	Discourse Organization, Cohesion, Coherence
Sociolinguistic Competence	Written Genre Appropriacy, Register, Tone
Strategic Competence	Audience/Reader awareness, Appeals, Pertinence of Claims, Warrants

We indicated earlier that linguistic competence was not the sole concern. According to our model, a greater emphasis in writing assessment needs to be placed on the masteries of discourse, sociolinguistic, and strategic competence. At the level of discourse competence, emphases should go beyond the structure of text and paragraph to cohesion and coherence. In terms of sociolinguistic competence, the focus should include written awareness of written genre appropriacy, tone, and register of text. Finally, in relation to strategic competence, issues of audience or reader awareness, appeals to the audience, and pertinence of claims are important.

ANNOTATED BIBLIOGRAPHY

Allaei Kurtz, S., & Connor, U. (1991). Using performative assessment instruments with ESL student writers. In L. Hamp-Lyons (Ed.), *Assessing second language writing in academic contexts* (pp. 227–240). Norwood, NJ: Ablex.

The chapter describes a new kind of writing assessment, performative assessment, for use with ESL students. Performative assessment is designed to describe students' writing performance in relation to specific tasks and discourse demands, unlike most ESL writing assessment that has been concerned with general proficiency in writing. Performative assessment is criterion-referenced rather than norm-referenced; students are not compared with each other but are judged according to how well the fulfill the expectations of a particular writing task. The chapter shows a step-wise method for constructing performative assessment assignments. It provides two actual writing tasks and corresponding rubrics to score the writing. Performative assessment tools focus on content and meaning, ignoring sentence structure and the mechanics of writing. Therefore, its positive feature is that it makes instructors and raters more aware of students' ability to respond to the demands of a particular writing task. Besides its potential as an diagnostic tool, performative assessment can also be used in classroom instruction.

Cohen, A. D. (1994). *Assessing language ability in the classroom* (2nd ed.). Boston, MA: Heinle & Heinle.

This book covers issues of language assessment in an extensive and up-to-date manner. The book starts out with placing language testing within the larger framework of teaching and learning, and then goes on to deal with the construction of language assessment instruments successively before discussing the testing of the four traditional language skills. The section on assessing writing goes beyond the construction of prompts to present and evaluate some of the main approaches to scoring writing. Because of the range and breadth of language testing issues covered, this is a most useful book.

Connor, U. (1991). Linguistic/rhetorical measures for evaluating ESL writing. In L. Hamp-Lyons (Ed.), *Assessing second language writing in academic contexts* (pp. 215–226). Norwood, NJ: Ablex.

The chapter describes a project in which the author developed an analytic system for evaluating students' writing. The system, based on Toulmin's (1958) model of argument, was used to analyze the holistic scoring of TWE essays completed by ESL students. Results indicate that the rhetorical writing measures of the model are a better predictor of essay quality than the previously accepted factor of fluency. The paper consequently advocates more incorporation of textual features in scoring guides for writing.

Connor, U., & Carrell, P. (1993). The interpretation of tasks by writers and readers in holistically rated direct assessment of writing. In J. G. Carson & I. Leki (Eds.), *Reading in the composition classroom: Second language perspectives* (pp. 141–160). Boston, MA: Heinle & Heinle.

Through protocol analysis, the study reported in this chapter examines the similarities and differences in writers and raters' perception of the importance of content, organization, and language in ESL essays. The study also seeks to determine how writers and raters conceptualized and interpreted the writing task, and whether they were aware of each others' role. Results indicated that both writers and raters highlight language use, content, and development of ideas. Little concern seems to be devoted by both writers and raters to organization, full compliance with the instructions of the prompt, and to considering the perspective of the writer or rater while rating or writing. The authors consider some implications of these findings for ESL writing.

Cumming, A. (1998). Theoretical perspectives on writing. *Annual Review of Applied Linguistics, 18*, 61–78.

This article presents a theory of second language writing that considers the diverse situations where people produce, learn, teach, and assess second language writing. The article reviews empirical studies that have analyzed the demands for writing that students of a second language encounter; discusses research that examines second language writing instruction; and, most importantly for the current topic, argues for text analyses of student writing for the purposes of instruction and testing. Cumming writes that: "systematic modes of analyzing students' written texts are needed because the rating scales typically used to evaluate students' writing in a second language are simply too imprecise, or lack the theoretical rigor or validation, to be able to provide useful indicators of students' achievement" (p. 65). The article provides numerous up-to-date references to analyses of students' texts in specific genres.

Hamp-Lyons, L. (1991). Scoring procedures for ESL contexts. In L. Hamp-Lyons (Ed.), *Assessing second language wniting in academic contexts* (pp. 241–276). Norwood, NJ: Ablex.

Appearing together with different other major articles on ESL writing assessment, this paper sets ESL writing in its specific before proceeding to review the most commonly used scoring procedures in testing writing. The article pertinently argues that it is important to have an appropriate method for the assessment of writing if one is to tap the full potential of writing instruction. Yet, this review of widespread scoring practices in writing suggests that many important discoursal features of texts throughout genres are hardly covered by these practices. The paper is recommended reading for anyone interested in ESL/EFL writing.

Kroll, B. (1998). Assessing writing abilities. *Annual Review of Applied Linguistics*, *18*, 219–240.

The chapter provides a review of issues in second-language writing assessment in the past couple of decades. Critical variables present in writing assessment are identified as the writer, the task, the written product, the reader/scorer, and the scoring procedures. The article acknowledges that "a number of product studies have focused on specific rhetorical features identifiable in essays written for exams" (p. 224). Yet, the article maintains that there is too much variation in products across genres and that there are too many genres to consider for us to be able to benefit from such text studies. The author admits, however, that "the field of contrastive rhetoric... has helped to illuminate the fact that the particular ways in which texts are deemed to be appropriate and successful in achieving their rhetorical goals are at least somewhat culturally determined" (p. 225).

OTHER REFERENCES

Alderson, C., Clapham, C., & Wall, D. (1995). *Language test construction and evaluation.* Cambridge, UK: Cambridge University Press.

Bachman, L. F., & Palmer, A. S. (1996). *Language testing in practice: Designing and developing useful language tests.* Oxford, UK: Oxford University Press.

Canale, M. (1983). From communicative competence to communicative language pedagogy. In J. C. Richards & R. Schmidt (Eds.), *Language and communication* (pp. 2–27). London, UK: Longman.

Canale, M., & Swain, M. (1980). Theoretical bases of communicative approaches to second language teaching and testing. *Applied Linguistics, 1,* 1–47.

Connor, U. (1990). Discourse analysis and writing/reading instruction. *Annual Review of Applied Linguistics, 11,* 164–180.

Connor. U. (1994). Assessing writing proficiency. In E. M. White (Ed.), *Teaching and assessing writing* (pp. 150–170). San Francisco, CA: Jossey-Bass.

Connor, U. (1996). *Contrastive rhetoric: Cross-cultural aspects of second-language writing.* Cambridge, UK: Cambridge University Press.

Connor, U., & Lauer, J. (1988). Writing across languages and cultures. In A. C. Purves (Ed.), *Cross-cultural variation in persuasive student writing* (pp. 138–159). Newbury Park, CA: Sage.

Crismore, A. R., Markkanen, R., & Steffensen, M. S. (1993). Metadiscourse in persuasive writing: A study of texts written by American and Finnish university students. *Written Communication, 10,* 39–71.

Educational Testing Service. (1989). Test of Written English Scoring Guidelines. Princeton, NJ: Author.

Hamp-Lyons, L. (Ed.). (1991). *Assessing second language writing in academic contexts.* Norwood, NJ: Ablex.

Jacobs, H., Zingraf, S. A., Wormuth, D. R., Hartfiel, V. F., & Hughey, J. B. (1981). *Testing ESL composition: A practical approach.* Rowley, MA: Newbury House.

Kinneavy, J. L. (1971). *A theory of discourse.* Englewood Cliffs, NJ: Prentice Hall.

Lloyd-Jones, R. (1977). Primary trait scoring of writing. In C. R. Cooper & L. Odell (Eds.), *Evaluating writing: Describing, measuring. judging* (pp. 33–66). Urbana, IL: National

Council of Teachers of English.

Martin, J. R., & Rothery, J. (1986). What a functional approach can show teachers. In B. Couture (Ed.), *Functional approaches to writing: Research perspectives* (pp. 789–808). Norwood, NJ: Ablex.

Purves, A. C. (1988). Introduction. In A. C. Purves (Ed.), *Writing across languages and cultures: Issues in contrastive rhetoric* (pp. 9–21). Newbury Park, CA: Sage.

Schneider, M., & Connor, U. (1991). Analyzing topical structure in ESL essays: Not all topics are equal. *Studies in Second Language Acquisition, 12,* 411–427.

Toulmin, S. (1958). *The uses of argument.* Cambridge, UK: Cambridge University Press.

Vande Kopple, W. J. (1985). Some exploratory discourse on metadiscourse. *College Composition and Communication, 36,* 82–93.

Weir, C. (1993). *Understanding and developing language tests.* New York: Phoenix.

White, E. (1985). *Teaching and assessing writing.* San Francisco, CA: Jossey-Bass.

Yancey, K. B., & Huot, B. (1997). *Assessing writing across the curriculum: Diverse approaches and practices.* Greenwich. CT: Ablex.

BIOGRAPHICAL INFORMATION ON CONTRIBUTORS

Ulla Connoy is Professor of English and Director of the Indiana Center for Intercultural Communication, Indiana University—Purdue University, Indianapolis. She has published extensively in the area of written discourse analysis and second language writing assessment. Her books include *Writing Across Languages: Analysis of L2 Written Text* (with Robert Kaplan; Addison-Wesley, 1987), *Coherence in Writing: Research and Pedagogical Perspectives* (with Ann Johns; TESOL, 1990), and *Contrastive Rhetoric: Cross-Cultural Aspects of Second-Language Writing* (Cambridge University Press, 1996). From 1989 to 1992, she served on the Test of Written English Core Group for Educational Testing Service (ETS) and in 1995 held an ETS grant to study writing prompts for development of the Test of English as International Communication (TOEIC).
Contact information: uconnor@iupui. edu

Susan Conrad is an Associate Professor in the Department of Applied Linguistics at Portland State University. Her interests include English grammar, writing in the academic disciplines, and the application of corpus linguistic techniques to a variety of teaching and research needs. Her publications in corpus linguistics include collaborations on an introductory text, *Corpus Linguistics: Investigating Language Structure and Use* (with D. Biber and R. Reppen; Cambridge, 1998), a reference grammar, *Longman Grammar of Spoken and Written English* (with D. Biber, S. Johansson, G. Leech, and E. Finegan; Longman, 1999), and an edited collection of multi-dimensional analysis studices, *Variation in English: Multi-dimensional Studies* (co-edited with D. Biber; Longman, 2001), as well as articles in journals such as *TESOL Quarterly*, *Linguistics and Education*, and *System*.
Contact information: conrads@pdx. edu

Geoff Hall is Lecturer in the Centre for Applied Language Studies, University of Wales, Swansea, United Kingdom. His research interests include literary stylistics and academic literacies, with publications in *Language Awareness*, *Language and Literature*, and *Language and Education*. His reviews have also appeared in *Applied Linguistics*, *Teaching in Higher Education*, and *English Language Teaching Journal*. Like his co-author of this *ARAL* survey, he is assistant editor of the journal *Language and Literature*. He is currently working on a volume entitled *Teaching and Researching Language and Literature*, to be published by Pearson Education.

Contact information: g. m. hall@swansea. ac. uk

Joan Kelly Hall is Associate Professor in the Department of Language Education at the University of Georgia where she teaches courses in second and foreign language acquisition, classroom discourse, and bilingualism and bilingual education. She is also on the faculty of the university-wide Linguistics Program. Her research interests include the study of classroom discourse, intercultural communication, and sociocultural identity as they relate to the learning of additional languages. She has published on her research in journals such as *Applied Linguistics*, *Modern Language Journal*, *Linguistics and Education*, and *Research on Language and Social Interaction*. In addition, she has co-edited two volumes: The *Sociopolitics of English Language Teaching* (with W. Eggington; Multilingual Matters, 2000), and *Second and Foreign Language Learning Through Classroom Interaction* (with L. Verplaetse; Lawrence Erlbaum, 2000). Her most recent book is *Methods for Teaching Foreign Languages: Creating a Community of Learners in the Classroom* (PrenticeHall, 2002).
Contact information: jkhall@arches. uga. edu

Kathryn Hill holds BA, Dip. Ed., and MA degrees from the University of Melbourne. A research fellow at the Language Testing Research Centre (LTRC) in Melbourne and, until recently, at the Australian Council for Educational Research (ACER). She has been involved in a broad range of assessment projects including AACESS (Australian Assessment of Communicative English Skills); the English Proficiency Test for Indonesia; the Australian Language Certificates; and the Programme for International Student Assessment (PISA). Her research interests include test-taker feedback, interviewer behavior, rater characteristics, language teacher proficiency, and foreign language learning in schools.
Contac information: k. hill@linguistics. unimelb. edu. au

Ken Hyland is Associate Professor at The City University of Hong Kong where he coordinates the MA in ESP. Before moving to Hong Kong, he taught in Sudan, Malaysia, Saudi Arabia, the United Kingdom, New Zealand, and Papua New Guinea. His articles on language teaching, writing, and academic discourse have appeared in several international journals. Recent publications include *Hedging in*

Scientific Discourse (Benjamins, 1998), *Disciplinary Discourses* (Longman, 2000), *Teaching and Researching Writing* (Longman, 2001), and *Writing: Texts, Processes, and Practices*, co-edited with Chris Candlin (Longman, 1999). He is reviews editor of *English for Specific Purposes* and co-editor of *The Journal of English for Academic Purposes*.
Contact information: enhyland@cityu. edu. hk

Sally Jacoby is Assistant Professor in the Department of Communication at the University of New Hampshire, where she teaches conversation analysis, language and social interaction, and ethnography of communication. Her research on co-construction, the turn, indigenous assessment, and the talk-in-interaction of physicists has appeared in *Research on Language in Social Interaction, The Journal of Linguistic Anthropology, English for Specific Purposes Journal, Issues in Applied Linguistics, Configurations*, and anthologies on grammar and interaction. She is especially interested in the interactional aspects of indigenous assessment practices and how participants make explicit the taken-for-granted moral order of communicative competence through these practices.
Contact information: swj@hopper. unh. edu

Irene Koshik is Assistant Professor in the Division of English as an International Language at the University of Illinois, Urbana-Champaign, where she teaches courses in conversation analysis, language and social interaction for language teachers, and second language teaching methodology. Her research uses a conversation analytic framework to analyze talk in L2 pedagogical contexts and ordinary conversation. She is especially interested in how teachers and students adapt praccices of ordinary conversation to accomplish pedagogical goals.
Contact information: koshik@uiuc. edu

Anne Lazaraton is a member of the MA in ESL program faculty at the University of Minnesota, where she teaches Courses in ESL Methods, Language Analysis, Discourse Analysis, and Practicum. With EVelyn Hatch, she co-authored *The Research Manual: Design and Statistics for Applied Linguistics* (Newbury House, 1991). Among her latest publications is the book *A Qualitative Approach to the Validation of Oral Language Tests* (Cambridge University Press, 2001).

Her research interests include conversation analysis of NS-NNS and NNS-NNS interaction, oral language assessment, research methodology for applied linguistics, and relationships between language ability, pedagogical performance, and cultural knowledge in ESL/EFL teachers who are nonnative speakers of English.
Contact information: lazaratn@ic. umn. edu

Allan Luke is Dean of Education at the University of Queensland, Australia, where he teaches literacy education, sociology and policy studies, and discourse analysis. He is author and editor of numerous books and articles including *Towards a Critical Sociology of Reading Pedagogy* (Benjamins, 1991), *Literacy in Contexts: Australian Perspectives and Issues* (Allen & Unwin, 1993), and *Constructing Critical Literacies* (Hampton, 1997). He was Deputy Director General of Education for Queensland in 1999–2000 and currently is Chief Educational Advisor to the Minister.
Contact information: a. lukc@mailbox. uq. edu. au

J. R. Martin is Professor in Linguistics (Personal Chair) at the University of Sydney. His research interests include systemic theory, functional grammar, discourse semantics, register, genre, multimodality, and critical discourse analysis, focusing on English and Tagalog, with special reference to the transdisciplinary fields of educational linguistics and social semiotics. Publications include *English Text* (Benjamins, 1992); *Writing Science* (with M. A. K. Halliday; Falmer, 1993); *Working with Functional Grammar* (with C. Matthiessen and C. Painter; Arnold, 1997); *Genre and Institutions: Social Processes in the Workplace and School* (edited with F. Christie; Cassell. 1997); *Reading Science* (edited with R. Veel; Routledge, 1998); and *Working with Discourse* (with D. Rose; Continuum. 2002). He is currently editing papers for Benjamins on functional language typology (with Alice Caffarel and Christian Matthiessen) and history discourse (with Ruth Wodak). He was elected a fellow of the Australian Academy of the Humanities in 1999.
Contact information: jmartin@mail. usyd. edu. au

Lynette May is a Lecturer in the English Language and Literature academic group at the National Institute of Education in Singapore. She is also currently undertaking postgraduate research in language testing at the University of Melbourne. She has

been involved in the development of tests of academic English proficiency for the University of Sydney, Nanyang Technological University, and the Ministry of Education in Singapore. Her current research is on the validity of the paired learner interaction in tests of oral proficiency for English for academic purposes.
Contact information: lamay@nie. edu. sg

Aymérou Mbaye is an EFL/ESL practitioner with experience in pre-university and university level L2 instruction, curriculum construction, and language assessment. He has an MA from Lancaster University, United Kingdom, and a Ph. D. from Oklahoma State University, where his dissertation research addressed the writing proficiency of college-level EFL students educated in French. At present, he is a Visiting Rescarch Associate at the Indiana Center for Intercultural Communication, Indiana University—Purdue University, Indianapolis, where he is furthering his research in text linguistics, cross-cultural literacies, teacher development, and achievement of quality in the delivery of language instruction.
Contact information: ambaye@iupui. edu

Mary McGroarty. Editor-in-Chief of *ARAL*, is a Professor in the Applied Linguistics Program in the English Department at Northern Arizona University and a past President of the American Association for Applied Linguistics (1997–98). A Woodrow Wilson Fellow, she has also received Fulbright and Mellon awards. Her articles have appeared in *Applied Linguistics, Canadian Modern Language Review, Language Learning. TESOL Quarterly*, and several anthologies. She has served on the editorial boards of *Applied Linguistics, ARAL, Journal of Language, Identity, and Education, Second Language Instruction and Acquisition Abstracts, and TESOL Quarterly.* Her research interests include theoretical and pedagogical aspects of language learning and teaching, bilingualism, language policy, and assessment of second language skills.
Contact information: mary. mcgroarty@nau. edu

Tim McNamara is Professor and Director of the Language Testing Research Centre in the Department of Linguistics and Applied Linguistics at the University of Melbourne. His language testing research has focused on performance assessment, theories of validity, and use of Rasen models. He is the author of *Language Testing*

(Oxford University Press, 2000) and *Measuring Second Language Performance* (Longman, 1996), and co-author of the *Dictionary of Language Testing* (Cambridge University Press, 1999). He also acts as a consultant with Educational Testing Service. With Chris Candlin, he is collaborating on research on the history of applied linguistics. A frequent speaker at international conferences, he has served on the editorial boards of the *Annual Review of Applied Linguistics*, *Applied Linguistics*, *Lauguage Testing*, and *TESOL Quarterly*.
Contact information: tfmcna@unimelb. edu. au

David Olsher is a doctoral candidate in applied linguistics at the University of California, Los Angeles. His dissertation focuses on speaking practices of language learners participating in small group project work. His research uses a conversation analytic framework for the micro-interactional analysis of classroom discourse, language learner discourse, and broadcast news interview talk. He is also interested in functional linguistic perspectives on the uses of grammar within interaction in both conversational and institutional settings.
Contact information: olsher@ucla. edu

Emanuel A. Schegloff is Professor of Sociology with a joint appointment in Applied Linguistics at the University of California, Los Angeles (UCLA). Educated at Harvard and the University of California, Berkeley, he has taught at Columbia University as well as UCLA. His interests center on the naturalistic study of interaction and what we can learn from it. Within the last five years, his articles have appeared in *American Journal of Sociology*, *Applied Linguistics*, *Discourse & Society*, *Discourse Processes*, *Discourse Studies*, *Journal of Narrative and Life History*, *Research on Language and Social Interaction*, and *Social Research*, among other venues.
Contact information: scheglof@soc. ucla. edu

Paul Simpson is a Reader in the School of English at Queen's University, Belfast, Northern Ireland, where he teaches undergraduate and postgraduate courses on English language and linguistics. Most of his published work deals with stylistics, critical linguistics, and related fields of study. His books include *Language, Ideology, and Point of View* (1993) and *Language through Literature* (1996), both

published by Routledge. Like his co-author of this *ARAL* survey, he is assistant editor of the journal *Language and Literature*. He is currently writing a book on the discourse of humor to be published by John Benjamins.
Contact information: p. simpson@qub. ac. uk

Merrill Swain is a Professor in the Department of Curriculum, Teaching and Learning at the Ontario Institute for Studies in Education of the University of Toronto. Her interests include bilingual education, particularly French immersion education, and communicative second language learning, teaching, and testing. Her present research focuses on the role of collaborative dialogue in second Ianguge learning. She was President of the American Association for Applied Linguistics in 1998–99 and is currently a Vice President of the International Association for Applied Lingusitics (AILA).
Contact information: mswain@oise. Utoronto. ca

Agustina Tocalli-Beller is a Ph. D. student in the Second Language Education program of the Department of Curriculum, Teaching and Learning at the Ontario Institute for Studies in Education of the University of Toronto. She completed her master's degree in applied linguistics at York University (Toronto)in 1999. Her research interests include communicative second language teaching and learning, vocabulary learning, language play, and sociocultural approaches to second language classroom research. She taught EFL in Argentina for over six years and currently teaches Spanish and English as a Second Language in Toronto.
Contact information: atocalli-beller@oise. utoronto. ca

Miles Turnbull is Assistant Professor in the Modern Language Centre, part of the Curriculum, Teaching and Learning Department of the Ontario Institute for Studies in Education of the University of Toronto. He teaches in both the pre-service education program in French and International Languages and also in the graduate program in second language education. Before joining the OISE-UT faculty, he worked in core and immersion French programs in three Canadian provinces. His research interests include core and immersion French program design, teacher beliefs and target language use, teacher education, project-based second language curriculum design, and multimedia technology in language teaching. He is associate

editor of the *Canadian Modern Language Review/ La Revue canadienne des langues vivantes*.
Contact information: mturnbull@oise.utoronto.ca

Meghan Walsh received a master's degree in Foreign Language Education from the University of Georgia in 2000 and is currently a specialist student in the Teaching Additional Languages program at the University of Georgia. A high school French teacher in Atlanta, she has also taught French at the middle school level for four years. As a graduate teaching assistant, she taught an Instructional Methods course for pre-service foreign language teachers. She has observed and evaluated student teachers and was actively involved with the Georgia Board of Regents Study Abroad Learning Outcomes project. Her research interests include classroom discourse, collaborative classroom community development, and foreign language teacher preparation. She has presented at several foreign language conferences in the Southeast.
Contact information: meghanw@mindspring.com

Richard F. Young is Professor of English Linguistics at the University of Wisconsin, Madison. His primary research interest is in the study of interactional competence in face-to-face interaction using the methods of conversation analysis and linguistic anthropology. He has published work on variation in second language acquisition, discourse approaches to the assessment of oral proficiency, and systemic linguistic analyses of classroom discourse. His books include *Variation in Interlanguage Morphology* (Peter Lang, 1991), and *Talking and Testing* (co-edited with Agnes He; Benjamins, 1998). He also edits the *Language Learning Monograph Series*. His current research project is *Discursive practices: Communication in face-to-face interaction*. He leads the planning for the 14th World Congress of Applied Linguistics to be held in Madison in 2005 and is current chair of the committee that advises Educational Testing Service on the Test of Spoken English.
Contact information: rfyoung@facstaff.wisc.edu

图书在版编目(CIP)数据

剑桥应用语言学年度评论.2002:话语和对话＝Annual Review of Applied Linguistics 2002 • Discourse and Dialogue:英文/(美)玛丽•麦克格罗蒂(Mary McGroarty)主编.—北京:商务印书馆,2016
(剑桥应用语言学年度评论)
ISBN 978-7-100-12678-6

Ⅰ.①剑… Ⅱ.①玛… Ⅲ.①应用语言学—研究—英文 Ⅳ.①H08

中国版本图书馆 CIP 数据核字(2016)第 258336 号

所有权利保留。
未经许可,不得以任何方式使用。

剑桥应用语言学年度评论 2002•话语和对话
Annual Review of Applied Linguistics 2002 • Discourse and Dialogue
　　主编　〔美〕Mary McGroarty
　　　　导读　王振华

商 务 印 书 馆 出 版
(北京王府井大街36号　邮政编码100710)
商 务 印 书 馆 发 行
北京市松源印刷有限公司印刷
ISBN 978-7-100-12678-6

2016年12月第1版　　开本 880×1230　1/32
2016年12月北京第1次印刷　印张 11⅜

定价:35.00元